In God
We Trust

To my granddaughter Kiki—
in hopes that, as she grows up,
she will come to understand
the roots of American history.

In God We Trust

The American Civil War, Money, Banking, and Religion

William Bierly

Foreword by
Q. David Bowers

Whitman
Publishing, LLC
PUBLISHING SINCE 1934
Whitman.com

In God We Trust

The American Civil War, Money, Banking, and Religion

© 2019 Whitman Publishing, LLC
1974 Chandalar Drive, Suite D, Pelham, AL 35124

ISBN: 0794845282
Printed in China

Correspondence concerning this book may be directed to Whitman Publishing, attn: In God We Trust, at the address above.

If you enjoy this book, we invite you to learn more about America's history by starting a new coin collection and reading as much as possible.

Whitman Publishing is a leading publisher of numismatic reference books, supplies, and storage and display products that help you build, appreciate, and share great collections. To browse our complete catalog, visit Whitman Publishing online at:
www.Whitman.com

You can join the American Numismatic Association (ANA), the nation's largest hobby group for coin collectors. Collect coins and other currency, learn about numismatics, and make new friends in the hobby. Explore the ANA at
www.Money.org.

Whitman®

Contents

LIST OF NUMISMATIC ILLUSTRATIONS

FOREWORD

Welcome to one of the most detailed, intricate, and fascinating books in the field of American numismatics—and in American history in general.

The national motto "In God We Trust" is familiar to all of us. Look in your pocket change or wallet and you will find it on every United States coin and paper bill. Before reading the manuscript to William Bierly's book I thought I knew all about "In God We Trust." Some years ago I wrote an article, "God in Your Pocket," for my local Presbyterian Church, telling of the motto's use on coins. I knew it appeared on pattern coins in 1863 and in 1864 made its first appearance on a circulating coin, the bronze two-cent piece, a new denomination introduced that year. I had the obscure knowledge that "In God We Trust" is the motto of the State of Florida and was used on certain National Bank notes issued in that state in the second half of the nineteenth century. I also knew that the $5 Silver Certificates of the Series of 1886 illustrate the reverse of a Morgan silver dollar of that year, with the motto as part of the design.

But what I *didn't* know were 101 other details—make that many more than 101 different details—as to how the motto came to be, how it was used over the years, and the wide cast of characters in the Treasury Department and elsewhere who participated in its use on money. All too often, books, newspaper columns, and magazine articles about popular subjects lack many details. For Whitman Publishing I wrote a volume on President Ronald Reagan, and I read every book and important study I could find. There were very few details about his personal day-to-day life. Not to worry about the historical personalities involved with "In God We Trust." While you might not learn the names of the protagonists' pet cats or their favorite dime novels, there is not much else missing herein. Dozens of cast members play cameo roles and small walk-on parts. It is probably correct to say that no other researcher could *add* to Bill Bierly's efforts! He collaborated with professional numismatists, leaving no stone (or coin) unturned in the creation of this book. Commonly believed myths and

"In God We Trust" has appeared on American money since the Civil War. William Bierly tells how the national motto came to be.

misunderstandings he examined, debunked, and corrected. Hundreds of historical images were collected, many of which have never been published in a numismatic reference, to which have been added beautiful photographs of rare coins, patterns, tokens, medals, and paper currency, including close-ups of important characteristics. All of this required a lot of work, creativity, and careful attention to detail.

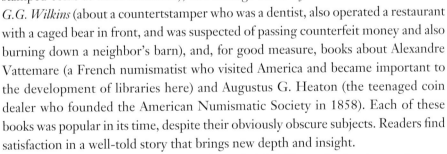

Further on the subject of detail: I enjoy learning about and digging deeply into previously unexplored subjects. I have written books on the Waterford Water Cure (a health spa in Waterford, Maine, that counter-stamped coins as advertisements), *The Strange Career of Dr. G.G. Wilkins* (about a countertamper who was a dentist, also operated a restaurant with a caged bear in front, and was suspected of passing counterfeit money and also burning down a neighbor's barn), and, for good measure, books about Alexandre Vattemare (a French numismatist who visited America and became important to the development of libraries here) and Augustus G. Heaton (the teenaged coin dealer who founded the American Numismatic Society in 1858). Each of these books was popular in its time, despite their obviously obscure subjects. Readers find satisfaction in a well-told story that brings new depth and insight.

That is precisely what we get with *In God We Trust*, the book now in your hands. Anyone with a combined interest in American history and numismatics will find a new world of important information, fascinating details, and previously unconnected relationships.

The motto "In God We Trust" is hardly history alone. It is so much more, and it means different things to different people. Today there are vocal critics who feel that it has no place on coins or paper currency. For that matter, some believe that

God has no place in public (and in some cases, private) life. On the other hand, many more people do indeed believe in the Supreme Being. Sometimes it just seems the naysayers get all of the publicity.

Bill Bierly's *In God We Trust* approaches the subject respectfully on all sides, with color, personality, dashes of humor, and dogged pursuit of the truth. He has given us a smorgasbord: there is a lot to choose from. If you are a collector and strictly so, with no interest in the million points where numismatics touches American history, you can simply immerse yourself in the coins, paper money, tokens, and medals. If you are like me, however, and enjoy every historical highway and byway connected to American money, you will read and find pleasure in the entire book from start to finish.

In the pages ahead there is much to enjoy!

Q. David Bowers
Wolfeboro, New Hampshire

Q. David Bowers is the award-winning author of more than 60 numismatic books ranging from 90-page monographs to 900-page encyclopedias, hundreds of auction and other catalogs, and several thousand articles including columns in Coin World, Paper Money, *and* The Numismatist. *He is a past president of both the American Numismatic Association (1983–1985) and the Professional Numismatists Guild (1977–1979). In his 60-plus-year career in numismatics he has earned most of the highest honors bestowed by the hobby community, including the ANA's Lifetime Achievement Award and induction in the ANA Numismatic Hall of Fame.*

AUTHOR'S PREFACE

This book is an effort to address different issues of the American Civil War than most histories do. Most deal with its military aspects, covering the battles and the generals. Others deal with the politics of the war. This book endeavors to illuminate two other aspects of the war. One is the religious, spiritual side, in which the Confederacy and the Union contested in an ideological struggle for what they viewed as "God's favor." Which side was the more Christian, the more righteous, the holier one, and how could they demonstrate their greater holiness? Indeed Abraham Lincoln discussed this in his second inaugural address. This struggle took various forms but included the Confederacy placing a religious reference in its new constitution, thus creating a contrast to the federal constitution, which was viewed as being "Godless." The reactions to this in the North had various manifestations, one of which was the ultimate adoption of the motto "In God We Trust" on federal coinage. The second aspect addressed herein is the financial and monetary side of the war. This includes the larger picture of how the war was financed through taxes, tariffs, and the issuance of bonds and "greenbacks," but also the issues of how ordinary people coped with everyday purchases during the coin shortages that developed during the war. As the story unfolds, the spiritual and monetary issues come together with the motto "In God We Trust" on the coinage.

I recall a quote from the prolific numismatic writer Q. David Bowers, stating that "mainstream" history and coin collecting seldom intersect. From the collecting side the focus is on the coins themselves, often neglecting the historical context from which they emerged or which they in turn influenced. From the history side, coins are largely ignored, regarded as insignificant parts of the bigger story. Bowers cites his conversation with a noted history professor, an expert on the Civil War, who was completely unaware of Civil War tokens, issued during the war as a means to alleviate coin shortages and now a popular collectible among numismatists. By the professor being unaware of these tokens, Bowers realized he was missing a significant element of what everyday life was like during the war, of which the tokens were evidence. In a similar way, the pattern coins highlighted in this book are artifacts that illustrate and help tell the story of how "In God We Trust" came about.

"In God We Trust" on U.S. coinage has become an iconic element of American culture. It has become in the years since the Civil War the official national motto of the United States. It has over the years excited both strong approval and strong opposition. Controversy surrounds it to the present day.

The financial issues of the war led to significant changes in the monetary system of the United States. These include the introduction of a standardized national currency issued under federal authority, and the development of a national banking system. These greatly facilitated the United States in emerging as a modern industrial and financial power in the nineteenth and twentieth centuries.

It is my hope that the discussion of these issues in this book will provide the reader with a fuller understanding and deeper perspective on the Civil War. I also hope that the reader will have a better understanding of how our money and banking systems came to be what they are.

Bill Bierly
La Porte, Indiana

PUBLISHER'S PREFACE

Sometimes in the numismatic world, it can seem like there's nothing new under the sun—as if every subject has been researched, every story told. This is an illusion. In reality, numismatics is a living, breathing discipline, rich with ongoing study, startling discoveries, and freshly revealed connections that span the depth and breadth of human experience. The story that William Bierly has woven together in his book, *In God We Trust*, illustrates this vibrancy.

I met Bill several years ago after a meeting of the Chicago Coin Club, held at the American Numismatic Association's annual World's Fair of Money. We were introduced by Robert Leonard (another member of the Club, and a Whitman author). Bob assured me that Bill had a very promising manuscript proposal. Our conversation that followed convinced me that he was on to something big, something new and significant.

Most coin collectors know little of the national motto, "In God We Trust," beyond the knowledge summed up in a single sentence in the "Two-Cent Pieces" section of the *Guide Book of United States Coins* (the *Red Book*): "The motto IN GOD WE TRUST appeared for the first time on the new coin, with the personal support of Treasury Secretary Salmon P. Chase." The words are factual. But that's like saying, "Abraham Lincoln was elected president of the United States in 1860 and served during the Civil War"—and allowing this to be the sum of your knowledge of the man!

Articles about the motto have been published in numismatic magazines and journals over the years. None have approached the detail and intricacy that Bill Bierly brought to his research. From time to time, mainstream (non-numismatic) writers also mention "In God We Trust," often when school prayer, public prayer, the separation of Church and State, atheist lawsuits, and similar subjects are in the headlines. Articles in popular publications often gloss over the details, and sometimes even get the facts wrong.

To set the record straight, Bill Bierly has followed leads, researched in archives and libraries, interviewed historians local and national, and gathered images. He has tracked down and dispelled rumors and half-true tales. And he has expanded the context of "In God We Trust" to show how the Civil War changed American banking, finance, and business forever. The result of his work is a fascinating exploration of a simple but profound four-word motto that has appeared on hundreds of billions of U.S. coins and paper-money notes. *In God We Trust* is an important addition to the body of historical research, and a sterling example of how numismatics touches every aspect of American life.

Dennis Tucker
Publisher, Whitman Publishing

A crowd gathered in front of the capitol building at Montgomery, Alabama, for the announcement of Jefferson Davis as the first president of the Confederate States of America. Earlier this was where the Confederate constitution was created.

CHAPTER 1

The Preamble

On the morning of February 8, 1861, an editorial appeared in the Montgomery, Alabama, *Weekly Mail*. It was entitled "No God in the Constitution." The piece described the "oversight" of the Philadelphia Founding Fathers in 1787 as they did not include any reference to God in their drafting of the U.S. Constitution. The editorial discussed "the longtime need of a statement expressing the people's dependence on God" and concluded by saying, "Let our rulers and representatives who are about to frame a new constitution of the Confederacy bear these facts in mind . . . then shall we be that happy people whose God is Jehovah."[1]

The "rulers and representatives" referred to were the Confederate delegates then gathered in Montgomery (the capital of the Confederacy at that time) for the purpose of writing the constitution of the newly formed Confederate States of America. Debates on the draft took place that very afternoon and evening and the representatives did indeed include, with little discussion, a reference to God in the preamble of their provisional constitution.

> We the deputies of the sovereign states of South Carolina, Georgia, Florida, Alabama, Mississippi, and Louisiana, *invoking the favor of Almighty God*, do hereby, in behalf of these states, ordain, and establish this Constitution for the provisional Government of the same. . . .

About a month later, on March 11, 1861, the permanent constitution of the Confederacy was adopted. Other states by that time had joined the secessionist movement. The preamble was modified somewhat but retained and slightly enlarged the invocation of favor from God, seeking also His guidance.

> We, the People of the Confederate States of America, each state acting in its sovereign and independent character, in order to form a permanent Federal Government, establish justice, insure domestic tranquility, and secure the blessings of liberty to ourselves and our posterity—*invoking the favor and guidance of Almighty God*—do ordain and establish this Constitution for the Confederate States of America.[2]

The motivation of the Southern delegates in including the simple phrase invoking Almighty God long predated the editorial in the morning newspaper. The federal Constitution did not reference a deity, but other American founding documents did.

The Declaration of Independence had at least three references:

> . . . all men are created equal, that they are endowed by their *Creator* with certain unalienable rights. . . .

> We . . . appealing to the *Judge of the world* for the rectitude of our intentions. . . .

> . . . with a firm reliance on the protection of *Divine Providence* we mutually pledge to each other our lives, our fortunes, and our sacred honor.

The Articles of Confederation, predecessor document to the Constitution, states in its concluding paragraph:

> And whereas it has pleased the *Great Governor of the world* to incline the hearts of the legislatures . . . to approve and authorize the said Articles of Confederation and Perpetual Union.

Going further back, the Mayflower Compact is permeated with references to God. In addition, virtually all of the states of the Union in 1860, before the Civil War, with the exceptions of Michigan and Kentucky, included such religious language in their constitutions.

Views of the Founding Fathers of the Constitution

All of this raises the question of why the Founding Fathers did not include some such reference to the Almighty in the federal constitution of 1789. The topic has been the subject of discussion and debate over the years. It relates to the hotly disputed questions of separation of Church and State and remains controversial down to the present day. Was it simple negligence, as the Montgomery editorial writer implied? Alexander Hamilton is said to have exclaimed, when asked in later years the reason for this neglect, "I declare we forgot it."[3]

A deeper study, however, leads to the conclusion that the exclusion was not accidental. The Constitution is quite secular, written as a legal document in a time when the authors were mainly concerned with securing secular and political freedom, not spiritual salvation. Just as most of the European nations had national churches, nine of the thirteen colonies (new states) had legally established churches. The Congregationalists, the heirs of the Puritan Pilgrims, were the official state church of New Hampshire, Massachusetts, and Connecticut. The Anglican Church was the establishment institution for Maryland, Virginia, North Carolina, South Carolina, Georgia, and large parts of New York. Connections between government

A sheet-music cover for the Confederate States' unofficial national anthem.

and religion in these states involved, among other things, imposing taxes for support for the churches and requiring religious tests for public office-holding. By the time the Constitutional Convention met these were, increasingly, sources of friction among the inhabitants of the states, and the trend was away from these kinds of provisions. In general, state laws favoring established churches were fading away, though they persisted, particularly in the New England states, into the early nineteenth century.[4] Vermont dropped them in 1807, Connecticut in 1818, and New Hampshire in 1819. Massachusetts persisted with its tax support of the Congregationalist Church until 1833.[5] Clearly the framers of the Constitution wanted to avoid any such federal churches, and silence left such matters in the hands of the states. The issue among the drafters focused on how to allocate and restrain power in a way that protected liberty. Pursuit of eternal truth was left to individuals and the churches.[6] There is minimal reference to religion in the Constitution, though there is an explicit prohibition of any religious test for holding *federal* public office. Later, Article 1 of the Bill of Rights stated that there should be "no law respecting an establishment of religion or prohibition of the free exercise thereof." For there to have been a federal establishment of religion would have immediately presented the question of, "Which religion?" Or more exactly, which denomination or group of denominations would be the chosen ones? Likely these were questions that the Founders didn't want to deal with.

Beyond this, scholars feel that the Founders were influenced by Deism—the belief that God created the universe but now remains apart from it. His creation is permitted to administer itself through natural laws. There are variations of Deism but in general it rejects supernatural aspects of religion such as belief in divine revelation. It stresses rationalist thinking and the importance of ethical conduct, social justice, and opposition to tyranny. Deism was a product of the Enlightenment, gaining prominence in the late 1600s in Europe and especially gaining influence around 1725 in America, with that influence continuing well into the middle to late decades of the 1800s. It was not an organized religion or sect but more of a philosophy or way of looking at the world. On the spectrum of Deist believers, none were atheists, but some were explicitly non-Christian, rejecting most or all of Christian beliefs in such things as the Trinity and the miracles of Jesus, things they could not reconcile with human reason. Most people, however, attempted to reconcile Deism and Christianity, viewing themselves as Christians, attending church, and generally assigning a positive attitude toward the teachings of Christ. Deists used many terms to refer to "God," including "The First Cause," "The Creator of the Universe," "The Divine Author," "The Supreme Architect," "Nature's God," "Divine Providence," and numerous related others. Indeed, terms such as "Creator" and "Nature's God" appear in the Declaration of Independence.

By its emphasis on rationalism and a non-interfering Creator, Deism tended to undermine personal religion. The need to read the Bible, attend church, pray, study theology, or seek a personal relationship with God was deemphasized. On the other hand, the emphasis on ethical behavior and promotion of justice inclined many to attend church and seek moral lessons from the teachings of Jesus and the Bible.

Another factor influencing the writers of the Constitution was Freemasonry. Masonic lodges grew in popularity during the Revolution and in the decades following. A full one-third of the convention's delegates were Freemasons. These included some of the most influential, such as George Washington and Benjamin Franklin. The Masons held views heavily influenced by Deism. Their rituals were full of architectural allusions and references to God as the Supreme Architect. Though a Bible was part of their ritual, they discouraged religious and political discussions in their lodge meetings, as well as personal religious expressions, feeling that these could lead to internal dissent damaging their goals of character improvement and brotherhood. The Masons strongly favored religious tolerance and rational thought. Washington took his oath as president on a Masonic Bible and laid the cornerstone of the Capitol building wearing his Masonic apron and using a Masonic trowel.[7]

About half of the delegates to the Constitutional Convention were Episcopalians, one-quarter were Presbyterian, and the remainder were scattered among Congregationalists, Quakers, and various other denominations.[8] In general they were not prone to open expression of personal faith. The majority operated under the assumption that the temporal and spiritual aspects of public life should be kept separate. Personal ethics were important, but in general they did not publicly express their religion and likely felt being openly emotional in their faith was in bad taste.

They were also very much aware of the growing diversity of religious sentiment in the country and were sensitive not to offend believers. The diversity sprung from the various immigrant groups that had come to America during the eighteenth century, bringing their own religions and ideas. Furthermore, a movement called "The First Great Awakening" had developed earlier in the eighteenth century. It involved a series of itinerant preaching tours by various ministers influenced by a fusion of English Puritanism and German Pietism. The Puritans emphasized a visible conversion, evidence of being "born again." Pietism emphasized avoidance of sin. The American movement was generally non-denominational but epitomized the fusion of the two ideas and was especially noteworthy for outdoor meetings that drew enormous crowds all through the middle colonies and New England during the 1740s. The First Great Awakening provided an alternative to the established churches of the upper classes and created a broader diversity of religious thinking. The movement was the beginning of the breakdown of traditional Calvinism, a doctrine which held that individuals were preordained from the foundations of the world for salvation or damnation and that personal efforts, piety, and conversion were for naught. This First Great Awakening was counter to Deism, but did not heavily influence the Anglicans, Lutherans, and Quakers. The men at the constitutional convention themselves were not likely heavily influenced by the movement except that they would have realized the growing diversity of thought and would have been encouraged to ensure tolerance for it.[9]

"Washington as a Freemason." In his Farewell Address George Washington said, "Of all the dispositions and habits which lead to political prosperity, religion and morality are indispensable supports."

For these various reasons the federal constitution did not contain explicit religious appeals or language. The lack thereof, however, did not go unnoticed, even at the time the Constitution was being placed before the states for ratification in the late 1780s. Among the more noteworthy critics was William Williams of Connecticut. He felt the document too secular and proposed that the preamble be rewritten rather extensively, expressing "a firm belief of the being and perfection of the one living and true God" and acknowledging "God's role in establishing our Independence." He furthermore believed that officeholders should be required to ascribe to those words, in effect creating a kind of religious test.[10]

Williams's arguments were effectively rebutted by others, including Oliver Ellsworth, a delegate also from Connecticut. He wrote regarding the exclusion of a religious test for office-holding:

> They have been afraid that this clause is unfavorable to religion. But my countrymen, the sole purpose and effect of it is to exclude persecution and to secure to you the important right of religious liberty.[11]

A writer using the pseudonym "Elihu" was even more direct in criticizing Williams's call for an "acknowledgement proper" in the Constitution. He wrote:

> A low mind may imagine that God, like a foolish old man, will think himself slighted and dishonored if he is not complimented with a seat or prologue of recognition in the constitution, but those great philosophers who formed the constitution had a higher idea of that "Infinite Mind" which governs all worlds than to suppose they could add to his honor or glory, or that He would be pleased with such low familiarity or vulgar flattery.[12]

George Washington, when responding to a letter from a group of New England Presbyterian ministers concerned about the moral perils of a godless constitution, encouraged them to stop relying on government for religious leadership and instead suggested reference "to the guidance of Ministers of the Gospel this important object is, perhaps, more properly committed." He also said, "The path of true piety is so plain as to require but little political direction."[13]

The secular view of the Constitution prevailed among the delegates in Philadelphia, but there were, from the beginning, elements of the population who thought it a serious omission. Numerous clergy and statesmen commented over the years. A Reverend Mason, who was a frequent critic of Thomas Jefferson, said in the 1790s that "from the Constitution of the United States, it is impossible to ascertain what God we worship or whether we own a God at all." In 1811 the Reverend Samuel Austin, president of the University of Vermont, said the "one capital defect" of the Constitution was that it "is entirely disconnected from Christianity." In 1820 the chaplain of the state legislature of New York said that the founding fathers showed "a degree of ingratitude perhaps without parallel" as they drafted the Constitution "in which there is not the slightest hint of homage to the God of Heaven." By the mid-1840s ministers began to suggest that the omission of God from the Constitution was the source of any and all American problems.[14]

As time went on, events led to an evolution in religious thought and culture that increased the number and influence of those elements doubtful about the lack of a religious reference. The creation of the Confederacy and its new constitution some 70 years after the Founding Fathers met offered a fresh opportunity for those of that opinion to remedy the "omission." The remedy took the form of the reference to the "Almighty" in the Confederate preamble.

The Second Great Awakening

Among the events leading to changes in American religious thinking was the "Second Great Awakening." It began in the 1790s and lasted well into the first half of the nineteenth century. Just as was the First, the Second Great Awakening was characterized by widespread emotional evangelical revivals usually held out of doors and led by itinerant preachers. Unlike the First, however, the Second had a follow-up institutional effect as converts at the revivals were not left alone afterward to cool in their religious ardor but instead were gathered into churches that were organized into ongoing entities. The Methodists and Baptists and, to a considerable extent, the Presbyterians were especially effective in this organizational effort and grew their numbers quite rapidly. At the end of the Revolution the largest denominations had been the Congregationalists, Anglicans, and Presbyterians. The Methodists and Baptists were at that time small sects on the fringes of American Christianity.

A camp-meeting scene from the Second Great Awakening.

But by early in the nineteenth century they outstripped the older, more established church denominations through their simple doctrines, plain preaching, and efficient organization. They reached out to and appealed to the common people and grew dramatically as a result.

John Wesley, the founder of Methodism in England, sent Francis Asbury and a small number of ministers to America in 1771. Asbury and the others had to go into hiding during the Revolution as many Americans regarded them as pro-British Tories. However, after the revolution, in 1784, Asbury changed the status of the organization from a group of Methodist "societies" to a formal church, entirely separate from the Anglican Church. At that time there were six Methodist ministers and about 700 members in the new country. It was said that after the war "Methodists would scarcely be numerous enough to fill a corncrib." By 1790 they had grown to approximately 57,000. By the time Asbury died in 1816 he had preached thousands of sermons along the frontiers, and the church had grown to 700 ministers and some 200,000 members. The Methodist Church was particularly noted for its organizational genius and was said to be the "most extensive national institution in antebellum America other than the federal government."[15]

At the same time the Anglicans and Congregationalists suffered as the last vestiges of church establishment and government support that they had enjoyed in pre-revolutionary days were swept away. They had been relatively untouched by the Second Great Awakening and had not benefited from its dynamic changes. These churches drew mainly from the upper classes, and the fading of the aristocracy, the rise of democratic feelings, and a stronger middle class led them increasingly into a minority status. The prevailing thought had been that for a church or

An outdoor camp gathering.

a religion to be healthy it required state support, but the Constitution in effect demanded a paradigm shift, away from public tax support and toward private support by the churches' congregations. By 1820 the Methodists and Baptists had 2,700 churches each and the Presbyterians 1,700. Each of these denominations individually outnumbered all the others.[16]

Formal church membership rose from 10 percent of the national population in 1790 to 40 percent by 1860. And of the 60 percent who were not formal members, many were pious people who declined formal membership for various reasons including reluctance to subscribe to a particular theology, or inability or unwillingness to submit fully to church discipline. Nevertheless a large proportion of those people attended Sunday services, read their Bibles, and prayed regularly. It was said ministers preached routinely to weekly attendees in numbers three to four times their official membership.[17] Salvation became more democratized and emphasis was placed on salvation through one's inner faith, practice of moral living, and more open expression of religious belief. A classic example of this is Abraham Lincoln, who never formally joined any church but subscribed to the fundamental Christian tenets and read the Bible such that his own political prose was affected by the rhythms of its language.[18]

The evangelical denominations grew rapidly everywhere but were especially successful in the South. At the time of secession, in 1860 and 1861, in the states making up the Confederacy, Methodists had 45 percent of the total number of churches, Baptists 37 percent, and Presbyterians 12 percent. The three denominations made up 94 percent of the churches in the region. The Presbyterians lagged the Methodists and Baptists probably due to stricter educational requirements for their clergy, which limited the number of clergy in the field. This may have slowed their growth relative to the others, but it may also account for their clergy's prominence in leading thought on the moral issues of the time in both the South and the North.[19]

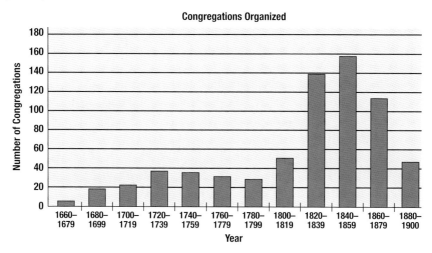

The Second Great Awakening and the Democratization of Christianity

The Second Great Awakening led to a kind of "democratization" of Christianity as the poor and poorly educated could feel part of the faith. The realization of this came to the author when he lived in a suburb north of Columbus, Ohio, years ago. A scenic rural road runs along the Olentangy River from Columbus north toward Delaware, Ohio. On the river's bank stands a small Presbyterian church, called Liberty Church. The congregation was established in 1810 with services rotating around at members' homes during the winter and in the woods outdoors in summer. In 1820 a church building was constructed. This is the building that still stands. A relatively well-off and prominent member of the church, Leonard Monroe, was especially zealous for the cause. He became a deacon in the church and frequently urged people of the area to attend services and join the congregation. One day he was lecturing a neighbor about attending. The neighbor commented that it was fine for Mr. Monroe to attend church as he had "proper clothes and shoes," unlike many of the residents of this wilderness area. Monroe was struck by this comment and began going barefoot to Sunday services to show that no one need be ashamed of attending for lack of shoes. It is said he would sit just inside the door of the church, clearly displaying his bare feet to make the point. All were welcome regardless of their economic or social condition. At least in part due to Mr. Monroe's efforts the small church prospered, expanding its congregation and surviving until this day.

This example illustrates the changes taking place during the early-nineteenth century as access to some established church denominations opened up and as the newer denominations grew with a more democratic and open approach to their memberships. It is hard to imagine a deacon of an Anglican church during the Revolutionary period doing as Mr. Monroe did in the 1820s. These trends were accompanied by greater emphasis on personal salvation and more open expression of personal faith. Both of the Great Awakenings, with their evangelical fervor, established these trends.

Liberty Church.

Even as these events unfolded, the influence of Deism declined. Freemasonry, one of the chief venues for Deistic thought, fell on hard times following the "Morgan Affair" in 1826. This murky situation involved a man named William Morgan in Batavia, New York. He fell out of favor with the local Masonic lodge and threatened to publish a book disclosing Masonic secrets. He subsequently disappeared and was presumed murdered by Masons. This crime was compounded by supposed cover-ups by fellow Masons protecting those who were accused of the murder. This incident and the reaction to it ultimately led to the creation of an anti-Masonic political party that was linked in opposition to presidential aspirant Andrew Jackson, who was a Mason. The net effect of all this was a dramatic fall-off in Masonic membership and general loss of influence. The organization did not recover until later in the nineteenth century.[20]

The Rise of Reform and Educational Efforts

The evangelical churches stressed the spiritual advancement of the individual. Virtues such as temperance, frugality, and the ethic of hard work were encouraged. This in turn led to an impulse to minister to the spiritual health of the larger society. Out of this, reform and educational movements arose. On the educational side, Sunday schools were created to teach the young. The American Sunday School Union was established in the late-eighteenth century to promote Sunday School classes, especially in rural areas. Bible societies (the American Bible Society was created in 1816) and missionary societies multiplied to promote Christianity both abroad and at home; educational groups established new colleges (virtually every American college founded in this time had church origins); and efforts came about to subsidize training of ministers. These efforts increased literacy as well as spreading the Gospel.

Related to this growth was the number of reform-oriented organizations founded in the first half of the nineteenth century. Groups promoting temperance, to suppress vice, to assist "fallen women," to press for prison reform, to minister to lonely seamen, to help the poor, and to generally improve society were typical. An important characteristic of most of these groups was that they were interdenominational, involving people of various faiths. In general they were not linked directly to the churches, but carried out missions that the churches favored. Reform groups also promoted a sense of national consciousness as many of them were national in scope.[21] Their publications constituted almost the only nationally circulated media. Indeed the explosion of such voluntary organizations was one of the main observations of Alexis de Tocqueville about the United States in his classic work *Democracy in America*.

Anti-Slavery Efforts

One manifestation of the reform efforts of the time was anti-slavery and abolitionist. Various groups were formed on a spectrum from those promoting general improvement of the slaves' lot (without destroying slavery itself) to those promoting gradual emancipation, returning blacks to Africa (American Colonization Society), or demanding immediate abolition. As might be expected, most of these groups were in the North, where slavery either did not exist or was not a significant factor in economic life. The South was, of course, a different story, with slavery being a major element driving an agricultural, plantation economy. There was, however, an element of Southern sympathy for mitigating the worse abuses of slavery and encouraging missionary efforts and education for blacks. Those ideas were not widespread in the South and the good intentions were not enough to erase the deep and rising differences in sectional attitudes toward slavery.

The event that effectively killed any Southern support for slavery-reform efforts was Nat Turner's Rebellion in August of 1831. This uprising manifested the worst fears of Southerners about slave rebellion and widespread massacre of whites. The rebellion was quickly suppressed, but not before 55 whites had been brutally killed. This united Southerners and many Northerners in a hysterical condemnation. Slave rebellion was an existential threat to white Southerners. After this any Northern anti-slavery expressions, however moderate, brought severe reaction in the South.[22] In light of this it is easy to understand the South's strong feelings about John Brown's raid on Harper's Ferry and his efforts to foment slave rebellion in 1859. Brown was openly financed and supported by New England anti-slavery groups.

Much of the mainstream clergy, both North and South, realized the explosive potential of the slavery issue and tried to avoid its controversy. But elements in the North increasingly pushed the issue, causing tensions to increase through the 1840s and 1850s. The famous abolitionist William Lloyd Garrison promoted the cause among the clergy and the general populace. He for example approached Lyman Beecher, a leading Northern clergyman,

BLOW FOR BLOW.

A Civil War–era image of
"blow for blow" vengeance.

A depiction of conspirators in Nat Turner's Rebellion.

for support. Beecher pointedly rebuffed him, realizing the subject was too danger-
ous to touch. Lewis Tappan and his brother Arthur, both abolition activists,
launched the "Great Postal Campaign" in 1835, through which anti-slavery material was mass-mailed to clergy in both the North and the South. This too created
severe reaction in the South. The post office in Charleston, South Carolina, was
broken into in July 1835 (the perpetrators in disguise, a la the Boston Tea Party).
All mail from New York was destroyed, as it contained anti-slavery literature.[23] In
the North the belief gradually grew that slavery was a sin. Among other things the
bestselling book *Uncle Tom's Cabin*, by Harriet Beecher Stowe (Lyman Beecher's
daughter), greatly contributed to this belief.[24] Over time the issue led to splits
within the churches themselves and religious arguments as to the relative righ-
teousness of their views.

The Churches Split

The abolitionist activists increasingly based their arguments on moral and religious values, and the Southern defense was necessarily also in moral and religious
terms. The churches were therefore increasingly drawn into the dispute, leading
to sectional splits. The first to separate was the Presbyterian Church in 1837. Initially their division was between the "Old School" and the "New School," largely
over doctrinal issues and not strictly along sectional or slavery-issue lines. The

A theatrical-poster rendering of the violence in *Uncle Tom's Cabin*.

doctrinal split began in the North. The New and Old School factions struggled for control of the General Assembly of the church. The New School tended to be faster-growing and held the majority prior to 1835. But in that year the Old School won back control and repudiated many of the New School programs. In the 1837 session the Old School enlisted the support of nearly all of the Southern delegates, who were generally offended by the New School's growing anti-slavery activities. The New School Presbyterians were in effect expelled from the Church and formed their own separate entity. In the North the Old School and New School factions emerged as of roughly equal size, though the New School was growing faster. The South became almost entirely Old School. The Presbyterian split of 1837 was a warning shot and resulted somewhat indirectly from the slavery issue.

The Methodist and Baptist splits in 1844 and 1845, however, were directly related to slavery issues and created more widely bitter sectional feelings.

The Methodist divide resulted from the refusal of the National Conference to permit a slaveholder to serve as bishop. The case was complicated as the individual, James Andrew of Georgia, had served as bishop since 1832. He had not himself owned slaves but inherited a mulatto woman and a young boy slave from his deceased wife. He tried to free them but was prohibited from doing so by Georgia law. He offered to resign as bishop to avoid a clash with Methodist authorities. However, Southern clergy and congregants would not permit him to do so, clearly regarding the situation as a test case. The conference meeting in 1844 held debates on the issue lasting nearly two weeks. Ultimately the vote went against Andrew by 110 to 68, completely along sectional North/South lines. The Southerners took this as reason to leave and form their own Southern Methodist entity. They divided their property and remained separate for a century.

The Baptists split in 1845 over whether a slaveholder could serve as a missionary, in a manner similar to the Methodists.[25]

The splits of the nation's three major denominations between North and South, in such rancorous ways, were recognized as harbingers of political disunity. Such prominent people as statesman Henry Clay (former secretary of State, senator, and founder of the Whig Party) and John C. Calhoun (former vice president, and states'-rights advocate) spoke of it. Just before his death in 1852 Clay said in an interview:

> I tell you this sundering of the religious ties which have hitherto bound our people together, I consider the greatest source of danger to our country. If our religious men cannot live together in peace, what can be expected of us politicians, very few of whom profess to be governed by the great principles of love? If all the Churches divide on the subject of slavery, there will be nothing left to bind our people together but trade and commerce. . . . That is a very powerful bond, I admit but when the people of these states become thoroughly alienated from each other, and get their passions aroused, they are not apt to stop and consider what is to their interest.

An abolition-themed copper token from the 1830s (cataloged as Low-54A).

Though Calhoun was often accused of exacerbating the tensions between North and South, in a Senate speech a few days before he died he expressed his fear of the consequences of the church splits:

> The cords that bind the States together are not only many, but various in character. Some are spiritual or ecclesiastical; some political; others social. . . . The strongest of those of a spiritual and ecclesiastical nature, consisted in the unity of the great religious denominations, all of which originally embraced the whole Union. . . . clergymen and lay members of the respective denominations, from all parts of the Union, met to transact business relating to their common concerns. It . . . extended to plans for disseminating the Bible, establishing missions, distributing tracts, and of establishing presses for the publication of tracts, newspapers, and periodicals, with a view of diffusing religious information—and for the support of their respective doctrines and creeds. All this combined contributed greatly to strengthen the bonds of the Union.
>
> The first of these cords which snapped, under its explosive force, was that of the powerful Methodist Episcopal Church. The . . . ties which held it together, are all broken and its unity gone. The next cord that snapped was that of the Baptists—one of the largest and most respectable of the denominations. That of the Presbyterians is not entirely snapped, but some of its strands have given way.
>
> If the agitation goes on, the same force, acting with increased intensity, as has been shown, will finally snap every cord, when nothing will be left to hold the States together except force.[26]

Henry Clay circa 1851, shortly before his death.

John C. Calhoun agreed with Henry Clay that the split in the churches boded ill for the nation.

Consequences of the Confederate Constitution

The national changes in religious culture promoted more open expression of piety and religious faith. In this light it is understandable that the Confederate constitutional delegates were more prone to include a reference to God in their work than the Founding Fathers had been. Perhaps of more immediate motivation, though, was the increasing split and frictions between Northern and Southern churches and clergy. These certainly encouraged a Southern effort to command the moral high ground. According to historian Harry Stout in his book *Upon the Altar of the Nation*, the Confederate lawmakers did not initially realize the significance of their introducing God explicitly into their constitution. But the significance soon became evident. First, it solidified the South's self-image and its claim as a religious, Christian republic. Second, and just as importantly, it served as a powerful Southern critique of a "godless Northern constitution" (and by implication a godless North). It allowed the South to take on a sense of moral superiority over its Northern opponents and provide a sense of cleansing. A South Carolina minister, William Prentiss, justified his state's secession in a sermon delivered in December 1860: "We cannot coalesce with men whose society will eventually corrupt our own, and bring down upon us the awful doom which awaits them."[27]

These points are illustrated by the reactions of two noted Southern clergymen. Reverend James Thornwell, a prominent Presbyterian minister from Charleston, was known before the war for his development of Biblical and theological justifications of slavery. Famous for his strong views and fiery oratory, Thornwell was called "the Calhoun of the Church." He had, however, been slower and more reluctant than many to advocate secession. He also tended to believe the clergy should be apolitical.

Despite this, on November 21, 1860, two weeks after Abraham Lincoln's election, Thornwell enthusiastically embraced secession and the Southern cause. He may have influenced the language of the Confederate preamble. Openly expressing his feeling that the federal constitution was flawed, he asked:

> May it not be that God is now punishing this nation for this practical atheism and national neglect and not . . . in a name acknowledging His supremacy?

As for the Confederate constitution, he said:

> We shall have a government that acknowledges God, that reverences right, and that makes law supreme. We are therefore, fighting not for ourselves alone, but, when the struggle is rightly understood, for the salvation of this whole continent.[28]

Eng.ᵈ by A.H.Ritchie

Reverend
James Thornwell
of South Carolina was
among the Southern clergy
who embraced secession.

Reverend Benjamin Palmer of New Orleans, also a Presbyterian minister, had been instrumental in earlier years in the breaking up of that denomination between Northern and Southern factions. A sermon preached by Palmer in late 1860 is credited with leading to Louisiana's decision for secession from the Union. In an 1861 sermon he stated:

> The Confederate constitution is a "truly Christian patriot's prayer" unlike "the perilous atheism of the U.S. constitution." The Founding Fathers had been too much influenced by "free thinking" and "infidel spirit" that was often associated with the "horrors of the French Revolution." The Confederate founders had made "a conscious effort to avoid the scandalous secularism of the U.S. constitution." The Confederate preamble had "clear, solemn, official recognition of Almighty God."

Reverend Benjamin Morgan Palmer of New Orleans.
His sermons helped spur the South to rebellion.

Palmer said that his "heart swelled with unutterable emotions of gratitude and joy . . . at length the nation has a God: Alleluia! The Lord reigneth, let the earth rejoice."

In another sermon in late 1860, Palmer criticized the anti-slavery aspects of the reforms preached by the Northern clergy.

> The Most High, knowing his own power, which is infinite, and his own wisdom, which is unfathomable, can afford to be patient. But these self-constituted reformers must quicken the activity of Jehovah or compel his abdication. It is time to reproduce the obsolete idea that Providence must govern man, and not than man shall control Providence.

Independence could allow the South to fulfill its duty "to ourselves, to our slaves, to the world, and to Almighty God . . . to preserve and transmit our existing system of domestic servitude, with the right, unchallenged by man, to go and root itself wherever Providence and nature may carry it."[29]

Thirty thousand copies of Palmer's sermon defending slavery and attacking Northern reformers were published and circulated over the South. It was said that Palmer did more than "any other non-combatant in the South to promote rebellion."[30] It is perhaps not surprising therefore that in 1862, after New Orleans was captured by the Union navy and occupied by federal troops, General Benjamin Butler, the federal commander (detested by the citizens of New Orleans), placed a bounty on Reverend Palmer's head, forcing him to flee the city.

Many of the clergy in the South felt the Confederacy and its new constitution represented a national rebirth as they believed they had been individually reborn in Christ, cleansed from sins and clothed in the strength of God and vindicating the right.[31]

On June 13, 1861, Confederate president Jefferson Davis proclaimed a fasting day, the first of many to come during the war, and asked the citizenry to call on God "to guide and direct our policy in the hearts and our efforts for the defense of our dearest rights, to strengthen our weakness, crown our arms with success, and enable us to secure a speedy, just, and honorable peace."

Prior to the war, fasts were more a Northern, perhaps more a New England, phenomenon. Beginning with this fast proclaimed by President Davis they became a common occurrence in the South. Davis proclaimed 10 of them during the war, and many others were organized and proclaimed locally. Meanwhile in the North, President Lincoln proclaimed three of them during the same period. On the same day as President Davis's proclamation, a sermon by Reverend O.S. Barten was published in Richmond, alluding to the Confederate constitution. It stressed that the new constitution promoted a close relation between religion and government. The Biblical grounding and constitutional circumstances of the Confederate

The Cabinet of the Confederate States of America,
June 1861. President Jefferson Davis is third from the right.

founding pointed to a glorious future and the birth of a unique Christian nation. God's purpose would be bound up with the nation.[32]

Indeed, numerous preachers and politicians drew contrasts between the new Confederate constitution and the Godless U.S. document that failed to acknowledge divine sovereignty. At least one, however, Methodist bishop George Pierce, believed the Confederacy had not gone far enough and that its Constitution was little more than a "deists' document." The new constitution required full acknowledgement of Jesus Christ, the Trinity, and use of the Bible as the basis of all law. We will see more of this line of thinking in a later chapter.

Beyond the borders of the Confederacy these events created a reaction and, among other things, inspired efforts in the North to get God into their own old federal constitution and correct the oversight of the Founding Fathers.

Among the early Northern reactions to the South's constitution was that of Horace Bushnell, a prominent theologian in Hartford, Connecticut. On the Sunday following the shocking Union loss at the Battle of Bull Run in July of 1861, he delivered a sermon entitled "Reverses Needed." It was published and widely circulated. In it Bushnell argued that the only way to make sense of the defeat was to place fault at the very foundation of American government. Defeats and reverses were needed to make people see the deficiencies of their constitution. It had been established without a moral or religious basis. It did not recognize that all power was from God. It provided "no feeling of authority, or even respect" among the people. By contrast the Confederate constitution acknowledged the authority of Almighty God. The time may have come to recognize the supremacy of God in the federal document.[33] A leading religious newspaper, the *Independent*, voiced support for Bushnell's thoughts.

Reverend Horace Bushnell (seen here in an 1847 portrait) expressed support early in the Civil War for a change to the federal constitution to provide for acknowledging God.

One group, the Reformed Presbyterian Church (a splinter from the mainstream Presbyterians), known as the "Covenanters," had long bemoaned the lack of recognition of God's authority in the Constitution. They believed civil officials only held power through God's authority, and governments were legitimate only to the extent that they acknowledged God's authority. Because the Constitution lacked an affirmation of God, they refused to vote or hold public office. The raising of the issue in the wider public through the *Independent*'s article prompted members of the group to meet in late 1861 in Allegheny, Pennsylvania. They drew up a petition deploring the absence of God and His laws in the Constitution and called for an amendment or change in some form to rectify the situation. Their petition caught the attention and support of Senator Charles Sumner of Massachusetts. Through Sumner's intervention, the Covenanters were able to arrange a meeting with President Lincoln and present their petition to him in early 1862. It is said Lincoln was non-committal. However, the effort had reached the highest levels of government, and there was widespread awareness of the issue, giving encouragement to the Covenanters. They and others would persist in their efforts and continue to raise the idea of an amendment with those in authority in the coming years.

Reverend Mark R. Watkinson.

CHAPTER 2

The Letter

In November of 1861 Reverend Mark R. Watkinson, a Baptist minister in Ridleyville, Pennsylvania, was a troubled man. The past year had brought unimaginable turmoil not only to the nation but to him personally as he was caught up in the national cataclysm. Watkinson was a native Northerner, born in Pemberton, New Jersey, on October 24, 1824. One of ten children, he had at an early age worked as a printer's apprentice in nearby Mount Holly. While in Mount Holly he had joined and been baptized in the local Baptist church. He moved in 1845 to Philadelphia, where he was active in the Broad Street Baptist Church. He came under the influence of the pastor there, who encouraged him to pursue a career in the ministry. With the support of the congregation Watkinson attended Lewisburg University, a Baptist college (now Bucknell University). Due to poor health he left the school after 18 months of study. But later he attended Columbian College (now George Washington University) in Washington, D.C., and completed his degree. Following college he worked for a few months as an evangelist at a Baptist church in Bristol, Pennsylvania. He was offered a position in Ridleyville, where he was ordained as a minister June 1, 1852. Today one can search a Pennsylvania map in vain, as no town of that name remains. However, a township bearing the name Ridley is part of Prospect Park, Pennsylvania, and a place of worship remains on the site of Watkinson's church, now known as the Prospect Hill Baptist Church.

The church in Ridleyville was known as The First Particular Baptist Church. "Particular" was applied due to an earlier doctrinal split among Baptists, with the other faction known as the "Regular Baptists." Watkinson met and baptized a young woman into the congregation. She was Sarah Isabella Griffiths. Their relationship clearly quickly moved beyond that of pastor and congregant, as they became engaged and married in 1853. Sarah was the daughter of Jesse Griffiths, a doctor at a government quarantine station nearby. The couple left Ridleyville later that year to take a position at the Schuykill Baptist Church in Philadelphia.[1]

They served in Philadelphia for three years, after which Watkinson was offered an interesting opportunity in Portsmouth, Virginia. Portsmouth was home to the Gosport Navy Yard (later named Norfolk Navy Yard). The region had suffered a devastating outbreak of yellow fever in 1855, with the population of the area falling from more than 27,000 to fewer than 10,000. In Portsmouth proper it is recorded that 1,080 of the population of 8,500 died. The Baptist church there (the Court Street Baptist Church) had suffered a dramatic decline in membership from the combination of yellow-fever deaths and the flight of the population. The church was searching for a minister willing to take up the challenge of rebuilding the congregation. They had made unsuccessful efforts to attract a new pastor in 1855 and early 1856. Besides the yellow-fever issues, the church had had a poor record of pastoral support. In July of 1856 the church unanimously elected Watkinson as pastor and offered him $1,000 per year in salary. Despite the conditions and the church's somewhat poor reputation, he accepted immediately. The $1,000 per year was a substantial increase from his days in Ridleyville, where he had earned $400 annually. Watkinson took up the position arriving with his wife in late summer 1856. In the following years he successfully built the church back up. He was highly regarded and popular with his congregation. It is reported that he was an energetic pastor who actively visited the homes of his congregants both

Prospect Hill Baptist Church today. The modern church is on the site of the Ridleyville church where Reverend Mark Watkinson preached and from whence he wrote his letter to Treasury Secretary Salmon Chase. A plaque commemorating Watkinson's letter to Chase was placed next to the door of the church in 1962 by the Delaware County Coin Club. A two-cent piece is pictured at the top of the plaque.

rich and poor and took a personal interest in their lives and families. He was also regarded as a strong preacher, delivering interesting and entertaining sermons drawing large and appreciative attendances. In addition he loved music and enlarged its role in the life of the church. In December 1856 Watkinson engaged a singing instructor who proceeded to give singing lessons and form a choir. Then in March of 1858 the church purchased an organ for $435. The church building was enlarged with a Sunday school room added in 1860 and another room enlarged, enabling Watkinson to lecture to large audiences one night a week in addition to his regular Sunday services.[2]

This happy situation was becoming cloudy as the tensions between North and South grew in the late 1850s. Watkinson would certainly have been aware of the deep splits over slavery and other issues both in the church and in the wider political arena. It is hard to know what his stand was on slavery during this period. He may have been conflicted, having Northern roots but a Southern congregation. Portsmouth itself was a conflicted, complicated place as the presence of the federal naval facility there meant that a larger portion of the population was pro-Union in their sympathies than would have been typical in most of Virginia.

Court Street Baptist Church. The present structure was built in 1903 on the site of the church where Reverend Mark Watkinson served. A historical marker displays pictures of the site's predecessor church buildings. The history does not mention Reverend Watkinson, though the church has a plaque inside commemorating the connection with him and "In God We Trust."

The presidential election of Abraham Lincoln in November 1860 brought matters to a head with even more tension. It was becoming clear that people would be forced to choose sides. Following the election Watkinson delivered a sermon on November 29, 1860, that seemed to make his thoughts clear. He said from the pulpit that he favored the South's position and blamed abolitionism for the state of national affairs. He may have called for secession. The sermon created a sensation and that evening a special meeting of the church council was held, the object of which was to appoint a committee of three men to approach the pastor to procure a copy of his sermon for publication. The committee reported that Watkinson "cheerfully and promptly consented to its publication."[3] The committee sought to have the sermon published in the *Daily Transcript* (a local paper), the *Religious Herald*, and "all other papers friendly to its sentiments." For whatever reason, however, there is no record of the sermon being published and there is no copy known of it. We do not therefore know in detail what it contained. However, it created division within the congregation and was regarded as inflammatory by many in the community.

By early 1861 several Southern states had seceded and by April even Virginia passed a secession bill dramatically affecting the Portsmouth area. The state seized the naval base and the American flag was torn down on April 20, 1861, replaced with the flag of Virginia. The federal commander of the navy yard, Commodore Charles McCauley had not evacuated the yard or made preparations to do so earlier, despite signs that trouble was coming. He was advanced in years and surrounded by subordinates who favored the South. In addition it seems there was a theory in Washington that they should not take radical action by evacuating ships or strengthening defenses as it might upset Virginia and tip the state toward secession while that issue was still in contention. By spring, however, the Navy Department began to grow uneasy and it sent 250 seamen from the New York Navy Yard to Portsmouth on March 31. There was special concern certain of the ships docked at Portsmouth might fall into hostile hands—in particular the *Merrimac*, a large modern steam frigate propelled by screw propeller, docked there for work on its engines. Also the large sailing warships, the *United States* and the *Pennsylvania*, were there. On April 11 a new captain, James Alden, was ordered to take command of the *Merrimac* and hasten completion of work on her. By the 17th her engines were in working order, but her departure and that of the other ships was delayed by McCauley's indecision, probably under the influence of his subordinates. The Navy then sent Commodore Hiram Paulding along with a Massachusetts volunteer infantry regiment on the warship *Pawnee* to Portsmouth to take over command of the base. Upon his arrival Paulding evidently viewed the situation as somewhat hopeless, as the yard workers were already turning hostile. Given his orders from Washington not to let anything fall into Confederate hands he made the decision to set torch to the ships and repair shops. Only the *Cumberland* and another smaller ship were towed out by the *Pawnee*, with the others being set afire on the night of April 20.

Admiral David D. Porter, in his *Naval History of the Civil War*, described the night:

> It was a beautiful starlight night, April 20, when all the preparations were completed. The people of Norfolk and Portsmouth were wrapped in slumber, little dreaming that in a few hours the ships and public works which were so essential to the prosperity of the community would be a mass of ruins and hundreds of people would be without employment and without food for their families.
>
> At 2:30 AM, April 21st, a rocket from the *Pawnee* gave the signal: the work of destruction commenced with the *Merrimac*, and in ten minutes she was one vast sheet of flame. In quick succession the powder trains to the other ships and buildings were ignited and the surrounding country brilliantly illuminated.
>
> The inhabitants of Norfolk and Portsmouth, roused from their slumber, looked with awe at the work of destruction, and mothers clasping their children to their breasts bewailed the fate that cut them and their offspring off from their supports. Yet this was but a just retribution for the treason which the inhabitants had shown towards the best government on earth. They had killed the goose that laid the golden egg.[4]

There were orders to also burn the large modern dry dock, but Paulding's forces failed to materially damage it. Many of the workshops survived the damage, and the frigate *United States* was not significantly damaged. The *Pennsylvania*, the largest ship in the navy, was burned. The *Merrimac* was burned to the water's edge and sunk. She of course was later raised by the Confederates and converted into an ironclad renamed *Virginia*. She and the federal ironclad *Monitor* would subsequently fight the first battle between iron ships.

According to Admiral Porter the greatest misfortune to the Union resulting from the destruction of the Gosport Navy Yard and its seizure by the Confederacy was the loss of at least 1,200 large guns. These were subsequently installed at various places around the Confederacy, including along the North Carolina sounds, at New Orleans, and even at Fort McHenry, Fort Donaldson, Island No. 10, and other fortifications along the Mississippi. Porter said, "Had it not been for the guns captured at Norfolk and at Pensacola, the Confederates would have found it a difficult matter to arm their fortifications for at least a year after the breaking out of hostilities. . . . Great as it was, therefore, the loss of our ships, it was much less than the loss of our guns."[5]

Riots and fighting in the streets followed the destruction of April 20 and 21, with numerous injuries and deaths. Watkinson himself had become controversial

The destruction and evacuation of the Gosport Navy Yard facilities at Portsmouth, Virginia, was carried out by federal troops on April 20 and 21, 1861. This followed the vote by Virginia for secession. The ship seen in flames here is the USS *Pennsylvania*.

and he seems to have felt some responsibility for the divisions and chaos in the community. Evidently he began to fear for the safety of his family in the turmoil even before the events of the 20th; he sent them back to Ridleyville, his wife's hometown, in early April. Watkinson followed his wife, catching the last ship north on April 23, 1861. Once back in Ridleyville, in early May he wrote a letter of resignation to his congregation. Most of them reacted with a sense of betrayal due to his sudden departure and resignation. They voted to expel him as their pastor for the misconduct of leaving his church. The minutes of the church conference meeting of May 10 reflect the depth of their unhappiness with Watkinson:

> After singing and prayers proceeded to business - Brother Armistead was chosen moderator - Several letters were read from Brother M.R. Watkinson (now in Pennsylvania) tendering his resignation to take effect August 1, 1861 - and asking for letters of dissociation for himself and his wife - On motion of Brother Morris his resignation was unanimously accepted, to take effect from date (May 10). A letter of dissociation was granted Sister Watkinson. Brother Armistead submitted the following preamble and resolutions, which after remarks by various brethren was adopted:

The Court Street Baptist Church of Portsmouth, now in regular monthly business meeting, feels called upon to place on account the expulsion of M.R. Watkinson.

On Monday the 23rd of April (last month) he left this place, giving contradictory reasons for so doing, and at the same time promising to return at an early day. It was a time of great trial to us, when we needed his sympathy, and if he had been true to his supposed sentiments, or grateful for our unfailing kindness to him he would have remained with us. A few days after he left he forwarded his resignation and shortly after wrote to a member of this church in terms designed to dissuade us and in truth proclaiming his hypocrisy in the past, and presenting himself as a bitter enemy. He asserts that he is now in a place of "happy content" that he is where he can "think and say what he pleases." He seems to rejoice at the thought that the Confederated States, as he explains it, will be "invaded and partially exterminated." He says it is was good of him to stay so long as he did with us and declares it is a great temptation for him to seek a "Military Reaction."

All that he has done and said in this communication has given us great pain and been deeply mortifying to us when with us he expressed the most ultra pro slavery sentiments and violent hatred of Northern opinions on that subject. He was among the first, practically or in effect, to put forth secession sentiments, and was most earnest in expressing sympathy with the South. All this was done without any urging on our part, made even in the face of qualified opinions as then held by many among us.

We feel called upon therefore to declare, that he has grossly deceived us and by voluntarily arraying himself against us has forfeited all claim to our personal regard and Christian fellowship, and therefore he be expelled from this church.

On motion of Brother Morris it was ordered that the vote be recorded on the above. The vote of the conference was 20 affirmative and only one negative.

On motion the Deacons were requested to make arrangements by which the pulpit can be regularly supplied.[6]

Certainly they were unhappy with him especially since his sermon just some four months earlier had led them to believe he was anti-abolition and pro-South, and he had influenced others' opinions. Why then had he fled back to the North when troubles came, when indeed they really needed him? We can imagine that parishioners needed comfort and that there may have even been funerals to be preached resulting from the local chaos. Some were more understanding and believed he had done it to protect his family. But the consensus on Watkinson's actions was negative.

In a diary entry quoted by Roger W. Burdette in his book *Renaissance of American Coinage 1905–1908* a 19-year-old member of the congregation, Annie Cox, wrote:

1861 – April 28th Sabbath afternoon. I did not go to church this morning as it commenced raining just about church time. Pa went down but there was no preaching. Alas! We are now left without a pastor. Mr. Watkinson has taken his departure, gone north & sent a letter of resignation to the church. I think it would have been much more manly & better for him if he had resigned before he left. I am very sorry that he has acted thus & that is after preaching and talking so much against abolitionists to go right among them. But we cannot judge him. God alone knoweth the heart.[7]

Soon after he joined his family back in Ridleyville, Watkinson's old church there took him back with the temporary minister stepping aside for him. The church agreed to pay him $5 per week and named him "supply minister," a title implying a temporary arrangement. This then was a drastic comedown from his salary and position in Portsmouth. It was a subsistence situation, and he relied upon the kindness of members of the congregation to provide his family with any food that could be spared. In later years Watkinson's granddaughter told of hearing her grandmother Sarah speak of living mostly on potatoes provided by church members during this time.[8]

We know that in July of 1861, some two or three months after leaving Portsmouth, Watkinson provided religious services for the 27th Pennsylvania Volunteer Infantry regiment at the time of the Battle of Bull Run. It seems now that he was all in for the Union.

This then was Watkinson's situation during the latter half of 1861. The mood in the North was at low ebb with more states having seceded, the Battle of Bull Run having been lost in July, Washington nearly captured, the country's finances strained. In November newspapers were full of news regarding the "Trent Affair" as a federal warship, the *San Jacinto*, under the command of Captain Charles Wilkes, stopped a British mail packet. The British ship, the *Trent*, had just departed Havana harbor. Wilkes had learned that two Confederates, Mason and Slidell, had been dispatched to England to act as Confederate commissioners seeking British assistance. On his own initiative, Wilkes had stopped the *Trent* and seized Mason and Slidell. This brought a strong reaction from the British, and there was real concern that the incident would bring them and possibly the French into the war on the side of the Confederacy.

Given the bleak circumstances of the Union at that time, any informed person would have to have been doubtful of the continuation of the United States in any form similar to what it had been a year earlier. On the spiritual side, the Confederacy, with its "religious constitution" and other actions, was clearly on the offensive. Watkinson would certainly have been aware of and disturbed by all of these events.

We can imagine that Watkinson's frame of mind, from political, religious, and personal perspectives, was deeply troubled. Very likely as a result of his mood he was moved to sit down and write a letter to Salmon Chase, secretary of the Treasury. This remarkable letter, dated November 13, 1861, was three pages long, as follows.[9]

Hon. S.P. Chase
U.S. Sec of Treasury
Dear Sir:

You are about to submit your annual report to Congress respecting the affairs of the National Finances.

One fact touching our currency has hitherto been seriously overlooked. I mean the recognition of the Almighty God in some form on our coins.

You are probably a Christian. What if our Republic were now shattered beyond reconstruction? Would not the antiquaries of succeeding centuries rightly reason from our past coins that we were a heathen nation?

What I propose is that instead of the goddess of Liberty we shall have next inside the thirteen stars, a ring inscribed with the words perpetual union. Within this ring the all-seeing eye, crowned with a halo. Beneath this eye the American flag, bearing in its fields stars equal to the number of the States United. In the fields of the bars the words God, liberty, law.

This would make a beautiful coin to which no possible citizen could object. This would relieve us from the ignominy of heathenism. This would place us openly under the Divine protection we have personally claimed. From my heart I have felt our national shame in openly disowning God as not the least of the causes of our present national disasters.

To you first I address a subject that must be agitated.

Yours, most respectfully,
M.R. Watkinson
Minister of the Gospel
Ridleyville, Del. Co., Pa.
Nov. 13, 1861

Perhaps the key line is: "From my heart I have felt our national shame in openly disowning God as not the least of the causes of our present national disasters." How did he think that the nation had disowned God? Given the context of the times he was almost certainly referring to the "Godless" federal constitution, now contrasted with the new Confederate document with its acknowledgement of reliance upon the "guidance of Almighty God." However, unlike many Northern clergy, he was not calling in his letter for amending the Constitution but rather for an alternative means of placing the country openly under the "Divine protection," through such an acknowledgement on the coinage.

Reverend Watkinson's Letter

Hon. S. P. Chase,
U. S. Sec. of Treasury

Dear Sir.

You are about to submit your annual report to Congress respecting the affairs of the National Finances.

One fact touching our Currency has hitherto been seriously overlooked. I mean the recognition of the Almighty God in some form on our coins.

You are probably a Christian. What if our Republic were now shattered beyond reconstruction? Would not the antiquaries of succeeding centuries rightly reason

The original letter in Reverend Watkinson's handwriting.

The journey of this letter following receipt by Secretary Chase is unclear. It was likely in the Treasury Department files for some time, but eventually resided in the Chase Manhattan Bank Museum of Moneys of the World in New York. It was on display there for many years, but in 1977 a decision was made to close the museum and most of its assets were transferred to the Smithsonian Institution in Washington. The letter is now in the Smithsonian's Museum of American History; however, it is not on display.

The Chase Manhattan museum was open to the public and produced a brochure that was given out to visitors viewing the letter. The brochure, dated 1957, was entitled "How the Phrase 'IN GOD WE TRUST' Came to be on the Coins and Paper Money of the United States."[10]

Watkinson remained at the Ridleyville church until 1864, when he moved to the Second Baptist Church in Camden, New Jersey. However, his story with the Court Street Church in Portsmouth was not over. In the spring of 1862 Union general George McClellan began the Peninsular Campaign, landing large numbers of troops in Virginia with some moving into the Norfolk–Portsmouth area. On May 9 Confederate troops burned the facilities and abandoned the base. The next day, May 10, 5,000 federal troops moved into Portsmouth and began a long occupation. The local Methodist church was burned, St. John's Episcopal Church was taken over by Northern Methodist missionaries for use by Methodists, and Trinity Episcopal was taken over for use as a hospital for escaped slaves. Court Street Baptist escaped destruction or takeover, perhaps because it had no pastor and couldn't be clearly identified as hostile to the Union. Nevertheless, as the occupation went on conditions became very difficult. The infamous General Benjamin Butler was in charge of the area. Butler had gained a reputation for cruel and arbitrary actions when he was in charge of the occupation of New Orleans earlier in the war. (He was nicknamed "Spoons" for rumors of his proclivity to steal the silver from dinner parties he attended, or for seizing silverware from a Southern woman crossing Union lines.) He built upon that reputation during his occupation of this part of Virginia. One of the elders of the Court Street Church was arrested and imprisoned by Butler for supposed traitorous attitudes or activities. In the church, during a prayer for President Lincoln, a lady coughed, was reported by informants to the provost marshal, and was arrested before the service ended.[11]

It is evident that Watkinson maintained contact with some in his old congregation and he decided in mid-1863 to travel back to Portsmouth. The July 12, 1863, minutes of the church contain this passage:

> Brother John D. Robinson offered the following. That there is a probability of Brother Mark R. Watkinson (our late pastor) visiting this city, and that we invite him to fill our pulpit during his stay among us. After considerable discussion, the question was taken, only four brethren voted. The Chair was unable to decide the question.[12]

A pre-war silver dollar. "One fact touching our currency has hitherto been seriously overlooked," wrote Reverend Mark Watkinson to Treasury Secretary Salmon Chase. "I mean the recognition of the Almighty God in some form on our coins."

Watkinson did visit the area in mid-August. We know little of whom he met or what conversations he had, but might imagine that he explored the possibility of returning to his pastoral position at the Court Street Church. Given the non-result of the vote to have him "fill the pulpit" during his visit, it seems unlikely that he was allowed to preach at the church when he was in the area.

Amazingly, Watkinson wrote a letter dated August 25, 1863, to President Lincoln, following his visit.

> Hon. A. Lincoln
> President of the United States
>
> Having just returned from a fortnight's visit to Norfolk and Portsmouth, Virginia, in the possession of valuable news of the Rebel plans derived from men I know to be trustworthy from a protracted acquaintance, allow me to give you in detail what I have learned. Most of this information I gave to a Naval Captain before leaving Portsmouth upon the promise that it should reach you. If that Officer's report has come this will corroborate it.

Watkinson continued with a fairly lengthy letter spelling out various bits of intelligence, political and military, that he believed would be of value to Lincoln. Near the end of the letter he wrote, "If I go to Portsmouth to preach for the Union men, who have desired me so to do, I may have occasion to send you letters from that point. If so, I shall sign them No. 1, 2, 3, 4, &c."[13] Certainly this letter confirms Watkinson's pro-Union sympathies at this point. His willingness to act in effect as a spy for Lincoln leaves no doubt. An intriguing aspect of the letter is his relatively familiar tone with the president, making us wonder if his earlier 1861 letters to Chase and Pollock (cited in chapter 4) had led to Lincoln and others in the administration having some knowledge of who he was.

Whatever conversations he had with the church during his August visit seem to have brought discussions within the church councils of his possible reemployment there. Minutes of September 13, 1863:

> Brother W.D. Robinson offered the following resolution, that we employ Reverend Mark R. Watkinson to fill this pulpit as a Supply (Minister) for twelve months and should he feel disposed to leave sooner he will be at liberty to do so. Question was taken up on Brother Robinson's motion and declared adopted. Two voted in the negative but passed. A committee was appointed to inform Brother Watkinson of his election.[14]

Just one week later a second meeting was held with the following minutes recorded:

President Abraham Lincoln.

September 20, 1863

Meeting called to take into consideration the action of a portion of the church on last Sabbath evening. Relative to the employing of Reverend Mark R. Watkinson as supply minister for this Church. . . . Owing to the inclemency of the weather and no previous notice of such were made known, but few members were present, and it being an improper occasion for such a resolution to have passed, and whereas it is deemed necessary for the members to have an opportunity to express themselves, upon this very important matter, this meeting is now called.

And be it resolved – that the Reverend M.R. Watkinson is not the choice of this Church and we will not employ him as a Supply or Pastor.[15]

The minutes do not record the number of votes pro and con, but we can imagine it likely would have been unanimous had they known of Watkinson's letter to Lincoln. Clearly memories of Watkinson's departure and perceived betrayal in 1861 had not faded and a majority of parishioners did not want him back. That majority felt strongly enough about it to reverse the decision made in his favor a week earlier.

As mentioned above, in 1864 Watkinson left the Ridleyville church and moved to the Second Baptist Church in Camden, New Jersey. It is evident that he still retained ties with the church in Portsmouth. An article dated December 14, 1865, appeared in the *Religious Herald*.

Reverend Mark R. Watkinson who was pastor in Portsmouth and went North soon after the war began has revisited his old flock; but our informant thinks there was less sorrow manifested when Brother Watkinson took his second departure than when Paul took his leave of the Elders of Ephesus who "all wept sore, and fell on Paul's neck and kissed him."

We can surmise from this that there remained elements of unhappiness with Reverend Watkinson! Then in 1867 the church needed a new pastor and thought they had found one, a Reverend N.W. Wilson. However, he received a call from another church and reneged on his tentative agreement with Court Street. In August of 1867 the church council voted thirty-nine to two to offer the position to Watkinson. Evidently he strongly considered the offer but declined, as he had committed to helping his Camden congregation build a new church. At that time he wrote that his leaving Portsmouth in 1861 had been "a violent and disagreeable event that has always been regretted." Ultimately it seems the Portsmouth congregation had liked Watkinson and, though the emotions of the early Civil War period had set a significant portion of the congregation against him, he remained popular with many. This thought is confirmed by the church minutes of July 8, 1871.

> The standing committee to whom had been assigned the case of Reverend M.R. Watkinson our late Pastor, relative to his being denied a letter of dismission, etc. at the May conference in 1861 offered the following preamble and resolution.
>
> Upon the case of Rev. M.R. Watkinson late pastor of this church referred to the standing committee at our last meeting, the committee begs leave to offer the following resolution.
>
> Resolved that all proceedings upon our records derogatory to the Christian character of the said brother be and the same is hereby rescinded.
>
> Our motions and preamble and resolutions were unanimously adopted.[16]

Watkinson and Court Street Baptist Church had found their peace. Inside the church today is a plaque stating:

Reverend M.R. Watkinson
Court Street Baptist Church
Pastor
1856–1861
His letter to the Treasury Department inspired President Lincoln
to add "In God We Trust" to all
U.S. currency.
Court Street Academy
February 12, 1969

With this plaque the church recognized Watkinson's role regarding "In God We Trust," although the statement on the plaque is not strictly accurate. Lincoln's role in the motto's adoption was limited, and not all U.S. currency (specifically, paper currency) bore the motto until nearly a century after Watkinson's service at the church.

Watkinson remained at the church in Camden until 1871. Apparently his health, never strong, was growing weaker and he took a position in Baltimore, at the High Street Baptist Church there. It seems this job was in the nature of ministering to a related private chapel and was less demanding on his time and physical condition. In 1873, however, he left that position due to further declining health.

Reverend Watkinson passed away on September 26, 1877. His lengthy obituary in the October 11 issue of the *Religious Herald* provided details of his last days, including the fact that in August he had traveled to Portsmouth, where

> [He] was invited to preach in the scene of his former labors. While there proclaiming the gospel to large audiences every night, he was seized with the fever which terminated his life. Animated with a warm heart and an energetic will, he continued to preach when he should have sought rest and recuperation.
>
> Returning home he endeavored to work on despite the malady which was upon him. But in a short time he was compelled to succumb. When I saw him first, some ten days ago, neither he nor I apprehended a fatal termination of his sickness. The fever was not violent, and all hoped that it would yield to treatment.
>
> He was not anxious about the result, and remarked: "I do not know what the Lord intends to do with me, but I am perfectly willing to have it as he wishes." . . . But the end was near. A short time before it came, he said to his devoted wife, "My troubles will soon be over." He fell asleep in Jesus we may well say of him; for he died so quietly that he seemed but to lay his head on the loving bosom of his Savior, and to breathe his life out sweetly there.[17]

There is no evidence that Reverend Watkinson was ever aware of his role in the story of "In God We Trust" on U.S. coinage. Some two and a half years had passed between his letter to Chase and the issuance of the two-cent piece bearing that inscription. Likely that passage of time and a motto different from anything he had proposed eliminated any thought of a connection for him. There is no mention in his obituary of his letter to Chase or his role in the creation of what would ultimately become the national motto of the United States. Neither does his tombstone reference any such role. He was buried back in his birthplace, Pemberton, New Jersey.

Evidently the cemetery was reconfigured sometime after his death in 1877, and newer burials, likely including that of his wife in 1916, were in a different location.

There is placed a larger tombstone displaying both their names. Watkinson's actual burial place is a few yards away. The stone on his burial site is very small and simple.

A section of the 1896 *Mint Director's Report* disclosed Watkinson's letter to Chase and Chase's memo to Pollock, thus bringing light to and recognition of his role in the story.

Today there is a modern marker in the Pemberton cemetery near his grave commemorating his letter and his connection to the motto. The plaque beneath the IN GOD WE TRUST marker says:

1864–1964

I would propose a religious motto be placed on our coins. So wrote the Reverend Mark R. Watkinson to the Secretary of the Treasury, Salmon P. Chase in 1861.

Rev. Watkinson suggested the words "God, Liberty, Law."
Chase himself selected the words "In God We Trust" which were placed on the 1864 Two Cent Piece.

Rev. Watkinson 1824–1877 lies at rest fifty yards behind this plaque. His suggestion for a religious motto will live forever.

As James Oliver once said "The world is blessed most by men who do things and not by those who merely talk about them."

Left: Reverend Mark R. Watkinson's tombstone. There is no indication on it of his connection to the story of "In God We Trust." It simply states, "He hath entered into his rest." His wife S. Isabella is also on the stone. She lived until 1916, some 39 years beyond her husband's death. *Below:* The smaller stone marking where the Watkinsons are physically interred.

Treasury Secretary Salmon P. Chase.

CHAPTER 3

The Memo

Reverend Mark Watkinson must have been well informed, as his letter was directed to the "right" person in Treasury Secretary Salmon P. Chase. The Mint, where coinage was designed and produced, was under Chase's purview. Watkinson's letter states, "You are probably a Christian," and Chase was indeed steeped in Christianity. He was born in 1808 into a devout Anglican family in New Hampshire, one of ten surviving children. He later said, "I was religiously educated but not under any severe restraint. I was baptized into the Episcopal Church and among my earliest recollections are those of a square pew in the little church . . . where however I did more sleeping than anything else."[1] His father passed away when Chase was only nine years old. His mother struggled to continue his and his siblings' educations. When he was twelve his uncle, Philander Chase, offered to care for the boy and provide an education for him. Philander Chase was an Episcopal priest and had recently been appointed the bishop of Ohio. He had moved to Worthington, Ohio, in 1817, as it had been settled in 1803 by New England people, many of whom were Episcopalians.

So in 1820, young Salmon travelled from New Hampshire to Worthington, a small town just north of Columbus, to join his uncle. Philander proved to be something of a taskmaster and the nephew worked hard at labor on the uncle's farm, but the uncle also provided a solid classical education and taught his nephew to be pious and religiously observant.

Life in Worthington was hard. Philander's wife, Mary, passed away in 1818, partly from the difficult conditions. He received nominal or no salary as bishop and worked to eke out a living from his small farm near the church. In 1822 he was offered the presidency of Cincinnati College. He accepted the position, bringing about the family's move (by that time he had remarried and had children of his own) some 100 miles south to Cincinnati. Cincinnati was a dynamic, fast-growing place on the Ohio River and soon to be largest city in the region.

Salmon Chase studied for about a year at his uncle's college, where he completed two years' worth of the curriculum. He was regarded by fellow students as solemn and self-righteous. Philander, the uncle, decided to leave his post as president in 1823 and travel to England to raise funds for the establishment of a new Episcopal college. He was successful in raising funds from Lord Kenyon and Lord Gambier. He returned to Worthington to begin work on the school but decided instead to establish it in a new place, further north in Ohio. With the $30,000 he had raised in England he started a new town, named it Gambier, and gave the name Kenyon College to the school. His efforts to establish this new college resulted from his frustration with the Anglican establishment in the East who refused to expand their education of Episcopal priests who were so badly needed in the West. Few newly graduated priests desired to pass up comfortable positions in the East for the rigors of the wilderness of Ohio and points further west. Hence the uncle chose the route of establishing a college in the West, where clergy could be locally recruited, trained, and assigned.[2]

With his uncle's departure from Cincinnati, Salmon decided to return to his family home in New Hampshire, with the aim of completing his education at nearby Dartmouth College. Though he struggled financially and worked at teaching on the side at local schools to make ends meet, he was able to graduate from Dartmouth. During the spring of 1826, while he was at Dartmouth, a religious revival occurred, a part of the Second Great Awakening. Chase was greatly influenced by this, shifting from his rather staid Anglican background to recognizing the power of the Evangelical movement. He found his religious faith, already strong, further strengthened. He told a friend at the time: "It has pleased God in His infinite mercy to bring me . . . to the foot of the cross and to find acceptance through the blood of His dear Son." Nevertheless his uncle's early influence kept him solidly Anglican in doctrine. He believed the Episcopal Church to be the one true church and in later years would point out doctrinal flaws of the Methodists and other Protestant denominations. Following graduation at age 18, Chase had to make a career decision. His uncle, Philander, urged him to pursue the ministry, but his older brother Alexander discouraged him from becoming "one of the band of hypocritical Reverends whose pride, lust of power and dominion . . . are the disgrace of the Christian

St. John's Episcopal Church in Worthington, Ohio. It was here that Philander Chase served as Episcopal bishop for Ohio. It was also here that his nephew, Salmon P. Chase, came to live with him. This portion of the church is original to the time Philander Chase was there. The priest's first wife, Mary, is buried under the chancel of the church.

Philander Chase, Salmon's uncle. He was the Episcopal bishop of Ohio and was instrumental in educating and raising his nephew.

church." Instead, "If you feel an ambition to be extensively useful to your species . . . if you wish for wealth, become an honest, conscientious and moral lawyer."[3]

Chase followed his brother's advice and, with the aim of studying for the bar, he moved to Washington, D.C. Again he taught school to finance his legal studies. Initially he struggled to find students and sought another uncle's assistance. The uncle was a senator and Chase asked for his help in finding a government job. The elderly uncle was as tough as his brother, the bishop, and refused to help his nephew, telling him he would give him a half dollar so as to buy a spade to begin a career with, "for then you might come to something at last, but once settle a young man down in a government office, he never does anything more—it's the last thing you hear of him. I've ruined one or two young men that way, and I'm not going to ruin you."[4] Soon afterward Salmon did succeed in starting a school to help finance his legal studies. Among his students were two sons of William Wirt, the attorney general under President John Quincy Adams. He became very close to Wirt and his family, regarding Wirt as a father figure. He spent a great deal of time with the family, especially with two of Wirt's daughters, one of whom he likely would have proposed marriage to, had he been in a sounder financial position. He read law with Wirt and passed the bar examination with his help. Following John Quincy Adams's loss of the presidency to Andrew Jackson in 1828, Wirt and his family left Washington to return to his private practice in Baltimore. Chase with his new law degree in hand decided to move back to Cincinnati and begin his legal career.[5]

When Salmon Chase asked an uncle to help him find a government job, his uncle instead offered him a half dollar—to buy a shovel and start a less ruinous career.

William Wirt, attorney general under John Quincy Adams. Chase studied law under Wirt and regarded him as a mentor and father figure. Wirt later ran for president on the Anti-Masonic Party ticket.

Kenyon College, founded in 1824 by Philander Chase.

For the first few years Chase struggled to build a practice and was financially quite strapped. Eventually he built a profitable practice and a good reputation. He became partner with another attorney who had work with the local branch of the Bank of the United States. Through this connection Chase gained some familiarity with banking. He earned notoriety in the legal profession by compiling the laws of Ohio in three volumes called "Ohio Statutes" during 1831 to 1834. It was deemed a monumental work and became a key text for the Ohio law profession. He prefaced the work with a history of Ohio that also received general praise. The books were not a financial success but established his legal reputation and greatly helped his practice.[6]

In 1834 Chase married Catherine Garniss, the only daughter of a well-to-do local businessman. He commented that he felt her understanding of literature was beyond that of most of the young women he knew. The marriage service was performed by Reverend Lyman Beecher, the minister who went on to become a leading Presbyterian clergyman and whose daughter was Harriett Beecher Stowe, who later wrote *Uncle Tom's Cabin.* Tragically, his wife Catherine died following childbirth in late 1835.[7] Their child, also named Catherine, survived but would die at age four.

Chase felt great loss at his wife's death, and strong guilt, as he had been absent on a business trip to Philadelphia when she went into decline and died. He was also haunted by thoughts that he had not sufficiently worked to make sure of her religious salvation. They had had conversations, and he had worked to promote her faith, but she had not joined the Episcopal Church, and he could not be sure she "had died in the faith."[8]

Catherine Garniss Chase, Salmon Chase's first wife.

A carte de visite of Salmon Chase.

Around the same time, during 1835, friction grew within Cincinnati regarding slavery. A relatively moderate abolitionist, James Birney, began publishing an anti-slavery newspaper. Because Cincinnati was just across the river from slave state Kentucky, many of the most prominent businessmen of the community had commercial ties with the South and wanted to avoid any anti-slavery activities that would offend their Southern business connections. Chase had good relations with the business community but also held anti-slavery ideas. He was therefore somewhat conflicted and generally agreed with Reverend Lyman Beecher, who was anti-slavery but favored colonization (returning freed slaves to Africa or other locations where they could establish new lives) rather than abolition. Tensions about slavery and its possible remedies surfaced over these years, with riots periodically breaking out. One of these led to the destruction of Birney's newspaper. Chase gradually became more anti-slavery but avoided being labeled an abolitionist. He kept himself in reasonable favor with both the anti-slavery and the business communities. He was outspoken in his opposition to slavery but took pains to deny he was an abolitionist. According to people who knew him well, his growing anti-slavery attitudes stemmed from what he felt to be religious duty. He regarded it as a moral wrong and was often frustrated at the apathy toward slavery shown by his own Episcopal Church.[9]

In 1839 Chase met Eliza Ann Smith, and he entered into his second marriage in September of that year. He said she had "a deeply religious turn of mind" that he found especially appealing. Chase said, "We are in a common dependence on the Savior and in a common hope of immortal life"[10] In August of 1840 she bore a baby girl whom they named Catherine Jane (Kate). In May 1842 another daughter, Elizabeth, was born, but she died at three months. In June of 1843 Eliza bore yet another daughter, whom they also named Elizabeth. Chase's record of family tragedies continued as that child too died, in July 1844, just over a year in age. His wife Eliza herself contracted tuberculosis and passed away in September of 1845.[11]

During this time the Fugitive Slave Law was a sensitive topic and controversial nationwide, but particularly so in Cincinnati. The law required free states and individuals therein to return escaped slaves to their Southern owners. Furthermore, slave catchers could operate in the North to capture fugitive slaves and return them to their owners for bounty rewards. Given Cincinnati's location across the Ohio River from slave state Kentucky, many slaves escaped to that city. Also many Southern slaveholders visited Cincinnati for business or recreation, often bringing their slave servants with them. There were frequent episodes of these slaves slipping away or inadvertently being left in Ohio, a free state. Some lived as free people for years before being identified, captured, and returned to the South and slavery. As a result there were many court cases in the area contesting and challenging aspects of the law. Chase became heavily involved in a number of such cases, including the

Van Zandt case, which he argued before the Supreme Court. He lost that case and most of the other such cases but worked at building legal bases for undermining and challenging the law. Through these cases he developed a national reputation as pleading for human rights. In 1845, after he represented a fugitive slave in the "Watson case," the congregation of a local African American church presented Chase with an engraved silver pitcher in recognition of his efforts. He earned the popular title of "Attorney General for Runaway Negroes."

Chase continued to assert that he was not an abolitionist but identified himself with efforts to stop the spread of slavery to new territories, supporting the Wilmot Proviso, being debated in Congress, which was intended to prevent that spread. He belonged to the Whig Party, with his first political position being on the Cincinnati City Council. His politics evolved during the 1840s. Chase identified with the Liberty Party and eventually the Free Soil Party. At the same time he maintained close ties with the Democratic machine in Cincinnati, trying to make himself palatable to Whigs and Democrats alike. He hoped for a union of anti-slavery Whigs and anti-slavery Democrats and that they would join with the Liberty Party and later the Free Soilers. "I hope for the best results from the organization of fused elements of Libertyism and radical Democracy (anti-slavery Democrats) and progressive Whigism in the Free Democracy."

Beyond Chase's anti-slavery efforts, he was involved in several reform movements that were textbook examples of those emerging from the Second Great Awakening, as described in chapter 1. He joined the Young Man's Temperance Society shortly after moving to Cincinnati. As a member of that group and as a city council member he worked to limit and control taverns in the city. He came to recognize that his efforts and attitudes against alcohol alienated many others, but he continued to believe his position was the right and ethical one.[12] He was active in church work, both within the Episcopal Church and in non-denominational causes. He assisted in organizing the Young Men's Bible Association of Cincinnati (associated with the American Bible Society) and helped to distribute the Scriptures to the public. He served as president of the group for ten years. He was a member of the American Sunday School Union. The group published books and literature for Sunday School use. He was

An enslaved supplicant in this abolition-related token (shown enlarged) implored the viewer: "Am I Not a Woman and a Sister?"

An 1850 print shows "The Effects of the Fugitive Slave Law." Four black men—possibly freedmen, possibly escaped slaves—are ambushed with musket fire. Below is a quote from Deuteronomy ("Thou shalt not deliver unto the master his servant which has escaped from his master unto thee.") and a passage from the Declaration of Independence ("We hold that all men are created equal. . . .").

superintendent of the Sunday School at his own church. Later, as a senator, Chase promoted legislation in support of Dorothea Dix, a crusader working to build hospitals and compassionate treatment for the insane. He also worked to reform and mitigate the severe and often cruel discipline employed in the U.S. Navy.[13]

In November of 1846, the year after second wife Eliza's death of consumption, Chase married for a third time. His new wife was Belle Ludlow. She was known to be artistic and to have a good and whimsical sense of humor.[14] In September 1847 she bore a daughter named Janette (Nettie), one of only two (the other being Kate) of the six children he fathered who would survive to adulthood. Belle bore another daughter, about a year later, who died in infancy. Then Belle herself fell ill, probably of tuberculosis, and died in January of 1852. Chase never again married but had his two surviving daughters whom he worked to raise over the coming years.[15]

In 1849, through his ties to the various parties and factions, Chase was able to arrange a deal in the Ohio legislature that gave majority control to the Democrats but in exchange obtained their agreement to repeal the worst aspects of Ohio's "Black Laws," which discriminated heavily against free blacks in the state. As part of the deal Chase got enough support from anti-slavery Democrats, Whigs, and Free Soilers to be elected senator. (The legislature chose senators at that time.) He was technically elected as a Democrat but was not accepted in the Democrat Senate caucus and was given an insignificant committee assignment.

His Senate career was not spectacular; the Democrat leadership often limited or prevented his efforts to speak on the Senate floor, as they knew his anti-slavery tendencies. Regarding slavery he maintained his stance that he only wanted to limit its expansion in the territories and that he did not intend to touch it where it existed or bring about its abolition. Nearing the end of his term it became evident that Chase would not be returned to the Senate. The Democrats had gained firm control of the Ohio legislature in 1853 and by election time 1855 did not need the factions that Chase had put together in 1849 to retain control. He gave up his efforts to bring about a combination of Democrats with various Whigs and Free Soilers and broke with the Democrats.[16]

Before he left the Senate he made a six-hour speech opposing the Kansas-Nebraska Act. In this effort he was directly confronting Stephen A. Douglas, the Democrat who was a leading proponent of the act. This legislation called for local elections to determine a state's status as slave or free and negated the Missouri Compromise of earlier years, which limited slavery's expansion geographically. Chase's speech scored points on Douglas and raised Chase's reputation further among anti-slavery groups.[17]

The political situation in Ohio was such that the Democrats were the largest party by a substantial margin. Their opposition was split among various parties:

the Whigs, the Free Soilers, the Know Nothings, and others. These parties for the most part were anti-slavery or contained large anti-slavery elements. But all had failed to organize on a large scale, and the Whigs in particular were fading organizationally and electorally as their pro-slavery elements went with the Democrats. Chase again had hopes that these factions could be combined into a viable party.

Stephen A. Douglas, a dominant force in American politics in the 1840s and 1850s. Chase opposed Douglas and the Kansas-Nebraska Act in the Senate, enhancing his reputation among anti-slavery groups.

There was indeed a movement afoot to do this, and a "fusion" convention was held in July of 1855. The Whigs, Free Soilers, Know Nothings, anti-slavery Democrats and various other parties and factions with whom he had worked off and on were coalescing into a new party, the Republican Party (Chase would have preferred the name "Independent Democrats"). The largest group at the fusion convention were the Know Nothings (officially known as the American Party), a nativist party that opposed immigration.[18] Chase received the nomination of this convention to run for governor. His campaign had to balance the anti-foreign stance of the Know Nothings with efforts to gain votes from the large number of German immigrants in Ohio. He emphasized that he had never been a member of the Know Nothing Party and that the new Republican Party was built on Liberty Party and Free Soil Party principles. In the election of October 1855 he won the governorship by 16,000 votes.[19]

Following his election, Chase worked to organize the Republicans into a national party. In February 1856 a meeting of party leaders was held in Pittsburgh to name a national committee and take steps to consolidate what was still only a loose coalition.[20] Much of the energy of the emerging party derived from reaction to the Kansas-Nebraska Act that Chase had opposed in the Senate. The passage of the law had resulted in armed struggle in Kansas, as pro-slavery and anti-slavery forces fought to win the new state for their respective causes.

In 1857 Chase was reelected governor, though by a smaller margin than in 1855, as the state treasurer, also a Republican, had been caught up in a scandal affecting the entire slate.

Chase had hopes of being the new party's nominee for president in 1856. Instead, former California senator John C. Fremont was chosen. Fremont lost the presidential election to Democrat James Buchanan but he and the Republican Party made a strong showing, giving hope for better things in 1860.

By 1860 Chase was one of the leading contenders for the Republican presidential nomination. However, again he failed to obtain it as he lost out at the Chicago convention to Abraham Lincoln, former U.S. representative from Illinois. Chase campaigned for Lincoln and, with Lincoln's victory, Chase became a leading candidate for a prominent cabinet position. He was considered for secretary of State but in the end Lincoln chose him as Treasury secretary, and he moved to Washington with his daughters in early 1861 to take up the post.

This then brings us to Chase's receipt of the letter from Reverend Mark Watkinson in November of 1861.

There is evidence that Chase wrote back to Watkinson expressing his general approval of the "principle" of a religious motto as proposed, though we do not have a copy of that letter. More importantly, Chase forwarded Watkinson's letter, along with a memo, to James Pollock, the director of the Mint, in Philadelphia.

Treasury Department, Nov. 20, 1861

Dear Sir:

No nation can be strong except in the strength of God, or safe except in His defense. The trust of our people in God should be declared on our national coins.

You will cause a device to be prepared without unnecessary delay with a motto expressing in the fewest and tersest words possible this national recognition.

S.P. Chase

James Pollock, Esq., Director of the Mint, Philadelphia, Pa.[21]

From our time and the distance of more than 150 years it may seem strange that the secretary of the Treasury would act in such a precipitous way to add a religious motto to the nation's coinage based on what appears a rather emotionally overblown letter from an obscure Baptist minister. However, given the religious sensibilities of Chase, it should not be so surprising. Beyond that lies the Confederate constitutional preamble. There can be little doubt that Chase was aware of the issue and of the reactions to it from both the Northern and Southern clergies and church congregations. He may very well have seized upon the suggestion in the letter as a way to redress the balance of the struggle "for God's favor" back toward the North. Whatever his motivation, Chase's memo to James Pollock at the Mint set in train serious efforts to modify the nation's coinage with a religious motto.

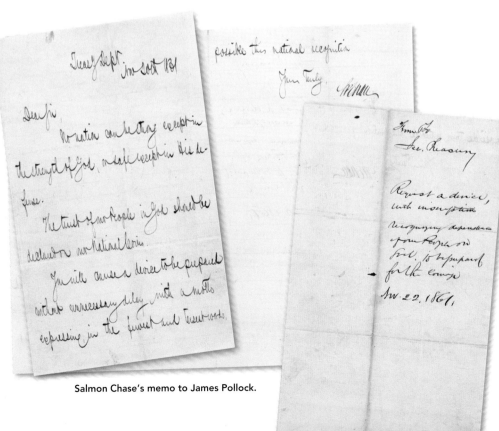

Salmon Chase's memo to James Pollock.

CHAPTER 4

James Pollock

We know that Treasury Secretary Salmon Chase wrote back to Reverend Mark Watkinson. While we do not have a copy of his response to the minister, it must have been encouraging, as evidenced in the letter Watkinson subsequently wrote, apparently at Chase's suggestion, to James Pollock, director of the U.S. Mint. The tone and content are similar to the letter Watkinson wrote to Chase.

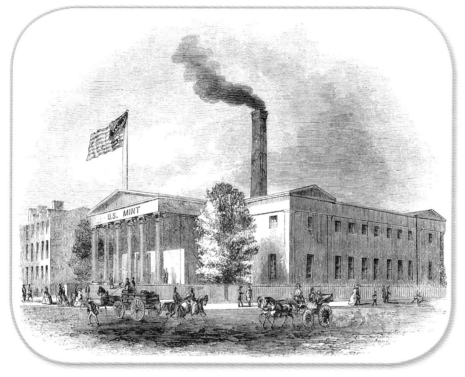

The second United States Mint building as it appeared in 1861, from a *Harper's News Monthly Magazine* print. This building was used from 1833 until 1901. It was where James Pollock was director and later Mint superintendent.

Opposite page: James Pollock, in his official portrait as governor of Pennsylvania (1855 to 1858).

Hon. J.H. Pollock
Director U.S. Mint

Dear Sir:

Will you allow a few suggestions respecting the devices upon our American coins. Is it not a burning shame that thus far in our national history our coins have been so thoroughly heathenish.

Suppose our governmental fabric were now dissolved; suppose in a future era some antiquary searching among the ruins of our public edifices, even of our churches, should alight upon the corner stone memorials of them, would he not justly pronounce us an idolatrous people worshipping the "goddess of liberty"; and perchance pantheistic also so far as to worship eagles?

Can God, the eternal arbiter of national destiny, have been pleased with this displacement and superseding of Himself?

Would it not be more in accordance with our actual Christian character, as England and other Christian nations, have done, in some form to recognize God on our coin. This I would not do in Latin, but in good plain English: let our watchwords be "God, Liberty, Law" either enstamped on the national flag, the folds of the stars and stripes, or in some other form – Let also the all-seeing "eye" with its surrounding halo be there somewhere – Let the present wreath be closed with the words "Perpetual Union" and closed into a ring.

Let some new Christian device, or one in which God shall be clearly acknowledged be prepared –

I have written to the Secretary of the Treasury, Hon. S.P. Chase, respecting the change, who informed me the general principle meets his approval.

I know of no single thing more pleasing to God than would be this, in our present civil strife.

Excuse a stranger's freedom and consider me

Yours, Most Respectfully,
M.R. Watkinson
Minister of the Gospel
Ridleyville, Delaware County, Pa.
January 6, 1862[1]

Director Pollock, having of course already received instruction from Chase to move this project forward, responded to Watkinson on January 10, 1862.

Jan. 10, 1862
Rev. M.R. Watkinson

Dear Sir:

Your letter of the 6th inst. in relation to the emblems and devices of our
national coinage has been rcvd.

I cordially approve the object you have in review, and I will most cheerfully
cooperate with the authorities at Washington in the adoption of such emblems
and mottoes as will recognize God as the Sovereign Ruler of Nations and as
our God. The subject is now under consideration.

Yours by . . .
J.A. Pollock
Director[2]

Reverend Watkinson had conceived of the idea of a religious reference on the
coinage, and Chase had responded positively, forwarding the suggestion to Mint
Director James Pollock. But, as we shall see, ultimately it was Pollock who picked
up the issue and persistently drove it over a period of years and through numerous
obstacles to final implementation.

James Pollock had had an impressive career before becoming Mint director. He
had served three terms in Congress, had been a district judge in Pennsylvania, and
had also served a term as governor of Pennsylvania.

Pollock was appointed to the directorship of the Mint by newly elected president Abraham Lincoln following his election in 1860. Pollock and Lincoln were
well acquainted through their overlapping terms in the House of Representatives
back in the 1840s. They had both been members of the Whig party and both had
stayed at the boardinghouse of Ann Sprigg located on Capitol Hill. In fact, for a
time they had shared a room there. Sprigg's was a favorite residence for the Whigs.
Clearly Pollock and Lincoln would have been in accord on the great issues of the
day, including opposition to the annexation of Texas and a general aversion to the
extension of slavery. There is no clear record, but it seems likely Pollock sought
the position as director of the Mint following Lincoln's election, and the presi-
dent-elect, personally knowing him to be a competent and politically compatible
person, granted it to him. As soon as Lincoln arrived in Washington, prior to his
inauguration, Pollock was among the very first he asked to his hotel to discuss
events and to seek advice on various appointments. While Pollock was with him,
Stephen Douglas called on Lincoln. Lincoln asked Pollock to stay during his

meeting with Douglas and in later years Pollock wrote a short paper, "Douglas the Loyal," recounting the meeting. Douglas, though long an adversary of Lincoln's, had pledged his support to preserve the Union. Indeed Douglas followed through on his promise, urging his constituents and supporters to stand with the Union. However, by June 1861 Douglas would be dead of pneumonia. In an interesting footnote, Douglas's young widow, in financial need, approached President Lincoln for assistance. Lincoln accommodated her by arranging the government's purchase of Douglas's farm south of downtown Chicago, on the shores of Lake Michigan. Some of the property became a small portion of what was later called Camp Douglas. This camp was used for training Union troops and, later, as a camp for Confederate prisoners of war. Douglas's burial place and large monument are there on his former land.

Pollock served in prominent roles during his life, but relatively little has been written about him. There are a few biographical sketches, and we can trace his career clearly, but he has not received the same detailed attention as other leaders of the era. In many respects Pollock held positions of stature equal to Salmon Chase's, and of greater stature than Lincoln's, before the Civil War, but he did not move into the higher circles of cabinet rank or Supreme Court Justice that Chase achieved. Pollock has not attracted the same fame or the biographers.[3] His story makes it evident that, in ability, he likely equaled Chase and others more famous. He seems, however, to have lacked the same driving ambition and love of electoral politics.

He was born in 1810 at Milton, Pennsylvania, one of seven children. His family were of Scotch-Irish Presbyterian extraction. With eerie similarity to Chase's story, James Pollock lost his father at age five. His mother (Sarah Wilson Pollock) somehow, in a manner like Chase's mother, managed to raise and provide for the education of James and his six siblings. She lived to age 94. James attended a local academy in Milton but went on to receive both a bachelor's degree and a master's degree (1831) from Princeton, with highest honors. He then studied law with an attorney, Samuel Hepburn, back in Milton. He was admitted to the local Northumberland County bar in 1833. The following year he set up his own practice in Milton.

In 1837 Pollock married Sarah Hepburn, daughter

The home of James Pollock. The house is gone now and there is a park on the site near downtown Milton, Pennsylvania.

Celebration of the driving of the last spike for the transcontinental railroad, 1869. James Pollock chaired the congressional committee in the 1840s recommending its construction, though it was nearly 25 years before the project came to fruition.

of Samuel Hepburn, with whom he had studied law. Sarah, four decades later, wrote a lengthy autobiography for their children. She said "I had never thought of him as a beau, but my father appreciated him and knew his worth, and told me I had better set my cap for him as he was the most promising young man in the county. I then began to look at him with different eyes and at last actually lost my heart with him."[4] They were married by Sarah's brother, James Curtis Hepburn, a Presbyterian minister. This brother and his wife went on to become missionaries in China and then in Japan. In Japan Hepburn developed and published the first major Japanese/English dictionary. It remains in print even today as a standard reference for students of Japanese.

Pollock's public career began in 1835 when he was appointed deputy attorney general for the county, serving in that position for three years. In 1844 Henry Frick, the congressman from his district, suddenly passed away (he collapsed on the House floor while delivering a speech). Pollock ran for his seat and was elected on the Whig ticket to serve out his term, even though the district was heavily Democrat. He was then twice reelected, serving in Congress from April 5, 1844, until March 4, 1849. He chose not to run for a fourth term.

While in the House Pollock had a strong record of achievements. Most notably he was chairman of a special committee appointed to study a transcontinental railroad. Although it would be another generation before the railroad was actually built, the committee's report was the first official recommendation for the project.

He also befriended and encouraged Samuel F.B. Morse in his efforts to seek assistance for construction of a telegraph line, though the inventor was regarded as a crank and a dreamer by most people. Pollock was able to obtain funding of $30,000 for Morse to construct a demonstration line between Washington, D.C., and Baltimore.

Following his congressional career, Pollock was appointed judge of the Eighth Judicial District of Pennsylvania. He remained in this position until 1854, when an amendment to the state constitution made his position elective rather than appointive. He chose not to run and returned to private law practice. Nevertheless, later that year he was nominated by the Whigs and the Know Nothing Party for the Pennsylvania governorship. Just as in Chase's race for governor of Ohio, the Democrats were the dominant party in Pennsylvania. And, just as Chase did, Pollock was able to pull together a coalition of Whigs, Know Nothings, Free Soilers, and others to win the election. In particular Pollock, being known as a highly moral man and a teetotaler, gained the support of the Temperance Party. This helped put him over the top as he defeated the incumbent Democrat governor, William Bigler, with 55 percent of the vote. Bigler struggled with the slavery issue. Just as with Chase in Ohio, the majority of Pennsylvanians opposed the Kansas-Nebraska Act and its pro-slavery implications. Bigler was unable to disentangle himself from the national Democrats supporting the bill and as a result lost the election.

James Pollock was a very competent governor, dealing with several serious issues during his three-year tenure. He sold off a significant portion of the state-owned canals and railroad properties. The canals in particular ran chronic losses, becoming huge liabilities to the state budget, creating deficits, and

Samuel F.B. Morse. James Pollock aided the inventor's efforts to develop the telegraph, obtaining congressional funding for an experimental line between Washington and Baltimore. Morse's first telegraphic message was, "What hath God wrought?"

fostering corruption. The sale of these properties greatly reduced the state's debt and improved its fiscal situation. Pollock was in this regard an early "privatizer" and was able to lower the state's taxes significantly while bringing the budget into line.

By 1856 he had evolved, as so many of his contemporaries did, from being a Whig into being a Republican. He advocated the Republican platform in 1856: leave slavery alone in the existing states but with no extension to the territories.

The Panic of 1857 brought financial crisis to the country and put many of Pennsylvania's state-chartered banks at risk of failure. Governor Pollock called a special legislative session which temporarily suspended the requirement that the banks back their notes with redemption in gold or silver. This saved the banks. The experience may have influenced Pollock's later position while Mint director regarding reducing the metal content of some coins below their nominal value.

Pollock also promoted education, with the establishment of teacher training schools and the institution that would eventually become Penn State University. He was quoted: "Ignorance is an enemy of Republics. Education is necessary with the Bible as the textbook alike of the child and the American Statesman" and "money liberally, yet wisely, expended in the pursuit and promotion of knowledge is true economy."[5]

A view of the inauguration of Governor James Pollock, in front of the Pennsylvania state capitol at Harrisburg, January 16, 1855.

Just as did many Whigs of the era, and in a similar manner to Chase, Pollock became active and instrumental in the creation and development of the Republican Party. He helped organize the party as the Whigs, Know Nothings, Free Soilers, anti-slavery Democrats, and others coalesced into Republicans.

As governor, Pollock was known for his honesty and his straightforward approach to issues. He became known as the "Christian Governor." His friend A.K. McClure in later writings said "conscientiousness was a prominent element of his character; honesty of intention was conceded by his opponents." On the other hand, he was regarded by some as overly rigid in his attitudes. McClure related a story about a dispute in Erie, Pennsylvania, involving the routing of a railroad. The Erie community was sharply divided and several unsuccessful efforts had been made to resolve the issue. Civil unrest resulted, and Pollock sent McClure to handle it, giving him authority to call out the state militia if needed. McClure invited the leading protagonists from both sides for dinner and drinks and a game of cards that continued through the night. By morning he had managed to arrange an agreement between them. He notified Pollock of his success and the means by which he had accomplished it. "While he (Pollock) was very much delighted at the restoration of peace, he left me greatly in doubt as to whether he would have not preferred peace by military force and the sacrifice of some lives to its attainment by a game of cards and several bottles of whisky." McClure continued in his comments: "He was a severe Roundhead in his religious views, and believed both cards

Pollock Road goes through the campus of Penn State University. James Pollock chartered the school as a teachers' college during his time as governor. Today there is also a computer center named for him.

James Pollock: "a commanding figure . . . and a countenance of intelligence and benignity." He would receive instructions from Treasury Secretary Salmon P. Chase to prepare pattern coins with a religious reference.

and whisky to be the invention of the devil himself. He was the only governor I ever knew who signed a death warrant without visible reluctance, as he held strictly to the old law of an eye for an eye."[6]

McClure also wrote of Pollock: "he was a man of fine address, delightful manners, and a popular orator of unusual attainments. His personal appearance had a commanding figure, somewhat above the average heights, with dark eyes and hair, smooth-shaven face and a countenance of intelligence and benignity. He was an eloquent speaker, graceful, persuasive, convincing and possessed remarkable tact in gaining the sympathy and approval of his hearers."[7]

An archive of Pollock's papers is held at Penn State University. Reading through them gives the impression of an evolution in his religious thinking. Letters in the 1840s between him and his wife, Sarah, while he was in Washington and she remained in Milton with their children, have a light, frequently humorous tone as he regales her with his observations of the latest women's fashions in Washington and descriptions of First Lady Julia Tyler's appearance and gowns. He relates to her his story of visiting the Executive Mansion (later called the White House) for President John Tyler's open house on New Year's Day. His description of the packed building (he could only enter through an open window) and the attendees high and low is humorous and good-natured. There are few religious thoughts expressed beyond comments about some of the prominent preachers and their sermons that he was hearing in Washington. By contrast letters during his governorship in the mid-1850s are full of religious language. It seems religion had become much more prominent in his thinking in the intervening years. A letter from Pollock to his wife on New Year's Day, 1857, demonstrates this.

State of Pennsylvania

Executive Chamber, Harrisburg, Pa.

January 1st, 1857

My Dear Wife:

A happy new year to you and many of them. A happy new year to children and friends, and might it be the best year of all the past. The old year has passed away, never to return. Its record we cannot change if we would—its misspent hours we cannot recall—its neglected opportunities will no more be ours. Know much of the past if it could be recalled, would we desire to live over again, that it might be better improved and devoted more to the service of God, and not to ourselves and our sinful gratifications. But it is gone, and all that remains for us to do, is to enter upon the new year with a renewed determination, by the help of God, to live more near to Him, under a constant sense of our responsibility to Him, in whose hands are the issues of life, and to whom we must render our final account.

Ja Pollock[8]

Pollock declined to run for reelection as governor when his term was finished, though it was considered certain he would win by a large margin. He deemed the duties of the office as too demanding, unpleasant, and he greatly disliked campaigning for votes. He returned again to private law practice. When he departed Harrisburg the entire legislature turned out to escort him to the train station, an unprecedented gesture.

By 1860 events brought James Pollock back into public life. Abraham Lincoln's election in November prompted several Southern states to secede, and clearly the issue of civil war was threatening in early 1861. In mid-January the legislature of Virginia (which had not yet seceded) called for "a final effort to restore the union and the constitution in the spirit in which they were established by the father of the republic." This effort took the form of a peace conference in Washington beginning February 4, 1861. Most of the states sent delegates. Pollock was sent as chairman of the Pennsylvania delegation. The conference was made up of many prominent people, including former president John Tyler of Virginia. The Washington Peace Conference, as it came to be known, met at the Willard Hotel. It adopted a proposal for a constitutional amendment drawing a line on the 36th parallel and allowing slavery to forever continue south of the line and to be prohibited north of it, across the continent. It made various concessions to the slave states in an effort to forestall the further breakup of the Union. Nothing came of all of this, of course, as events had already moved too far, and Southern states continued to secede.[9]

It is interesting that Salmon Chase also attended the peace conference, as a delegate from Ohio, and that he and Pollock met during the proceedings. We can be

certain that they talked of the incoming administration, their roles within it, and the dark uncertainty of the future.

Both men took their offices in March of 1861.

When the war broke out in April 1861, James Pollock returned to Milton, Pennsylvania, and presided over a mass meeting where hundreds of men volunteered to form the "Pollock Guards." As Pennsylvania's quota had already been filled, the unit was declined for service. Later, however, as the war needs grew, these men were accepted and served under Pollock's nephew, John McVeery.

Pollock went back to Washington and took up his Mint duties full-time in May.

The gentlemen's parlor, reading, and sitting room at the Willard Hotel, 1861.
A peace conference was held at the hotel in a fruitless attempt to avert secession.

THE
STAR SPANGLED BANNER

A PARIOTIC SONG.

Baltimore. Printed and Sold at CARRS Music Store 36 Baltimore Street.

Air, Anacreon in Heaven

Con Spirito

O! say can you see by the dawn's early light, What so proudly we hail'd at the twilight's last gleaming, Whose broad stripes & bright stars thr perilous fight, O'er the ramparts we watch'd, were so gallantly streaming. And the Rockets' red glare, the Bombs bursting in air, Gave proof through the night that o

(Tssb.)

(Adapd. & Arrd. by T.C.)

(Pl

"The Star Spangled Banner" invoked the nation's motto as "In God is Our Trust."

CHAPTER 5

GOD OUR TRUST

Treasury Secretary Salmon P. Chase's memo to Mint Director James Pollock dated November 20, 1861, cited in chapter 3, instructed Pollock to prepare a device with a motto declaring "in the fewest and tersest words possible" the recognition of national trust in God. He gave no explicit instruction or suggestion as to what that motto might be or how it might appear on the coinage.

There is no written record, but it is clear that Pollock, in following up on Chase's memo, consulted with James B. Longacre, the Mint engraver. Longacre was long experienced and well respected, having been chief engraver since 1844. He had designed and engraved dies for many pattern and regular coins for the Mint, most notably the gold dollar of 1849, the Liberty Head $20 gold piece in 1849, the Flying Eagle cent in 1856, and the Indian Head cent in 1859.

Pollock informed Longacre of Chase's instructions and showed him Reverend Watkinson's letter. After studying and considering the issue, Longacre drafted a letter to Pollock dated December 13, 1861. He spelled out his thoughts and outlined the issues for placing such a motto upon the coinage.

> The idea should be unmistakeably expressive, and at the same time the letters should be distinctly and easily legible, to unite these desiderata within the limits presented on the face of the coin in combination with the required arrangement of the legal devices as established by law, demands more ingenuity than may at first be apparent—our present devices may be altered in form but not in character, without impinging the provisions of the law on that subject. . . .
>
> From these considerations, it has seemed best to me, in attempting to introduce the suggestion of the Secretary of the Treasury, to contrive as little interference with the present and legal devices as possible. The most appropriate place for such a motto is found in connection with the national inscription, which on all our larger coins is on the reverse; the device of which is the Eagle with the heraldic accompaniments appropriate to the arms of the union as adopted by law, dispensing at present with the motto (E Pluribus Unum) and the crest, except on the Double Eagle: The place of the crest offers the best

position for the insertion of such a motto as is now required as on all the other coins which are large enough to admit of such an addition, this space is now vacant—and a motto if sufficiently brief, may be introduced with the least disturbance of the devices as now arranged. . . .[1]

Longacre referred to the motto "E Pluribus Unum." This had appeared on U.S. coins in the late-eighteenth century and early-nineteenth century. On some in the 1790s and early 1800s it was placed on a banner stretching across the eagle's neck from wing to wing. On others (of the Capped Bust design) from about 1810 until 1837, it was on a scroll just above the eagle's head. These are the coins Longacre was referring to when he said "dispensing at present with the motto. . . ." E Pluribus Unum had been dropped in 1837 with the introduction of the Liberty Seated design. The space above the eagle's head (the "crest," as Longacre termed it) was therefore vacant.

An 1803 dollar with the motto E PLURIBUS UNUM on the reverse.

An 1830 half dollar displaying E PLURIBUS UNUM, and an
1844 half with the space on the reverse, above the eagle's head, vacant.

The Great Seal of the United States

In July of 1776 the Continental Congress appointed a committee to design a seal to be used on official documents. By that August the committee proposed a design to Congress that included the motto *E Pluribus Unum*. The committee was made up of Benjamin Franklin, Thomas Jefferson, and John Adams. They sought the advice of Pierre Eugene Du Simitiere, who was born in Switzerland but lived for many years in the West Indies before migrating to the United States. Du Simitiere was considered eccentric but knowledgeable, particularly about ancient symbols and mottoes. He suggested the motto *E Pluribus Unum* ("Out of Many, One") for the obverse of the seal. This was included in the committee's proposed design. However, Congress tabled the issue and in 1780 a second committee was appointed; they also proposed a design. That design too was rejected, and in May of 1782 yet a third committee was formed and a third design proposed by late May. Again Congress did not approve the committee's proposal. They then assigned their secretary, Charles Thomson, to come up with still another design. He evidently studied the prior proposals and produced a seal that combined elements from all of them. Importantly he retained *E Pluribus Unum* on the obverse, with the image of an eagle, probably taken from a book of emblems owned by Benjamin Franklin. On the reverse of the seal Thomson added the mottoes *Annuit Coeptus* ("He Smiles With Favor") above an all-seeing eye and an unfinished pyramid, implying Providence overseeing events, and *Novus Ordo Seclorum* ("A New Order of the Ages") beneath the pyramid. Congress finally accepted this design and these mottoes on June 20, 1782. Some say that the all-seeing eye and the pyramid on the reverse were promoted through the influence of the Freemasons, perhaps Benjamin Franklin in particular. This image certainly was used by the Masons, though some experts say the Masons did not use it until the 1790s, after its adoption by Congress.

As for E Pluribus Unum, there is a general consensus that Du Simitiere picked up the idea from a popular periodical of the era, *Gentleman's Magazine*. This magazine, published in London, was widely read in both England and America. The magazine had *E Pluribus Unum* on its title page. The motto was deemed appropriate for the 13 colonies, who were endeavoring to act as "one," and it also reflected the various nationalities that had settled in North America and were in the process of forming a new nation. The magazine, while going through many iterations since the eighteenth century, is the ancestor of today's *GQ Magazine*. On the seal, the eagle on the obverse is holding in its beak a ribbon that bears *E Pluribus Unum*. Even though the Congress during this period never made this the official motto of the United States it was used on U.S. coins from early times along with the eagle.

The seal adopted in 1782 remains the official Great Seal of the United States. We are most familiar with it on the reverse of the dollar bill.

Of interesting contemporary note, there is a group that has organized something called the "Original Motto Project." They reject In God We Trust as a proper legal motto for the United States and promote E Pluribus Unum as the "original motto" that should replace what they view as an unconstitutional religious motto. They sell a small stamp that can be used to stamp over In God We Trust with E Pluribus Unum on the reverse of the dollar bill, and urge their supporters to use it on all the currency they handle.

Charles Thomson's first design for the obverse of the Great Seal of the United States, 1782.

The Great Seal of the United States. It bears the motto *E Pluribus Unum*.

The title page of *The Gentleman's Magazine*, 1731.

A dollar bill bearing the stamp issued by the Original Motto Project, a group that contends E Pluribus Unum should be the official motto of the United States.

Longacre then continued, discussing what the motto should be:

> This motto "Our Trust is in God" which was the first suggested, was found however—in attempting to apply it to the Eagle and the Half-Dollar reverses—contained too many letters to insert in the place of the crest without crowding them too much for good taste: and we therefore selected for greater brevity the words "God Our Trust" which carries the same idea, in a form of expression according with heraldic usage—and probably as readily understood as the more explicit form of the other.

These excerpts from the letter are very interesting and enlightening, as Longacre had determined the best location for the motto to be on the reverse of the coins, on the "vacant" crest above the eagle's head. The motto's insertion there would "cause the least disturbance of the devices as now arranged." He would not have to move the eagle or modify other parts of the existing design.

Longacre's statement that the first suggested motto was "Our Trust is in God" is confusing and contradicts other references to "In God is Our Trust" being the first motto considered, given its ties to "The Star Spangled Banner." Perhaps Longacre was misremembering the motto as he wrote, or perhaps "Our Trust is in God" was another motto that they considered. The author's opinion is that, for whatever reason, Longacre misstated the motto in this letter.

Longacre did not say who suggested the motto or whence it originated. In any case, however, he said it was necessary to abbreviate it so as to avoid "crowding them [i.e., the letters of the motto] too much for good taste." Perhaps even more

James Barton Longacre, highly respected chief engraver of the Mint, pictured with some of his early coinage designs. He was named to the position in 1844 largely due to his connections with John C. Calhoun. Was it Longacre who thought of "God Our Trust" as the motto on pattern coins sent to Salmon P. Chase?

interesting is that the original text of the letter first states "*I found* however in attempting to apply it to the Eagle and the Half-Dollar reverses—contained too many letters. . . ." In his letter's handwritten text "*I found* . . ." is scratched out and the sentence made to read "*was found.*" Also regarding the motto itself, the original text reads "*I therefore selected for greater brevity the words 'God Our Trust'. . . .*" Again "*I*" is scratched out and "*we*" substituted. Did Longacre first write what really happened, i.e., he had made these decisions himself, but, having second thoughts, didn't want to claim the credit for himself? If so, with whom did he feel the credit should be shared? Pollock? Or some Mint assistant? In any case "God Our Trust" had become the suggested operative motto.

Longacre continued his letter:

> I have caused this motto to be struck on reverse dies of the Eagle and Half-Dollar, and impressions, in copper of the Eagle, and in silver of the Half-Dollar are presented herewith (in company with these remarks) which will serve to show the effect as proposed. This motto in the same letters can be placed on the four larger denominations i.e. the Silver Dollar, the Double Eagle, the Eagle, and the Half Dollar; and by reducing somewhat the size of the letters, perhaps on the Half-Eagle and Quarter-Dollar, if that should be thought necessary.

Note that Longacre said he had caused the motto to be struck on *reverse dies* of the eagle (the term applied to the $10 gold piece) and the half dollar, and he concluded his letter by stating that "the smallest changes of the permanent devices or legends on the face of the coin requires the making of new hubs for all the dies on which it is to be placed, which will be the work of some months." The implied meaning of this is that Longacre had simply stamped the motto into existing working dies in the vacant space above the eagle for the half dollar and the $10 gold piece. He had not prepared new hubs. This was the most efficient way to quickly make the dies with which to strike specimen Motto coins. Longacre advised that should Pollock or Chase desire any other modification, new hubs for every denomination involved would be required, and their creation would consume a lot more time and effort.

Thirteen days after Longacre's letter, on the day after Christmas, Mint Director Pollock wrote a lengthy letter to Treasury Secretary Chase. Much of Pollock's letter was simply repeated from Longacre's letter. He informed Chase that the best place for the new motto was the crest above the eagle on the reverse of the coinage. He also elaborated on the legal aspects, stating that any modification of designs excluding the eagle would require congressional action. Design changes needed to be minimal.

He exactly repeated Longacre's words that the first suggested motto, "In God is our Trust," had been deemed to contain "too many letters to insert in the place of the crest . . . and *we* therefore, selected for greater brevity the words 'God Our Trust'. . . ." However, Pollock disclosed more as he related to Chase that the

idea had come from "our great National Hymn—'The Star Spangled Banner'."
He explained:

> A number of mottoes have been suggested some of which are appropriate, but
> lack the necessary brevity. The motto adopted was selected in consideration of
> its having become familiar to the public mind by its use in our great National
> Hymn—the "Star Spangled Banner"—In that National Song which has
> thrilled the hearts and been sung by the lips of millions of American freemen—
> our motto declared to be "In God is Our Trust."[2]

Indeed, the final stanza of the "Star Spangled Banner" (which in our time is little
known and almost never sung) goes as follows:

> Oh, thus be it ever when free men shall stand between their loved homes and
> the war's desolation! Blest with victory and peace may the Heaven-rescued
> land praise the power that hath made and preserved us a nation! Then conquer
> we must when our cause it is just, *And this be our motto: "In God is Our Trust!"*
> And the star-spangled banner in triumph shall wave o'er the land of the free
> and the home of the brave!

Pollock's letter also repeated Longacre's words: "I have caused this motto to be
struck on the reverse dies of the eagle and half dollar, and impressions, in copper
of the eagle, and in silver of the half dollar are presented herewith which will serve
to show the effect proposed."

1861 GOD OUR TRUST, Plain Letters,
half dollar pattern, cataloged as Judd-279.

1861 GOD OUR TRUST, Plain Letters, $10
eagle pattern struck in copper. (Judd-287)

1861 GOD OUR TRUST, Plain Letters,
half dollar pattern in copper. (Judd-280)

However, Pollock's letter went on to disclose yet more:

> It will be seen that on one of the impressions of the Eagle and the half dollar, the motto appears within a scroll. While deferring the choice entirely to the taste and judgement of the Department, a preference is here felt for the scroll device, as presenting a more artistic appearance than the other, which is perhaps too naked and conspicuous. There is also a certain uniformity to the style of the old "E Pluribus Unum" which shall fall gracefully upon the public eye.

From Pollock's December 26 letter, therefore, we learn that the pattern coins produced by Longacre display the motto in two ways: in plain letters above the eagle, and on a scroll above the eagle.

It is something of a mystery that Longacre's earlier letter to Pollock did not mention these two ways of presenting the motto. Also the passage of 13 days between the Longacre letter to Pollock and Pollock's letter to Chase raises the question as to whether Longacre initially produced and sent examples of both styles to Pollock, or only one of them. Could it be that Longacre first only produced patterns in the Plain Letters style, almost certainly the quickest and easiest, as it would have involved just stamping the individual letters into a working die? Could it then be that suggestions from Pollock or others led Longacre to produce the motto in a second format (i.e., the scroll)? The scroll device likely required the creation of a single punch with the entire scroll and motto combined. It would have been stamped into

1861, GOD OUR TRUST, Scroll Type, half dollar pattern in silver. (Judd-277)

1861, GOD OUR TRUST, Scroll Type, $10 eagle pattern in copper. (Judd-285)

1861, GOD OUR TRUST, Scroll Type, half dollar pattern in copper. (Judd-278)

the die above the eagle. This could explain the 13-day gap between the letter from Longacre to Pollock and the letter from Pollock to Chase. This probably would have been sufficient time for a second pattern variation to be produced.

In their letters Longacre and Pollock referenced enclosing "impressions in copper of the Eagle and in silver of the Half Dollar" for Chase's review. In reality examples of the half dollars also exist in copper. Furthermore, there are rumored specimens of the $10 eagle struck in gold. There were gold examples of both types dated 1861 listed in the King Farouk sale in Cairo in the early 1950s; however, the lots were not sold, leading to the current suspicion that they were not gold but perhaps gold-plated or gilt examples. No gold examples of 1861 GOD OUR TRUST eagles have ever surfaced.

Further mysteries surround these coins as the obverse of the Scroll Type half dollar was struck in two die varieties, one with the point of the shield over the 1 in the date and the other with the shield point over the 8 in the date. Clearly two different obverse dies were used to make these coins. Given that the total quantity known of both date-position varieties is very small, probably no more than seven or eight coins, the question comes up as to why the Mint would have used two different obverse dies in making so few coins. Were they struck at different times? The Shield Point Over 8 variety, with only two or three specimens known, seems to be slightly rarer than the Shield Point Over 1. There were no known examples in copper of the Shield Point Over 8 variety until 2001, when one surfaced in the Vermeil Collection sold by Stack's Rare Coins in New York City. Since then a second example has been discovered. For the Plain Letters half dollar, of all known specimens, only one obverse die was used.

The $10 eagles also hold a mystery related to die variety. Both the Plain Letters variety and the Scroll Type have High Date and Low Date position variations. This raises the same question as it does for the Scroll Type halves. Were they struck at different times? Why were two obverse dies developed when so few coins were made?

The next mystery is the lack of any recorded response from Treasury Secretary Chase to Mint Director Pollock regarding the Mint's suggestions and the pattern coins that Pollock had sent him. There would be a lapse of some six months before any further correspondence on the issue. Why would Chase not respond relatively quickly, given that he was the one who had made the request? The next chapter may shed light on Chase's non-response.

| 1861 GOD OUR TRUST, Scroll Type, half dollar pattern (Shield Point Over 1 variety). (Judd-277, Pollock-326) | 1861 GOD OUR TRUST, Scroll Type, half dollar pattern (Shield Point Over 8 variety). (Judd-277, Pollock-328) | A Low Date variety GOD OUR TRUST eagle pattern (left) and a High Date variety. Both the Plain Letters and the Scroll Type eagles exhibit the date position variations. |

"General Kearney's Gallant Charge, at the Battle of Chantilly, Va., 1st of September 1862." One scene of conflict among many—with no end in sight.

CHAPTER 6

Demand Notes and Legal Tender Notes

During late November and early December 1861, at virtually the same time that Mark Watkinson's letter stirred activity on a religious motto, other matters began to distract Treasury Secretary Salmon Chase, causing a fairly long detour in our story of "In God We Trust." A serious financial situation was developing. When Chase assumed office on March 7, 1861, he had existing authority under previous acts of Congress to negotiate loans up to $40,964,000. By March 22, he was advertising for some $27 million in funding under that authority. The funds raised by these borrowings were consumed quickly as the war effort scaled up. A special session of Congress had to be called in July to deal with the situation. During this session the Loan Act of July 11, 1861, was passed with only nominal opposition. It authorized Chase to borrow up to $250 million. Clearly the Treasury secretary was kept busy with these matters.[1]

Treasury Secretary Salmon P. Chase.

In addition to borrowings an income tax was imposed starting at a rate of 3 percent on incomes of $800 (an average middle-class income of that era) or more and increasing to 5 percent for incomes over $10,000 per year. Rather than the federal government directly collecting the taxes, quotas were set for the individual states. Total quotas for all the states were set at $20 million. The states had the option of appointing their own collection agents or allowing the federal government to provide agents. Most states chose to appoint their own agents. An interesting side note to this is that collection quotas were imposed not only for the Northern states remaining in the Union but also for the 11 Southern states that had seceded. Provisions were made for their collection by boards of tax commissioners. The amount apportioned to the Southern states was $5,153,891.33. Needless to say the seceded states did not cooperate and collected no taxes for the federals. However, some property seized by federal troops during the war was auctioned off and the proceeds taken toward those quotas. Following the war the obligations remained and the federal tax commissioners continued to work to collect what was due. Well after the war, by 1874, about half remained uncollected.

Besides income taxes, tariffs were increased dramatically and also imposed on goods that had previously been duty-free. Tariff rates overall increased from 19 percent to 48 percent from fiscal 1861 to fiscal 1865.[2] Before the war substantially all the revenues needed to operate the federal government had been raised through the tariff and through sales of Western lands. The Southern states had generally been opposed to tariffs as a great proportion of their goods, especially

$5, $10, and $20 Demand Notes. Their green color gave rise to the term *greenback*. The Demand Notes were printed only in these three denominations. Later the Legal Tender Act of February 1862 mandated withdrawal of the Demand Notes; as a result they are today very rare and in great demand by collectors.

cotton, was exported. They did not want to risk higher tariffs being imposed by their foreign customers on their cotton and other goods in retaliation for high U.S. duties. In addition, high tariffs would reduce price competition for Northern manufacturers, making goods overall more expensive. In effect this raised the costs of manufactured goods in both the North and the South—to the advantage of Northern manufacturers and disadvantage of the South in general, as it had a far smaller manufacturing base. Hence the Southerners in Congress had moderated the federal tariff charges. But now with the Southerners out of the Union and no longer voting in Congress, the door was open to increase duties with the dual purpose of raising revenues and protecting Northern industry from foreign competition.[3]

Beyond borrowing, taxes, and tariffs, a further means of financing the war was to simply print the money. The Act of July 17, 1861, bill authorized issuance of up to $50 million in Demand Notes, which bore no interest but which could be used for payment of salaries or other government obligations. These Demand Notes were the first and earliest issuance of U.S. currency intended to circulate in the economy

(with the exceptions of Continental Currency and of notes issued during the War of 1812, the latter of which circulated but were of a very limited and temporary nature).[4] The Demand Notes were issued in denominations of $5, $10, and $20. The reverse side of these notes was printed in green, giving birth to the term *greenback*. The notes were first issued in August of 1861, and were paid to the clerks of various government departments for their salaries, as well as to other creditors. On their first appearance there was reluctance on the part of government employees to accept them, as they were accustomed to being paid in gold or silver coin. In reality the notes officially were convertible into gold and were frequently so converted. The authorizing legislation of July 17, 1861, did not specify that they were convertible to specie, but a subsequent Treasury Department circular declared them payable in gold if the bearer so requested. The notes could also be used to pay tariff duties which normally were payable only in gold. It was reported that some Washington merchants, railroads, and others refused to accept them. Evidently Secretary Chase issued the circular allowing the redemption to gold in order to overcome these objections to the paper and to maintain their par value with gold.[5] With time they gained general, but not universal, public confidence. They did, however, become preferred to existing state-bank currency (today termed "obsolete currency"). It is estimated that $35 million of these notes was in circulation by the time of specie payment suspension in December, and the entire authorized amount had been printed and issued by April 1, 1862.

Chase realized printing paper currency was only a partial solution to funding the war and would indeed create massive inflation if overdone. He knew he needed the cooperation of the banks to purchase and hold or distribute the enormous quantity of bonds forthcoming to finance the war. He called a conference in New York of the leading banks on August 19, 1861. They discussed the issues from both sides: the government's desperate need to raise funds, and the banks' constraints of disposable capital. The banks were also unhappy with Chase's limits on interest rates. Chase pressed them for as much assistance as they could provide and issued a veiled warning when a banker said the banks might issue an "ultimatum." Chase replied, "No, it is not the business of the Secretary of the Treasury to receive an ultimatum, but to declare one if it shall become necessary." If the banks did not cooperate? "If not, I will go back to Washington, and issue notes for circulation; for it is certain the war must go on until the rebellion is put down, if we have to put out paper until it takes a thousand dollars to buy a breakfast."

In the end the banks agreed to advance $50 million on three-year bonds yielding 7.3 percent. A second $50 million issuance under essentially the same terms soon followed. However, a third ran into difficulties in November of 1861, with banks having trouble funding it, and Chase was forced to sell a further $50 million at a discount to par, creating a somewhat higher effective yield.[6]

Jay Cooke, "The Financier of the Civil War"

No story of money during the Civil War would be complete without noting Jay Cooke and his remarkable marketing of U.S. government bonds during the war. Due to his efforts Treasury Secretary Salmon Chase was able to keep the armies and the navy funded adequately to maintain the struggle. Cooke became known to historians as "The Financier of the Civil War."

In early 1862 Chase and the Treasury Department were struggling to sell the bonds authorized by Congress. They had endeavored to do it through the existing process of involving the large banks through a bidding process, but the banks were unable to readily fund the issues. Furthermore, European markets were skeptical of U.S. bonds and actually favored Confederate bonds early in the war.

Jay Cooke. His innovative methods for selling government bonds led to his being called "The Financier of the Civil War."

Jay Cooke came to Chase's attention as he appeared to have better success than other bankers in assisting the Treasury in the early bond issues. Cooke was originally from Sandusky, Ohio. He had worked at various jobs including clerking at a hotel, at a steamship company, and later at the banking company of E.W. Clark in Philadelphia. He was well regarded in the bank and rose to become a partner by the late 1840s. In January of 1861 he had started his own firm, Jay Cooke & Company. The bank was engaged in buying and selling state-bank notes, gold trading, foreign exchange, and related banking activities. As Cooke was unusually successful in bond sales, he convinced Chase to name him as "Special Fiscal Agent" for the Treasury. It was agreed that he would receive 3/8 of 1 percent of the par value of whatever bonds he sold. Out of this commission he was responsible for any marketing costs. Cooke implemented highly innovative methods for promoting the bonds. He developed a network of 2,500 sales agents across the country and supported them with a sales campaign of promotional newspaper articles, advertisements, handbills, and favorable editorials expounding both the personal financial advantages of investing in government bonds and the fulfillment of patriotic duty in so doing.

Typical of Cooke's promotion was this article in the Pittston, Pennsylvania, *Gazette*, in which the editor or a reporter wrote about discussing federal bond issuance and the growing confidence in them. Undoubtedly Cooke provided the material and narrative for the article.

NEWS and OTHER ITEMS.

THE BEST WAY TO PUT MONEY OUT ON INTEREST.

The following information we insert in our columns
for the benefit of the readers:

[From the Philadelphia Ledger, March 27.]

One of the most surprising things in the recent conversation of greenbacks notes into the popular Five-Twenty six per cent, Government loans at par, is the universality of the call. We happened in yesterday at the office of Jay Cooke, who is the agent for the sale of these loans, and the conversion of the greenbacks and found his table literally covered with orders and accompanying drafts for almost all amounts, from five thousand to a hundred thousand dollars each, and from all parts of the Union. The little States of Delaware and New Jersey are free takers, as are also Pennsylvania, New York and the New England States. But the West is most especially an active taker, as well through her banks as by individuals. The amount of orders lying before us, all received during the day, amounted to over *fifteen hundred thousand dollars*. With this spontaneous proffer of money, Secretary Chase must feel himself entirely at ease, and will take care to put himself beyond these money sharpers, whose chief study is how to profit themselves most from the troubles of the country and the necessaries of the treasury. There are millions of dollars lying idle over the country, and while the uncertainty existed as to what Congress would do, and the bullion brokers were successful in running up gold to the discredit of the Government issues, capital was clutched close. But as the policy and the measures of the Secretary of the Treasury are gradually developed, confidence in the Government and in the future is strengthened, and holders are now anxious to make their long unemployed means productive; the ready and liberal investment in the Five-Twenty loans at par. Almost every town and village throughout the country has individual holders of money to larger amounts probably than ever before at one time, for which satisfactory takers cannot be found. Many of those are now investors in these loans, and the number of such is likely to increase, until the demand shall put all the Government loans on a par with, at least, the loans of the various incorporated companies. The country banks are also free takers for themselves and their customers. On the 1st of July this Five-Twenty year loan will, under the law, be withdrawn.

Then following this article was a letter from a reader of the paper written to Jay Cooke stating that the reader might "have shortly a few thousand dollars to spare" and asking about the federal bonds as an investment, with a list of questions that might have commonly been in people's minds about them.

DEAR SIR:—I see by our papers that you are selling for the Government a new Loan called 'Five-Twenties.' I expect to have shortly a few thousand dollars to spare, and as I have made up my mind that the Government Loans are safe and good, and that it is my duty and interest, at this time, to put my money into them in preference over any other loans or stock I write to get information, of you as follows:

1st. Why are they called 'Five-Twenties'?

2nd. Do you take country money or only Legal Tender Notes, or will a check on Philadelphia, or New York, answer for subscriptions?

3d. Do you sell your bonds at par.

4th. As I cannot come to Philadelphia, how am I to get the Bonds?

5th. What interest do they pay, and how and when and where is it paid, and is it paid in Gold and Legal Tenders?

6th. How does Secretary Chase get enough Gold to pay this Interest?

7th. Will the face of the Bond be paid in Gold when due?

8th. Can I have the Bonds payable to Bearer with Coupons, or registered and payable to my order?

9th. What size are the bonds?

10th. Will I have to pay the same tax on them as I now pay on my Railroad or other bonds?

11th. What is the present debt of the Government, and what amount is it likely to reach if the Rebellion should last a year or two longer?

12th. Will Secretary Chase get enough from Custom House duties and Internal Revenue, Income Taxes, &c., &c., to make it certain that he can pay the Interest punctually?

I have no doubt that a good many of my neighbors would like to take these Bonds, and if you will answer my questions I will show the letter to them.

Very Respectfully,

S— M— F—.

Cooke of course wrote the questioner back, answering his questions in detail and assuring him of the safety of the bonds. "[Our] National debt will be small compared with Great Britain or France, while our resources are vastly greater."

Office of Jay Cooke, Subscription Ag't Jay Cooke & Co., Bankers 113 S. 3rd St. Philadelphia, March 23, 1862

Dear Sir: - Your letter of the 20th, inst. is received, and I will cheerfully give you the information desired by answering your questions in due order.

1st. These Bonds are called 'Five-Twenties,' because while they are twenty year Bonds, they may be redeemed by the Government in GOLD at any time after five years. Many people suppose that the Interest is only 5:20 per cent. This is a mistake – they pay Six per cent Interest.

2nd. Legal Tender notes or checks upon Philadelphia or New York that will bring Legal Tender, are what the Secretary allows me to receive. No doubt your nearest Bank will give you a check or Legal Tenders for your country funds.

3d. The Bonds are sold at Par, the Interest to commence the day you pay the money.

4th. I have made arrangements with your nearest Bank or Banker, who will generally have the Bonds on hand. If not, you can send the money to me by Express, and I will send back the Bonds at cost.

5th. The Bonds pay Six per cent Interest in Gold, three per cent every six months on the first day of May and November at the Mint in Philadelphia, or any other sub-treasury in New York or elsewhere. If you have Coupon Bonds, all you have to do is cut the paper Coupon off each six months and collect it yourself or give it to a Bank for collection. If you have Registered Bonds, you can give your Bank a power of Attorney to collect that interest for you.

6th. The duties on imports of all articles from abroad must be paid in Gold and this is the way Secretary Chase gets his gold. It is now being paid into the Treasury at the rate of two Hundred Thousand Dollars each day, which is twice as much as he needs to pay the Interest in Gold.

7th. Congress has provided that the Bonds shall be Paid in Gold when due.

8th. You can have either Coupon Bonds payable to the Bearer, or Registered Bonds payable to your order.

9th. The former are in 50's 100's 500's and 1000's – the latter in the same amounts, also $500's $10,000.

10th. No! You will not have to pay any taxes on these Bonds if your income from them does not exceed $600: and on all above $600 you will only have to pay one-half as much Income Tax as if your money was invested in Mortgages or other Securities. I consider the Government Bonds as first of all – all other bonds are taxed one-quarter per cent to pay the interest on the Government Bonds, and the Supreme Court of the United States has just decided that no State or City or County can tax Government Bonds.

11th. The present bonded debt of the United States is less than THREE HUNDRED MILLIONS, including the seven and three-tenths Treasury Notes: but the Government owns enough more in the shape of Legal Tenders, Deposits in the Sub-Treasuries, Certificates of Indebtedness, &c., to increase the debt to about eight or nine hundred millions. Secretary Chase has calculated that the debt may reach one thousand seven hundred millions, if the Rebellion lasts eighteen months longer. It is, however, believed now that it will not last six months longer; but even if it does, our National debt will be small compared to that of Great Britain or France, while our resources are vastly greater.

12th. I have no doubt that the revenue will not only be ample to pay the ordinary expense of the Government and all interest on the debt, but leave at least one hundred millions annually towards paying off the debt again as it has twice before—in a few years after the close of the war.

I hope that all who have idle money will at once purchase these Five-Twenty

Year Bonds. The right to demand them for Legal Tender will end on the first day of July 1863, as per the following authorized notice.

Cooke also ran straightforward advertisements offering bond issues.

U.S. 7-30 LOAN.

By Authority of the Secretary of the Treasury, the undersigned has assumed the General Subscription Agency for the sale of United State Treasury Notes, bearing seven and three-tenths per cent. Interest per annum, known as the

SEVEN-THIRTY LOAN.

These notes are issued under date of August 15th, 1864, and are payable three years from that time, in currency, or are convertible, at the option of the holder, into

U.S. 5-20 SIX PER CENT. GOLD-BEARING BONDS.

These Bonds are now worth a premium of nine per cent, including gold interest from Nov., which makes actual profit on the 7-30 loan, at current rates, including interest, about ten per cent per annum, besides its exemption from state and municipal taxation, which adds from one to three per cent more, according to the rate levied on other property. The interest is payable semi-annually by coupons attached to each note, which may be cut off and sold to any bank or broker.

The interest amounts to:

One cent per day on $50 note
Two cents per day on a $100 note
Ten cents per day on a $300 note
20 cents per day on a $1000 note
$1 per day on a $5000 note

Notes of all denominations named will be promptly furnished upon receipt of subscriptions. This is

The Only Loan in Market

now offered by the Government, and it is confidently expected that its superior advantages will make it the

Great Popular Loan of the People.

Less than $200,000,000 remain unsold, which will probably be disposed of within the next 60 or 90 days, when the notes will undoubtedly command a premium, as has uniformly been the case on closing the subscriptions to other Loans.

In order that citizens of every town and section of the country may be afforded facilities for taking the loan, the National Banks, State Banks, and Private Bankers throughout the country have generally agreed to receive subscriptions at par. Subscribers will select their own agents, in whom they have confidence, and who only are to be responsible for the delivery of the notes for which they receive orders.

JAY COOKE,

Subscription Agent, Philadelphia
Subscriptions will be received by the
First National Bank, Hartford, Conn
Charter Oak National Bank, "
Phoenix National Bank, "
Aetna National Bank, "
National Exchange Bank, "

Instead of relying on the large money-center banks, his campaign sold directly to individuals, smaller banks, and companies. It is estimated that more than 1,000,000 individuals bought government bonds through Cooke's sales during the war. Cooke sometimes felt the 3/8 of 1 percent commission was too little when taking into account his marketing expenses. However, it is believed this was made up for by the market insights his bank was privy to through its special arrangement with the Treasury Department. Cooke was extremely successful and between October 1862 and January 1864 he sold out the $500 million issue of 5-20 bonds (callable in 5 years and maturing in 20). By January of 1865 the government again struggled to fund the war effort and again employed Cooke to handle sales of its 7.3 percent bond issue. By that time Chase was out of the Treasury, but his successors recognized Cooke's ability to raise money. He sold more than $600 million of the bonds within six months, enabling the federal government to make the final military push to end the war.

Cooke and Chase became close personally and Chase came to rely on Cooke for his own personal investments. Cooke was liberal in lending to Chase over the years, even after Chase was out of the Treasury secretary position. There often were accusations of Chase favoring Cooke for personal gain and vice versa, but Chase was scrupulous in keeping his personal business separate from government business and very sensitive to any accusations of special dealing.

Cooke of course became very wealthy through his bond sales, and after the war became involved with development of railroads in the West. In particular he invested heavily in the Northern Pacific Railroad. By 1872 the railroad was in trouble and this helped precipitate the Panic of 1873, which cost Cooke his fortune. In later years he was able to recoup much of his wealth through investments in silver mining. He died in 1905.[7]

As the amount of paper currency and debt exploded and the banks struggled to sell bonds, it became evident there was not enough gold and silver coin to meet the demand for people wanting to convert their paper currency. The bank-note circulation could not be sustained at par value for coins. Finally, on December 27, 1861, the banks agreed among themselves to suspend specie payments, and all in New York did so by December 30. Other banks throughout the country quickly followed this action. Note that the specie suspension on December 27 was just one day after Mint Director James Pollock's letter to Secretary Chase, enclosing the "God Our Trust" pattern coins. Thus we have the likely explanation for Chase's non-response to Pollock regarding the With Motto pattern coins. He was consumed by the financial crisis.

Contributing to the crisis was the fact that the war was going badly for the North, and Congress authorized troop levels to be increased to 500,000 from the previous 300,000. Chase estimated the needed expenditures for the fiscal year ending June 30, 1862, at well over $500 million. The Union loss in July 1861 at the Battle of Bull Run came as a major shock in the North. It shook confidence but perhaps more importantly showed that the war would not be quickly over, nor inexpensive.

The Trent Affair in November 1861, mentioned earlier, was unfolding and threatening to bring Britain and probably France into the war on the side of the South. This seriously hurt public confidence. The sense was that the military was being badly managed as the Union armies lay inactive, the one exception being that under Brigadier General Ulysses S. Grant in the west. President Abraham Lincoln took the opportunity to dismiss Simon Cameron as secretary of War. (Lincoln wrote Cameron saying he accepted Cameron's resignation, even though Cameron had not submitted one!)[8] Not only was Cameron less than effective, he also was surrounded by rumors and incidents of corruption. In particular his connections with the railroads led to overcharges for movement of troops and supplies.[9] The president replaced Cameron with Edwin Stanton on January 13, 1862. Time would prove him to be an effective and honest War Department secretary.

The war was now spinning far beyond all expectation. Significantly higher troop levels would be required. The Navy needed extensive enlargement to enforce the blockade of Southern ports and to support the Army's efforts. And the Treasury was nearly empty. A "hard money" war was now becoming impossible. Indeed Congress was already inclined to move toward "Legal Tender" issuance, meaning currency to be issued with no provision for conversion to coin. Public acceptance of such currency in payment of financial obligations would in effect be dictated by the government saying it was legal tender and must be accepted in payment of all debts "public and private." Chase was at heart a hard-money man, and in his December 9, 1861, report to Congress had expressed an aversion to circulation of United States notes even when convertible to coin. However, he was reluctantly dragged to the conclusion that there was no alternative. Congress ran ahead of Chase on the issue and was considering a bill in mid-January 1862, House Bill no. 240. This bill was titled "An Act to Authorize the Issue of United States Notes, and for the Redemption and Funding Thereof and for Funding the Floating Debt of the United States." Congressman Elbridge G. Spaulding of New York had proposed it and said:

> It is a war measure; a measure of necessity and not of choice, presented by the Committee of Ways and Means to meet the most pressing demands upon the treasury, to sustain the army and the navy until they can make a vigorous advance upon the traitors and crush out the rebellion. These are extraordinary times, and extraordinary measures must be resorted to in order to save our Government and preserve our nationality.

Congress sought the opinion of Chase before passing such legislation, knowing he had doubts on the issue. Chase hesitated but finally on January 29 wrote to Thaddeus Stevens, chairman of the House Ways and Means Committee:

I have the honor to acknowledge the receipt of a resolution of the Committee of Ways and Means referring to me House Bill No. 240, and asking my opinion as to the propriety and necessity of its immediate passage by Congress.

The condition of the Treasury certainly makes immediate action on the subject of affording provision for the expenditures of the Government both expedient and necessary. The general provisions of the bill submitted to me seem to be well adapted to the end proposed. There are some points in it, however, which may perhaps be usefully amended.

The provision making United States Notes a legal tender has doubtless been well considered by the committee, and their conclusion needs no support from any observation of mine. I think it my duty to say, however, that in respect to this provision my reflections have conducted me to the same conclusions they have reached. It is not unknown to them that I have felt, nor do I wish to conceal that I now feel, a great aversion to making anything but coin a legal tender in payment of debts. It has been my anxious wish to avoid the necessity of such legislation. It is at present impossible, however, in consequence of the large expenditures entailed by the war and the suspension of the banks, to procure sufficient coin for current disbursements; and it has therefore become indispensably necessary that we should resort to the issue of United States notes. The making them a legal tender might still be avoided if the willingness manifested by the people generally, by railroad companies and by many of the banking institutions, to receive and pay them as money in all transactions was absolutely or practically universal; but unfortunately there are some persons and some institutions which refuse to receive and pay them, and whose action tends not merely to the unnecessary depreciation of the notes, but to established discriminations in business against those who—in this matter—give a cordial support to the Government and in favor of those who do not. Such discriminations should, if possible, be prevented; and the provision making the notes a legal tender in a great measure, at least prevents it by putting all citizens in this respect upon the same level both of rights and duties.[10]

Congressman Elbridge G. Spaulding of New York. He worked energetically on questions of the nation's currency.

Chase continued the letter by saying he expected the committee to accompany the legal-tender legislation with other provisions that would secure "the highest credit" and ensure circulation of the notes. He believed funding them with interest-bearing bonds and by judicious and adequate taxation would sustain the credibility of the currency. In conclusion he said:

> Such legislation, it may be hoped, will divest the legal tender clause of the bill of injurious tendencies, and secure the earliest possible return to a sound currency of coin and promptly convertible notes.
>
> I beg to add that vigorous military operations, and the unsparing retrenchment of all unnecessary expenses, will also contribute essentially to this desirable end.

A few days later, on February 3, 1862, Chase wrote to E.G. Spaulding, on the Ways and Means Committee, further on the topic:

> Mr. Seward said to me on yesterday that you had observed to him that my hesitation in coming up to the legal tender proposition embarrassed you; and I am very sorry to know it, for my anxious wish is to support you in all respects.
>
> It is true I came with reluctance to the conclusion that the legal tender clause is a necessity, but I came to it decidedly and I support it earnestly. I do not hesitate when I have made up my mind, however much regret I may feel over the necessity of the conclusion to which I came.
>
> Immediate action is of great importance. The Treasury is nearly empty. I have been obliged to draw for the last installment of the November loan; so soon as it is paid, I fear the banks generally will refuse to receive the United States notes. They will see the necessity of urging the bill through without more delay.[11]

On February 4 Chase wrote a letter to William Cullen Bryant, editor of the *New York Post*, in response to an editorial Bryant had written opposing issuance of Legal Tender Notes:

> Your feelings of repugnance can hardly be greater than my own, but I am convinced that, as a temporary measure, it is undispensably necessary.[12]

Despite Chase's support, the bill faced heavy opposition in Congress. The national experience 85 years earlier, during the Revolutionary War, with the nearly unlimited printing of Continental Currency, lingered in the nation's memory. That paper currency had become essentially worthless, had created runaway inflation, and caused general pain on the population. The bill, however, passed on February 25, 1862. It authorized an initial issue of $150 million. Of this, $50 million was to be in lieu of $50 million in Demand Notes authorized by the July 1861 and February 1862 acts. The Legal Tender Notes were not convertible at par to silver or gold, and also could not be used to pay import duties. The Demand Notes were to be retired and withdrawn from circulation. By June of 1862, less than six months after passage, it was clear $150 million was not enough and, on June 7, authority to issue another $150 million was passed. Also authorized was up to $35 million (out of the $150 million) to be issued in denominations of less than $5, since the absence of smaller money for making change was becoming a significant problem. In practice this allowed for printing of $1 and $2 bills. With the suspension of specie payments by the banks, coins could not be readily obtained. So money denominated between 1¢ and $5 (previously the lowest note denomination) had in effect become unavailable.

Only a month later, yet another $150 million was approved. By war's end $1.25 billion of Legal Tender Notes had been authorized and issued. The consequence of so much printing was of course the depreciation of paper money against gold

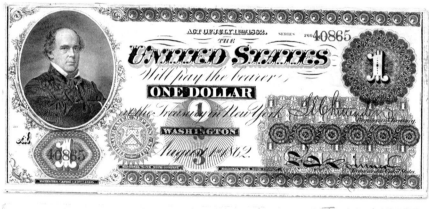

Above: A $1 Legal Tender Note picturing Treasury Secretary Salmon P. Chase.
Opposite page: A $2 Legal Tender Note featuring Alexander Hamilton, first secretary of the U.S. Treasury; a $5 Legal Tender Note with a portrait of Alexander Hamilton; a $10 Legal Tender Note picturing President Abraham Lincoln and an allegory of Art; and a $20 Legal Tender Note showing Miss Liberty with a sword and shield.

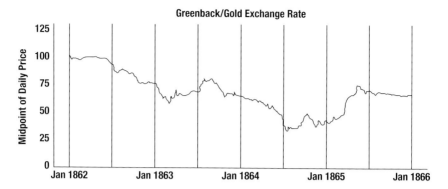

Note that the value of the greenback against gold declined significantly and steadily until July/August 1863, when Union victories at Gettysburg and Vicksburg raised hopes (and the greenback values). It resumed its decline into mid- to late 1864, when Atlanta fell. Then it increased sharply after Appomattox. It would not recover par value with gold, however, until the late 1870s.

and silver. The exchange rate between paper and specie fluctuated over the course of the war, largely depending on the success or failure of the Union armies on the battlefield. The chart above shows the greenback vs. gold rates over the course of the war.

The Legal Tender Act authorized retirement of the Demand Notes. With the Legal Tender Notes not convertible to silver or gold, the Demand Notes remained highly prized and began trading at significant premiums. The Treasury Department moved to retire them as quickly as possible. Within a year they became rare in circulation. An 1880 Treasury Department report showed only $60,535 in Demand Notes had not been redeemed.[13]

The constitutionality of the Legal Tender Act was in some dispute and eventually it was challenged in court, though not until after the war. The case *(Hepburn vs. Griswold)* reached the U.S. Supreme Court in December 1868. A decision was not reached until the December 1869 term, when it was declared unconstitutional. Salmon Chase, by then chief justice of the Court, did not disqualify himself though he had been involved in the notes' original issue. But amazingly he voted with the majority that they were unconstitutional! Initially the case and the ruling was believed to only apply to contracts made before the war. The realization soon came that the implications were wider, and an effort was undertaken to have the court review the question. Eventually, following a complex series of legal challenges, re-arguments, and changes in judges that occurred on the court, the ruling was reversed by a vote of 5 to 4, keeping the Legal Tender Notes legal. Chase maintained his previous stance this time, voting with the minority in deeming the Legal Tender Act unconstitutional.[14]

Civil War Bank-Note Companies

Aside note to this story of paper-money issuance is how the currency was actually produced. Initially the production was contracted out to two companies, the American Bank Note Company and the National Bank Note Company. The notes were printed in sheets of four and shipped to the Treasury Department. There some 70 workers were employed to count them, inspect them, and cut them into individual bills. The notes initially required hand-written signatures as well. It is said that President Lincoln teased Secretary Chase that he would have to sign all the notes himself.[15] This operation continued for some six months when an employee, Spencer Morton Clark, had printing plates engraved with the signatures and showed that they could be printed on the bills, saving an enormous amount of labor. Clark had started his government career in 1856, working in the Bureau of Construction of the Treasury Department. He had become interested in the production and finishing of the new currency and gradually assumed responsibilities in that area.[16] In July of 1862 he convinced Chase that the companies printing the notes were overcharging the government and that it would make sense to bring the entire operation in-house. Clark took on this project, hiring an engraver, acquiring printing equipment, and establishing the National Currency Bureau. He became superintendent of this entity, which later was to become the Bureau of Engraving and Printing. He hired more employees including nearly 300 women, the first ever to be employed by the federal government. Clark said that the women's work was neater than men's and that they were less "boisterous."[17]

Counterfeiting was a constant issue during this era and Clark was looking for ways to prevent it. An inventor approached him with an idea for banknote paper that would

supposedly make counterfeiting more difficult. The inventor was Stuart Gwynn, and his "membrane paper" did not require damping with water before printing as did the standard paper used for notes. Clark was quite taken with Gwynn's idea and new specialized presses were acquired at high costs. As things turned out the paper required extremely high pressure and the whole thing became a fiasco. There were rumors of corruption surrounding Gwynn that tainted Clark as well. Gwynn ended up in jail for fraud and non-payment of his suppliers.[18]

Spencer Morton Clark, first superintendent of the National Currency Bureau.

At about the same time rumors began to circulate of illicit activity surrounding the women working at the Treasury Department. Clark himself may have been involved with one or more of the women working there. Late hours, drinking, and carriage rides with men to nearby hotels brought disrepute, and the term "Treasury Woman" became a euphemism for prostitute. Chase heard these stories and questioned Clark. Clark denied them, but Chase quietly had the noted detective/spy Lafayette Baker conduct an investigation. Baker's report came down hard on Clark, but a competing congressional report expressed confidence in Clark, and ultimately he escaped censure, continuing in his office until the late 1860s.[19] Related to this was the fact that a Chase political rival, the Blair family, was inciting the congressional investigations in order to embarrass and damage Chase. The charge was that "The Treasury Department has been converted into a house of orgies and bacchanal" and Clark led "a sort of carrousel in the Treasury building" (late in the evening) "where liquors were used freely and some of the female employees participated in the frolic." It was "a kind of Government house of ill fame where pretty women toiled until morning over ale and oyster suppers." The congressional committee responsible for investigating the matter had James Garfield, the future president, as chairman and other Chase allies in its membership, packed by Chase ally House Speaker Schuyler Colfax. They succeeded in delaying and allowing the matter to drift inconclusively.[20]

Another incident regarding Clark was his placing his own picture on the 5¢ Third Issue Fractional Currency note. There are conflicting versions of how this came about. There may have been confusion on the part of Francis Spinner, treasurer of the United States, thinking he was approving placing the portrait of William Clark of Lewis and Clark fame on the note rather than Spencer Morton Clark.

Another version of the story is that the American Bank Note Company had placed his picture on the note in an effort to flatter Clark and gain his influence for retention of their very profitable business printing the notes. This story is related in Ted Schwartz's book *A History of United States Coinage*.[21] The story cannot be true as the Treasury Department had taken the printing in-house (on Clark's recommendation) with the beginning of the Second Issue in July of 1863. The Third Issue, which included the Clark note, did not begin until December of 1864, about a year and a half later. The American Bank Note Company would not have had any role in producing Clark's note.

In any case Congress was not happy with what had transpired and passed legislation soon thereafter forbidding portrayal of living persons on coins or paper currency going forward.

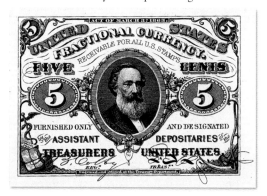

A Proof of a Third Issue
5¢ Fractional Currency note,
picturing Spencer Clark.

National Banking

Secretary Chase had laid out his ideas for financing the war in his December 9, 1861, annual report. In it he proposed the measures discussed above, i.e., bond issues, tax increases, and higher tariffs. Another proposal included in his report was establishment of a national banking system. Congressman Elbridge Spaulding of New York, a man knowledgeable in banking and who had actually initiated the Legal Tender bill, called on Chase to follow up and learn details of his proposal for a national banking act. He learned that Chase had nothing in detail prepared, and Spaulding took it upon himself to draft a bill over the Christmas holiday. However, he and Chase quickly realized there was powerful opposition from the state-chartered banks and that such an act would take at least several months to pass and much longer to implement.[22] That part of Chase's measure was therefore put on hold.

The background to the idea of national banking dated back to the Founding Fathers, particularly Alexander Hamilton. Hamilton favored establishment of a central bank that would hold U.S. government funds, issue standardized currency, and lend both to private entities and to the government to cover liquidity gaps. Such a bank was established in 1791 with a 20-year charter. (The government held a minority ownership interest; thus it was not a "national bank" in the sense that European central banks were.) When it came up for renewal in 1811 the Senate tied on its vote and the vice president broke the tie, voting against the renewal. In 1816 the Second Bank of the United States was chartered along the lines that Hamilton had envisioned, also for 20 years. It had been the well-known target of Andrew Jackson, and he succeeded in stopping the renewal of its charter when it was up for extension in 1836. Since the Second Bank of the United States had been killed off by Jackson there were no federally chartered banks. All banks were state-chartered institutions. Even with the new federal Demand Notes and Legal Tender Notes of 1862, the great preponderance of money circulating in the country was still made up of state-chartered bank and company-issued notes.

Nearly all of the state banks issued paper currency, but there was no standard. Instead there was a hodgepodge of different notes with a great variation in physical appearance. There was also great variation in the reliability of the money, depending on the strength of

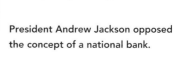

President Andrew Jackson opposed the concept of a national bank.

A Gallery of Obsolete Paper Money

Two toddlers play among gigantic silver dollars on the face of this $2 note of the West River Bank, Jamaica, Vermont.

A panorama of farming activities on a $5 note of the Freehold Banking Co., New Jersey.

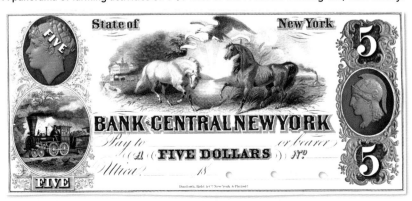

A scarce $1,000 note of the Canal Bank, New Orleans. This was Louisiana's most prolific issuer of paper money.

Cattle and other livestock populate the face of this $3 note of the Drovers Bank, Salt Lake City, Utah. The bank itself is something of a mystery, with almost nothing known about its operations.

The Bank of Cape Fear, North Carolina, issued odd denominations including this $9 note.

Opposite page: A $5 note of the Bank of Central New York in Utica. Horses and railroad scenes were popular motifs in obsolete paper money.

the individual bank. In general, notes were of a local nature, where people could be familiar with the issuing bank and be able to judge its management's reputation and financial strength. When a note was transferred any distance from the locale of its issuer, it was likely to be questioned and accepted only at a discount, if accepted at all. This localization and lack of a standard national currency had long been a hindrance to commerce. There was a high rate of bank failures among the state banks, which were often poorly or fraudulently managed. The states varied in their regulatory oversight, with the older Eastern states of New England and New York generally doing a better job, usually requiring real security backing their notes, and the newer Western states often very loose in their regulation and security requirements. Paper currency was issued not only by banks but also by companies, particularly canal companies, railroads, and plank-road toll-collecting companies that were able to receive state charters. These notes, both bank-issued and company-issued, are known today as "obsolete currency" or "obsolete paper money."

Beyond the question of the soundness of the issuing bank was the problem of counterfeiting, which was very widespread. There was no uniform appearance or quality in the state-bank–issued notes, making them easy targets for counterfeiters.[23] The result of all this was that it was difficult for sellers to judge the currency they were being offered for their products or services. Every transaction carried an extra element of risk. Chase likely had given this a lot of thought, as when he was a young attorney in Cincinnati his first major client was the Cincinnati branch of the Bank of the United States. He had realized that that bank's currency was standardized and accepted at par at all its branches around the country. It was therefore more safely accepted in business. The demise of the bank had eliminated those notes.

President Lincoln also took a personal interest in this issue, as he understood the importance of a national currency and bank credit to support a healthy economy. As a young man on the Indiana and Illinois frontiers he had seen the ways that unreliable paper money and inadequate credit frustrated the ambitions of his

A $20 note of the Bank of the United States, with a hand-engraved adaptation of the Great Seal of the United States.

neighbors, often cheating them of the fruits of their labors. These experiences influenced his political outlook and perhaps guided him toward supporting the Whig Party, which had opposed Jackson's destruction of the National Bank.[24]

While the Legal Tender Notes overcame some of the deficiencies of the state bank notes, Chase disliked their unsecured nature, viewing them as but a short-term expedient. In national banking he was seeking an alternative both for providing a standardized, secure currency and for financing the war. Chase's thought was that notes issued by national banks would require backing with federal bonds, therefore creating demand for the bonds and helping government finance the war. In his December 1861 report he viewed a national banking system as "a system of notes bearing a common impression and authenticated by a common authority . . . and the security of redemption by the pledge of United States stocks, and an adequate provision of specie." Chase believed that national banks' note circulation being backed by deposits of U.S. Treasury bonds would assure their relative security, as the notes would then be indirect liabilities of the U.S. Treasury.

There would be "advantages of uniformity in currency; of uniformity in security; of effectual safeguard . . . against depreciation; and of protection from losses in discounts and exchanges; while in the operations of the government the people would find the further advantage of a large demand for government securities, of increased facilities for obtaining the loans required by the war, and of some alleviation of the burdens on industry through a diminution in the rate of interest, or a participation in the profit of circulation, without risking the perils of a great money monopoly."[25]

Second Bank of the United States headquarters. The building still stands in Philadelphia.

Chase's reference to "perils of a great money monopoly" likely is an allusion to the defunct Bank of the United States. Jackson and the anti-bank people frequently had attacked it for what they deemed its monopolistic characteristics. Under Chase's plan there would be many national banks, not just one, and they would be owned by private interests, not the government. Though national banking was put on hold in early 1862, Chase, Congressman Spaulding, Senator John Sherman, and others knew the importance of the issue and continued to push for it. Senator Sherman (brother of General William Tecumseh Sherman) in particular argued for such a bill and presented one to the Senate on January 26, 1863. There remained strong opposition from the state banks, particularly from those in New York and on the East Coast. Sherman made the case that a national-bank system would not only provide a uniform currency but would create a new market for U.S. Treasury bonds, as banks would have to buy them to back their issuance of notes. He couched it therefore as an emergency measure to help finance the war, much the same argument that had been used to pass the Legal Tender legislation.[26] He also said that a common currency would create greater national unity and that the lack of such a national currency and predominance of state bank notes had contributed to stronger states' rights and contained the seeds of the Civil War.[27]

Senator Sherman worked to rally Senate Republicans to the cause. President Lincoln, too, personally intervened, convincing two Republican senators to swing their support to the bill.[28] The bill passed by the narrow margin of 23 to 21. Only two Democrats voted for it, and nine Republicans voted against it, greatly influenced by lobbyists for the state banks, who were fearful that a national banking system would ultimately force them to give up their unrestrained ability to issue circulating notes. In the House the bill was sponsored by Elbridge Spaulding and Samuel Hooper and was passed also by the fairly close vote of 78 to 64, on February 20, 1863. It was signed by President Lincoln on February 25. The bill, originally the National Currency Act, became known as the National Bank Act of 1863. It provided for establishment of national banks and permitted those banks to issue a standardized national currency in amounts up to 90 percent of the market value of U.S. Treasury securities that they held on deposit with the Treasury. Total currency issuance was limited to $300 million and remained at that level for several years.[29] Further legislation in June of 1864 established the office of the Comptroller of the Currency to charter, examine, and regulate the federally chartered banks. Chase named Hugh McCulloch, an Indiana banker, to the position. It was an interesting choice, as McCulloch had originally been opposed to the national bank concept but had come to support it.[30] Following the 1863 legislation many state-chartered banks changed over to federal charters, but many others did not, as clearly there was closer regulation under the federal provisions. A further act therefore was passed on March 3, 1865, that imposed a 10 percent tax on any notes

Hugh McCulloch, first Comptroller of the Currency, would later become secretary of the Treasury after the war.

issued by the state banks. This was so onerous that it forced the state banks to either change over to federal charters or cease issuing notes. The 10 percent tax was challenged in a court case, *Viazie vs. Collector of Internal Revenue*, in which a bank refused to pay the tax, claiming it to be unconstitutional. The Supreme Court came down in favor of the tax legislation, and the state banks quickly fell in line. The number of nationally chartered banks rose from 66 right after the acts were passed to 7,473 by 1913.

State bank numbers fell from 1,466 in 1863 to 247 in 1868. They were widely believed to be on the way to near extinction. However, the state banks made a resurgence in later years as the various state reserve requirements and other regulations were not as stringent as for the national banks, often making them more competitive vis-a-vis the national banks. In addition the state banks developed demand deposit accounts that allowed for checks to be drawn by customers on their accounts. Checks then substituted for notes in payments and offset the state banks' disadvantage of no longer being able to issue currency. By 1871 the deposits of non-national commercial banks were roughly equal to those held by national banks and they remained so in the years following.[31] The number of state banks grew rapidly in the latter part of the nineteenth century and reached more than 15,000 by 1913. By 1890 only 10 percent of the nation's money supply was in the form of notes as the checking system flourished.[32]

A check, dated 1874, drawn on Jay Cooke & Co. Bank from General William T. Sherman's account. It has "In God is Our Trust" on a vignette. The development of the checking system in the late 1860s and 1870s reduced the need for physical currency.

Salmon P. Chase's role in establishment of the national banking system is one of his major claims to fame. It truly revolutionized banking and greatly facilitated commerce. Chase had pressed for its passage, threatening Congress that he would resign as Treasury secretary if it failed. It is also clear that such congressional leaders as E.G. Spaulding and John Sherman were instrumental in developing and promoting the details of the enabling legislation.

As noted earlier, besides Chase, Lincoln also favored the development of a national banking system with a uniform national currency. In his 1864 State of the Union speech he highlighted the passage of the legislation and the changes occurring in banking:

> The national banking system is proving to be acceptable to capitalists and to the people. On the 25th day of November 584 national banks had been organized, a considerable number of which were conversions from State banks. Changes from State systems to the national system are rapidly taking place, and it is hoped that very soon there will be in the United States no banks of issue not authorized by Congress and no bank-note circulation not secured by the

An 1882 National Bank Note from Buffalo, New York.

A 1902 note of the First National Bank of Fairbanks, Alaska.

Government. That the Government and the people will derive great benefit from this change in the banking systems of the country can hardly be questioned. The national system will create a reliable and permanent influence in support of the national credit and protect the people against losses in the use of paper money. Whether or not any further legislation is advisable for the suppression of State-bank issues it will be for Congress to determine. It seems quite clear that the Treasury cannot be satisfactorily conducted unless the Government can exercise a restraining power over the bank-note circulation of the country.

A painting by N.C. Wyeth depicting Abraham Lincoln and Salmon P. Chase working on national banking legislation.

The changes wrought by the war on the nation's finances were staggering. An article in a 2011 issue of *Barron's* entitled "The High Cost of War" gave a good summary of the numbers. In 1850 federal government expenditures averaged about $1 million per week. By mid-1861, after the war began, government was spending $1.5 million *per day*. By war's end it was $3.5 million per day. Spending was over $1 billion per year by the war's end. About 21% of revenues came from taxes and about two-thirds (67 percent) from bond sales, with the balance from issuance of greenbacks, tariffs, and other sources. In 1860 the national debt was $64 million. By 1866 it was $2.68 billion, up some 40 times! Inflation was high but manageable at about 180 percent over the course of the war.

By contrast, the South borrowed and printed currency massively, raising only 6 percent of expenditures through taxes. While early in the war Confederate bonds were considered more attractive to European lenders than federal bonds, this changed as the war and relative financial conditions of the two parties evolved. The Confederacy experienced 700 percent inflation during the first two years of the war and more than 9,000 percent by the war's end, when its currency became worthless.[33] The Confederate constitution had allowed states to issue currency but prohibited any "legal tender" measures, allowing that status only to gold and silver, of which the Confederacy had very little. This led to uncontrolled issuance of paper money from both central government and state sources. The lack of legal-tender status also allowed for any of their currency to be declined in commerce. Furthermore the lack of printing facilities and shortage of paper in the South led to poor-quality notes, easily counterfeited (mainly by Northern printers motivated both by greed and by the desire to undermine the Confederate money). Often the quality of the counterfeit notes was superior to the genuine Confederate currency. Initially Confederate authorities were troubled by the counterfeiting and tried various means to curtail it. However, the Confederacy was having problems producing enough currency to facilitate commerce and, by late 1862, Confederate Secretary of the Treasury Christopher Memminger suggested that counterfeit currency should be honored as genuine. He wrote to Vice President Alexander Stephens that many of "the notes were so well counterfeited that they will be freely received in business transactions." Indeed, legislation was passed to that effect. By the middle of the war, federal greenbacks were the preferred currency when they could be obtained. Newly captured Union prisoners of war reported being approached and offered as much as $15 Confederate for any $1 in federal currency they might have on their persons. By 1864 the Confederate government recognized this as a problem and their Congress passed legislation prohibiting its citizens from "dealing in the paper currency of the enemy."[34]

A Notable Instance of
IN GOD IS OUR TRUST

It is interesting that there were no efforts that we know of to place a motto on the newly produced Demand Notes or Legal Tender federal currency. However, an 1864 Compound Interest Bearing Note actually carries the motto "In God is Our Trust" on a vignette to the left of George Washington, who stands in the center. The note is extremely rare, with fewer than a half dozen examples believed to exist.

In an enlarged view the words IN GOD IS OUR TRUST are visible on the shield in the vignette. As discussed in chapter 5 this had been the original idea for the motto on U.S. coinage, drawn from the "Star Spangled Banner," but the thought was that it took up too much space to fit neatly and be visible on coins, hence "God Our Trust" and eventually "In God We Trust" was used. But on currency, where space was less of a limitation, "In God is Our Trust" clearly fit perfectly well. There is one report, mentioned later in chapter 17, that President Lincoln had his doubts about a religious reference on paper currency. This may be the explanation for its not being used for that purpose until the 1950s, some 90 years later. This Compound Interest Bearing Note (cataloged as Whitman-3245 and Friedberg-199) was therefore well ahead of its time.

A close-up view of the note's motto.

An 1864 Compound Interest Bearing Note.

CHAPTER 7

1862 "God Our Trust" Patterns, Coin Shortages, and the Search for Alternatives

As noted in chapter 5, Treasury Secretary Salmon Chase did not respond to Mint Director James Pollock's December 26, 1861, letter proposing "God Our Trust" as the motto to be placed on the coinage and enclosing the pattern half dollars and $10 pieces to demonstrate its appearance. We can suppose from what we learned in the last chapter that the financial crisis had distracted Chase at the time he received the letter. Perhaps he laid it aside intending to deal with it later. However, with the passage of some months we might also surmise that he had either forgotten or lost interest in the motto project altogether. Likely the matter would have died there but for Director Pollock reviving it. Pollock sent a letter reminding Chase on June 16, 1862:

> Sir:
>
> On the 26th of December last I had the honor to submit at your request some coins in relation to the introduction on the face of our coinage a motto expressive of national reliance upon Divine Support. Not having heard from you in relation to the matter and as the time is now at hand when the preparation of the dies for the coinage of 1863 must be commenced I beg to call your attention to my letter, and to request that you will furnish me with your idea on the issue in question as soon as convenient.
>
> *I am most respectfully*
> *Your obedient servant*
> *Jas. Pollock*
> *Director of the Mint*[1]

Opposite page: A patriotic Civil War lithograph showing "volunteers in defence of the government against usurpation."

Even after Pollock's prompting we have no record of a response from Chase but, again, Pollock was persistent in keeping the issue alive. The Mint director was required to provide an annual report, usually produced in autumn of each year, for fiscal year-end June 30. He used this report for 1862 (dated October 27) to again bring the subject up:

> The distinct and unequivocal recognition of the divine sovereignty in the practical administration of our political system is a duty of the highest obligation. History unites with divine revelation in declaring that "Happy is that people whose God is the Lord." In exercise of political sovereignty our nation should honor him; and now in this hour of peril and danger to our country and its liberties, it is becoming to acknowledge his power and invoke his protection. Our national coinage in its devices and legends should indicate the Christian character of our nation, and declare our trust in God. It does not do this. On the contrary, ancient mythology, more than Christianity, has stamped its impress on our coin. It is however gratifying to know that the proposition to introduce a motto on our coins, expressing a national reliance on divine support has been favorably considered by your department, and will not doubt be approved by an intelligent public sentiment. The subject is under the control of Congress; and without a change in existing laws, no alternation in the legends and devices of most of our national coins can be made; a motto however may be added without additional authority or violation of the present law.[2]

In referring to ancient mythology, Pollock's language echoed Watkinson's thoughts about worshipping the "goddess of liberty" and "pantheistic worshipping of eagles," as that bird appeared on the reverses of the larger U.S. coins, reminding him of ancient "heathen" coins. Pollock then reiterated the provisions of the Mint Act of 1837 and how they applied to placing a motto on the coinage, i.e., the reverse of each of the larger gold and silver coins should have the representation of an eagle along with "United States of America" and the denomination inscribed.

An ancient tetradrachm from Ptolemy VI depicting an eagle on the reverse. Watkinson and Pollock felt the eagle on U.S. coins was more about ancient mythology, as shown on such coins, than any Christian theme.

The consequence of this was that "it will be necessary to interfere as little as possible with the present legal devices." Much of this was a repeat of James B. Longacre's letter to Pollock in December of 1861, as quoted in chapter 5.

Besides drawing attention to the issue through his annual report, Pollock had more pattern coins produced. He had already struck and provided 1861-dated pattern coins enclosed with his letter to Chase in late 1861, demonstrating the placement and appearance of the motto. But he had more struck dated 1862. They were done in the same denominations and in the same formats as the 1861 coins, the only change being that of the date. These were the half dollar struck in silver (examples were also struck in copper) and the $10 gold piece in copper. Again the motto "God Our Trust" was placed above the eagle on the reverses of the coins in the two different formats, in plain letters and on a scroll device.

The 1862 pattern coins were struck in greater numbers than the 1861 pieces, which are very rare. There are no official records showing the numbers struck, but we can arrive at some estimate from the numbers of surviving pieces observed in auctions and other sales venues. According to the standard reference work on pattern coins, *United States Pattern Coins*, by J. Hewitt Judd (updated by Q. David Bowers), there are likely 7 to 10 pieces known of each of the 1861 coins, that is:

1. silver half dollars with the motto, Plain Letters type,
2. silver half dollars with the motto on a scroll,
3. same as 1., but in copper,
4. same as 2., but in copper,
5. $10 eagle with Plain Letters motto, struck in copper,
6. $10 eagle, Scroll Type, struck in copper.

Both the 1861 and 1862 $10 eagles have High Date and Low Date varieties. In contrast with the 7 to 10 pieces estimated for 1861, those dated 1862 are known in substantially higher numbers. According to the Judd reference book the 1862 halves in silver, both types (Plain Letters and Scroll Type), are Rarity-5 on the Sheldon Rarity Scale, meaning between 31 and 75 are believed to exist. The $10 eagles in copper, both types, are estimated as Low Rarity-6 or approximately 21 to 30 believed extant. According to an auction catalog dated May 1863, by the well-known auctioneer W. Elliot Woodward, 25 sets were struck. There were likely later restrikes made of these issues, accounting for the estimated number of survivors being somewhat over the 25 sets specified for 1862. We do not know to whom Pollock may have distributed the pattern coins, but it is likely he provided them to congressmen and Treasury Department officials he believed might be in positions of possible influence on the matter. Coins provided to them would make them aware of the issue and would promote the concept. Many patterns also were secretly sold by Mint officials to coin dealers for their personal profit.

A Gallery of 1862 Pattern Coins

1862 GOD OUR TRUST, Plain Letters, half dollar pattern, struck in silver (Judd-295). The same design was also struck in copper (Judd-296).

1862 GOD OUR TRUST, Scroll Type, half dollar pattern, struck in copper (Judd-294). The same design was also struck in silver (Judd-293).

1862 GOD OUR TRUST, Plain Letters, $10 eagle pattern (Judd-298). Both the Plain Letters and the Scroll Type 1862 GOD OUR TRUST eagles had High Date and Low Date varieties, just as the 1861 patterns had.

1862 GOD OUR TRUST, Scroll Type, $10 eagle pattern (Judd-297). Both the Plain Letters and the Scroll Type 1862 GOD OUR TRUST eagles had High Date and Low Date varieties, just as the 1861 patterns had.

In the Mint's 1862 annual report Pollock repeated his earlier explanation as to how "God Our Trust" was the preferred motto choice. While "In God is Our Trust" would be an appropriate one due to "its use in our national hymn, 'The Star Spangled Banner' . . . it contains too many letters to insert in the place of the crest, without crowding too much for good taste." Hence for greater brevity the words "God Our Trust" had been substituted. He also reiterated that the "crest offers the best position for inscribing a motto." This would not require changing the eagle and other devices and therefore congressional action would not be needed. He concluded this discussion with:

> The adoption of this motto "God Our Trust" or some other words expressive
> of national reliance upon divine support, would accord fully with the sentiment
> of the American people, and it would add to the artistic appearance of the coins.

Coin Shortages

Going back to the financial issues: Prior to the suspension of specie payments the public had eagerly been converting whatever paper currency they could into gold and silver, especially gold. The New York banks' gold reserves sank by more than one third in the three weeks before suspension. Gold had been hoarded and disappeared from circulation very quickly in December of 1861, leading the banks to no longer convert the paper. Silver coinage also almost immediately began to be hoarded and it largely disappeared by June of 1862.[3] As early as January of 1862 the problem was becoming evident. The Detroit *Free Press* carried an article dated January 16, 1862:

> On motion of Mr. Vallandigham, the Committee of Ways and Means were
> instructed to arrange to prevent hoarding of coin and bullion, and to enquire
> into the expediency of reviving the acts authorizing the currency of foreign
> coin, and making them legal tender, and whether any law regulating the value
> of domestic or foreign coins is necessary.

Prior to 1857 foreign coins had been treated as legal tender and freely circulated in the country. This had been changed by the Act of 1857, which had led to their withdrawal and melting mainly for reminting into U.S. coins.[4] Representative Clement Vallandigham's hope was that reinstating those coins as legal tender would alleviate the problem. However, no action was taken on his motion as it became evident the problem was bigger than any such authorization could fix.

The silver coins, with their precious-metal content, began to carry significant premiums over paper currency of equal stated denominational value. Many of them were melted and sold as bullion to realize the premiums. However, most were sold and exported to Canada or South America as another means to take advantage of the premium.[5] The exports to Canada came about as quirks in the exchange rates among the currencies, gold, and silver enabled people to carry U.S. silver coins into

Canada and exchange them at a favorable rate for gold that could then be brought back into the United States and exchanged for U.S. paper currency at an advantageous rate. The paper currency was then used to purchase silver coins and the whole process started again.[6] Montreal was the main center of this trade and some 30 or more brokers operated there. It is said that more than $80,000 in U.S. silver coins traded there every day.[7] The result was that enormous quantities of U.S. silver coins ended up in Canada, contributing to the shortage of change in the United States. This situation lasted until near the end of 1862, when Canadian commerce was saturated with U.S. silver coins, and they began to trade at a discount.[8]

The greater quantity of coins were exported to Latin America, as the economies of Spain's former colonies were based on the Spanish dollar, and their subsidiary coinage was very similar to U.S. quarters and halves in weight and values. None of these countries were producing large coinages of their own at that time, and the U.S. silver freely circulated, often at a premium. The exports mostly came from California, though they also came in large quantities from New York and Philadelphia. Silver was being mined in California and other Western states. It was especially advantageous to have the silver minted in San Francisco and shipped to Latin America.[9]

Concrete evidence of the large outflows to Latin America includes the hoard of San Francisco–minted half dollars found around 1956 in Guatemala. They were dated from 1860 through 1865, probably reflecting the years they were brought into Guatemala. There were several thousand of them of various grades and with many of them having been cleaned with baking soda or some other abrasive.[10]

Beyond the exports, the uncertainties of the war led large quantities of silver coins to simply be stashed away by average Americans seeking some hedge against the even worse times they feared might come. It is estimated that $25 million in small change disappeared from commerce in the space of only the few months of early 1862. Making small purchases and providing change in such transactions became difficult, and even copper-nickel cents began to be hoarded.

This situation caused people to seek substitutes for small change, and numerous ideas quickly emerged. Every conceivable substitute for coins came into use. Bank notes cut into fractional parts, private bills of credit, merchant scrip, foreign coins (until they too were hoarded for metal content), and postage stamps were among the vehicles used. Of course prices for the full range of goods and services were much lower than today, and even small change was of considerable value. Beef in 1860 cost 12¢ per pound; sugar and coffee were around 8¢ per pound.[11] A beer and a sandwich could be bought for 5¢. A carriage ride might be 3¢. A dime or a quarter were considerable amounts of money and to not be able to receive change from a purchase was a serious issue.[12] Seeking solutions to this became a distraction in people's everyday lives that consumed a lot of time and energy. One quotation of the day said the small-change panic "apparently absorbs the entire attention of the people to the exclusion of the war, the condition of the army, the new call for troops, the doings of Congress, or even the policy to be pursued with regard to the Negro."[13]

Stamps became a favorite choice in the spring of 1862 as they carried stated denominations similar to coins: 1¢, 3¢, 5¢, 10¢, etc. Other stamps carried denominations irregular to coins, such as 12¢, 24¢, 30¢, 90¢, and so forth, but they at least provided some means of carrying on transactions. Some merchants began accepting stamps in commerce as they were regarded as perhaps the best of whatever options were available. Stamps also had the practical value of being usable to mail letters. The public began to make runs on the local post offices, creating shortages of stamps. This was exacerbated by the fact that the government had repudiated the stamps current when the war began and had started a new series to prevent the Confederacy from using or benefitting from stamps held in the South. So the ramped-up printing of a new series of postage stamps to replace those repudiated was still going on. Furthermore the new taxes imposed to finance the war included requirements for revenue stamps to be placed on certain legal documents and on certain products, for example patent medicines. The government at this time did not have its own facilities for printing either postage stamps or revenue stamps and relied on outside contractors to produce them. These contractors were hard pressed to keep up with the new demands.[14]

As it was becoming evident that people were in practice using stamps in place of coins during the spring of 1862, Congress legalized their use as currency, on the recommendation of Secretary Chase. He wrote to Congress on July 14 suggesting the "receiving of postage and other stamps in payment of fractional parts of a dollar." The situation was regarded as serious enough that Congress remained in session an extra day before its summer recess to pass the legislation. It was signed by President Lincoln on July 17. Under the legislation stamps were monetized and, as of August 1, 1862, would be acceptable for payment of amounts due the government of less than $5. The act also prohibited issuance of private scrip and tokens (denominated as less than $1) by banks, merchants, and others. This type of money substitute was rapidly proliferating.

Examples of Civil War–era postage stamps that were used as substitutes for coins in making small change. The stamps depicted here were new issues used to replace the pre-war stamps that were invalidated to prevent the Confederate states using those that remained in the South.

Even before this Act of July 17, 1862, there had been pressure on the post offices to provide adequate supplies of stamps. With its passage the public descended in huge numbers to buy them. Chase had acted without consulting or even advising Montgomery Blair, the postmaster general, and post offices across the country were totally unprepared. The New York City main post office, for example, prior to passage of the act, sold on average $3,000 worth of stamps per day. The day after passage, sales rose to $10,000, the next day to $16,000, and the third day to $24,000.[15] Blair was furious at Chase and instructed post offices to restrict sales to levels prevailing before the legislation had passed and to only sell them for postage purposes. In some cases post-office patrons had to swear that their purchases were only for mailing.[16]

The *Washington Herald* on July 22 carried this comment:

> Much difficulty is experienced in carrying out the law authorizing the issue of postage stamps for currency. The act appears to have been hastily drawn, without consultation with the Postmaster General.
>
> It inaugurates a conflict of authority between the Post Office and the Treasury departments. The details in reference to the issue of stamps has not yet been arranged.

The conflict between Blair and Chase was mediated by the Internal Revenue Department, and Blair was persuaded to issue larger numbers of postage stamps with their costs of production to be paid for by the Treasury Department rather than Blair's department. (Interesting to note is the fact that Chase and Blair continued their feud well after this issue was resolved, with both vying for a Supreme Court position in later times. See also Blair's hounding of Chase described in chapter 6.) It is estimated that more than $20 million in postage stamps for use as currency was issued by the spring of 1863.[17] An article in the *Pittston Gazette* (Pittston, Pennsylvania), dated July 31, 1862, discussed the new legislation and its implications:

> There appears to be a very general apprehension with regard to the act authorizing payments in stamps, and to prohibit the circulation of notes of a less denomination than one dollar, which was approved July 17 last. Under the provisions of this act the Secretary of the Treasury, and not the Postmaster General, is directed to furnish postage and other stamps to the assistant treasurers and such designated depositaries of the United States as the former may select, to be exchanged by them on application for U.S. notes, and from and after the 1st day of August next such stamps shall be received in payment of all dues to the United States less than five dollars and shall be received in exchange for United States notes when presented in sums not less than five dollars, to any assistant treasurer or designated depository selected as aforesaid. Hence the law does not make postage stamps "legal tender," nor does it require postmasters to receive them in exchange for United States notes. It is expected that the Secretary of the Treasury will

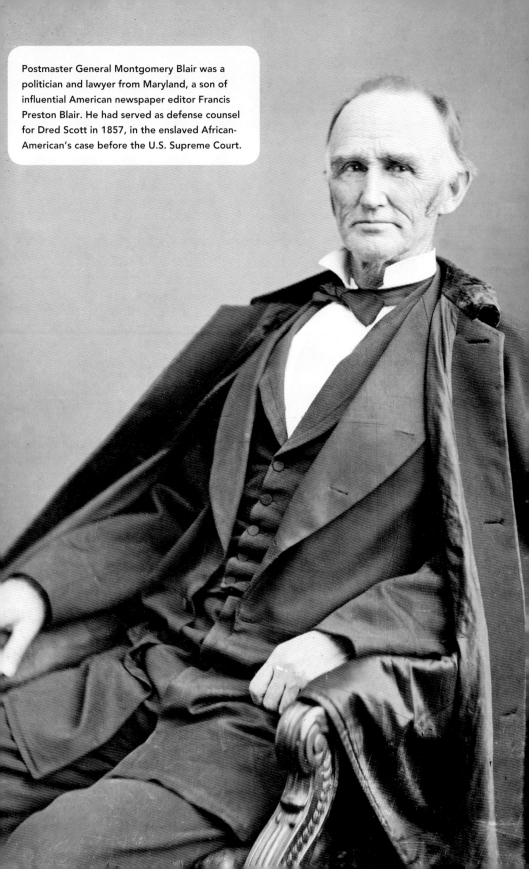

Postmaster General Montgomery Blair was a politician and lawyer from Maryland, a son of influential American newspaper editor Francis Preston Blair. He had served as defense counsel for Dred Scott in 1857, in the enslaved African-American's case before the U.S. Supreme Court.

> furnish postage stamps to be used as a circulating medium, under the law, in such form that they cannot be attached to letters or other mailable matter . . . and if such stamps are gummed to pasteboard or other paper, which spoils or renders them unfit to be used to be used in the prepayment of postage, they will be rejected for postage, because when so soiled they cannot be distinguished from stamps that have already been used for postage. . . . This is absolutely necessary to prevent frauds. Already defaced postage stamps are being bought up and passed at their nominal values, after having had this defacing ink extracted and being pasted on paper to conceal loss of gum.
>
> A number of businesses are already buying stamps to use as change. They can be purchased at the Post Offices everywhere. With these in circulation as a small currency, the motive for hoarding silver coin will cease, for there is no demand for its exportation, and there will be no profit in speculating in it where postage stamps will answer all the purposes of currency, and where they can be procured in unlimited quantities at par.

However, the drawbacks of using stamps for change quickly became obvious. They were small, fragile, and became dirty gummed masses with even minimal circulation. Private enterprise soon stepped up to attempt to solve this problem as stationery shops everywhere advertised small envelopes with a stated value of postage stamps contained within. These provided the practical function of protecting the stamps and keeping them relatively clean and intact. They could be ordered with a business's name, address, and advertising printed on them as well.[18] While the envelopes were an improvement, they were not a panacea. Those receiving them almost inevitably would open the envelope and count the stamps within to make sure they were not being cheated. Hence the stamps still became worn and sticky, especially in humid or rainy weather.

Another private-sector initiative to mitigate the problems with stamps was the Encased Postage Stamp. A very entrepreneurial inventor, John Gault, developed this product. In the 1850s he had spent time in the California goldfields, finding some gold but not enough to make him rich. Upon returning east to Boston he had developed a sewing machine that solved the problem of "lock stitching"—but he had been up against the major sewing-machine makers, Singer and Howe, and had not made money at it. When the Civil War began he immediately started working on artillery shells and invented new types that fragmented more effectively. However, the Union Army leadership preferred the older standardized shells, and this invention too failed to make Gault a wealthy man. He may have witnessed a confrontation in New York in mid-1862 between a cab driver and a rider trying to pay with postage stamps. The story is that this incident gave him the idea of a device to make the postage stamp more acceptable in commerce. He invented and patented a brass shell

Examples of Civil War–era envelopes used
to contain stamps of the value printed on them.

similar to a button, open on one side and covered with a mica insert, making it transparent. A stamp could be placed inside and protected by the brass and the mica. The stamp was visible through the mica with its denomination evident. Approximately the same size as a quarter, the result was coin-like in the way it handled and appeared. Further, the back of the brass case could be impressed with advertising.

Horace Greeley, in the August 19, 1862, issue of the *New York Tribune*, took note of Gault's invention and commented that the encased stamps were "a happy solution to our common plight." Gault began to have the encasements manufactured immediately upon receiving the patent. He contracted with Scovill Manufacturing Company in Waterbury, Connecticut, for their production. Scovill manufactured buttons and had a booming business for brass buttons for military uniforms. The materials and production processes for the encased postage stamps were virtually the same as for buttons. Making large numbers of the encased postage stamps quickly and efficiently was therefore relatively easy for Scovill. Gault began with an initial order in August of 25,000 pieces. Public acceptance was generally positive. In September he had another 100,000 produced. Gault was marketing his "New Metallic Currency" to merchants looking for ways to make change. His first major customer was the Irving House Hotel located at Broadway and 12th Street in New York. The initial order was for $1,000 or about 10,000 encased stamps mostly in 5¢ and 10¢ denominations. The "currency" was well received and the hotel quickly ordered another $1,000 worth, mostly in higher denominations, 25¢, 50¢, etc. The hotel paid Gault $750 face value for the stamps and $200 for the cases ($20 per 1,000).[19] By

An encased postage stamp,
1¢, with the back of its
case displaying "J. Gault"
and a patent date, along
with an advertisement
for Ayer's Sarsaparilla.

October more newspapers were beginning to pay attention. The *Washington Correspondent* said on October 25:

> Proposed New Postal Currency. – A Washington correspondent says that parties in New England propose a new style of postal currency. It is to enclose the Post Office stamp in a circle of white metal, covered by a piece of mica making a circular metallic case with the stamp protected from the wear and tear of use. It has been approved by all who have seen it. It is stated that, at the present rate of issue of the postal currency, it will take eight years to bring out the fifty millions authorized by Congress. The inventors of this new style of currency propose to get up the stamps themselves at their own cost if allowed to issue these metallic currency. They think that by employing the button factories of New England they can very nearly supply the demand at such an advance as will be satisfactory to the bankers and to the public.[20]

The *Chicago Evening Journal* on October 31, 1862, went even further, suggesting that the government adopt encased stamps as official currency:

> Stamp and Mica Currency – It is stated that the Commissioner of Internal Revenue is disposed to think the mica cases for stamps, designed to facilitate their use as currency, well suited to the purpose intended and sufficiently cheap to justify the Government in their adoption. They are but little larger than the nickel cent, silvery clean and beautiful in appearance.

Indeed there were indications that official adoption was being considered in October of 1862. The key player in this was George S. Boutwell. He had been governor of Massachusetts and had worked as a patent attorney for some time. He later served in Congress and would become secretary of the Treasury in the Grant administration after the war. The Internal Revenue Service had been established by an act of Congress dated July 1, 1862, to collect the newly passed income taxes. Chase immediately appointed Boutwell commissioner of Internal Revenue. He took office July 12 and was quickly overwhelmed with establishing the procedures of the bureau. Among the many duties he was charged with was implementing the Act of July 17, monetizing postage stamps. Besides this he had to work out ways to provide revenue stamps for the various products that congressional legislation now required. Chase was preoccupied with the larger issues of funding the war and entirely turned these "small change" matters over to Boutwell. If he sought guidance on any issue from Chase, he was told "decide for yourself."[21] Boutwell was familiar with Gault's encased stamps, probably from two separate sources. First, he was close friends with James C. Ayer, a fellow Massachusetts man. Ayer had a company producing a variety of products from sarsaparilla drinks to patent medicines. Ayer had become a customer of Gault as he had similar change needs as other merchants but also was required under the Act of July 1, 1862, to purchase revenue stamps for many of his products. Likely Ayer discussed the encased stamps with Boutwell. Second, Boutwell's background in patent law made him aware of Gault's invention and his patenting of the encased stamps.[22]

Boutwell had another option on the table besides the encased postage stamps. This was the idea of printing small-currency bills in denominations under $1. This "fractional currency" had the advantage of simpler production—not requiring both stamps and a metal case, as well as the assembly required, to complete the product. (Production in the massive quantities required would be problematic with the encased postage. There were already problems in printing enough postage stamps. This would be compounded with production of the cases.) In addition, fractional currency would eliminate the involvement of the Post Office and the resultant feuding between it and the Treasury Department. Probably for these reasons Boutwell came down on the side of fractional currency.[23]

The idea of fractional currency had been originated by Francis E. Spinner, the treasurer of the United States. He had noted some of the problems of using postage stamps and had the idea of pasting stamps to Treasury Department paper indicating the value. He even signed some of these to add further legitimacy and used them to make small payments to Treasury vendors. By pasting the stamps in this way, he destroyed their usefulness for postage, but the idea of such "notes" being used for small change caught on with Congress. With Boutwell's blessing the first issue of this currency began in late 1862. The notes of the first issue were printed under the authority of the Postal Currency Act of July 17, 1862, discussed earlier, though clearly the letter and intent of the legislation were stretched to do this as these small bills were not stamps. The notes were printed with direct copies of the postage stamps then in use. So, for example, the 5¢ note had a picture of a 5¢ stamp, the 10¢ note the picture of a 10¢ stamp, the 25¢ note the pictures of five 5¢ stamps, and the 50¢ note the pictures of five 10¢ stamps. Some of the earliest of the issues were perforated to make the connection with the stamps even clearer while those printed later in the issue eliminated the perforations. The first-issue

First Issue Postage Currency Notes of various denominations.

notes were printed by the American Bank Note Company and the National Bank Note Company under special license from the government. Chase commented in his annual report for 1862:

> An arrangement was made with the Postmaster General for a supply of postage stamps to be distributed for use in such payments. It was soon discovered, however, that stamps prepared for postage were not adapted to the purposes of currency. Small notes were therefore substituted.

His comments were not strictly correct as there was never such an "arrangement," and Treasury had in effect begun issuing "fractional greenbacks" without congressional approval. The first notes were rather inaccurately called "Postal Currency" and were first issued to Army paymasters on August 21.[24]

By early 1863 the notes were deemed successful enough that another congressional act was passed on July 11 of that year authorizing the Treasury Department to issue the notes directly, without further involvement with the Post Office. It was no longer referred to as Postal Currency (or Postage Currency) but simply as Fractional Currency. The second issue of the currency was printed by the Treasury Department itself, as were all the subsequent issues. Spencer Morton Clark was involved with this just as he had been with the greenback currency notes. There were a total of five issues of fractional notes stretching until April of 1876.

Probably for lack of any other good alternatives, the Fractional Currency notes found general public acceptance and circulated widely. The exceptions to this were the 3¢ note (only produced during the third issue) and the 5¢ notes (produced in all issues except the fifth). Probably due to their small denominations, they were unpopular and regarded as nuisances. This unpopularity eventually inspired special efforts to replace them, leading to production of three-cent and five-cent coins made of nickel, as we will see in a later chapter.

By 1876 the nation's finances had recovered such that the premium of silver vis-a-vis paper currency had disappeared and silver coins were being produced in quantities adequate to meet everyday needs. Congress ordained that all Fractional Currency notes could be redeemed with silver coin. The Fractional Currency notes gradually disappeared from circulation.[25]

Before this rebalance was achieved, the Mint continued to crank out silver coinage despite the fact that it was exported, hoarded, melted, or otherwise removed from circulation almost as soon as it was struck. Following large mintages in 1861, however, coin production was reduced and stayed at lower levels until the mid-1870s, when parity between paper currency and silver coinage came again, and the Fractional Currency was eliminated.

Other ideas to stop hoarding and mitigate the shortages were put forward. Mint Director Pollock early on suggested reducing the weight of the coinage to keep it circulating. In his October 1862 annual report he raised the idea:

In regard to our minor currency, usually called "small change," it is difficult to realize the fact that, with over forty-five millions of dollars in silver coin now in the country, we should be driven to a substitute, which, however useful as a temporary measure, cannot enter into comparison, in point of convenience and durability, with small coin, not to speak of intrinsic value. Why cannot silver change be issued on a basis somewhat similar, yet more than that which the copper coin is issued, namely, not to give a full bullion value, but to afford a public benefit? The cent we issue costs the government scarcely half a cent; but for its purposes, and with the stamp of authority, it is worth its nominal value to everybody: it is largely sought after, notwithstanding so many have been issued, and would purchase no more if it were three times as heavy. Would the half dime, dime, or quarter dollar be any less acceptable if it were, say three-fourths of the present weight of those coins? At all events, we could most safely and reasonably issue ten millions of dollars in five and ten cent pieces, of the present nine-tenths fineness, but of reduced weight, and of legal tender to the amount of five or ten dollars. The new pieces would, of course, be not worth that much abroad, but they would be at home, which is all we are concerned about. A legal provision to this effect, prospective perhaps, to follow the wearing out of the stamp currency, would at once bring to the mint a supply of the old coin and silver bullion from the Washoe mines and other sources, by holders desirous of realizing a premium and of accommodating their own business. So much of the gain as would be necessary to draw the material should go in that direction; the remainder would pay expenses of recoinage and transportation. The three-cent pieces already out, and considerably coined, might be left to fulfill their mission, without calling them in or adding to their number, the cents being sufficient to fill the space between one cent and five. It would be best at present to limit the new issue to the dime and half dime, leaving the larger coins for future consideration, or, probably, to return to their par value on the return of better times.

But Pollock's idea was not adopted, or even seriously considered by Secretary Chase. Instead the printing of Postal Currency adopted in the Act of July 17, 1862, continued on. Fear on the part of some Mint employees that small-denomination paper currency would eliminate the need for coinage and that coin production might cease altogether (shutting down the mint) prompted them to experiment with reduced-weight coins in 1863. The Mint assayers Jacob Eckfeldt and William DuBois came up with the idea of dimes and quarters being minted in non-precious metals, or in alloys of low precious-metal value, or simply of lower weight, per Pollock's thoughts. They submitted a report to Director Pollock dated May 15, 1863. Evidently on their own volition they secretly produced pattern ten-cent pieces about half the weight of the regular dimes and in a range of experimental alloys including aluminum combined with copper, silver, and others. They were similar in size to the dime. Only in recent years has metallic analysis of these patterns revealed the range of experimental alloys that they tried.[26] The engraver, James Longacre, was especially pleased with examples struck in silver with a five percent alloy of aluminum instead of copper. He felt the alloy made the coins hard and durable but with a better color.[27] The change in metallic content would take the coins' intrinsic value well below their denominational value and eliminate incentive for melting or hoarding. The patterns were inscribed with "Exchanged for U.S. Notes" on the obverse and "Postage Currency Act July 1862" on the reverse. Mint staff convinced Pollock with the thought that the July 1862 Act did not specify the material from which the postal notes were to be made, therefore making the proposed coins legal under that act. Hence they would be a kind of metallic postal/fractional currency that could replace the paper money without risk of being hoarded, exported, etc. Pollock realized the standard weight and fineness of gold and silver coins were fixed by law and would, on the surface at least, require legislation for a change. Employing his lawyerly skills (and as suggested by Eckfeldt and Dubois), Pollock wrote: "Now whilst this [weight and fineness standard] is true of the mint law or laws relating to our national coinage, permit me to suggest, whether under the Act of Congress of July 17, 1862 a metallic currency similar in character and value to the present 'postal currency' might not be introduced?"[28] In other words, coins referencing the term "Postal Currency" might be an expedient for avoiding the need for congressional action to change the standards. Of course this was another stretching of the meaning of the Act of July 17, 1862. Pollock provided the pattern coins and the concept to Chase. Chase and Congress, however, did not buy into the idea, and striking of regular-weight silver coinage continued throughout the war—as did the coins' hoarding, melting, export, and non-circulation.[29]

At the same time printing of Fractional Currency continued apace. It has been said that after June of 1862 the Philadelphia Mint had become, at least in regard to silver coins, a mere establishment operated for the benefit of New York bullion dealers.[30]

Pattern ten-cent pieces were designed and struck by Mint employees in weights of about 20.0 grains (compared with the standard legal weight of the dime of 38.4 grains) with the idea being that they would eliminate the need for paper Fractional Currency and would preserve Mint production and jobs. Note the reference to "POSTAGE CURRENCY ACT JULY 1862" on the pattern. (Judd-330)

Printing and distribution of the paper Postal Currency took time and the supply remained inadequate until the spring of 1863. By the end of May, just over $20 million in the small notes had been issued, and they began to relieve the coin shortages.

In the meantime postage stamps themselves had been circulating. Under the provisions of the July 17, 1862, law they were redeemable, and by late 1862 people were endeavoring to redeem them. Postmaster General Montgomery Blair refused to take back the stamps, by now often dirty masses of paper and glue. The law technically required the Treasury Department to redeem those stamps that Treasury had issued. The reality was that Treasury had never actually issued any stamps, and people had bought what they had from the Post Office. The law did not require the Post Office to redeem them, putting the general public in a catch-22. Eventually Blair, under public pressure, redeemed (or exchanged) large quantities. Redemption began December 15, 1862. The post offices were again swamped by people bringing in stamps just as they had been when people were purchasing them. Given the terrible condition of most of the stamps, the postmasters could not determine whether the stamps were unused and redeemable or if they were unredeemable by having been cancelled through actual use in mailing of letters. Also in some cases the cancellation marks had been chemically removed from used stamps. Clearly huge amounts were redeemed fraudulently.

A fairly lengthy article in the Brooklyn *Daily Eagle* dated November 14, 1862, did a good job of relating the situation of small change, stamps, and the Fractional Currency at that time.

The Withdrawal of the Postage Stamps from Circulation.

The Railroad Companies of New York have given notice that on and after tomorrow they will refuse to take postage stamps. It is understood that the Railroad & Ferry Cos. of this city will do likewise. We presume that the example of these corporations will be followed by the public. It is only a question of time about the discarding of the troublesome "stamps." The government is issuing the postage currency as fast as possible, and if there be not enough of it in circulation for the public demands at present, there will be very shortly. Thousands of dollars have been paid out to the army; this is fast finding its way into circulation. If any embarrassment be created it will be but temporary. In the meantime retail dealers will find it to their interest to be as accommodating in taking or making change as possible. Everybody will find use for postage stamps: no one who has a limited amount on hand need to be in "a panic," to get rid of them therefore. The chief of difficulty will be experienced from the want of currency of a lower denomination than five cents. In the panic for hoarding "hard" money, the copper coin has been stowed away. There can be no possible advantage in retaining copper or nickel pennies. The currency of the world is gold and silver. They are intrinsically of a certain value, whether in a half dollar or in a candlestick. The copper and nickel pennies are not worth intrinsically the amount for which they pass.

Gold and silver are sent abroad, copper is not. Like postage stamps, they are little more than a token, accepted by mutual consent for a certain value, which they do not intrinsically possess. Our nickel and copper pennies are worth no more abroad as currency than our shinplasters. It is true that pennies have advanced two or three per cent; but this is only because they are more convenient as currency than postage stamps, and not liable to be rendered worthless by frequent or careless handling. . . . Within a week or two there will be a full supply of postage currency then we shall have pennies in abundance, for the reason that then we shall not need them. By a desire on all hands to do the best we can until that time there will be no trouble consequent upon the withdrawal from circulation of the postage stamps with which—notwithstanding the fact that they saved it from a great deal of trouble—we are all more or less disgusted.

To sum up, the use of stamps as small change authorized under the Act of July 17, 1862, was a fiasco, but it did eventually lead to the production of the Postage Currency and Fractional Currency notes that succeeded by mid-1863 in at least partially alleviating the small-change shortage problems.

With the Fractional Currency going through five different issues over the more than a decade that they were used, the notes varied greatly in their appearance. This led to a lot of confusion in the public as to what they were supposed to look like. As a result counterfeiting was easier, and it became widespread. A brief article in the October 12, 1865, *Daily Milwaukee News* illuminated the problem in describing the situation of a young man with two 50¢ Fractional Currency notes:

Lost His Dollar—A day or two since a young man of this city having two fifty cent pieces of postal currency that differed widely in appearance supposed very naturally that one of them must be a counterfeit and accordingly made a wager with a friend as to which was genuine. They proceeded to a bank for the purpose of ascertaining to a certainty, when the cashier very coolly took the stamps and marked both of them as counterfeits.

In a later effort to mitigate the confusion over the notes and provide some defense against counterfeiting, the Treasury Department produced specimen notes pasted on a cardboard back. The cardboard back was printed with the image of a shield and the notes attached within it. These "Fractional Shields" were issued in 1866 and offered to banks and other institutions (at a price of $4.50) so that they could check currency presented to them against the official specimens. They included the first three issues but not the fourth and fifth, as those issues came after 1866. Often the shields were framed and hung on the wall so the notes could be easily viewed and compared. The demand for the Fractional Shields was not as great as anticipated and many sat in the basement of the Treasury building for years before being sold. A flood there in the late 1860s led to many being water-stained. Today the Fractional Currency shields are rare and popular as collectibles, with estimates of 200 to 300 still in existence.

A Fractional Currency Shield. These were sold by the Treasury Department to banks and others to facilitate identification of authentic notes and help avoid counterfeits.

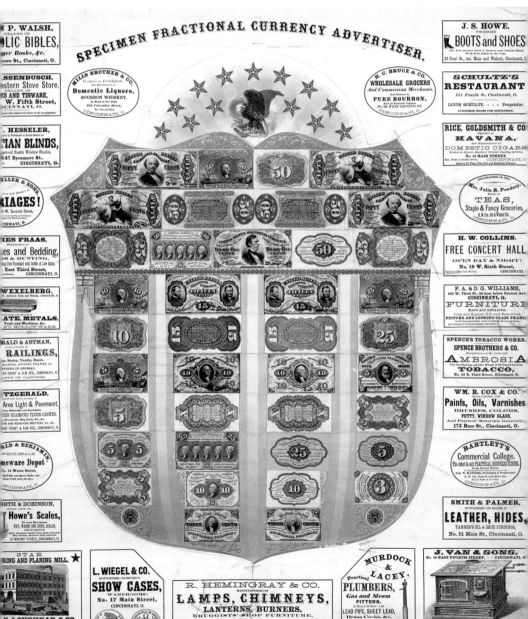

AESCULAPIUS.

HEBE.

GIBSON & CO. LITH. CINCINNATI.

CHAPTER 8

The Cent Shortage

A s seen in the previous chapter, the fractional paper currency relieved, or at least mitigated, the shortage of silver coins for change by early to mid-1863. The Fractional Currency, however, did not relieve the one-cent coin situation. The cent shortage began later and ended later than the shortage of the larger-denomination coins or their paper substitutes.

It is estimated that there were more than 100 million cents in the country at the start of the war. Production of the old large copper cents that had been struck since 1793 had ceased in 1857. They had been replaced by a much smaller copper-nickel coin (88 percent copper and 12 percent nickel). The new cents were struck in large numbers and were initially popular as they were smaller and more conveniently carried than the old large cents. However, by about 1860 the new cents were in oversupply and were often regarded as a nuisance. Some merchants would accumulate more of the coins than they needed; banks often declined to accept them; and businesses in larger Northern cities would sell them at a discount to brokers to get rid of them. It is said that a store in New York accumulated so many of the coins that the floor upon which they were stored collapsed from their weight.[1]

The first new copper-nickel cents were of the Flying Eagle design. During the design's three-year run (1856 through 1858) some 42 million were produced. The design was changed in 1859 to the Indian Head type. Just during 1859 and 1860 nearly 57 million of this new type were struck. These numbers were many multiples of the total number of large cents produced during their last few years. Looking at these quantities, the massive oversupply can easily be understood.

This oversupply situation, however, quickly reversed as circulating silver coins disappeared in 1861 and 1862 and the cent coins were called upon to pick up the slack in commerce. Besides being spent one or two at a time, they were tied in bundles of 25, 50, or 100 pieces and substituted for their larger-denomination brethren quarters,

Opposite page: An early 1860s apothecary lithograph, and several tokens issued to serve as small change during the widespread coin-hoarding of the Civil War. Many individuals and merchants—druggists, saloonkeepers, dry-goods merchants, tobacconists, jewelers, physicians, barbers, brewers, and others—made and distributed such tokens.

A copper cent of
the larger format
(in this case, actual
size 27.5 mm) minted
from 1793 to 1857.

A cent of the Flying Eagle
style—minted as patterns in 1856
and in much larger numbers, for
circulation, in 1857 and 1858.

An Indian Head cent,
minted from 1859 to 1909.

halves, etc. By mid-1862 brokers were paying premiums of 2 to 4 percent for them in some places. The Philadelphia *Public Ledger* dated July 18, 1862, carried an article:

> The difficulty among small shopkeepers, provision dealers in the markets and the city generally, in making change, has caused an extraordinary demand for cents, and all that can be commanded at the Mint are eagerly bought. . . . Though many of those who desired cents stood in line for hours, waiting an opportunity to get into the Mint, they had to go home without them, as the supply on hand was exhausted before half the applicants were accommodated.[2]

Unlike the silver coinage, cents were in short supply due not to the value of their metallic content but rather to their convenience value. Though the price of nickel in particular fluctuated over the Civil War era, the cents were generally worth only half a cent in the value of the nickel and copper they contained, and it never would have made sense to melt them to realize a metallic premium. But having a few of these cents in hand could make the difference between having to walk and being able to take a cab or a horsecar or of losing out in a transaction for lack of proper change.

As noted above, shortage of coins larger than one cent was eventually dealt with by Fractional Currency. The cents or "pennies" were another matter. James Pollock discussed this in his October 1862 Mint director's report. He mentioned the continuing exchange of the old copper large cents for the smaller cents made of copper-nickel. He said, "The number of old cents is rapidly diminishing, and that coin will soon disappear altogether from circulation." Regarding the new smaller cents he said:

The demand for the nickel cent has largely increased. The disappearance of small silver coins from circulation has caused the new cent to be extensively used, and every effort has been made to meet the demand. Large amounts have been sent to every part of the country, and orders, beyond our ability to fill, are constantly forwarded to the mint. The profits of the cent coinage have been fully adequate to meet all expenses of material, production, and transmission to the parties ordering them.

Although the copper-nickel coins only contained 12 percent nickel content, they had a whitish appearance, and they were referred to by the general public as "nickels." Of course this was before the five-cent piece that we today refer to as the "nickel" existed (the latter would debut in 1866). The nickel content of the cent was, under ordinary circumstances, not a problem. Even with the overproduction since 1856 nickel supplies had been sufficient to meet that production.

However, as Pollock said, the demand was increasing and supply was soon inadequate. At the end of April 1862 the Mint had 940,000 cents on hand, but by the end of August its stocks were down to only 368 pieces.[3] This then was the situation Pollock referred to in his report. Orders beyond the Mint's ability to fill were constantly forwarded to them.

The situation only worsened over the following year, and the Mint archives contain many letters regarding the problem. Two examples follow:

Mint of the United States

Philadelphia, June 12, 1863

Hon. S.P. Chase
Secretary of the Treasury
Washington City

Sir:

I have to acknowledge the receipt of your letter of the 6th inst. with the endorsed letters in relation to a supply of cents for the use of the Post Master at New York.

I have from the beginning given a preference to public officers in the distribution of cents, and although in consequence of the great demand from all sections of the United States from official and private persons, we cannot furnish the Post Office at New York with $200 per week, we will endeavor to furnish half of that amount weekly and have so informed the Post Master, Mr. Wakeman today.

Respectfully Your Obt. Svt.
Jas. Pollock, Director

Mint of the United States

Philadelphia, Nov 18, 1863

M.B. Field Esq.
Asst Sec of Treasury

Sir:

Your communication of the 17th inst. with enclosures, has been recvd.

The rule of the Mint is to furnish Treasury of the U.S. Paymaster, Collectors, cents in sums of $50 as promptly as practicable, without the delay incident to private orders.

The demand from private and official sources is very great, some delay is unavoidable but officials are first served.

I am Very Respectfully Yours,
Jas. Pollock, Dir. U.S. Mint[4]

Just as was the case with the shortage of silver coins, private enterprise and entrepreneurship, fueled by necessity and spurred by profit, emerged and led to substitutes and at least partial solutions to the cent problem. These came in the form of private tokens similar in size and, in many cases, in appearance to the regular cents coined by the Mint. They were developed and produced by a variety of private die sinkers and shops across the country, beginning early in the war. Some of these makers produced other tokens before the war, generally as advertising items or as collectibles. For example, in New York City, George Lovett designed and struck a series of tokens in the late 1850s depicting Revolutionary War events. They were popular and were collected actively. Another die sinker, Frederick Dubois, in Chicago around 1858 began producing tokens the same size as the regular cent. The reverse bore a wreath, similar to that of the federal cent, but carried the caption "Business Card" within the wreath. The obverse then bore the name of whatever store or business was doing the advertising. These were known as "store cards." Numismatic historian Q. David Bowers quotes a piece that Dubois wrote about his token business:[5]

> I did all this work myself so the cost of it was very small and more than half of what I sold them for was profit. I sold them to people who wanted to advertise for nine dollars a thousand, and they passed them off in their business for pennies, making a profit of ten percent. I don't recall how many of these pennies I made, but made them for the Chicago businessmen and county merchants until it ran into the hundreds of thousands and they were in general circulation all around. They attracted the attention of Chicago newspapers where they were described as a nuisance, so I stopped making them. The public never knew where they came from, but I made quite a little money from the project to help my weak business.

Dubois thus had laid out the model of how the business worked. The diesinker could sell the tokens at high margins, still allowing the merchant to buy at discount to nominal value and pass them as full value cents in change, netting a profit. They were profitable to both diesinker and merchant so long as the public accepted them for the value of one cent.

But it was only when the war came and the cent shortage arose that these tokens were circulated on a much wider scale. Public need in ordinary commerce grew dramatically. Numerous die cutters and private minters stepped up to meet the demand implementing the model Dubois had laid out. Among the noteworthy token-makers were Childs Manufacturing Company in Chicago, John Stanton in Cincinnati, William Bridgens in New York, and Robert Lovett Jr. in Philadelphia.

The tokens were of two broad general types: "store cards," which bore on one side the store or merchant's name, address, or whatever other information they wished; and "patriotic" tokens, which were of general designs and carried no specific merchant names or information. They usually featured patriotic slogans and/or images. The patriotics were generally priced more cheaply as they could be made from stock dies and did not require cutting new dies with specific merchant information.

Childs Manufacturing Company in Chicago began producing tokens for sale to merchants early in the war. The company sold them in enormous numbers, mostly to merchants around the Midwest. Evidently Childs salespeople traveled to towns and cities along the railroad routes out of Chicago, promoting the tokens to local shop owners.

In Cincinnati, John Stanton in 1862 began striking advertising tokens with merchants' names on the obverse and an Indian Head design on the reverse, similar to that on the regular government-issued Indian Head cents. They were sold and distributed widely, mainly in the Midwest but also in the East. These were dated 1862. Stanton in time became the largest producer of Civil War tokens, with a great variety of designs.

More and more diesinkers got involved in this business as the cent shortage worsened in 1863. In New York William Bridgens began making tokens, supplying merchants mainly in the New York City area and on the East Coast. Another maker in New York, Emil Sigel, began producing tokens, including many patriotics. It is believed he struck more tokens than any other entity in New York. His token are mostly dated 1863.

The number of individuals and companies who made these tokens is too large to give every detail here. They are a separate study in themselves and numerous references exist about them. Estimates of the total number issued during the Civil War period vary but range from about 25 million to 40 million.

The quality of Civil War tokens varied dramatically, with some being finely cut and struck with attractive designs, and others crude and produced with little quality control. Some were quite roughly made. Perhaps the most noteworthy of the latter are the "Indiana Primitives" made by Henry D. Higgins of Mishawaka, Indiana. Their designs and lettering are relatively crude but they have a certain charm that has made them highly collectible. Childs Manufacturing and Higgins worked together on some tokens with, for example, a Childs reverse and a Higgins obverse sometimes combined.

Civil War tokens were made of various metals, but the vast majority were copper or bronze. Their metallic content probably averaged about one-fifth of a cent in intrinsic value. The prices charged to merchants varied but were in the general range of 60 to 70 cents per 100, somewhat lower than the 90 cents Dubois said he charged earlier. The merchants dispensed them as change for the value of one cent, so there was good profit for both the die sinker and the merchant. The general public seems for the most part to have accepted these tokens in change. Likely people felt they had little choice, as government-issued cents simply were unavailable. There was also a tacit understanding, though not a legal one, that the merchant would accept his tokens back for future merchandise purchases. The tokens therefore in general circulated freely.

Technically the tokens were illegal, as the Act of July 17, 1862, which legalized Postal Currency for use as small change, had a provision banning private scrip and such private tokens. However, the law was largely ignored and unenforced, and ever larger numbers of the tokens were produced and circulated. In nearly every case, the tokens bore no denomination and could not therefore be construed as counterfeit cents. In a few cases the tokens bore "One Cent" preceded by the word "Not," thus trying to avoid any possible appearance of counterfeiting.

Examples of patriotic Civil War tokens. Phrases glorifying the Union, and portrayals of President Lincoln, General McClellan, the ironclad *Monitor*, and other military and political motifs were common on these pieces.

Gustavus Lindenmueller's Famous Civil War Tokens

An often-told story of problems relating to Civil War tokens' legality and ultimate legal demise is about one token issuer, Gustavus Lindenmueller, a German-American barkeeper in New York City. He distributed enormous numbers of tokens, perhaps as many as one million, with his establishment's name on them. While details are sketchy, it seems he honored them as they were redeemed for drinks by individual customers. Many of his tokens were circulated generally by the public and, as one version of the story goes, great numbers were used to pay fares on a streetcar operated by the Third Avenue Railroad of New York. The railroad accumulated huge quantities (one version of the tale says 300,000 tokens) and approached Lindenmueller to redeem them for cash. He refused to do so. The railroad had no legal recourse, but it did have political influence. This incident purportedly resulted in Congressional action during 1864, outlawing issuance and circulation of such tokens.

This Lindenmueller story, in various versions, has been told since as far back as the 1880s and given as the trigger for the demise of Civil War tokens.[6] An article in the Civil War Token Society *Journal* (Fall 2010 issue) by Donald Erlenkotter debunked the story. Certainly Lindenmueller did issue large numbers of tokens, but there is no evidence of involvement by a streetcar company or of any connection with federal legislation affecting issuance of the tokens. So far is as known there was never a problem with non-redemption of his tokens.

Gustavus Lindenmueller's famous token (shown enlarged).

"A German Beer Garden in New York City on Sunday Evening."

But Erlenkotter uncovered other facts that make Lindenmueller's story even more intriguing and at least tangentially relevant to the religious side of our story. Before the war, in 1858, Lindenmueller operated a saloon / beer garden which was open on Sundays, in violation of local laws prohibiting serving of alcohol on the Sabbath. The laws had been on the books for some years but had been laxly enforced. Changes in the police-department administration led to stricter enforcement. Lindenmueller was arrested on August 8, 1858, and, according to the *New York Times*, some 500 to 800 customers were "cleaned out" of his "disorderly" establishment, "a notorious gambling and dance house."[7]

In 1859 Lindenmueller opened another saloon combined with a theater. There was resistance to the Sunday laws, particularly in the German-American community. For the German working classes, Sunday was their only day off, and it was part of their culture to socialize, seek entertainment, and drink beer. The issue was couched as a violation of the U.S. Constitution, in their view an imposition of religious views different from their own. In 1860 the controversy sharpened as the New York legislature passed a law that banned all Sunday theatrical performances in New York City. Lindenmueller and other German-American saloon owners raised money with the aim of challenging the law's constitutionality. He and several others were arrested in April of 1860 for selling liquor and presenting dramatic exhibitions on Sundays in violation of the laws. Lindenmueller claimed he had founded a new free German church called the "Shaker Congregation." He stated, "If I give moral representations on Sunday, decent and instructive, I am a preacher, and my actors are orators; no church is anything but a different kind of theater." An injunction was obtained against Lindenmueller by the Society for the Reformation of Juvenile Delinquents prohibiting any further performances in his saloon. On November 20, 1860, his trial took place, and he was found guilty. He appealed his case to the New York Supreme Court but lost his appeal in May of 1861. His case was a landmark in establishing the legality of the legislation prohibiting various Sunday activities. Over the following many years some of these laws were relaxed, but not entirely removed until 2004, when everyday liquor sales were legalized in New York.

In light of Don Erlenkotter's research, the Lindenmueller tokens remain perhaps more as reminders of religious and cultural issues than of monetary redemption problems.

An 1862 scrip note "Good for 10 Cents in Meals" at Lindenmueller's restaurant.

Beyond the role of the Civil War tokens in mitigating the cent shortage, they also influenced significant and permanent change in the metallic content of the cent denomination. The tokens' general acceptance by the public and their low intrinsic metallic value relative to regular federal cents was noted by Pollock in his October 1863 *Mint Director's Report*, as he gave the history of the cent's content:

> The coinage and issue of the nickel cent has been very large, and almost unprecedented. The demand still continues, and every effort has been made to supply it. This coin has been distributed to every part of the country, and orders for large amounts are daily received. The profits pay all expenses of the coinage and distribution of the cent. A great benefit to the country was effected by the act of 1857, reducing the size of the cent. It is to be regretted the idea still prevailed that it was necessary to put into the coin, if not an equivalent, at least a large proportion of real value. To this end, and for other reasons, an alloying metal was sought which should command a comparatively high price in the market, without being properly a precious metal. Nickel, possessing the requisite value and suitable qualities, was selected. It was then worth about two dollars per pound; though it has also been much lower in price. Our cent was, by decreasing the size, reduced in weight from 168 to 72 grains; the former simply copper, the latter an alloy of 88 percent copper with 12 percent nickel, making a coin of convenient size and neat appearance, containing a half cent's worth of metal, more or less, according to market fluctuations. The change was well intended, but the experiences of other countries, and, *indeed of our own*, has taught us that it was an unnecessary liberality, and that all the nickel we have thus used has been so much money wasted.

Pollock continued and described the French experience with their minor coins and their conversion to "bronze," which he explained is a mixture of 95 percent copper and 5 percent tin and zinc. He extolled its virtues as "less oxidable and more clean than copper." He referenced the private tokens and went on to the heart of his argument for a change in the cent's content.

> Whilst people expect a full value in their gold and silver coins, they merely want their inferior money for convenience in making exact payments, and not at all for the value of the copper, tin, or nickel which may be present. If the law makes it a cent of legal tender to a proper and sufficient extent, then it is a cent to every one using it, even if its intrinsic should be only the one tenth of its nominal and legal value. If any further proof of this fact should be demanded, we have only to refer to our recent experience, when illegal cent tokens of the size of the legal cent were made and freely passed, although they contained no nickel, weighed on the average about 51 grains, and worth not more than onefifth of a cent. Not less than three hundred varieties of these false and illegal tokens or cents have been made and issued, and until suppressed, and were

freely used as coin by the public. They were in direct violation of the laws of the United States; and prosecution of certain parties issuing them has deterred others and will soon drive them altogether from circulation.

It is hard to know what Pollock meant by "suppression" of the "illegal" tokens. As noted earlier they were technically illegal under the legislation of 1862, but there is no indication of active suppression. In fact, these tokens were probably at the height of their production and use at the time Pollock was writing in October 1863.[8]

The copper and bronze tokens were indeed widely accepted and circulated freely, but the regular-issue copper-nickel cents still were preferred by the public. They traded for as much as a 20 percent premium in 1863. It seems that Gresham's Law was operating, as when people had both a private token and a federal cent in their pocket, they would spend the token and hold the cent.[9] The Mint produced prodigious volumes of the cent in 1862 (more than 28 million) and in 1863 (nearly 50 million) but could not keep up with the demand.

Pollock went on in his *Annual Report* to discuss nickel further:

> We have therefore used a great deal of nickel to little purpose; and much of it from foreign countries, for which we have had to pay in gold or its equivalent. We have given it away under the mistaken notion that value was essential to secure the circulation of our inferior coinage and to prevent its being counterfeited. The law regulating the cent coinage required it. Experience proves that an alloy more valuable than the principal metal may be safely omitted.

Pollock's argument that the intrinsic metallic value of the cent was unrelated to people's willingness to accept it in circulation is reminiscent of his argument in the 1862 report calling for reduction in the silver content of the other, larger-denomination, coins discussed in chapter 7. Beyond nickel being unnecessary to ensure circulation of the cent, Pollock also enumerated nickel's deficiencies and the problems it caused in coinage operations, implying its name derives from Old Nick (i.e., the Devil):

> Nickel derives its name from a certain unpleasant allusion, indicating its character, and which, in a metallurgic sense, it honestly deserves. It is very obstinate in the melting pot, requiring the fiercest fire, even when in alloy with copper. It commonly makes a hard mixture, very destructive to dies, and all the contiguous parts of the coining machinery. Perhaps as great as any to the further use of this alloy is its limited use in the arts. With the addition of zinc it would make good German silver, and could be worked up into plated ware. Beyond this, and a few other applications, copper with 12 percent of nickel is of no more value to the artisan than copper alone; it is even a deterioration, and more difficult to melt. On the whole, it may now be advised, and even

urged that the law of coinage be modified, so as to provide that the cent, retaining its present size and devices, shall be composed of 95 per cent of copper; the
remainder tin and zinc in suitable proportions.

Clearly Pollock had become convinced that bronze (95 percent copper and 5
percent tin and zinc, as he said) should replace the copper-nickel alloy for the
cents. He increasingly pressed for this change as he believed it held the solution
for the cent shortage. Besides increasing difficulties in obtaining nickel and difficulty in working it, as he said in the October 1863 report, it wore out the dies at a
much greater rate. A single pair of cent dies could produce about 150,000 of the
copper-nickel pieces while the softer bronze metal would allow production of
nearly 300,000 before wearing out a die pair.[10]

As was typical, Pollock had no (known) response from Treasury Secretary
Salmon Chase in regard to his recommendation in the *Annual Report*. Pollock
therefore pressed the matter further a few weeks later, in a letter dated December
8, 1863. He included at least three pattern coins with the letter: a cent struck in
bronze using the regular Indian Head dies normally used for the copper-nickel
pieces; a two-cent piece in bronze bearing on the obverse a portrait of George
Washington and the motto GOD AND OUR COUNTRY; and a two-cent piece
in bronze bearing a shield with arrows on the obverse with the motto GOD OUR
TRUST. This latter motto of course was the same as that used on the half dollar
and $10 eagle patterns of 1861, 1862, and 1863. A note from Assistant Assayer
George Eckfeldt in the Mint archives states: "November, 1863, Struck 2 cent
pieces – 2 varieties, one with 'God and our Country' Washington head. The other
is God our trust with two spears and shield and palm wreath, with the same reverse
as the Washington head with the wheat leaf wreath."

Sir: In my last annual report I recommended the disuse of nickel in the cent
coinage, and the substitution of the alloy lately introduced in France and England called bronze. It is composed of copper, tin and zinc, and makes a beautiful
and ductile alloy. This change in the material of the cent is not only desirable in
itself, but has become a necessity from the advance price of nickel (for a supply
of which we are present entirely dependent upon the foreign market, paying for
it in gold or its equivalent), and the great uncertainty of procuring an adequate
supply for the future from any source at a price within the legal limit.

Besides this, nickel is itself objectionable as an alloying metal. It is harsh,
brittle, most difficult to melt, requiring the fiercest fires even when in alloy
with copper, and is very destructive of dies, machinery, &c., thus increasing
the cost of production, which will soon exceed the value of the product if the
price of copper, labor, coal, &c., continues to advance, as it is almost certain to
do. In that event, the coinage of the cent must cease.

It is not proposed to change the size or devices of the cent, only the weight. The weight of the new coin would be forty-eight grains or one tenth ounce troy. This will secure a coin in every respect superior to the slumpy nickel. I also propose for your consideration the coinage of a two cent piece, same material and double the weight of the cent, and with such devices and motto as may be approved by you.

The piece would be a great public convenience, and its coinage, in my opinion, should be authorized. I enclose some specimens. The devices are beautiful and appropriate, and the motto on each such, as all who fear God and love their country will approve. I prefer the "shield and arrows" to the "head of Washington" on the obverse of the coin. They are submitted for your consideration.

If you approve of the proposed change in material and denomination, the enclosed bill, prepared with care, can be submitted to Congress for their action.

Permit me respectfully to suggest that immediate action is necessary, for if nickel is retained it will be impossible to meet the enormous demand for cents, and the increasing cost of production may compel a cessation of that coinage. The demand for cents is now far beyond our ability to supply it. The substitution of bronze for the nickel alloy was examined by the commissioners of the last annual assay in February, and was then cordially approved. The commission consisted of professors Joseph Henry, Washington, District of Columbia; John Torrey, New York; Alexander, Baltimore; Rogers and Rand, Philadelphia; Judge Putnam, Boston; Hon. H. McCulloch, Washington, District of Columbia; and the three ex officio members from Philadelphia. The opinions of such gentlemen, though not officially expressed, are deserving of consideration.

Yours, etc. Jas Pollock
December 8, 1863[11]

Secretary Chase responded quickly to Pollock's letter in a brief but important note dated December 9, 1863.

I approve your mottoes, only suggesting that on the Washington obverse the motto should begin with "OUR" so as to read "OUR GOD AND OUR COUNTRY" and that on that with the shield obverse it should be so changed as to read "IN GOD WE TRUST", or how would it do to substitute for the shield the motto "GOD IS OUR SHIELD"?[12]

This note is significant since, as far as is known, it is the first response to Pollock's various efforts to elicit Chase's thoughts on a religious motto since Chase's initial memo of December 1861, some two years earlier, instructing Pollock to come up with such a motto. So by intentional plan or otherwise Pollock had succeeded in bringing back the issue of the motto, under the issue of metallic change in the cent and on the vehicle of a new two-cent piece.

An 1863 Indian Head cent pattern struck in bronze. It is believed 300 were struck with probably 150 to 200 known today. They were struck with medallic turn, meaning the obverse and reverse are 180 degrees off alignment so as to be easily distinguishable from the regular-issue copper-nickel cents. Cataloged as Judd-299.

The "Head of Washington" specimen piece referred to in Mint Director James Pollock's letter. It carries the motto GOD AND OUR COUNTRY. It is fairly common as far as pattern coins go, with perhaps 100 to 150 examples known. James B. Longacre designed both this coin and the Shield and Arrows type. This pattern is cataloged as Judd-305.

The Shield and Arrows pattern two-cent piece of the type enclosed in Pollock's letter to Chase, along with the Head of Washington piece. It, too, is relatively common for a pattern, with around 150 still believed extant. Note that it has the same reverse as the Washington pattern and that the word CENTS is sharply curved. It is listed as Judd-312.

1863 Patterns

On November 16, 1863, before the December correspondence between Mint Director James Pollock and Treasury Secretary Salmon Chase, the coiner George Eckfeldt noted in his journal that he had "struck 30 sets of silver 'God is Our Trust' half dollars [he meant 'God Our Trust'] and 20 sets of copper for Gov. Pollock. Date 1863." Then on November 17, Eckfeldt further noted: "Struck 20 sets of 10 dollar pieces 'God is Our Trust.'"[13] Pollock clearly still had in mind "God Our Trust" as of mid-November, when he had these patterns produced. It seems that, in Pollock's mind, the issue of a religious motto, whatever it might be, was still in doubt as he was motivated to continue promoting it with more patterns.

Estimated numbers of surviving half dollars in both silver and copper are two dozen each. This is true for both the Plain Letter and the Scroll Type halves. The same applies for the copper $10 pieces, with roughly two dozen surviving examples of both types. This would indicate either a high survival rate for these coins from their striking in November of 1863, or that some were struck in later years. Unlike the 1861 and 1862 $10 patterns which have High Date and Low Date varieties, there is only one date position for the 1863 coins. Another distinction of the 1863 $10 patterns is that a single example of each type (Scroll Type and Plain Letters) was struck in gold. Their strikings were also noted by Eckfeldt as being on August 2, 1863. They were made for the chief coiner, Mr. Broomall.[14] Of course these coins are deemed great rarities and have been in the John Hopkins University Collection, the Garrett Collection, the Woodward Collection, and other significant collections over the years.

1863 GOD OUR TRUST, Plain Letters, half dollar pattern in silver (Judd-340).
The same design was also struck in copper (Judd-341b).

1863 GOD OUR TRUST, Scroll Type, half dollar pattern in copper (Judd-339).
The same design was also struck in silver (Judd-338).

1863, Plain Letters, eagle pattern in copper. (Judd-352)

1863, Scroll Type, eagle pattern in copper. (Judd-350)

Furthermore, the December 9 note contained the suggestion of In God We Trust. The operative motto on all of the earlier patterns had been God Our Trust, except for the Head of Washington piece, which carried God And Our Country. What brought In God We Trust to Chase's mind? We will speculate on this in a later chapter.

Pollock responded to Chase's note on December 15, 1863. In his response he rejected Chase's suggestion of Our God And Our Country, saying it created a "sense of limitation and appropriation," reducing the "grand idea of God over all nations and the only God of the nations." Pollock deemed both In God We Trust and God Our Trust appropriate and equally expressive but said "I prefer the latter because of its brevity and compact expressiveness—But these questions can be determined when the coinage is authorized. It is not proposed to adopt both the Shield and the Washington Head, they are my specimens, one or the other, or some other, but only one to be selected and adopted."[15]

Pollock added that he had enclosed a draft of a law that could be presented to Congress "embracing the objects proposed." That draft formed the basis for the Mint Act of April 22, 1864. As we shall see in the next chapter, that act passed, but only with some difficulty. The act succeeded in providing for the cent to be produced in bronze rather than copper-nickel, and for the introduction of the new two-cent piece. Ultimately these actions resolved the cent shortage. The act also contained a clause that led to a religious motto on the new two-cent coin.

Julia Ward Howe, author of "The Battle Hymn of the Republic," the unofficial war anthem of the Union.

CHAPTER 9

The National Reform Association

As noted in chapter 1, a splinter group of Presbyterians called "Covenant-ers" had long been troubled by the "Godless" federal constitution. They had raised the issue even before the Civil War and the Confederacy's rati-fication of its new constitution. However, the Confederacy's inclusion of a reference to God in its preamble stirred the group to greater efforts. Beyond this the group was moved to further action by a sermon delivered by Reverend Horace Bushnell on the Sunday following the disastrous Union battlefield defeat at Bull Run on July 21, 1861. The sermon was published in the and became widely quoted. Bushnell was a leading theologian of the era, known for his reformist ideas in both theology and society in general. He was a minister at a Congregational church in Hartford, Con-necticut, and became a prolific and well-known writer on religious topics. In his ser-mon, called "Reverses Needed," he placed fault "at the very foundation of American government established without a moral or religious basis." The Founding Fathers had created a government "without moral or religious ideas . . . a merely man-made compact." As a result of these errors the nation was now paying the price and "there must be reverses and losses" as "without shedding of blood there is no grace pre-pared."[1] Furthermore, given that the Confederate constitution acknowledged the authority of "Almighty God," Bushnell proposed that "it might not be amiss, at some fit time" to amend the preamble of the U.S. Constitution with a declaration of God's authority.[2] The *Independent*, widely considered the most important religious publication in the country, published an editorial supporting Bushnell's proposal and calling for immediate action as a correction to "this atheistic error in our prime conceptions of Government" and to the "atheistic habit of separating politics from religion."[3] Moved by these developments, the Covenanters held a conference in late 1861 in Allegheny, Pennsylvania, where they drew up a petition deploring "the absence of God and his laws in the Constitution" and proposing that it be amended to correct the problem. Senator Charles Sumner of Massachusetts became aware of this petition and managed to arrange a meeting between two Covenanter ministers, representing the group, and President Abraham Lincoln. The meeting took place in early 1862. The ministers presented the petition and urged their case upon the president. We do not have any detailed record of their conversations, but it seems Lincoln was noncommittal and probably did not assign much significance to the meeting. The Covenanters nevertheless were encouraged and, joining with other like-minded religious groups, continued their efforts.[4]

In February of 1863, less than a year after the meeting with Lincoln, another conference was held in Xenia, Ohio. The Covenanters were joined by eleven Protestant denominations from seven states, showing a broadening of support. The conference continued for three days. The highlight seems to have been on the second day, when a Presbyterian attorney and wealthy businessman, John Alexander, addressed the convention. His thesis was that the nation had a terrible "original sin" which had led to its current woes. This sin was not slavery, but was "the neglect of God and his law, by omitting all acknowledgements of them in our Constitution." Alexander believed the key to rectifying this sin was to amend the Constitution. In his address he read a draft of a proposed amendment to the Preamble:

> We the People of the United States recognizing the being and attributes of Almighty God, the Divine Authority of the Holy Scriptures, the law of God as the paramount rule, and Jesus, the Messiah, the Savior and Lord of all, in order to form a more perfect union, establish justice, insure domestic tranquility . . . do ordain and establish this Constitution for the United States of America.[5]

The convention unanimously approved this proposed amendment and agreed to continue the effort and to schedule another meeting. At almost the same time as the Xenia convention another and similar gathering was held in Sparta, Illinois. At the time the meetings were held, neither group was aware of the other. The Sparta conference was also made up of ministers and laymen of several denominations. They passed a resolution calling for "faithful administration of the government according to the principles of the Word of God" and acknowledging Christ's authority in the political realm.

In January of 1864 yet another meeting was held in Allegheny, Pennsylvania, that combined representatives from the previous Xenia and Sparta sessions along with others of similar mindset. They formed what was called the Christian Amendment Movement. This was formalized soon after and renamed the National Reform Association. The key purpose of the organization was to press for a constitutional amendment acknowledging in some form the importance of God and Christ in the nation's life. The NRA had been formed by people from various Protestant denominations, but the leadership was mainly Presbyterian. The Allegheny convention elected John Alexander as president of the new organization and formally approved his proposed constitutional amendment to be presented to Congress. They had some success picking up congressional interest as senators Charles Sumner, Gratz Brown, and John Sherman supported their efforts. They again expressed support, and numerous prominent individuals including some federal judges, governors, bishops, and college presidents joined in.[6] By February the organization was able to arrange a second meeting with President Lincoln. According to their reports of the meeting, the president promised to give their proposal attention. They reported his reaction:

> To a few of the men who were on the Committee of the National Reform Association he privately said "Gentlemen, in your former visit you requested of me two things. During the first term of my administration I was able to secure your first request [emancipation]. It is my hope that during my second term I will be able to secure your second request."[7]

At this time leaders of the NRA were greatly encouraged and believed an amendment might be imminent. However, as the potential reality of such an amendment became apparent, many backers became soft in their support of it in practice. Horace Bushnell, who had urged an amendment in 1861, changed his attitude, believing that the nation had been already redeemed through the blood of its massive battlefield casualties. Senator Charles Sumner, an early congressional supporter, came under pressure from Jewish constituents who opposed it. In December 1864 he wrote to a Jewish supporter saying he was "astonished" by accusations that he "favored any proposition to disenfranchise anybody. . . . I have said that I should not object to a recognition of God by formal words in the Constitution. . . . That is all, I take it no Hebrew would differ with me on this point." He also asked his constituent to "quiet your Hebrew associates with regard to me."

By March of 1865 even the *Independent* reversed its support and opposed those who sought "to engraft the Christian religion into the Constitution." It stated that religious skeptics "have ground for apprehending the formation of an ecclesiastical party to act distinctly in political affairs."[8]

Probably the most interesting test of support came from President Lincoln himself. Many doubted that the Covenanter's NRA efforts to convince him on the issue had been effective, despite the somewhat vague statements of support they had attributed to him in early 1864. However, a quote from Gideon Welles's diary indicates something different. Welles was secretary of the Navy and he kept a detailed diary of the Civil War period, providing much insight into the personalities and events of the Lincoln administration. His diary entry for December 3, 1864, discussed the cabinet meeting called to go over Lincoln's proposed State of the Union address:

Charles Sumner was a strong abolitionist and early supporter of a constitutional amendment referencing God. He became concerned, however, that some of his Jewish constituents were opposed to such an amendment and felt the need to clarify his position.

December 3, Saturday. The President read his message at a special Cabinet-meeting today and general criticism took place. His own portion has been much improved. The briefs submitted by the several members were incorporated pretty much in their own words. One paragraph *proposing an Amendment to the Constitution recognizing the Deity in that instrument* met with no favorable response from any one member of the Cabinet. The President, before reading it, expressed his own doubts in regard to it, but it had been urged by certain religionists.[9]

So from this we are led to believe Lincoln may have been willing to entertain proposing an amendment, but, given negative reactions from his cabinet members (and his own doubts?), he did not move forward with it.

Certainly Lincoln was aware of and gave a lot of thought to the religious struggle between North and South for God's favor. Indeed, his Second Inaugural Address was very explicit in making it a major theme:

Each looked for an easier triumph, and a result less fundamental and astounding. Both read the same Bible and pray to the same God, and each invokes His aid against the other. It may seem strange that any men should dare to ask a just God's assistance in wringing their bread from the sweat of other men's faces, but let us judge not, that we be not judged. The prayers of both could not be answered. That of neither has been answered fully.

The Almighty has His own purposes.

By the time of the December 3 cabinet meeting Salmon Chase was gone from the administration. One wonders how he would have reacted to the discussion and the president's thoughts.

We might surmise that, as the Union gained the upper hand on the battlefields and Lincoln's reelection the previous November ensured that the war would be pressed on to a victorious conclusion, support for changing the Constitution to seek further favor from God had already peaked by mid- to late 1864. By this time

Abraham Lincoln delivering his Second Inaugural Address.

the two-cent piece with its motto "In God We Trust" had been issued and was beginning to circulate. Is it possible that Lincoln and others in the administration, and even those in the general public, may have regarded that coin as adequately addressing the issue of recognizing the Almighty? Susan Jacoby in her book *Free-thinkers: A History of American Secularism* takes the view that "The affirmation on coins of America's trust in the deity was intended as a harmless sop by Lincoln to ministers who, during the Civil War, wanted to bully Congress and the President into amending the Constitution to include God. . . ."[10]

The National Reform Association, while missing its chance for a "Christian Amendment" in 1864–1865, did not go away. It held periodic meetings during the late 1860s and early 1870s and began a publication, the *Christian Statesman*. It worked in Congress for various amendment proposals in 1871 and 1872, though it failed to bring congressional action. It worked in several states for the goal of amending state constitutions with Christian amendments. It had at least a partial success in Pennsylvania in 1873, and it hoped to use this as a springboard for another effort at the national level. A petition was presented and debated in committee. In the meantime, however, a new organization had been established with the goal of opposing such an amendment. This was the Free Religious Association, founded by Unitarian preacher Octavius Frothingham and theologian Francis Abbot. They created a publication in 1870 known as *The Index* to counter the *Christian Statesman*. The FRA gathered more than 35,000 signatures opposing an amendment, present-ing it to the congressional committee involved. This made an impression on Con-gress, and the NRA's amendment was tabled in early 1874.[11] However, the NRA did not go away; we will hear more of it in a later chapter, some 80 years further on.

Developments in the Confederacy

Confederate clergy had certainly rejoiced in the spring of 1861 with their new nation's constitution and the reference in its preamble to "Almighty God." But even so there were efforts to go further. In December of 1861, Reverend James Thorn-well, at the behest of the Presbyterian Conference, drew up a memorial to the Con-federate Congress titled "Relation of the State to Christ." In it Thornwell reiterated the familiar criticism of the Founding Fathers for having forgotten God and for having opened the American Republic to the will of the majority. "A foundation was thus laid for the worst of all possible forms of government—a democratic absolut-ism which in the execution of its purpose, does not scruple to annul the most solemn compacts and to cancel the most sacred obligations." He then thanked and congrat-ulated the Confederacy in the memorial for having moved to rectify those mistakes:

> The changes which your honorable body had made in the Constitution of the United States and which have been satisfied and confirmed by the various states of the Confederacy have received the universal approval of the Presby-terian population of these states. . . . We congratulate you on your success.

"The Battle Hymn of the Republic"

Another event, besides placement of "In God We Trust" on U.S. coinage, unquestionably helped tip the balance of "Godliness" toward the Union. This was the composition of "The Battle Hymn of the Republic," written on the night and in the early morning of November 18–19, 1861. It is a striking and perhaps haunting coincidence that this was written at virtually the same time (November 20) that Reverend Mark Watkinson's letter was passed from Treasury Secretary Salmon Chase to Mint Director James Pollock, urging recognition of God on the nation's coinage.

Julia Ward Howe. Her "Battle Hymn of the Republic" became an anthem for the Union cause, expressing its religious and moral purpose.

The Hymn was written by Julia Ward Howe, a noted Boston poet. She was visiting Washington, D.C., and had attended a troop review. On her way back into the city that evening her carriage passed thousands of troops, some marching, some around campfires. Many were singing "John Brown's Body," written a year or two earlier with words in praise of the anti-slavery martyr John Brown. Upon her return to the Willard Hotel, near the White House, Howe found she was still stirred by the sights and sounds she had experienced during the day. She was unable to sleep and rose to write out words that came to her. She later recalled, "I awoke in the gray of the morning twilight; and as I lay waiting for the dawn, the long lines of the desired poem began to twine themselves in my mind. Having thought out all the stanzas, I said to myself, 'I must get up and write these verses down, lest I fall asleep again and forget them.'" She scribbled the verses on the back of a piece of stationery. She did fall asleep and, when waking later, realized she had indeed forgotten the words that had come to her in the night. But she found her verses written out on the desk in her room and realized they fit the "John Brown's Body" tune.[12]

However, Thornwell went on to argue for more. Vague recognition of God would not do.

> But gentlemen, we are constrained in candor, to say that, in our humble judgement, the Constitution, admirable as it is, in other respects, still labors under one capital defect. It is not distinctively Christian. . . . in the way of respectful petition, to pray that the Constitution may be amended so as to express the precise relations which the Government of these States ought to sustain the religion of Jesus Christ.

Howe had her work published in the *Atlantic* magazine in early 1862. The Hymn became immediately popular and was sung and recited widely in the North. The circumstances of its creation, as though from a divine visitation, combined with its powerful apocalyptic words associating the Union cause with God's will, made a strong message that "stirred men's souls" then and yet today.

> Mine eyes hath seen the glory of the coming of the Lord:
> He is trampling out the vintage where the grapes of wrath are stored;
> He hath loosed the fateful lightning of His terrible swift sword:
> His truth is marching on.
>
> Glory! Glory! Hallelujah! Glory! Glory! Hallelujah!
> Glory! Glory! Hallelujah! His truth is marching on.
>
> I have seen Him in the watch-fires of a hundred circling camps,
> They have builded Him an altar in the evening dews and damps;
> I can read His righteous sentence by the dim and flaring lamps:
> His day is marching on.
>
> I have read a fiery Gospel writ in burnished rows of steel:
> "As ye deal with My contemners, so with you My grace shall deal;
> Let the Hero, born of woman, crush the serpent with His heel,
> Since God is marching on."
>
> He has sounded forth the trumpet that shall never call retreat;
> He is sifting out the hearts of men before His judgment seat:
> Oh, be swift, my soul, to answer Him! be jubilant, my feet!
> Our God is marching on.
>
> In the beauty of the lilies Christ was born across the sea,
> With a glory in His bosom that transfigures you and me:
> As He died to make men holy, let us die to make men free;
> While God is marching on.
>
> He is coming like the glory of the morning on the wave,
> He is wisdom to the mighty, He is honor to the brave;
> So the world shall be His footstool, and the soul of wrong His slave,
> Our God is marching on.

Your honorable body has already, to some extent, rectified the error of the old Constitution, but not so distinctly and clearly as the Christian people of these States desire to see done. We venture respectfully to suggest that it is not enough for a state which enjoys the light of Divine Revelation to acknowledge in the general terms the supremacy of God; it must also acknowledge the supremacy of His Son whom he hath appointed heir to all things by whom also He made the worlds. To Jesus Christ all power in heaven and earth is committed. To Him every knee shall bow, and every tongue confess. He is the Ruler of the nations, the King of kings, and Lord of lords.

Thornwell's memorial continued on in that vein and ended by proposing an amendment to the Confederate constitution. It was intended to be included in the new constitution's existing section providing for liberty of conscience.

> Nevertheless we, the people of these Confederate States, distinctly acknowledge our responsibility to God, and the supremacy of His Son, Jesus Christ, as King of kings and Lord of lords, and hereby ordain that no law shall be passed by the Congress of these Confederate States inconsistent with the will of God as revealed in the Holy Scriptures.

This proposal was put forward to the Presbyterian Conference for their approval before presentation to the Confederate Congress. However, it was done late in the session, on the eighth day, near the end. While it may have had majority support, it was opposed by some who doubted its propriety and wisdom. Thornwell withdrew the measure on the ground that there was not time for its discussion. He felt it should not be pushed through unless it could be adopted with "cordiality and unanimity."[13] He did not give up on it, however, and intended to raise it in future sessions. He believed that it had wide support. There can be little doubt that, even if not officially endorsed by the Presbyterians, the Confederate Congress was aware of it.

Soon after the Conference, in late 1861 and early 1862, Thornwell wrote another tract called "Our Danger and Our Duty" that was widely circulated in the South. In it he laid out the importance of the Confederacy winning the war. With victory, "We shall have a Government that acknowledges God, that reverences right, and that makes law supreme. We are, therefore, fighting not for ourselves alone, but, when the struggle is rightly understood, for the salvation of this whole continent." He wrote of the French Revolution and how its leadership had "begun the fabric of a new Government, or the reformation of an old" but had made the "capital omission" of forgetting God and therefore failed in its efforts. This in his view was a warning for the Confederate people and government.

All of Thornwell's well-publicized writings and efforts to further and more explicitly tie the Confederacy to Christianity were happening at the same time that Reverend Mark Watkinson's letter was under consideration by Treasury Secretary Chase and Mint Director Pollock. We can certainly speculate that the letter itself and Chase's response were in part motivated by these developments in the Confederacy.

Fate dictated that Thornwell was unable to pursue his intended efforts to amend the Confederate constitution. His son Gillespie joined the Confederate army as a cavalryman early in the war. He was only 16, underage to join, but his father signed off, providing parental permission for him. On May 5, 1862, the son was wounded by a saber cut at the Battle of Williamsburg, one of the many fights that were part of the Peninsular Campaign. He was transported to Richmond for treatment. His father and mother traveled from their home in Columbia, South Carolina, to Richmond to attend to him and by May 26 brought him home to Columbia. Though the son recovered, the journey to Richmond and back affected the father's health, which was never strong. Thornwell wrote to a friend and fellow minister in late May:

> My son continues to improve. He stood the journey remarkably well, better even than I did. For I had to go to bed upon reaching home and have not been worth a chew of tobacco since my arrival. If I had not felt so good for nothing I would have written you before.

Indeed, Thornwell did not recover and he died on August 1, 1862. With him went the strongest advocacy to make the Confederacy constitutionally Christian.

In a tragic footnote, his son Gillespie returned to the army and was killed in combat about a year later.[14]

The Confederate Seal and Motto

The Great Seal of the Confederate States of America was intended to authenticate various documents issued by the Confederate government. It seems it was designed in April 1863 and the official seal manufactured in London sometime after May 20, 1863, when the Confederate secretary of State ordered it. The seal displays George Washington on horseback, copied from the Virginia Washington Monument on the grounds of the Confederate capitol in Richmond, Virginia. The statue predated the Confederacy, having been erected in 1858. The seal bears the date 22 February, 1862, the day the Confederacy was officially established and Jefferson Davis inaugurated as its president.

Most important for our story is that the seal bore the Confederate States motto "Deo Vindice." The Latin phrase is variously translated as "Vindicated by God," "With God as Our Champion," or "Delivered by God." The general sentiment was that the Confederacy was justified and supported by God. It was another indication of the efforts to identify the Confederacy with the Deity.

The Great Seal of the Confederate States of America.

53 Lehigh Zinc Works.

Pennsylvania industrialist Joseph Wharton
was instrumental in bringing nickel into
greater use in U.S. coinage.

CHAPTER 10

Joseph Wharton

Much of the nickel used in the nation's new copper-nickel cents at first came from the Gap Mine in Lancaster County, Pennsylvania. This was the only domestic source at the time. The facility had operated as a copper mine perhaps as far back as the early 1700s, but had more actively been exploited beginning in 1849. Besides copper the mine contained another, little-known, ore that the miners identified as "mundic" (the Cornish word for common pyrite), viewing it simply as mine waste. This material was mostly discarded, but in 1853 it was studied more deeply and found to be nickel. As copper production was dropping the operation shifted to nickel and was renamed the Gap Nickel Mine Company. When the U.S. Mint's changeover from copper large cents occurred in 1857, the mine began supplying nickel for the new copper-nickel cent. The mine shut down in 1860 for reasons that are unclear, but it was likely due to poor management and lack of profitability. It was selling its production to the Mint at 42¢ per pound. Following the closure, the Mint began importing its nickel from England at higher prices. By 1863 it was paying $1.75 per pound. As Mint Director James Pollock noted in one of his reports (October 27, 1862), the cent production remained profitable with costs running at 50¢ to 60¢ per 100.[1]

In 1863 a man named Joseph Wharton acquired the Gap Nickel Mine. Wharton was from a prominent Philadelphia Quaker family and had been involved with another mining operation, the Pennsylvania and Lehigh Zinc Company. He was the manager and largest shareholder of that company and, under his guidance, it had become the first successful producer of zinc metal in the United States. Seeing opportunity in the Gap Nickel Mine he sold his zinc interests to raise funds for its development. He paid just $1,000 to buy stock in the mine. He hired an experienced mine engineer to refurbish it and concentrate on nickel mining. He also invested in a refinery, the Camden Works in New Jersey, and worked to improve the metallurgical process, greatly enhancing the metal's purity and malleability. Between the mine and the refinery Wharton invested some $200,000.[2]

Pollock's efforts to eliminate nickel from the cents and make the switch to bronze during 1863 and early 1864 must have come as a surprise to Wharton. He

Thaddeus Stevens, "The Old Commoner," was a powerhouse in the House of Representatives: a fierce opponent of slavery, and, as chairman of the House Ways and Means Committee, a leader in financing the Union's war effort. He and Joseph Wharton both hailed from Pennsylvania.

was not without political influence as an active Republican and having connections with individuals in Congress. In particular Thaddeus Stevens, the prominent anti-slavery congressman, was from Lancaster County, Pennsylvania, where Wharton's Gap Nickel Mine was located.

It soon became evident to Pollock that there was opposition in Congress to his proposal and on January 27, 1864, he again wrote to Treasury Secretary Salmon Chase urging action on the bill he had earlier provided:

Hon S.P. Chase
Sec. of the Treasury

Sir

Permit me, respectfully, to call your attention to my former communications on the subject and necessity of substituting bronze for nickel in the composition of the Cent.

It is not only very difficult to obtain a supply of nickel, but almost impossible, and with the advancing price, the cost of production will soon exceed the value of the product.

I had the honor, a few weeks ago, to forward you a bill prepared at your request, embracing not only the change in metal, but authorizing the coinage of a two cent piece etc. If approved by you, it is desirable that Congress should be requested to take immediate action upon it – at least so much thereof as authorizes the substitution of bronze for nickel in the cent, which is of the first necessity, if the making of that coin is to be continued. The demand for cents is very great and cannot be met under existing circumstances. The substitution of bronze will enable us to mint it, and at the same time secure a fair profit for the government. If you deem it advisable, I will go to Washington and aid in procuring the early action of Congress on this subject, by furnishing such information, as I may be able to communicate.

Yours very truly &
Respectfully
Jas. Pollock
Director

There followed a series of letters among the principal actors involved in the decisions to be made. Wharton wrote a letter to Chase dated February 15, 1864, that countered Pollock's various arguments against nickel:

Hon. S.P. Chase, Secretary of the Treasury

Sir

The Director of the Mint urges the abolition of the Nickel alloy coinage for the following reasons: viz

1st that the alloy is too expensive, and that a coin of equal weight made of copper alone would answer every purpose of our present cent coin.

2nd That the Nickel has to be bought abroad and paid for in gold.

3rd That the Nickel alloy is hard to melt and to work.

To these arguments I reply

1st That the cent coinages now pays a handsome profit to the government, but that a larger profit may be got if desired by merely reducing the thickness of the cent coin, having everything else unchanged.

2nd I am ready to begin selling Nickel to the Mint, though not immediately to the extent of the usage.

3rd The difficulty in getting and working Nickel is the surest prevention of counterfeiting.

4th Unnecessary changes in the coinage of a great Nation are very much to be deprecated; especially changes for the worse.

5th I am willing to contract to make all of the cent coins required by the government at a price below their nominal value.

After expending a large capital and much labor, I have begun to produce good Nickel, and I expect to continue and to enlarge the business.

Very Respectfully,
Joseph Wharton[4]

Wharton argued that he could supply adequate nickel to the Mint but admitted that he could not *immediately* meet the full demand even though he had cut off his other customers.

Whether through Secretary Chase's intervention or, more likely, through earlier arrangement, Wharton did begin sales to the Mint. In a letter to Mint Director Pollock on March 5, 1864, he wrote as follows:

Camden Nickel Works

Camden, N.J., March 5, 1864

Mr. James Pollock

Dear Sir:

I send you herewith 200 lbs. of nickel, also duplicate bills for the same amounting to $900. I propose to be able to give you a larger quantity this day make, but this will depend to a great extent upon what I can do with my other customers. Some of them I have already cut off, so as to give sooner and more freely to you, and you will I trust always find me able to do what is possible to meet your wishes.

The approximation of the present lot is below my present assays arising to my having been decisive as to the quality of the charcoal.

Very Respectfully,
Joseph Wharton[5]

On March 2, 1864, Pollock again wrote Chase, reiterating much of what he had said in earlier letters and reports, requesting authorization to switch to bronze and to begin production of a two-cent piece. At the end of the letter he argued for a religious motto, not just on the two-cent piece as covered in the bill he enclosed but also on the larger-denomination silver and gold coins. He may have been hoping for Chase's approval to modify the bill to make that change. We have no record of a response from Chase on this point. The letter, with its repetition of earlier arguments for bronze, was certainly intended for Chase to pass to Congress in support of the bill that he had prepared and enclosed.

Mint of the United States

Philadelphia, March 2, 1864

Hon S.P. Chase
Sec. of Treasury

Sir

In my last annual report I recommended the disuse of nickel in the cent coinage and the substitution of the alloy lately introduced in France and England, called bronze. It is composed of copper, tin, and zinc, and makes a beautiful and ductile alloy. This change in the material of the cent is not only desirable in itself, but has become a necessity from the advanced price of nickel for a supply of which, we are at present entirely dependent upon the foreign market, paying for it in gold or its equivalent, and the great uncertainty of procuring an adequate supply for the future from any source, at a price within the legal limit.

Besides this, nickel is itself objectionable as an alloying metal. It is harsh brittle – most difficult to melt, requiring the fiercest fires even where alloyed with copper – and is very destructive of dies, machinery and thus increasing the cost of production, which will soon exceed the value of the product, if the price of copper, labor, coat, etc. continues to advance, as it is almost certain to do. In that event the coinage of the cent must cease.

It is not proposed to change the size or devices of the cent, only the weight. The weight of the new coins would be 48 grains or one-tenth oz troy. This will secure a coin in every respect superior to the slumpy nickel.

I also propose for your consideration the coinage of a two-cent piece, same material and double the weight of the cent. The size of this coin would be much less than the old copper cent,—be a great public convenience—and its coinage in my opinion should be authorized.

If you approve of the proposed change in material and denomination the enclosed bill, prepared with care, can be submitted to Congress for their action.

Permit me respectfully to suggest that immediate action is necessary, for if nickel is retained it will be impossible to meet the enormous demand for cents, and the increasing cost of production may compel a cessation of that coinage. The demand for cents is now far beyond our ability to supply it.

The substitution of bronze, for the nickel alloy was examined by the commissioners of the last Annual Assay in February, and was by them cordially approved. . . .

Would it not be proper to authorize the introduction upon our gold and silver coins of the larger denominations, a motto expressive of a National reliance upon the divine Sovereignty? The times seem to demand. I hope it may receive the sanction of law.

> *Yours Most Respectfully*
> *Jas. Pollock, Director*[6]

On March 5 Chase did indeed submit Pollock's letter and bill to William Fessenden, chairman of the Senate Finance Committee. However, there was no action on the part of the Senate and, evidently in some frustration, Pollock wrote another letter to Chase, dated March 16:

Hon. S.P. Chase, Sec of Treasury

March 16, 1864

Sir:

The continuance of the cent coinage is now not only a question of price but supply. Our present stock of nickel will be exhausted in a few days, and an adequate supply cannot be obtained from any source. Our foreign correspondents inform us that nickel cannot be furnished at present prices, nor can any considerable amount be had for some months.

We are thus shut up to the home supply, from the works of Mr. Wharton; but if we could receive all made at his establishment the amount would be wholly insufficient, would be from five hundred to eight hundred pounds per week, not more than one half the amount required under ordinary circumstances. Something must be done by Congress, and that at once, to meet the constant and overwhelming demand; our daily orders range from two to five thousand dollars; our daily production about one thousand dollars. We cannot increase it, for we cannot procure the material. The wants of the public could be fully met by substituting bronze for the nickel alloy. *But private interests have induced opposition to this proposition.* Can these private interests be reconciled, and at the same time the public interests and convenience be promoted? I think they can, by reducing the weight of the nickel cent from seventy-two to forty-eight grains, and continuing the coinage of the nickel alloy at this reduced rate, making a more convenient and desirable coin, and at the same time authorizing the coinage of a two cent bronze piece. This will meet the wants of the people and the Government, and be satisfactory to Mr. Wharton and his friends. Although every consideration of public interest and convenience requires the abandonment of nickel, yet the plan now proposed, if adopted, will greatly aid the Mint in meeting a demand that is unceasing and increasing. I enclose an amendment or new section to the supplement forwarded some weeks ago, embracing the present proposition. If bronze is substituted, or the submitted plan be adopted, a clear revenue of at least two hundred or two hundred and fifty thousand dollars will, under the present demand for cents, annually accrue to the Government. I hope the subject will receive the early and favorable action of Congress.

Yours etc.
Jas Pollock[7]

Though Wharton was not able at this point to provide adequate supplies of nickel (note his first shipment had only been 200 pounds), Pollock recognized Wharton's influence and the political difficulties Congress was having with the change to bronze. Pollock was in effect offering a compromise to "reconcile" the interests. The Mint would continue using copper-nickel for the cents but would reduce their weight from 72 grains to 48 grains by striking them on thinner planchets, just as Wharton suggested in point 1 of his February 15 letter. This change would cut the need for nickel by one-third. The new two-cent piece would be of bronze, and Pollock still preferred the cents also be bronze, but it is clear he was trying to make the best he could of the situation.

The day after writing this letter, on March 17, Pollock wrote another brief letter to Chase, enclosing pattern copper-nickel cents of the reduced 48-grain weight:

Hon S.P. Chase

Sec. of Treasury

Sir:

I enclose four Specimen nickel cents of 48 grains, or reduced weight, as suggested in my communication of yesterday. They are much more desirable than the present thick and heavy cent—and would be, if introduced, a decided improvement. There is no reasonable objection to the reduction of weight. This, or the bronze would be universally accepted and will reduce the cost of production.

Yours Very Truly,

Jas. Pollock, Dir.[8]

Chase seemed to grasp the gravity of the situation and he forwarded Pollock's letter to Senator Fessenden. He sent a cover memo stating, "I concur with the Director in thinking that the public interests and convenience require the abandonment of nickel and the substitution of bronze for one and two cent pieces, as provided by the

A Thin-Planchet
Copper-Nickel Pattern Cent

Mint Director James Pollock's March 17, 1864, letter gives evidence that at least four Indian Head cent patterns on thin copper-nickel planchets weighing 48 grains were struck and provided to Treasury Secretary Chase. An example of this pattern cent appeared in the April 2013 Heritage Auctions sale of pattern coins from the Eric P. Newman collection. Therein, lot number 3942 was described as being struck from "the regular dies for the 1864 Indian cent without Longacre's initial L, struck in an alloy of 88% copper and 12% nickel." This was, of course, the standard alloy for the copper-nickel cents. The catalog commentary continues: "This may better be classified as a mint error than a pattern, as it purports to be a regular issue 1864 copper-nickel Indian cent, except it is struck on a thin planchet that weighs 47.8 grains compared to the standard of 72 grains. A similar piece weighing 51 grains appeared in the Floyd Starr collection." The provenance given of the Newman coin showed it coming from the Colonel Green Estate. The letter from Pollock to Chase enclosing four of these cents shows the coin was not a "mint error." This coin is listed in the Judd pattern book as J-356b.

Judd-356b

bill already submitted." Chase's pressure brought results and the bill was introduced in the Senate on March 22. Pollock's letters were read in support. The bill passed after three readings without debate.[9] The idea of the reduced-weight copper-nickel cent, which Pollock had offered as a compromise, was evidently not seriously considered, and bronze was chosen, per Pollock's original preference.

The bill then went to the House of Representatives. Before the House had a chance to consider the matter, Wharton drafted a paper, presented as a brochure dated April 15, 1864. It was titled "Project For Reorganizing the Small Coinage of the United States of America." In it he discussed the various materials available for producing "token" coinage, meaning coinage whose intrinsic value was less than its nominal value. Wharton recommended that coins of 25 cents or more should contain intrinsic value at least approximately equal to their nominal value. However, for those coins under 25 cents, he argued that the intrinsic value was meaningless and that people would accept them and circulate them for purposes of convenience. This argument was similar to Pollock's discussions in his earlier annual reports. Wharton proposed the issuance of $20,000,000 in coinage in denominations up to and including 10 cents, over a five-year period. This coinage would be made of copper-and-nickel alloy. He estimated the amount of nickel required for this $20,000,000 in coinage would be 1,000,000 pounds, or 200,000 pounds per year. He claimed that his mining and refining operations would be able to meet these production targets and cover the Mint's needs over the next five years and probably for the next fifty years. He estimated that his production could rise to some 120,000 pounds per annum within three months and to 200,000 pounds within six months. He stated that he did not intend to make such investments to reach those production levels without some absolute assurance that the government's demand would be high enough and over a long enough period to justify them. He committed to providing the nickel at prices that would assure large profits to the government.

He summarized his paper by stating eight conclusions:[10]

1. That our small coins, or change, should not pretend to intrinsic value, but should be a system of tokens.
2. That these tokens should be redeemable or convertible into larger money, as our postage notes now are.
3. That the alloys of nickel and copper are the proper materials for these coin tokens on account of their beauty, durability, cheapness, and the very great difficulty of counterfeiting them.
4. That several nations have adopted nickel alloy token coinage with perfect success, and that others are now preparing to do so.
5. That our token coinage should go to the denominations of 10 cent pieces, but not higher, as the system should be suitable for continuance after a return to specie payments.

6. That the total amount to be issued might properly be $20,000,000, distributed through five years.
7. That such an issue would yield to Government a profit of $15,000,000, reckoning at present prices, and not taking into view the almost certain extension of the issue, or the replacing of coins lost and destroyed.
8. That the nickel needed for the purpose can be had in our own country, and at a moderate price.

Joseph Wharton, circa 1890.

Wharton circulated his paper in Congress and his plan was reviewed by the House Committee on Coinage, Weights, and Measures. However, on April 20 the committee rejected Wharton's proposal, and Pollock's bill was unanimously endorsed. Still, in the House at large there was opposition to the Pollock bill. Thaddeus Stevens, the representative from the Lancaster area, argued for his constituent Wharton's position. He claimed that previous government actions "had induced several gentlemen to embark on the difficult project of working nickel mines" and that Wharton had spent $200,000 investing in his mine and machinery expecting continuing government purchases. He asked rhetorically, "Shall we destroy all this property because by coining with another metal more money may be saved to the Government?" He also claimed that the "brass" (he meant bronze) would rust, unlike the copper-nickel alloy.

Representative John Kasson of Iowa, who was chairman of the committee recommending Pollock's bill, countered by saying that the idea of the government, by purchasing an article from a producer, was bound by him in perpetuity to continue such purchases "was without precedent."

The bill was put to a vote and passed, becoming the Coinage Act of April 22, 1864.[11]

Nevertheless Joseph Wharton's pioneering work with nickel and his paper advocating its use in coinage had their effect. We will see in later chapters that nickel was to become an important metal in U.S. coinage. It should be noted that, beyond the United States, the German imperial government adopted nickel-alloy coinage in 1873, and Wharton became a wealthy man through his nickel operations. His metallurgical research resulted in purer and more malleable nickel, for which he held various patents, and he was placed in the National Mining Hall of Fame for his accomplishments. He co-founded the Bethlehem Steel Company in later years and was known for his generous philanthropy. He founded the Wharton School at the University of Pennsylvania, still regarded as one of the nation's leading business schools. He also was one of the founders of Swarthmore College in Pennsylvania.[12]

JUSTICE!

THE GUARDIAN OF OUR LIBERTY.

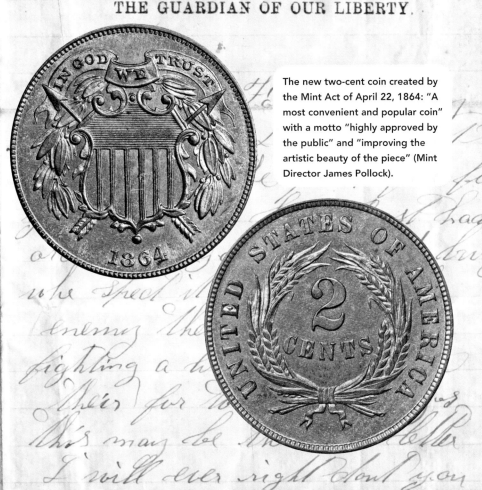

The new two-cent coin created by the Mint Act of April 22, 1864: "A most convenient and popular coin" with a motto "highly approved by the public" and "improving the artistic beauty of the piece" (Mint Director James Pollock).

The Mint Act of April 22, 1864

The new Mint act, passed despite influential businessman Joseph Wharton's opposition, was actually an amendment to the Mint Act of 1857. The 1864 legislation contained five sections. The first section called for the reduction in weight of the cent to 48 grains (1/10 troy ounce), with the composition to be 95 percent copper, 5 percent tin and zinc, the latter two elements in such proportions "as shall be determined by the director of the mint." Section 1 also called for the striking of a two-cent piece of the same composition as the cent, with a weight of 96 grains (double that of the cent). Furthermore, *the shape, mottoes, and devices of said coins shall be fixed by the director of the mint, with the approval of the Secretary of the Treasury. . . .*"

Section 2 stated that all laws then in force relating to U.S. coins would be extended to the newly authorized coinage. This included the penalties for debasement and counterfeiting.

Section 3 prescribed suitable regulations be established by the director of the Mint to ensure conformity to the required weights and composition. This included the usual trials by the assayer with reports to the director of the Mint.

Section 4 stated that the cents were legal tender in any payment up to the amount of 10¢, and the two-cent piece up to the amount of 20¢. It also called for expenses related to "exchange, distribution, and transmission" to be paid out of the profits of the coinage. "Net profits of said coinage shall be transferred to the treasury of the United States."

Section 5 stated "That if any person or persons shall make, issue, or pass, or cause to be made, issued, or passed, any coin, card, token, or device whatsoever, in metal or its compounds, intended to pass or be passed as money for a one-cent or a two-cent piece, such person or persons shall be deemed guilty of a misdemeanor, and shall on conviction thereof, be punished by a fine not exceeding one thousand dollars, and by imprisonment for a term not exceeding five years."[1]

IN GOD WE TRUST

The implications of the act were significant to our story for several reasons. First, the change in weight and composition of the cent brought the bronze cent into being. Its composition of 95 percent copper and 5 percent tin and zinc would prove highly satisfactory and would be the standard for 118 years (from 1864 until 1982) with the exception of the year 1943, when need for copper during World War II led to the use of zinc-coated steel for the coins. The new bronze composition did enable the Mint to increase production and reduce costs dramatically. Only well over a century later, in 1982, would the rising price of copper force a change to a copper-plated zinc cent.

The seigniorage profits to the Mint from the new bronze cents were even greater than Pollock had expected. In the fiscal year ending June 30, 1864, they were $146,000, and the following year they rose to $558,000.[2]

The introduction of the bronze two-cent piece also helped mitigate and ultimately end the small-change shortage. Related to the two-cent–piece authorization was the provision that the director of the Mint could "fix the shape, mottoes, and devices" of the coin with "the approval of the Secretary of the Treasury." This left the door open for Mint Director James Pollock to put a religious motto on U.S. coinage through the vehicle of the new two-cent piece. It is interesting that the wording of the act gave no hint as to what such a motto might be. There was certainly no reference to God, trust, or any religious allusion whatsoever in the act itself. We are left to wonder if the congressmen voting had any awareness of the implications of their votes and if there would have been objection, or more specific instructions on the coin's mottoes, if they had been more aware. Certainly the only debate on the bill had to do with the elimination of nickel. Of course President Lincoln signed the legislation. Was he aware of the intent of Treasury Secretary Salmon Chase and Mint Director Pollock to use the provision "to fix the shape, mottoes, and devices" to place a reference to God on the new coin?

Numismatic historian R.W. Julian, in his article "All About the Two Cents" in the December 2009 issue of *The Numismatist*, said that Chase consulted with Lincoln about the coinage changes. While there is no definitive account of their conversation, it seems unlikely Chase would have taken such a significant action without making Lincoln fully aware of the intent.

Lastly, section 5 of the act targeted the private Civil War tokens. A fine of up to $1,000 and imprisonment up to five years was included for even passing them, let alone producing them. This served as a deterrent at least to their production, though they continued to circulate for years after the war. Unlike the July 1862 legislation banning the tokens, which was largely ignored, this 1864 legislation was taken seriously. Notices warning against their production and use were published in many newspapers.[3] Further legislation in June of 1864 increased the maximum penalties related to their production to $3,000 and five years' imprisonment, demonstrating the government's seriousness in eliminating private competition to the Mint.[4]

In a few cases striking of the tokens continued, as it was too good a business to give up easily. But their production and circulation was carried on in a much more limited way. Some makers had already prepared 1864-dated dies, and a few tokens were issued before the legislation took effect. But in some cases the makers likely reverted to 1863-dated dies so as to avoid possible evidence of their breaking the new law.

A privately issued 1864- dated Civil War token.

Of the vast number of storecard tokens outstanding, many were redeemed over time by their issuing merchants, whether in merchandise or in exchange for regular federal cents. Mint-issued cents became plentiful by early 1865 both through large production numbers of bronze cents and through the older copper-nickel cents coming out of hiding as motivation for hoarding ended. The patriotic tokens were redeemed to a lesser degree as it was impossible to identify, or at least to prove, which merchant had issued them. The tokens continued to circulate well into the 1870s and beyond.[5]

An 1864 bronze Indian Head cent, produced by the Philadelphia Mint.

We can certainly suppose that the provision in the act for the use of bronze in the cents and the issuance of two-cent pieces was of the most immediate interest to Pollock, as he was eager to realize the efficiencies expected through use of the new metal. We might assume passage of the bill would have been communicated to him by Chase or others in the Treasury Department, or even by someone in Congress. However, this was not the case, as a letter dated May 2, 1864, from Pollock to Chase shows:

> The bill proceeding for the coinage of one and two cent pieces in bronze having become law *as I have learned through the newspapers*, I would respectfully ask that you will cause a certified copy to be sent to this institution.

So Pollock learned about the passage of the bill through the newspapers some ten days after the event and had to prompt Chase to provide a certified copy so that he might get on with the work of the conversion. He continued in his letter to Chase:

> In the meantime and to avoid delay, I would suggest as heretofore proposed in my earlier correspondence on this subject, that the present devices of the nickel cent be retained and used on the new cent, thus avoiding the expense of new dies, and that the devices of the two cent pieces be the shield as in the specimens already sent to you and now enclosed—*changing the motto "God Our Trust" to the legend "In God We Trust", if you prefer the latter*. With your approval of these suggestions we will be able in a few days to get the one cent bronze

cents in production and in about two weeks from this date the two cent coinage. As our stock of nickel will be exhausted in two or three days, may I ask your immediate attention to the subject matter of this communication. Your approval is respectfully requested.

Yours very respectfully,
James Pollock[6]

As had happened so often before, Chase did not respond to Pollock's letter despite Pollock's indicating urgency and requesting that Chase pay immediate attention to the subject matter. So, a week later, on May 9, Pollock again wrote to the Treasury secretary:

Philadelphia May 9, 1864

Hon. S. Chase
Secretary of Treasury

Sir:

Permit me respectfully, to ask your attention to my letter of the 2nd instant, in relation to the coinage of the one and two cent pieces in bronze. Our stock of nickel is exhausted and the coinage of the nickel cent must cease, so soon as the clippings and grains of the nickel alloy are connected into cents which will be in the course of two or three days. The demand for the one and two cent coins is great. We can only rectify this with the immediate commencement of the bronze coinage. A suspension of the operations in the cent coinage will involve a lot in labor and profit of about nine thousand dollars per day. Your approval of the proposition made in my former letter, or of some other under this law, will enable us to commence at once, the coinage of the one cent and two cent piece. We wait your action and approval. We are all ready with dies, machinery, and material. Hoping you will concur in the heretofore expressions.

I am yours very respectfully,
James Pollock[7]

The May 2 letter is highly significant in that it determines that the motto will be In God We Trust. Pollock is referring back to the letter of December 9, 1863, from Chase (as shown in chapter 8), in which Chase had written, "I approve your mottoes, only suggesting . . . that on the shield obverse it should be changed as to read 'In God We Trust'."

We have no copy of Chase's response, whatever it was, to the May 9 letter. He must have sent some communication authorizing Pollock's switch to bronze and beginning two-cent piece production under the new legislation, as Pollock did proceed with the changes. Whether or not such a communication further confirmed Chase's preference for In God We Trust, clearly Pollock proceeded on that assumption. Chief Engraver James Longacre therefore in early 1864 produced a new die for the Shield and Arrows obverse design virtually the same as the 1863 pattern version but changing the motto from God Our Trust to In God We Trust. It is the author's belief that the first patterns struck in 1864 with the new motto retained the reverse of the 1863 patterns—that is, with CENTS highly curved beneath the 2 and lacking the small ribbons under the wreath. This 1864 pattern with CENTS highly curved is referenced in the Judd pattern book as Judd-366. Numismatic researcher Kevin Flynn's reference on two-cent pieces reinforces the author's view. This pattern is quite rare, with the 10th edition of the Judd book estimating fewer than six specimens known.

Reverses of two 1864 patterns, with CENTS in different arcs. (Judd-367, top; and -371, the style adopted for regular coinage)

The 1863 patterns, Head of Washington and Arrows and Shield, both exist with the two reverse types (sharply curved and less curved). The sharply curved reverse version of both the Arrows and Shield pattern (Judd-312) and the Head of Washington pattern (Judd-305) were struck in relatively large numbers, as pattern coins go. Estimates are approximately 150 known of Judd-312 and 80 to 100 of Judd-305. The 1863 less-curved CENTS versions of both, Judd-315 and Judd-309, are far rarer, with estimates of only 5 or 6 known of the former and 2 or 3 of the latter in bronze, though perhaps 8 or 9 of the same design are known in coppernickel (Judd-310).

A Washington Head 1863 two-cent piece pattern, with less-curved CENTS. Was it made in 1864? (Judd-310)

1863-dated Arrows and Shield two-cent piece pattern bearing GOD OUR TRUST with less-curved CENTS. This may have been produced in 1864, as the less-curved CENTS reverse die might not have been made until early in that year. (Judd-315)

It is a question whether the less-curved reverse design was actually produced in 1863 or not until early 1864. Had the new less-curved reverse type dies been made yet? Were the existing specimens dated 1863 with the less-curved CENTS version restrikes? Were they not made until 1864 or later? In the letter of Pollock to Chase dated December 8, 1863, which referenced Pollock's enclosure of two-cent piece specimens, there is no reference to variations in the appearance of CENTS on the reverse. If only one variety was enclosed, which one was it? Given the great disparity in numbers of still-existing specimens, it seems fairly certain that it was the sharply curved variety. We might therefore speculate that the straight (less curved) cent reverses, though dated 1863, were struck in 1864. Further evidence of this is in a note dated November 1863, from Assistant Assayer Jacob Eckfeldt, regarding the striking of two-cent patterns:

> November, 1863, Struck 2 cent pieces – 2 varieties, one with "God and Our Country" Washington head. The other is "God Our Trust" with two spears and shield and palm wreath, with the same reverse as the Washington head with the wheat leaf wreath.

There is no reference to two reverse varieties being used at that time.[9]

The first bronze cents were struck on May 20, 1864, while two-cent piece production started about ten days later at the end of May. The motto on the 1864 two-cent pieces appeared in two varieties: a small-letter version and a large-letter version.

Without doubt the Small Motto variety was the first struck and is significantly rarer than the Large Motto type. The 1864 pattern, Judd-366, with sharply curved CENTS also has the small motto, indicating it was struck early in the sequence of events. The first delivery of the two-cent pieces at the end of May 1864 was for 25,000 coins.[10] It is clear that these were all of the Small Motto variety. They are prized by collectors of two-cent pieces. For whatever reason the size of the motto was increased on later strikes. Information on early deliveries of the new two-cent coins leads to the conclusion that the total mintage of the Small Motto variety was about 25,000.

The Mint moved quickly to increase production of cents as well as to initiate and ramp up production of the two-cent coins. More than 39 million of the bronze cents were struck in 1864—quite a high mintage, especially considering that production only began on May 20. Combined with the nearly 14 million copper-nickel cents made prior to May, total production was about 53 million one-cent coins, higher than the previous record year of 1863, when 49 million copper-nickel cents were made. More than 19 million two-cent pieces were struck, also impressive considering there were only seven months of production. Of course the new two-cent pieces bore the motto IN GOD WE TRUST, fulfilling Mint Director Pollock's longtime efforts to have such a religious motto on the coinage.

The Small Motto variety of the 1864 two-cent piece.

The Large Motto variety of 1864 and later two-cent pieces.

A Clandestine Pattern?

Another intriguing two-cent piece pattern from this era is the 1863-dated coin with IN GOD WE TRUST as the motto and with the less-curved CENTS on the reverse, appearing just like the regular-issue coins of 1864. It is quite rare, with perhaps a dozen examples known.

For many years this coin (designated Judd-316) was believed to be a true proto-type or "transitional," meaning that it was a bridge between the GOD OUR TRUST pieces and IN GOD WE TRUST regular issues of 1864 and later years. However, as the correspondence between Pollock and Chase cited above has come to light, it is clear that the motto IN GOD WE TRUST was not determined until early 1864 and that no dies with it would have been produced until then. Furthermore, the motto on Judd-316 is of the large-lettered variety. We know that it too did not exist until 1864. In addition, numismatic writer Walter Breen noted that the top serif on the D in UNITED STATES was missing on these patterns. This missing serif feature was not seen on regular-issue two-cent pieces until those dated 1866 and later. It is there-fore clear that these patterns, though dated 1863, were not made until 1866 or after. The reason for their being made was likely for sale outside official Mint channels to collectors of the time. They may have been made under clandestine circumstances, with the proceeds of any sale going to a Mint employee (or employees) who had access to the Mint's tooling and equipment. It would not have been an easy project, as no 1863-dated pattern obverse bore IN GOD WE TRUST. A new die would have been required. It would not have been as simple a task as just putting two old pattern dies together.

Judd-316, and
a close-up view
of the D in UNITED.

Pollock highlighted the change to bronze and the new religious motto in his annual *Mint Director's Report* for fiscal year ending June 30, 1864:

The substitution of the bronze alloy for the nickel mixture, as authorized by Congress, has been highly successful. The demand for the one and two cent pieces has been unprecedented, and every effort has been made to meet it. . . . The two cent piece is a most convenient and popular coin. Its size and its weight contribute to its usefulness. The motto "In God We Trust," stamped upon this coin, has been highly approved by the public, not only as improving the artistic beauty of the piece, but also as an expression of our nation's reliance upon the "God of Nations" in this hour of peril and danger. Why should this distinct and unequivocal recognition of God of Him who is "The King of kings, and Lord of lords" be confined to our bronze coinage? The silver and gold are His, and upon it should be impressed by national authority, the declaration of our nation's trust in Him, "who maketh war to cease unto the ends of the earth, who stilleth the raging of the sea, and the tumult of the people." Let our nation, in its coinage, honor Him, in Whom is our strength and salvation.

This certainly puts on full display Pollock's deep religious feelings and his enthusiasm for the motto. He states that it "has been highly approved by the public." He is pleased with the new motto, but he is not entirely satisfied and urges its placement not only on the bronze two-cent piece, but also beyond and to include the coins made of gold and silver.

A sampling of newspaper articles from the time provides some idea as to the actual public reactions to this new religious motto. Many of them were simply descriptive, perhaps positive toward the coin generally without being either positive or negative on the motto.

The *Reading Times* of Reading, Pennsylvania, ran an article on April 26, following passage of the legislation but before actual production had begun:

The New Two Cent Piece—We have seen a cut representing the new species of coin, which is destined to have immense circulation in the absence of silver and gold. The design of issuing such a coin at present is to avoid the immense expense attendant upon the coinage of the nickel cents, which at present monetary quotations, are worth more than their facial significance. The new two cent-piece is but a little larger and thicker than the present one cent coin, and contains less nickel, an abundance of copper, with five parts of tin. In size it may be compared to the silver quarter dollar, and resembles as much as anything can, a gold coin, and is really beautiful. On one side there is a wreath of wheat, in the centre of which is stamped "2 cents" and around which are the words "United States of America." On the other side there is the Shield of Liberty bearing the words "God our Trust." It is a very pretty coin and will no doubt receive the sanction of Congress.

The writer clearly described the coin and was positive about it but didn't specifically comment on the new motto, which he believed to be "God Our Trust."

The *Urbana Union* of Urbana, Ohio, in an article dated April 27, 1864 (taken from the Wheeling, West Virginia, *Wheeling Intelligencer*), also reacted favorably to the coin. They also believed the motto would be "God Our Trust" and referred to seeing a specimen of the new coin. We are led to believe, therefore, that they had seen a pattern coin (of 1863?) with "God Our Trust."

The New Two Cent Piece—We have seen a specimen of the new two cent piece which has been recommended for the sanction of Congress. It resembles as much as anything can a gold coin, and is really beautiful. On one side there is a wreath of wheat, in the centre of which is stamped '2 cents,' and around which are the words 'United States of America.' On the other side is the shield of liberty, bearing the words 'God our Trust.' It is a very pretty and very convenient coin, and we hope it will be adopted and generally circulated. – *Wheeling Intelligencer*

The *Pittsburgh Gazette* on May 10, 1864, ran a very straightforward description of the coin without expressing approval or disapproval. It noted the motto as being "In God is our Trust." Obviously confusion reigned as to what the new motto really was.

The Two-Cent Coin—This new coin, to be made of bronze, is in size about midway between a Spanish shilling and an American Quarter of a dollar. On one side is a shield resting against crossed arrows, with the motto, in a scroll above, "In God is our Trust"—underneath, "1864." On the other side a wreath of corn, &c., inclosing a large figure 2 above the word "cents," and around the margin "United States of America."

On May 12 the *Daily Empire* in Dayton, Ohio, commented positively on the coin, especially happy that it would be of bronze rather than paper, and believed it would help relieve the scarcity of coins. They said the motto was "God is our Trust."

The Two Cent Piece—The new two cent piece which has been recommended by Congress resembles very much in appearance a gold coin: On one side there is a wreath of wheat in the centre of which is stamped "2 cents" and around which are the words "United States of America." On the other side there is a shield of liberty, bearing the words "God is our Trust." It was feared that this new issue of money, like that which has been circulated for three years back, would be made of paper. It will be a refreshing sight to see a new issue of coin— an article of great scarcity now-a-days.

The *Alton Telegraph*, Alton, Illinois, described the coin and had the motto correct, as "In God We Trust." It was published rather late, January 27, 1865, well after the coin was in circulation. The writer made a perhaps cynical comment that it resembled a $5 gold piece, but that "in reality it approaches as near to that as a copperhead newspaper editor does to a loyal and patriotic citizen" (in other words, not the same.)

News about the coin spread to the Confederacy fairly quickly and the June 30, 1864, issue of the Wilmington, North Carolina, *Wilmington Journal* reported it.

The Yankees are getting out a new two cent coin—It is somewhat smaller than the old fashioned cent. On one side are two crossed arrows, over which is a shield with the date 1864, and the motto, "In God we trust." A wreath nearly surrounds the shield. On the adverse side is a wreath surrounding the inscription "Two Cents." Outside of the wreath are the word "United States of America."

Some articles were more explicitly approving of the motto itself.

The *Wheeling Daily Intelligencer* of April 26, 1864, noted that the motto would be "God Our Trust" and deemed it becoming to affix "such a simple expression of our abiding faith and reliance on, the Almighty Sovereign of the Universe." It also advocated that it be extended to all the coins, whether of gold or silver or bronze.

The New Two Cent Piece—The new two-cent piece will doubtless have an extensive circulation in the absence of gold and silver. . . . On the other side there is the Shield of Liberty, bearing the words "God our Trust." It will be observed that this is the first on of our national coins which recognizes the existence of God, in either legend or device. In this day of tribulation and suffering, it is becoming for us thus to affix on our money tokens a simple expression of our abiding faith in, and reliance on, the Almighty Sovereign of the Universe. And we hope that the design may be extended as to embrace all our coins, whether of gold or silver, or bronze.

A rather lengthy but creative story on the new coin, titled "A New Acquaintance," appeared in the Zanesville, Ohio, *Zanesville Daily Courier* on July 15, 1864, written by a Reverend John Todd. It also advocated that the motto "hereafter put thy text on all our coin."

A NEW ACQUAINTANCE
BY THE REV. JOHN TODD, D.D.

It would be a curious history could we tell when and how and where we first met this and that acquaintance and especially how very different he appeared, if we had heard of him before, from what we expected! How seldom is he as noble, or as handsome, as we thought he would be!

A few days since I was sitting in the store of a friend, engaged in conversation, when suddenly there leaped upon the counter a little bright-faced fellow whom I had never seen before. He came down with a ringing sort of laugh, and in his gladness actually bounded two or three leaps upon the counter.

Very politely my friend introduced me to him and I soon saw that he was deaf and dumb. But his face was so bright and fresh, that he could hardly think of his condition.

"This is Mr. Penny, sir, who has just arrived in town."

"Mr. Penny! Why have I seen many of that name. They are a modest, quiet family, and great favorites with children."

"How is that?"

"I suppose it is because they are so generous, and are often giving candies and apples, and such things to children. But this one seems different from any I have ever met before. Let me see. He has a kind of double face, and what is no less curious, he has words stamped on each! On one face, I see a beautiful shield, laid upon two arrows, and a vine hung over it, and the words In God we Trust, 1864. On the other side United States of America with a vine and arrows and in the center, *2 cents.*"

This then is Mr. "TwoPenny," a new friend—the last child of the Mint, the new coin of my country! How many hands will receive and pass this very penny! How many poor men and poor children will it feed! — How many patches will it put on the poor man's garment! I greet you, Mr. Twopenny, for the good you will do in this way! But, my good friend, if you can help it, don't help the drunkard to injure himself and family! But I hail you, good fellow, and welcome you above any coin I ever saw in my life! You are a little preacher! You are a catechism—a kind of walking Bible—to every man that will ever see you! *You are the first coin of my country that ever acknowledged God! You are a perpetual proclamation! You are a lithe cable to anchor a great nation to the throne of God!*

Oh, little coin! Thy text is very short, thy words are very few, but how many will read them! How many children in the future will read them, and learn that in "1864" our whole nation proclaimed to the world the great truth that "in God we trust." And that

short proclamation will do more to bring God's blessing upon us, than armies and navies. Go thy way, little preacher! Thou hast already cheered one heart, and created new hope. — Go thy way! and show thy bright face as often as thou canst. The poor widow and orphan child will gain strength from thee, and the lofty man will learn that there is one loftier than himself. Go thy way, Oh coin of my country, adding patriotism, adding to love of our own dear, dear country, and adding to our confidence that the God in whom "we trust" will never forsake us.

Oh, herald of better things! We shall hereafter put thy text on all our coin, for surely we shall not write "holiness to the Lord" on our copper, and not on our silver and gold! Surely we shall not want to say to the bright silver and the yellow gold, "Our confidence and trust are not in you, but in God we trust." And this, the voice of the nation, will teach the miser in his greed, and the politician in his schemes, and ruler in his power, that we hope only in the living God. And it may be found in the history of the world, as God shall write it, that this one little act of our Government has become a blessing unspeakably great to all future generations.

Not all reaction was positive. An article in the *Liberator*, located in Boston, carried a piece on June 24, 1864, entitled "Liberty." While it did not specifically criticize "In God We Trust," it bemoaned the loss of the word "Liberty" on some U.S. coins and its absence from the new two-cent piece. The *Liberator* was the strong abolitionist publication by William Lloyd Garrison.

"LIBERTY."

A few of the two-cent pieces just coined are in circulation in this city. The new coin is a handsome one, a little less in size than the gold eagle, and probably composed of the same materials as the small cents. It bears on one side a shield, encircled with an olive

wreath, and two crossed arrows behind it. Below the shield is the date, "1864," and above it is a scroll bearing the motto, "In God we trust." The other side bears the domination of the coin, "2 cents," surrounded by a wreath of wheat, which again is surrounded by the inscription, "United States of America."

Our old cents used to bear the beautiful word "Liberty" upon them. When the first small cent was coined (under the Presidency of Franklin Pierce, I believe), that word was omitted from the coin, and eagle being sub- stituted for the head that bore it. Afterwards the eagle gave place to the head of an Indian queen, and the word "Liberty" was restored, though so small as to be nearly illegible. Now, under the Presidency of Abraham Lincoln, that significant word is again omit- ted. – C.K.W.

Another article had a political tinge to it. The *Times-Democrat* in New Orleans, Louisiana, wrote on October 21, 1864 (shortly before the November election), that "Mr. Secretary Chase, in getting up his new brass two cent piece . . . has exchanged our favorite old motto, 'E Pluribus Unum' for a quotation from scripture." It also criticized the efforts by Senator Gratz Brown to amend the U.S. Constitution "in order to incorporate what he considers a reasonable quantity of godliness and spir- ituality." These comments preceded the paper's criticism of Abraham Lincoln and its advocacy of George McClellan for president. Of course McClellan, the failed Union general, was the Democratic candidate opposing Lincoln's reelection. New Orleans, though a Southern city, had been in Union hands since early in the war. Evidently the Union occupation forces were not censoring the local papers.

Not least among the reasonable fears of the probable future we may reckon that if we lose our admirable constitution and form of Gov- ernment, our religious liberty will be in dan- ger. Already we discover in certain prominent abolitionists, indications that something of the sort is covertly intended. As for example, Senator Gratz Brown wants to knead over the United States Constitution, in order to incorporate therein what he considers a rea- sonable quantity of godliness and spirituality; and Mr. Secretary Chase, in getting up his new brass two cent piece, of ninety-six grains weight, appreciating the signs of the time, has changed our favorite old motto, "E Pluri- bus Unum," for a quotation from scripture.

We, the American people, are in a peril- ous condition. Our liberties are endangered and our most cherished rights and immuni- ties are put in jeopardy. I am afraid Abra- ham Lincoln is not the man to help us out. He stands now fully committed to the aboli- tion policy, and is so much under the influ- ence of his office holders, civil and military, of radical factions, of army contractors and secret Union leagues, that it is not probable he can speedily end this war. The declared policy of George B. McClellan, the other Presidential candidate, harmonizing with the Constitution of the United States, is such as to deserve the approval of every American citizen who desires the Union to be preserved; and should he be elected, I will venture to predict that peace and Union will be substantially restored to the land, within the first year of his administration.

A notable individual reaction to the new motto was that of Mark Twain. He said, "It is not proper to boast that America is a Christian country when we all know that five-sixths of our population could not enter in at the narrow gate." He

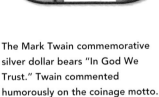

The Mark Twain commemorative silver dollar bears "In God We Trust." Twain commented humorously on the coinage motto.

proposed using the phrase "The god we trust in" and perhaps "Within certain judicious limitations we trust in God." When it was suggested the coin might not be big enough to fit his words on, he said, "Why, enlarge the coin!" It is ironic that the Twain silver commemorative dollar issued by the Mint in 2016 bears "In God We Trust" right in front of his face above the pipe he is smoking. Put that in your pipe and smoke it, Mr. Twain![12]

Whether or not James Pollock was right in his assessment that the motto was "highly approved by the public," there is no evidence of mass opposition to it. And certainly there was some vocal support for it. His efforts therefore to place the motto on the other coins (the silver and the gold as well as the bronze) proceeded without noticeable opposition.

From a purely aesthetic viewpoint the two-cent piece is a beautiful coin symbolic of the time in which it was designed and produced. Art historian Cornelius Vermeule, who was a collector of both great art and of coins, commented on the two-cent piece in his classic work *Numismatic Art in America: Aesthetics of the United State Coinage*:

The coin that is most Gothic and most expressive of the Civil War is the two-cent piece, especially the pattern of 1863 with GOD OUR TRUST as opposed to the regular issue of 1864. The shield, arrows, and wreath of the obverse need only flanking cannon to be the consummate expression of Civil War heraldry. On the reverse, the manner in which the CENTS curves against the tondo of wreath and legend recalls monumental lettering, like inscriptions on tombstones in the second half of the nineteenth century. The wreath meets in a form of Gothic arch above the denomination. The same combination of shield in this shape, curve and counter curve of lettering, and pointed arch is found in the standard tombstones provided by the United State for burial of the fallen and veterans of the war between the stares in local cemeteries through the North.[13]

The legislation in 1865 which approved the new three-cent piece composed of nickel provided the opportunity for Pollock to insert a provision allowing "In God We Trust" on whatever coins "as shall admit of such legend thereon." This provision was Section 5 of the March 3, 1865, Act to Authorize Coinage of Three-Cent-Pieces, and For Other Purposes.

> And it shall be further enacted That, in addition to the devices and legends upon the gold, silver, and other coins of the United States, it shall be lawful for the director of the mint, with the approval of the Secretary of Treasury, to cause the motto "In God We Trust" to be placed on coins hereafter to be issued as shall admit of such legend thereon.

This act and its passage will be covered in more detail in a later chapter.

Of course, by the time this legislation was passed, Chase was gone from the Treasury post, and it was filled by William Fessenden. We must assume that Fessenden supported Pollock's efforts to expand the motto to the other coins or at least that he had no objection to it.

From a letter written by Director Pollock to Congressman John A. Kasson we know that Pollock was communicating directly with Congress for the facilitation of passage of the legislation. The letter was dated February 6, 1865, just 28 days before Congress voted on the legislation for the motto on all of the larger coins.

> I enclosed as suggested a draft of a bill authorizing the introduction of the Motto "in God We Trust" upon the gold and silver coins of the United States.[14]

The legislation was passed on the very day that Fessenden left office as Treasury secretary. He had not wanted the office but had taken it at Lincoln's behest the previous July. As soon as he felt he could, he left the office and returned to the Senate. He was succeeded by Hugh McCulloch, the Indiana banker who had been serving as Comptroller of the Currency for the new national bank system. This legislation would have been one of the last acts to be signed by President Lincoln, as he was assassinated the following month.

In his annual Mint director's report for fiscal year ending June 30, 1865, Pollock highlighted the passage of the bill and the motto's placement on gold and silver coins:

> By the 5th Section of the Act of Congress of March 3, 1865, already referred to, the Director of the Mint, with the approval of the Secretary of Treasury, was authorized to place upon all the gold and silver coins of the United States, susceptible of such addition, thereafter to be issued, the motto, "In God We Trust." The direction was at once given to prepare the necessary dies, and it is confidently expected that before the close of the calendar year, the gold and silver coins of the Mint of the United States will have impressed upon them by national authority, the distinct and unequivocal recognition of the Sovereignty of God, and our Nation's trust in Him. We have added to our Nation's honor by honoring Him who is "King of kings and Lord of lords."

Pollock was once again displaying his enthusiasm for the motto and celebrating his success in getting it on the gold and silver coinage. The work on the new motto dies evidently took longer than Pollock expected and, though there are 1865-dated patterns with "In God We Trust," the motto did not appear on regular coinage until 1866.

A medal issued by the Pennsylvania Association of Numismatists (PAN) commemorating the 150th anniversary of the passage of the Mint Act of April 22, 1864, which enabled the placement of "In God We Trust" on the two-cent piece. The medal portrays Reverend Mark Watkinson, Treasury Secretary Salmon Chase, and Mint Director James Pollock, the three primary actors in the origins of "In God We Trust."

179

TO MY COUNTRYMEN.

Huntingdon County is moving too slowly, and being persuaded in my own heart that I am actuated by an eye single to God's glory, and my country's welfare, and encouraged by several incidents coming under my notice to believe, that it is "God who worketh in me to will and to do of his good pleasure," I therefore thus publicly intrude myself upon your notice.

Who controls the issues of battles? I answer—GOD.

Does success depend upon the numbers engaged? I answer—Not when God is with us. (Gideon with the sword of the Lord on his side, with 300 men, put 135,000 Midianites to flight.

What will make a man invincible in battle? Answer—A righteous cause with the assurance of God's inspiring presence.

Will God dwell in camps where drunkenness, profanity and vice are permitted? I answer—No. He is pure and hates sin, and punishes it, and our cause will not meet with *permanent* success until our armies are purged of all that is morally offensive to God. (The invincible Joshua was defeated once in as holy a cause as ours, because sin was found in his camps; he put it away and led his men to victory.)

To what cause shall we attribute the Bull Run panic and slaughter and other reverses? I answer—By reason of vice and immorality in our army, God assuredly was not with us to direct in counsel, or to strengthen our hearts in the shock of battle, and we were taught what a cowardly, terror-stricken thing man is if left to his own strength.

I firmly believe, therefore, that the best and only way to put down this unholy rebellion, is to humble ourselves in the sight of the Lord, and to so deport us that He will dwell with us, guide our counsels, go out before us, and strengthen our hearts in the shock of battle. I therefore propose to you, my countrymen, to raise a company of which I will be one, every man of which shall take his BIBLE with his musket, (he that has none shall be supplied.) The Captain shall, every morning and evening, (when not absolutely impossible,) assemble his men in order and read with them by alternate verse the Holy Scriptures, and then in prayer beseech the care and protection of Almighty God, just as every Christian household is in the habit of doing, or should do. So far from being influenced by a desire for high position in the company thus raised, I shall esteem it an honor to *drum* such a company on to victory.

All men who who will not subscribe to these terms, who will not put their trust in Almighty God, had better stay at home, for their hearts will fail them in the hour of battle, and they will only encumber the God-sustained.

"A little leaven leaveneth the whole lump" and who knows but that our example would spread through the whole army and God would work a great moral victory for us upon the consciences of the rebels.

COME ON MEN, COME ON, even if it is decreed in the wisdom of Almighty God, that our blood shall fertilize southern soil, this brief life is not worth purchasing at the price of the overthrow and destruction of our government, framed in infinite wisdom and the best ever handed down to man, the righteous inheritance from our fathers, inaugurating instead thereof, lawlessness, anarchy, and such principles as are rife in Hell. No. We must die sometime and we cannot die a nobler death, or one more acceptable to God, than while battling for our country in a righteous cause. I say again, come on, we will have in each other comrades who will be brothers in the highest, noblest sense, in peril, in pain, in death; the dying will be borne upon the prayers of the survivors to the Mercy Seat.

All who will unite with us in this spirit, will report themselves at once to the undersigned, and have their names enrolled.

WM. W. WALLACE.

Huntingdon, Pa., July 30, 1862.

OUR BATTLE CRY--
IN GOD IS OUR STRENGTH!

A recruiting poster for Company C of the 125th Pennsylvania volunteer infantry regiment. Was there a connection between Company C and "In God We Trust" on U.S. coinage?

CHAPTER 12

Why the Words "In God We Trust"?

In earlier chapters we learned that the operative coinage motto from late 1861 had been "God Our Trust." These words had been used on the pattern half dollars and pattern $10 eagles of 1861, 1862, and 1863, as well as on the first two-cent patterns of 1863. "God and Our Country" had also appeared in 1863 on other two-cent piece patterns with a head of George Washington on the obverse, probably done by Chief Engraver James B. Longacre. Also Treasury Secretary Salmon Chase had suggested in his December 9, 1863, letter "God Is Our Shield," but it had been considered by Mint Director James Pollock as not fitting with the rules of heraldry because such a motto referenced the shield design on the coin. It therefore never appeared on any patterns. "God Our Trust" was the motto that persisted through the three years that the idea was promoted. We cannot be certain who came up with this motto, but it was likely either Longacre, the Mint's chief engraver, or Pollock, the Mint's director, in November of 1861, and it was explicit from correspondence that they had derived it from a phrase in "The Star Spangled Banner."

The letter of December 9, 1863, from Chase to Pollock, however, changed all of this, as Chase brought up "In God We Trust." Pollock's comments in a return letter to Chase on December 15 were that both "In God We Trust" and "God Our Trust" were "equally appropriate and equally expressive." He said that he still preferred "God Our Trust" because of "its brevity and compact expressiveness." Pollock did not argue the point, however, saying "these questions can be determined when the coinage is authorized." The legislation itself did not specify a motto or even require one, but it had in effect allowed a motto, stating that "the shape, mottoes, and devices of said coins shall be fixed by the director of the mint with the approval of the Secretary of the Treasury."

In his letter to Chase dated May 2, 1864, requesting official confirmation of the passage by Congress of the legislation authorizing the two-cent piece, Pollock enclosed more of the same two-cent patterns that he had already provided Chase in December of the previous year. He probably didn't include the Washington Head design but only the Shield and Arrows patterns, as he recommended that design as preferable: "the shield as in the specimens already sent to you and now enclosed, changing the motto 'GOD OUR TRUST' to the legend 'IN GOD WE TRUST' *if you prefer the latter.*" Likely Pollock wanted to refresh Chase's memory regarding the patterns sent him earlier, and their previous motto discussions. He therefore enclosed examples to illustrate what he was talking about. It is also interesting that in this letter Pollock did not argue anymore for "God Our Trust," despite his earlier expression of preference for it. Perhaps, in the four or five months intervening since their last known correspondence on the issue, Pollock had come to like Chase's suggestion, or perhaps he didn't want to risk delay of the whole project by contesting the wording of the motto.

So while Pollock had driven the efforts for the motto, in the end Chase is the one who came up with "In God We Trust," with Pollock quietly acquiescing to it. But where did Chase get those words that are now so familiar and iconic to us? There are theories and stories explaining it that are worth exploring.

Brown University

The most commonly and widely disseminated explanation was originated by the famous numismatic writer Walter Breen. In his monumental *Complete Encyclopedia of U.S. and Colonial Coins*, published in 1988, he covered the authorization of the motto and the role of Reverend Mark Watkinson's 1861 letter to Chase. Breen stated that Watkinson's letter:

> directly led to Chase's choice of the wording IN GOD WE TRUST rather than its various proposed alternatives (GOD AND OUR COUNTRY, GOD IS OUR SHIELD, GOD OUR TRUST). Chase was doubtless influenced by the wording of the motto of his alma mater (Brown University in Providence, Rhode Island) which was IN DEO SPERAMUS, 'In God We Hope'; this in turn derived from the motto of colonial Rhode Island.[1]

Breen's explanation of the origin of this motto in Chase's mind as being derived from that of his alma mater, Brown University, has been widely accepted and repeated endlessly in secondary sources, auction catalogs, etc. It is true that Brown's motto is "In Deo Speramus." However, Chase did not attend Brown University, nor to anyone's knowledge did he ever have any connection with that school. As noted in chapter 3, Chase attended and graduated from Dartmouth College. Dartmouth's motto is "Vox Clamatis in Deserto" ("A voice crying out in the wilderness"), quoted from a verse in the Book of Isaiah and certainly having nothing to do with "In God We Trust." Chase definitely felt a connection with Dartmouth, as he left $10,000 to the school in his will.[2] It is hard to know if Breen simply was misinformed about Chase's real alma mater or if he made the story up to provide a more interesting narrative for his book. In any case it is not the factual explanation.

The seal of Brown University.

William Sprague and Kate Chase

A possible explanation for Chase's putting forward "In God We Trust" relates indirectly to Breen's story, for Brown University is located in the state of Rhode Island, and there was a connection between the Chase family and that state, formed beginning with a celebration in Cleveland, Ohio, in September of 1860. The celebration was held to commemorate the Battle of Lake Erie, the victory of Commodore Oliver Hazard Perry over the British fleet during the War of 1812. The battle was critical in securing the Great Lakes region and large territories for the United States. Chase, governor of Ohio at the time of the celebration, and his daughter, Kate, attended the event. Also attending was the soon to be elected governor of Rhode Island, William Sprague. As Rhode Island was Commodore Perry's native state, Sprague was there as the head of a military contingent providing official representation.

Governor Chase's daughter Kate was beautiful and cultured. Her father had lavished his attention on her and her younger half-sister, Nettie, his only surviving children. As a three-time widower, Chase likely regretted that the lack of a mother for them in the home might put them at a disadvantage. He worked to compensate by making sure they were well cared for, religiously observant, and well educated. He sent Kate to Miss Haines' School, an elite private boarding school in New York. Chase may have been influenced to send her there by Catherine Beecher, sister of Harriet Beecher Stowe. Chase had known Catherine and the Beecher family well in Cincinnati, and Catherine had advocated for young women

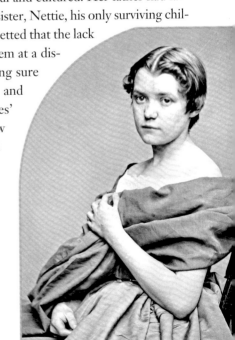

Katherine "Kate" Chase met her future husband, William Sprague, shortly before the Civil War began, when her father was governor of Ohio.

to be sent to such boarding schools to "not only learn home economics but to receive instruction in the natural sciences and language arts so they might develop a parlor based culture that would spread their influence over the entire nation."[3] Kate's four years there certainly contributed to making her into a cultured and charming young woman capable of engaging in conversation on nearly any topic. Following her education under Miss Haines, Kate returned to Columbus, Ohio, where she served as hostess for her father during his time as governor.

So fate led to Sprague and Kate Chase meeting at a ball held the evening following the Perry / Lake Erie ceremony. William Sprague was heir to a family fortune dating back four generations based on ownership of textile mills and related industries in Rhode Island. The family was among the wealthiest in the nation. Moreover, Sprague must have been impressive in his uniform. According to Richard Parsons, the Cleveland attorney who introduced them to each other, Kate and William were "quite taken with each other and spent most of the evening together."[4]

They were to meet again a few months later in Washington following Abraham Lincoln's election, as Kate's father took office as secretary of the Treasury, and as critical events early in the Civil War brought Sprague to the city. Even prior to the actual start of war there was concern that Southern forces would take control of Washington before any effective defense could be organized. Sprague at age 30 was elected governor of Rhode Island in November of 1860, bringing him notoriety as the "Boy Governor." While events unfolded and tension with the South increased, Sprague saw fit to raise a Rhode Island militia regiment and equip it with his own funds. He wrote Lincoln the day before Fort Sumter was fired upon:

> We have a Battery of Light Artillery with Horses and Men complete and a force of 1000 men completely disciplined and equipped, unparalleled or at any rate not surpassed by a similar number in any country, who would respond at short notice to the call of the government in defense of the capitol. . . . I would be ready to accompany them. Would God grant his protecting care and guidance to you Sir in your trying and difficult position and a safe deliverance from our unhappy difficulties is the constant prayer of
>
> *Your obedient servant,*
> *William Sprague*[5]

Immediately after Sumter, Sprague telegraphed the president: "Will you accept the First Rhode Island Regiment?" Lincoln responded simply, "Yes, send them quickly." And so it was that Sprague arrived at the head of his troops on April 18 of 1861. His regiment was one of the very first to arrive in the capital, receiving much attention and a great many accolades. On May 1 his regiment was sworn in on the front lawn of the White House with Lincoln himself witnessing the exercise.[6] Even old General Winfield Scott took note that Sprague left his troops to pay his respects

The dashing William Sprague, Rhode Island's "Boy Governor,"
won the heart of the Treasury secretary's daughter.

at the Chase carriage, where Kate was watching the review. She was frequently seen at the Rhode Islanders' headquarters tent appearing to act in the role of hostess.[7]

In the meantime Kate was carving out a prominent role for herself in Washington society to such an extent that First Lady Mary Todd Lincoln viewed her as a rival, leading to Mary's rather open dislike for her. Kate and William quickly became reacquainted and a courtship developed over the ensuing months. There were ups and downs in the relationship and extended periods when Sprague was away in Rhode Island conducting state business, or, perhaps more often, his companies' business. Kate was very much caught up in the social whirl of wartime Washington. She was clearly one of the leading belles, perhaps *the* leading belle, of the time, and her company was sought by many prominent men. Among those she spent time with was James Garfield, a friend of the Chases' from Ohio. Garfield was invited to stay with the Chases while he was awaiting his next military assignment. He was a very impressive young man of 30 years who would later rise to the rank of major general and, in 1880, be elected president—and then, tragically, be assassinated in September of 1881. Garfield was treated almost as a son by Salmon Chase, and Kate also was clearly enamored of him. He stayed with the Chases for some six weeks in the fall of 1862. Garfield and Kate took long rides in Rock Creek Park and attended many balls and other functions together. It was clear that he was smitten with her, and all said they made a great couple. The problem with this was that James Garfield was already married, with his wife remaining in Ohio.[8] Garfield eventually moved out of the Chases' home, and Sprague returned to Washington in early 1863 on a more permanent basis as senator from Rhode Island.

Mary Lincoln, after the death of her son Willie in early 1862, was in mourning and, while still officially head of Washington society, she was far less active than before. Furthermore Secretary of State William Seward's wife, who normally would have been the First Lady of the Cabinet, was a semi-invalid and stayed most of the time at their home in Auburn, New York, seldom even visiting Washington.[9] Kate Chase, due both to the circumstances and to her beauty and wit, became the sovereign queen of that society during this period. Visiting the Army camps around Washington and attending the many military reviews was much in vogue, and Kate was frequently seen engaging in these activities accompanied by high-level officers.[10]

James Garfield and Kate Chase took an interest in each other—despite his already being married.

In March of 1863, as noted, Sprague resigned as governor and became a U.S. senator from Rhode Island. This of course brought him to stay in Washington for longer stretches of time and enabled him to again spend time with Kate and more actively pursue her hand. It seems their relationship had cooled, due likely in part to the stories surrounding her and James Garfield. But his presence back in Washington revived the attraction between them. According to Peg Lamphier, author of *Kate Chase and William Sprague: Politics and Gender in a Civil War Marriage*, the correspondence and courtship ritual that Kate and William engaged in was typical of the period and much more based on concepts of romantic love and its open expression than in the eighteenth century and earlier in the nineteenth century, when such ideas were deemed of dubious value. This Lamphier attributes to "various cultural factors, chief among them the heightened value and expression of emotions in America's First and Second Great Awakenings."[11] So we can see the impact of the Great Awakenings not only in religious expression but also in courting and romance!

In any case their courtship renewed and progressed. By late May of 1863 the couple became engaged. On the evening of Thursday, November 12, 1863, their wedding was held at Chase's residence at 6th and E streets in Washington. It was the social event of the Civil War era, combining the wealth of Senator Sprague with the political influence of Secretary Chase, and highlighted by the beauty and style of Kate. No expense was spared. Arrangements consumed most of the summer and autumn as Kate made numerous trips to New York on extensive shopping sprees beginning shortly after their engagement. Beyond New York, dresses were ordered from Paris from noted European designers. Cases of wine, champagne, brandy, and other libations were ordered. The finest foods were laid in for the event. The United States Marine Band was engaged to provide music. The "Kate Chase Wedding March" was composed especially for the occasion by Frederick Kroell, a noted

Kate Chase in camp visiting General John Joseph Abercrombie and staff outside Washington in 1862. Visiting the camps was part of the social scene early in the war.

composer of the time. The groom's gifts to the bride were highlighted by an ornate tiara made by Tiffany & Co. from pearls and diamonds, along with many other matching pieces of jewelry. The *New York Herald*, alluding to the well-known ambition of Kate for her father's presidential aspirations, wrote a cynical piece suggesting that Mary Lincoln, "with her usual good nature," might permit Miss Chase to hold her wedding reception in the East Room "in order that in view of a certain possible event [i.e., Chase becoming president] she may have an opportunity of judging how its associations suit her."[12] President Lincoln certainly was aware of Chase's ambitions and once commented that it was like a worm eating at Chase's brain.[13]

There were 50 invitees to the ceremony held at Chase's home and 500 to the reception immediately following. The attendees were the elite of the nation.[14] Nearly all of the Cabinet attended, with the notable exception of Montgomery Blair, the postmaster general, with whom Chase had clashed on the issue of Postal Currency earlier in the administration. President Lincoln attended, though unaccompanied by Mrs. Lincoln, who begged off with the excuse that she was still in mourning for Willie. It was reported that, when the ceremony ended, "the President bent over from his great height and kissed the bride awkwardly on the cheek."[15] We do not know the total cost of the event, but Chase indicated in correspondence to a friend that on the day of the wedding his bank account was overdrawn $156.98![16]

Perhaps telling of James Garfield's strong feelings for Kate, though he was in Washington at the time of the wedding and was repeatedly invited to attend by Kate's father, he did not do so. This was despite the fact that virtually everyone of note in the capital was desperately seeking an invitation.

Cynics would say that the match between Sprague and Kate Chase was opportunistic. William was attracted to Kate for political advantages and Kate to him for mercenary reasons. A mutual acquaintance, Henry Villard, later wrote in his memoirs that "Sprague had very limited mental capacity but had reached political distinction at an early age through the influence of real or reputed great wealth. . . . She was superior to him in every way and married him for the enjoyment and power of his money."[17] Still, in their correspondence certainly affections were expressed, and we have to believe there was a strong degree of attraction between them. There were, however, warning signs as William was a heavy smoker and drinker, vices that her beloved father abstained from. It is clearly true that Sprague did not have the intellectual depth of Kate herself or of her father. These issues eventually played out in disastrous ways, as we shall later see.

The relevance of this relationship between the Chases and Sprague to our story and to "In God We Trust" lies in the fact that during the course of this courtship and after the wedding, Salmon Chase and Sprague spent a great deal of time with one another. Sprague was a constant dinner guest at the Chase home, and after the nuptials he bought the house that Chase had been renting and remodeled it such that Chase and the newlywed couple could live under the same roof. This was the exact time period (late 1863) that Mint Director James Pollock and Treasury Secretary Chase were corresponding about the issue of bronze cents, two-cent pieces, and a religious motto. And it is exactly the time Chase first raised the words "In God We Trust." Is it not conceivable that in the course of their dinner conversations Chase brought up the issue, and that the son-in-law mentioned that the motto of Brown University in Rhode Island was "In Deo Speramus"? And, jumping back to Walter Breen's idea, was it not an easy transition in the translation from something like "In God We Hope" to "In God We Trust"? We have no documentary evidence of any such conversation or connection, but the timing is intriguing and suggestive.

Brown University, in a document on the history of its seal and motto published in 1993 by its Office of University Communications, refers to the story that its motto "In Deo Speramus" inspired "In God We Trust" on the coinage, as Chase may have become familiar with it through the connection of the marriage of his daughter to Sprague. The university does not have any concrete evidence of this and deems this story and others connected with the motto "apocryphal."[18]

Chase did visit Rhode Island with his daughter following the engagement, for the purpose of meeting Sprague's family, but we have no direct evidence of his visiting Brown. Any connection made with Brown's motto may indeed be far-fetched.

The Huntingdon Bible Company

Yet another theory as to how Chase arrived at "In God We Trust" relates to Company C of the 125th Pennsylvania volunteer infantry regiment from Huntingdon, Pennsylvania. A tale connecting this regiment to the "In God We Trust" story appeared in the Huntingdon *Daily News* on November 2, 1963. It was written by Jeanne Singer, a writer for the newspaper, and based on the discovery by Katherine Bard, a local librarian, of an account of the origin of the motto in a chapter contained in the regimental history of the 125th published in 1906. The regimental history is a mixture of general history, official records, rosters listing the members of the unit, pictures of many of them, and accounts of the regiment's reunions at Antietam in 1888 and 1904. A monument to the regiment was erected in 1904 and dedicated on the Antietam battle-

William Sprague and Kate Chase Sprague
soon after their marriage.

field at their reunion that year. Most important to our story is that the history included reminiscences of several of the more notable members of the regiment.

One of the reminiscences in the history was written by William W. Wallace, who, besides being the captain of the 125th's Company C, had also been its recruiter and organizer. Wallace was from Huntingdon, Pennsylvania, and he worked for his family business, which operated a coal mine in the area. He had raised Company C in July and August of 1862, mostly with men from Blair and Huntingdon counties in central Pennsylvania. He was a devout Presbyterian and felt that clean living and religious observance would be essential for the success of the unit and of the Union army in general. Wallace, in his chapter of the 1906 regimental history, quoted the recruiting appeal he issued to the community as follows:

TO MY COUNTRYMEN

Huntingdon County is moving too slow, and being persuaded that I am actu-ated by an eye single to God's glory, and my country's welfare, I am led thus publicly to ask:

Who controls the issues of battles?

To what cause shall we attribute the Bull Run panic and slaughter and other reverses?

(God assuredly was not with us to direct in council or to strengthen our hearts.)

In responding to OUR COUNTRY'S CALL for more men, let us humble ourselves in the sight of the Lord, and to deport us that he will dwell with us, guide our counsel, go out before us, and strengthen our hearts in the shock of battle. I therefore propose to you, my countrymen, to raise a company, every man of which shall take his BIBLE with his musket, and go out in His fear.

All who will unite with us in this spirit, will report themselves at once to the undersigned, and have their names enrolled.

Wm. W. Wallace
Huntingdon, Pa., July 30, 1862

Wallace recorded that 170 men were raised, 100 of whom were placed in Com-pany C of the 125th Pennsylvania Volunteer Regiment, for nine months' service. He said "Mine was the color company (bearing the flag), and was also known as the Bible Company because every member of it had been presented with a pocket Bible by the good people of Huntingdon, in consequence of a suggestion made in my public circular, that we should carry our Bibles in camp with our muskets."[19]

Another of the reminiscences was written by Theodore H. Flood. He had been recruited by Wallace and over the course of his service rose in rank from sergeant to second lieutenant. Following the war he became a Methodist minister. Flood, in his chapter of the 1906 regimental history, provided his version of Company C's organization:

Captain Wallace invited the writer into his office, where he talked about the war and the duty of young men to stand up for the Government by responding to the call of the President, and as the only direct way to do this was by enlisting in the army, Captain Wallace suggested that we open books and recruit as many men as possible in one or more companies, and his characteristic way also suggested that we ought to do it in the name of God and religion. So he proposed that we organize the Huntingdon County Bible Company, every man to take his Bible with his musket, and that when we enter the service we have company prayers in the morning after roll-call, *and that the company ought to have a motto, which was selected then and there—"In God We Trust."* This motto was afterwards placed on the coin of the United States at the Mint in Philadelphia, and remains there to this day.[20]

In September 1862, only a few weeks after the company was organized, it was thrown into the Battle of Antietam. Flood related the action of the regiment:

> . . . we went into that awful conflict early on the morning of Wednesday, the seventeenth day of September. While waiting in line of battle for orders to advance and fire, Adjutant Johnston, of our regiment, was mortally wounded and died in a few hours. The battle was on in full force. Confederate pickets were shooting down our officers, shells were flying over our heads, horses and men lay dead on the field. We were ordered forward in line of battle, and *Captain Wallace stepped out in front of the company, waving his sword and called out "Boys remember our battle cry, 'In God We Trust.'"* This was taken up as a battle cry by adjoining companies along the line, until we reached the edge of a woods, where we were halted and ordered to fire. The enemy met us with a heavy charge.[21]

The attack Flood described was across the famous cornfield at Antietam, toward the woods behind the Dunker Church. The regiment moved into the woods but were suddenly met with a counterattack by forces under the command of Stonewall Jackson. The 125th initially held its ground but additional Confederate troops came in and hit the regiment simultaneously in front and on its flank. The regiment broke and was driven back across and beyond the cornfield, with very heavy losses. Colonel Jacob C. Higgins, in command of the regiment, later reported, "Had I remained in my position two minutes longer I would have lost my whole command."[22]

Flood's account stated that in this action the regiment lost 229 men killed and seriously wounded, with another 84 wounded to a lesser degree.

Flood's 1906 recounting of Wallace stepping in front of Company C, shouting "In God We Trust," with the cry being taken up along the lines, was noted by a local librarian and picked up in the 1963 Huntingdon newspaper account.

The following year further attention was brought to the story by an article in the April 1964 issue of *Civil War Times*. The article, "The Huntingdon Bible

Company," was written by Edward M. Greene on the 100th anniversary of the placement of "In God We Trust" on the two-cent piece. It was largely based on the Flood chapter in the regimental history. Greene may have realized the story needed more corroboration and he included a note in the article asking any readers who "might have any information bearing on the question of whether the Huntingdon Bible Company's motto inspired that on U.S. coins are invited to write" to him at his home in Greenwich, Connecticut.

Then in the early 2000s a history writer named Richard E. Gardiner followed up these writings with a 23-page Internet article addressing the subject. It is titled "The Ultimate Originations of the Phrases 'In God We Trust' and 'Under God.'" The article was published at www.pennswoods.net, but it has long since been removed from the Internet site. The piece began by recounting the story of Reverend Watkinson's letter to Chase, and Pollock's proposed "God Our Trust," "God and Our Country," etc., as well as Chase's December 9, 1863, letter calling for the motto to be "In God We Trust." Then Gardiner proceeded to discuss Flood's account of the action of the 125th Pennsylvania at Antietam and how during a tour of the battlefield a few days after the battle President Lincoln may have heard the story of Company C from General George McClellan. Lincoln then may have conveyed that story during a Cabinet meeting that, of course, Chase would have attended. Gardiner admitted that there is no record of these conversations, but he also showed linkages between members of the regiment and the governor of Pennsylvania, Andrew Gregg Curtin. Curtin had two cousins, Thomas and Henry Gregg, who were members of the 125th Regiment and who were from Huntingdon. Some ten days after Antietam, Curtin visited the White House and met with Abraham Lincoln. Presumably Curtin might have heard the story of Company C from his cousins and conveyed it to the president. Furthermore, Curtin was a personal friend of William Wallace's, with both attending the Presbyterian church in Huntingdon—creating another connection.

Gardiner emphasized the close relationship between Curtin and Lincoln and gives various instances of their meetings where the governor may have conveyed the story to the president. These include Curtin and Lincoln sharing dinner in November 1863 on the night before Lincoln delivered the Gettysburg Address. Gardiner argued that the timing of Chase's letter to Pollock in December is more than coincidental.

Gardiner stated, "In short the potential connections between the soldiers at the Dunkard church at Antietam to Lincoln's cabinet in the White House are numerous." He went further and said, "The idea that no one at the White House ever heard the story of the brave 125th Pennsylvania Volunteers and their widely used battle cry on the front lines in the conflict at Antietam is highly unlikely."[23]

Opposite page: A monument to the 125th Pennsylvania Regiment at Antietam, erected in 1904. The Dunker Church is not far from here.

The story on the surface has plausibility. There is no question about the regiment's attack across the cornfield at Antietam and its heavy sacrifice of life. Gardiner clearly and thoroughly documented the connections between members of the regiment, Governor Curtin, and President Lincoln. However, subsequent to Gardiner's writing, Robert Cree, a Huntingdon resident and amateur historian familiar with the history of the 125th Pennsylvania, searched for further evidence to corroborate the claim of connection with the motto on the coinage. After lengthy efforts including extensive research on accounts of the Battle of Antietam he found no evidence of such a motto being shouted during the attack across the cornfield toward the Dunker church and into the woods beyond. Interviews with battlefield historians and National Park rangers at Antietam National Battlefield disclosed no evidence of Flood's version of events having ever occurred. In 1904, during the 42nd-anniversary observance of the battle, a monument to the 125th was dedicated. The speeches delivered at that event contained no mention of such a happening or such a motto. These include the addresses given by both Flood and Wallace. Furthermore, the monument itself records nothing to suggest such a story, only having inscribed on it the words "Virtue, Liberty, and Independence." Cree argues that by 1904 "In God We Trust" was already iconic and had there been any genuine connection it would almost certainly have been highlighted. There is no mention of "In God We Trust" in any of the writings or speeches of William Wallace, the unit's captain. Yet in 1906, just two years after the reunion and dedication, Flood wrote his reminiscences relating the before-unheard story.

Perhaps the most convincing evidence against Flood's story was the discovery of an original recruiting poster published by Wallace and dated July 30, 1862. It repeats some of the language he used in his public appeal on the same date. The poster does indeed express strong reli-

Andrew Gregg Curtin, governor of Pennsylvania during the Civil War. He had served as secretary of the Commonwealth (and, as part of that high office, as state superintendent of public instruction) when James Pollock was governor in the 1850s. Although Curtin suffered a nervous breakdown from the stress of the Civil War during his own first gubernatorial term, he was one of Abraham Lincoln's stalwart "war governors" and was able to rally himself to win a second term.

OUR BATTLE CRY--
IN GOD IS OUR STRENGTH!

The battle cry from William Wallace's recruiting poster—notably, not "In God We Trust."

gious and patriotic sentiments and does call for recruits to take their Bibles with them to war and to read Scriptures and pray together every morning and evening. This certainly legitimizes Company C's being called the "Huntingdon Bible Company." However, on the bottom of the poster is boldly imprinted: "OUR BATTLE CRY - - IN GOD IS OUR STRENGTH!" No mention of "In God We Trust."

It is unclear why Flood wrote his 1906 account of Wallace shouting "In God We Trust." There is no other independent mention of this incident in any other account. Robert Cree states that "It would appear that the use of these words constituted either a gross error or a gross fabrication on the part of Flood." Another local Huntingdon historian, Albert Rung, had extensive discussions with Cree regarding the motto issue. Rung for many years wrote a history column for the *Huntingdon Daily News* and was considered very knowledgeable about Huntingdon's Civil War history. Though he wrote thousands of local-history articles for the paper over the years, he never used the "In God We Trust" story as a subject for one of his columns, because he strongly doubted the veracity of Flood's account. Cree quoted Rung's opinion that "The entire 'In God We Trust' thing was just a figment of Theodore Flood's imagination."[24]

So we are left with stories that explain why Salmon Chase chose "In God We Trust" as the coinage motto, but they are all open to serious doubts at best and likely are completely bogus. Perhaps the words simply came to him and he preferred them to "God Our Trust" and the other mottoes that had been discussed.

There is an intriguing letter dated October 22, 1863, that gives some insight into the timing of Chase's thoughts about "In God We Trust." It may demonstrate confusion on his part about the pattern coins and mottoes that Pollock had previously provided to him. It is from Chase, addressed to Pollock, instructing Pollock to send "specimen" coins to George Opdyke, the mayor of New York City and a close political ally of Chase's.

Prior to the war, Opdyke was a businessman involved in clothing manufacture and merchandising as well as banking. He was anti-slavery and active in the Free Soil Party. As the Republican Party was formed in the late 1850s he became more

A Confederate Regiment's Claim

An April 8, 1863, newspaper article in *The Message* from Greensboro, North Carolina, relates the story told by the colonel of the 14th Texas Regiment about their regimental flag being inscribed with "In God We Trust." It is notable that a Confederate regiment may have utilized the motto well before it became iconic to the Union.

I called, just before preaching, on Col. Camp, of the 14th Regiment, a courageous Christian gentleman. I found him reading his Bible and ready to enter upon religious conversation with delight.

The Banner of his Regiment is inscribed with the motto "In God we trust." While in gallant charge at Murfreesboro many of his command were cut down by a galling fire. The flag was planted in an open space and the brave Standard Bearer was pierced by a ball—yet the banner was borne aloft without a single shot penetrating its folds on which was inscribed their trust in the God of battles.

politically active and supported Lincoln in the 1860 presidential election. In December 1861 Opdyke ran as a Republican for mayor of New York. Normally it would have been a hopeless endeavor as New York City was heavily Democratic. However, the Democrat factions split and Opdyke was narrowly elected by some 600 votes. He aggressively supported the Union war effort as mayor, blocking bills passed by the City Council exempting New York citizens from the draft by paying from city funds the $330 required for such exemptions. He worked to suppress the 1863 New York draft riots and suffered personally as the mobs burned one of his factories and attempted to burn his house. All of this hurt his reelection efforts and he was defeated in the December 1863 elections as Democrats returned to power in the city. Opdyke was also close to Salmon Chase during Chase's time as Treasury secretary, and worked with the failed movement to replace Lincoln with Chase for the 1864 Republican presidential nomination. After the war he went on to further business successes.

The Opdyke letter called for Pollock to provide Proof sets of "specimen pieces" dated 1862 and 1863 with quarters and halves struck in silver and the "series of gold coins" struck in copper. All the coins were to bear the motto "In God We Trust."

Opposite page: Secretary Chase's October 22, 1863, letter to James Pollock, regarding George Opdyke.

Treasury Department.

Oct 22d 1863

Sir:

You will please to furnish to Hon. George Opdyke, Mayor of New York, a proof set of the specimen pieces struck at the Mint for the years 1862 and 1863, as follows: Half dollars and Quarter dollars in silver, and the series of gold coins struck in copper, all bearing the legend, "In God we trust," on his paying the expense of the same.

New York City mayor George Opdyke had an early interest in the new "In God We Trust" coins.

I am very respectfully,

Salmon Chase

Secretary of the Treasury

James Pollock Esq.

Director of Mint

This letter raises many questions. Why did Chase request the sets with "In God We Trust" when no such coins had been struck and there were no dies at that time to strike such coins? Furthermore, how was it that Opdyke was aware of and requested such sets? Did Chase have a conversation with him that referenced the addition of a religious motto to the coinage? Did Opdyke hear about such patterns from some other source and use his connection with Chase to request them? Did Chase have a memory lapse about what the proposed motto had been on the pattern coins that Pollock had previously sent him? Was he confusing "God Our Trust" with "In God We Trust?" and imagining the latter was what he had been provided by Pollock? Did he not remember that only half dollar and $10 eagle patterns with "God Our Trust" had been produced? There had been no full 1862 or 1863 Proof sets with either "God Our Trust" or "In God We Trust," such as Chase described in his letter to Pollock. Pattern coins (quarters through dollars) with "In God We Trust" dated 1863 do exist but, as discussed elsewhere, they were almost certainly made in the late 1860s. The one certainty that we can know from this October 22, 1863, letter is that Chase had "In God We Trust" in his mind at least several weeks before he wrote the December 9, 1863, letter to Pollock.

CHAPTER 13

Chase's Departure, 1865 Patterns, and 1863 and 1864 "Transitionals"

As we learned in the last chapter, Mint Director James Pollock, with congressional passage of the Act of March 3, 1865, succeeded in the goal of obtaining approval of placement of "In God We Trust" on all coin denominations that were large enough to display it. This moved the motto beyond simply the two-cent piece and guaranteed far wider circulation of its message. Mint staff were quickly put to work on new reverse dies for the quarter, the half dollar, the dollar, and the $5, $10, and $20 gold pieces. This work would take several months.

In the meantime much happened politically in mid-1864. The most significant development was the departure of Salmon Chase as Treasury secretary. Late in 1863 various of Chase's allies had begun organizing committees in several states to promote Chase him as a challenger to Abraham Lincoln for the Republican presidential nomination in 1864. The efforts were largely financed by Chase's son-in-law, William Sprague, and by Jay Cooke, the close Chase ally who had built his fortune through sales of government bonds. From our modern perspective, in which Lincoln is such an iconic figure, it is hard to realize how politically vulnerable he was considered to be. The war was dragging on with no conclusion in sight. In northern Virginia, generals Ulysses Grant and Robert E. Lee continued to grapple in stalemate, with massive losses on both sides. Union general William T. Sherman had successes but was stalled in front of Atlanta. The popular mood viewed President Lincoln as a failure.

Salmon P. Chase.

The Salvation and Death of Heb Pollock

During the time the dies inscribed with "In God We Trust" were being made, James Pollock was going through a difficult ordeal in his personal life. His eldest son, Samuel Hepburn Pollock, was severely ill as a result of his service in the war. Samuel, or Heb, as he was nicknamed, had graduated from Princeton with honors in 1859, following which he had studied law with his father. When the war began in April 1861, Heb volunteered (probably with the Pollock Guards mentioned in chapter 4) but was declined as Pennsylvania's quota was considered full at the time. He then chose to follow his father to the Mint, where he worked as a clerk. By mid-1862 he again felt the urge to serve in the war. He joined the 131st Pennsylvania Volunteer Infantry Regiment and saw action at Antietam, Fredericksburg, and Chancellorsville, as well as other less noted engagements. It was reported that he behaved with coolness and bravery, and he was honorably discharged when his regiment's term of service was completed. In 1864 he returned to work at the Mint. He was soon promoted to chief clerk, a position to which he was nominated by President Lincoln. In this job he worked closely with his father. His health, however, had been seriously affected during his time in the Army. He had contracted dysentery from which he was unable to recover. His condition steadily deteriorated with severe

Chase endeavored to keep his efforts quiet so as not to provoke a reaction from Lincoln before he could build an effective base of support. However, in February 1864 a circular highly critical of the president and calling for the nomination of Chase in his place appeared in public. This was known as the Pomeroy Pamphlet, as it was signed by Samuel Pomeroy, Republican senator from Kansas, and distributed by him and others to various party functionaries. The pamphlet largely backfired as many Lincoln allies defended the president and condemned the arguments made against him. Chase, realizing the blunder, felt he owed an explanation to Lincoln. He wrote him on February 22 denying his involvement with the pamphlet itself but offering his resignation. Lincoln did not respond immediately, leaving Chase in some suspense, but within a few days he wrote a letter to Chase declining his resignation and praising his efforts at the Treasury. Nevertheless the incident took its toll on their relationship, as it became clear Chase was seeking Lincoln's defeat.

weight loss, and he became unable to work by mid-October 1865. Despite careful nursing by his parents, he died on October 25, 1865. James and Sarah took the loss very hard. They had also been very concerned with his spiritual health as it seemed, in their eyes, he had not actively practiced the Christian faith. Following Heb's death his parents wrote a several-page memorial to him. In it they described his last days and how he had developed faith and in the end died in salvation.

> On the evening of the 23rd of October AD 1865 – being the 27th anniversary of his birth – as he was lying upon his bed and suffering much pain, he uttered the prayer "God help me." His father, sitting at his bedside said "Heb, you have asked help from the true source – He is always ready and willing to help." He repeated the verse "Call upon me in the day of trouble and I will deliver thee." Later Heb spoke with his mother and told her "I am seeking my soul's salvation." She was overjoyed to hear this good news and told him Jesus was always ready to save – "the thief on the cross was saved at the last hour." He said he trusted in Jesus, and He was precious to him, "I have been the Chief of Sinners – have been a wicked man – but I have prayed more than you have any idea of Mother. I have asked God to save my life, but, if not, to give me repentance. I am not afraid of death now . . ." He was buried in the Milton Cemetery on Friday October 27th, 1865. "His End was Peace."[1]

Perhaps more than a tribute to Heb's deathbed conversion, this document illuminates the strong beliefs of his parents and their concern with the fate of their son's soul.

Soon after publication of the Pomeroy Pamphlet another situation developed. The politics of it were rather convoluted. John Cisco, the assistant treasurer in the New York Subtreasury office and a close Chase ally, submitted his resignation due to bad health. This led to a factional struggle to name his replacement. The William Seward–Thurlow Weed faction of the Republican Party in New York wanted to name Cisco's replacement and control the substantial patronage around the Treasury office there. Chase nominated another of his own allies, but pressure on Lincoln from opponents of Chase led to the president's disapproval of his nominee. Chase, fearing he

Samuel Pomeroy, U.S. senator from Kansas, secretly circulated a paper (the Pomeroy Pamphlet) calling for Abraham Lincoln to be replaced by Salmon Chase as the 1864 Republican nominee.

would lose his patronage advantage in the New York office, then persuaded Cisco to delay his departure, despite the health issues that had led him to resign in the first place. Cisco agreed, and Chase wrote Lincoln on June 29 saying that the difficulty was behind them as there was no need for a replacement at that time. Almost as an afterthought, Chase again offered his resignation to Lincoln at the end of the letter. He had offered his resignation or threatened resignation numerous times before, any time he felt he was not getting his way or not getting Lincoln's full respect. It had become almost a ritual, as Lincoln always refused to accept it. This time, however, Lincoln had had enough and, in a major surprise, he accepted the resignation. The cumulative effects of Chase's under-the-table efforts to take the Republican nomination, constant struggles over patronage in Treasury, the Pomeroy Pamphlet, and Chase's persistent badgering of the president over various issues (particularly Chase's relatively radical anti-slavery ideas and reconstruction policies) finally pushed Lincoln over the edge. The president wrote Chase on June 30, saying:

> Your resignation of the office of Secretary of the Treasury, sent me yesterday, is accepted. Of all I have said in commendation of your ability and fidelity, I have nothing to unsay; and yet you and I have reached a point of mutual embarrassment in our official relation which it seems cannot be overcome, or longer sustained consistently with the public service.[2]

Lincoln wrote to Ohio governor John Brough that he was tired of Chase's many resignations and no longer felt obliged to "continue to beg him [Chase] to take it back, especially when the country would not go to destruction in consequence."[3]

Chase's sudden departure, and the uncertainty about his possible successor, rattled the financial markets with gold rising against greenbacks. Lincoln initially nominated David Tod, former governor of Ohio, but lack of confidence in his qualifications led to congressional outcry and further market problems. Lincoln realized he needed to act quickly to avoid a financial crisis and persuaded Senator William Fessenden, the widely respected head of the Senate Finance Committee, to take the post. Fessenden initially resisted, preferring to stay in the Senate. Chase, realizing the potential crisis situation, also urged Fessenden to take the post. Unlike Tod, Fessenden had been understanding of and supportive of Chase's financial policies and was likely to continue them. He took office July 5, 1864, just five days after Chase's departure, and stability returned to the markets.[4]

As for Chase, he deeply regretted offering his resignation and giving Lincoln the opening to remove him. He was cooperative with Fessenden, briefing him, advising him, and supporting him as he struggled to learn the new job and gain effective control of Treasury. Chase also campaigned for Lincoln during the fall before the November 1864 elections. As events of the war unfolded, General Sherman captured Atlanta in September, and it became evident that the war was moving toward a conclusion with Union victory a near certainty.

Also, the Democratic candidate, former general George McClellan, proved weak as he shifted from the Democratic platform of quickly reaching accord with the Confederacy (even if that meant agreeing to the division of the Union and the continuation of slavery) to a murky position that he might go on with the war. Lincoln won reelection in a landslide with McClellan only carrying three states.

Long before his resignation, Chase had expressed to Lincoln his interest in a Supreme Court position. In October of 1864 longtime Supreme Court chief justice Roger Taney passed away, leaving a vacancy. In December 1864, following his reelection, Lincoln nominated Chase to the position, showing his overall appreciation for Chase's financial contributions to the war effort and his desire to be reconciled with him. Lincoln told Congressman Augustus Frank of New York that "We have stood together in the time of trial, and I should despise myself if I allowed personal differences to affect my judgement of his fitness for the office of Chief-Justice." Montgomery Blair, the longtime Chase adversary from the days of the postage-stamp fiasco, was unhappy and tried to thwart the nomination, hoping it might go to him instead. Oddly enough, Kate Chase too was unhappy with this nomination, as she still had the presidency in mind for her father. When his close friend Senator Charles Sumner excitedly came to inform Chase that the Senate had unanimously confirmed his appointment to the Court, Kate is reported to have shaken her finger at him and said, "You too, Mr. Sumner? You, too, in this business of shelving papa? But never mind, I will defeat you all." Other sources challenge this, holding that Chase was very happy to have received the appointment and that Kate would have had the same attitude as her father about it.[5]

Senator William Fessenden took the reins at the Treasury Department after Salmon Chase departed.

General William T. Sherman. His capture of Atlanta in the fall of 1864 assured President Lincoln's re-election.

Salmon P. Chase in later life, as chief justice of the U.S. Supreme Court.

Chase would serve on the court the remainder of his life. In that role he was involved in the landmark cases regarding Reconstruction and also presided over the impeachment trial of President Andrew Johnson. Chase's ambition for the presidency never died. With daughter Kate's urging and assistance, he made an unsuccessful try for the Democratic presidential nomination in 1868. Then again in 1872 Kate directed an effort to obtain the Democratic nomination for her father. By that time age and effects of a stroke had taken their toll and any likelihood of success had passed him by. His health continued to decline and he passed away May 7, 1873, at age 65.

To give an overall assessment of Salmon P. Chase's career is not an easy task. His efforts as secretary of the Treasury, including introduction of Demand Notes and Legal Tender Notes, bond issuance, income taxes, and other innovations, were significant. It can be argued, however, that he was slow in moving on them and that he was frequently prodded and guided by Congress. Much the same can be said about his landmark achievement, the national banking system. He clearly favored such a new system; he introduced the idea, and advocated for it, but he was slow and perhaps lacked enough financial knowledge to work out the details. Knowledgeable people in Congress provided much of the actual groundwork and content of what was adopted. Still, in the overall scheme of things, Chase succeeded in providing the measures needed to successfully finance the war. Certainly some inflation and dislocations resulted, but it never reached hyperinflation, as it did in the Confederacy. It did not cause undue financial damage, nor was the Union war effort ever unduly impeded for lack of money. For this Salmon Chase deserves very high praise. In a June 1874 eulogy delivered at his alma mater, Dartmouth College, the memorial service by William Evarts, who served in later years as attorney general and secretary of State, stated:

> For a great part of the wisdom, the courage, and the overwhelming force of will which carried us through the stress of this stormy sea, the country stands under deep obligations to Mr. Chase as its pilot through its fiscal perils and perplexities. Whether the genius of Hamilton, dealing with great difficulties and with small resources, transcended that of Chase, meeting the largest exigencies with great resources, is an unprofitable speculation. They stand together, in the judgment of their countrymen, the great financiers of our history.[6]

Indeed there were many comparisons made between Chase and Alexander Hamilton. Chase brought great changes to the financial system the foundations of which had been laid by Hamilton. A national currency and a federally chartered system of banks were significant in bringing the United States into the modern financial world.

Chase's contributions to the Mint's work and to U.S. coinage are certainly more dubious than those he brought to the nation's finances. He did little or nothing to solve the wartime shortage of small change. His recommendation to use postage stamps as a substitute for coins was a disaster, not only in its conception but also in its implementation, as he totally disregarded the need to involve Postmaster General Montgomery Blair in it. His role in the initiation and development of Fractional Currency was also limited. That innovation originated from Francis Spinner, the treasurer. It caught the attention of Congress, which moved forward with it. Mint Director Pollock's suggestions to reduce the weight and precious-metal content of the coinage, at least as a temporary measure to prevent its hoarding and melting, were largely ignored by Chase. He evidently regarded issues of the coinage as significantly less important than other financial issues, and he paid little attention to

Alexander Hamilton, first Treasury secretary, laid the foundations for the U.S. financial system. Salmon P. Chase is often compared with him for the changes he brought to the American monetary and banking systems.

them. Numismatic historian Don Taxay, in his book *The U.S. Mint and Coinage*, says of Chase, "during the whole of the war he conceived no greater reform in the coinage than the addition of a religious motto."[7]

As for that religious motto, Chase certainly got the ball rolling by passing Reverend Mark Watkinson's letter to Pollock in late 1861 along with a memo instructing him to produce "specimen coins" with some undefined religious motto. However, Chase did not follow up on the issue despite Pollock's repeated efforts to elicit a response or further instructions from him. It was only through Pollock's ongoing pressure and persistence that in 1864, some two years later, legislation came about, leading to a changeover in metallic content of the cents and the initiation of the two-cent piece. Pollock's burying a provision in that legislation for an undefined motto on the two-cent piece enabled the inclusion. This was all accomplished though Pollock's persistence and de facto threats that cent production would cease without a change to bronze. The portion of the legislation referencing a motto was definitely initiated by Pollock, and the impression is that Chase rather passively acquiesced to it. On the other hand, it is clear that Chase did come up with the words "In God We Trust" and deserves either credit or blame for them. He pressed them in preference over "God Our Trust," which had been on the earlier pattern pieces. Chase does not seem to have made a big issue of being responsible for the motto, and it generally is not mentioned by his biographers. Pollock, on the other hand, clearly was proud of his role, even having the words carved on his tombstone.

The Sad Decline of Kate Chase

There were doubts on the part of many people about the marriage of Kate Chase and William Sprague. Those doubts unfortunately were realized in subsequent years. Sprague was a heavy drinker, given to violence and jealousy. Kate was strong-willed and often uncompromising. She began to spend extended absences from her husband on European stays. There were periods of reconciliation and they had four children together, a son and three daughters. But over time there was estrangement. Kate's father, Salmon Chase, was deeply troubled over their relationship and often tried to help them reconcile, frequently taking the husband's side and urging his daughter to be more understanding and tolerant. But it was a hopeless cause, and Sprague began having affairs, in particular with a woman named Mary Viall. The Sprague family fortunes took a major hit, as happened with many others, during the nationwide financial panic of 1873.

It was in 1873 that Kate's father passed away, a loss from which her friends said she never recovered. Then in the mid-1870s Kate became involved with Senator Roscoe Conkling from New York in what became a scandalous affair. He was married but long estranged from his wife, who never moved to Washington, remaining in Utica, New York. Some believe their relationship influenced the outcome of the disputed presidential election of 1876 in which Rutherford Hayes ultimately defeated Samuel Tilden. Kate felt Tilden had earlier betrayed her father in his efforts for the presidential nomination and persuaded Conkling to work against Tilden's interests in a crucial Senate vote.

In August of 1879 there was a famous confrontation between William Sprague and Conkling which eventually led to Kate's filing for divorce. It was finalized in 1882. Over time Kate's finances were depleted, and she lived on the outskirts of Washington in a house called Edgewood that her father had bought before his death. She lived there with her youngest daughter, Kitty, who was mentally challenged and never developed beyond a child's intellect. Her son Willie committed suicide in 1890 having, like his father, fallen into alcoholism and depression. Kate did whatever she could to

Senator Roscoe Conkling of New York. He and Kate Chase were involved in a scandalous affair in the 1870s.

remain financially solvent, mortgaging Edgewood and raising chickens and selling eggs and milk locally. She was eventually able to work out an arrangement with old friends of her father's to put the house, by then in decay for lack of repair, into a trust, which gave her enough money to survive on for several years. She passed away in 1899 at age 58, after living as a recluse with only her daughter Kitty for companionship. She was buried near her father in Cincinnati.[8] Kate's fall from the heights of wealth and fame to the poverty of having to live on egg money was unimaginably tragic. Through it all she retained her dignity and did what she needed to do to survive. Her story has made her the subject of several biographies over the years, the most recent being published in 2014. In 1940 a movie by MGM about her life, to star Joan Crawford as Kate, was planned but never produced.

Following their litigious divorce, William Sprague remarried and to a great extent got his act together, stopped drinking, and recovered financially, though never to former levels. He moved to Paris not long before the beginning of World War I. He died there in 1915. In his last year he opened his home as a hospital for wounded soldiers and gave what help he could to the French and British effort against the Germans in the war.

The March 3, 1865, act was passed well after Chase's departure as Pollock's boss. He had been replaced as Treasury secretary by a reluctant William Fessenden. It is unclear to what degree Fessenden paid attention to coinage issues. He certainly approved and supported the act, likely on the advice of Pollock. Fessenden left the Treasury post on the same day the act was passed, having only been in the office about eight months.

The March 3 act did four major things:

1. It authorized the copper-nickel three-cent piece.
2. It banned production and passing of tokens in lieu of coins (marking the beginning of the end of the Civil War token production and circulation).
3. It disallowed Fractional Currency under 5¢ in value.
4. It enabled placement of "In God We Trust" on coinage beyond the two-cent piece.

1865 IN GOD WE TRUST "Transitional" Patterns

In pursuance of the provision placing the motto on more coins than the two-cent piece, the Mint staff's work on the dies with "In God We Trust" for the larger denominations continued through the middle and latter months of 1865. Pattern coins with the motto were likely struck in November or early December. The terms of the March 3 legislation required approval of the motto and design by the secretary of the Treasury before regular production could begin. Following Fessenden's resignation in March, Hugh McCulloch came into the secretary position and was the person whose approval Pollock would need. Therefore, on December 15, 1865, Pollock wrote to McCulloch the following letter:[9]

Mint of the United States

Philadelphia, December 15th, 1865

Hon. Hugh McCulloch

Secretary of the Treasury

Sir:

By the 5th section of the Act of Congress approved March 3rd, 1865, entitled "An act to authorize the coinage of three-cent pieces, and for other purposes," it is enacted, that in addition to the devices and legends upon the gold, silver, and other coins of the United States, it shall be lawful for the Director of the Mint, with the approval of the Secretary of the Treasury, to cause the motto "In God we trust," to be placed upon such coin, hereafter to be issued, as shall admit of such legend thereon.

In pursuance of this authority, I directed the engraver of the mint to prepare dies with the motto for such gold and silver coins as would admit of the addition. The execution of this order required time, care, and skill, and I now forward to you specimens in copper of the Double Eagle, Eagle, and Half Eagle (gold coins) and the Dollar, Half Dollar, and Quarter Dollar (silver coins) with the motto "In God we trust," on the reverse of each coin, for your approval or otherwise, as required by law. The other gold and silver coins are too small to receive the motto, so as to be legible. The retention of the existing legends and devices will not admit of greater prominence being given to the motto on the coins, but the addition as now presented on the specimens add much to the appearance of our coinage. Should you approve the specimens submitted, I will at once cause to be struck, with the motto, gold and silver coins of the denominations represented by the specimens.

I propose to direct the engraver to revise and remodel the dies for the gold and silver coins, so that, retaining the legal devices and legends, he may, by change of size, position, &c., give to the coins with the motto a more artistic and elegant appearance. I think it can be done. If successful, I will submit them to you for your judgment and approval. For this purpose no additional legislation is required.

Yours, very respectfully,
Jas. Pollock, Director.

Obviously McCulloch approved the motto and the designs, and the motto appeared on all of the regular-issue coins in 1866 and beyond. However, we do not have a copy of McCulloch's approval, and do not know what date he provided it.

Pollock's letter to McCulloch mentions only specimens "in copper." However, pattern coins with the motto dated 1865 also exist in silver in the specified silver denominations: quarter, half dollar, and dollar. The $5, $10, and $20 also exist in gold as well as in copper.

For this reason and others, controversy surrounds the 1865 "In God We Trust" patterns, particularly those done in silver. Pollock's letter indicating only copper strikings, contradicted by coins known in silver and other metals, raises suspicion as to whether these coins in other than copper were really produced in 1865 or if they were later restrikes. Or perhaps they were done in 1865, but "unofficially." Another reason for doubts was the discovery of over-dated 1865 pattern coins with the motto. All of this has led to a very interesting story of numismatic mystery, research, and discoveries causing changing interpretations over the years as to the origins of these coins. There are two routes to finding answers, or at least insights into the mystery. One is examination of the coins themselves, especially their die characteristics and sometimes the number of survivors of the particular types. The other route is studying the documentary evidence. This includes correspondence and whatever other written records might be relevant.

As for the overdated coins, in 1977 an example of an 1865-dated With Motto dollar in silver (Judd-434) was found that appeared to be struck over a regular 1866-dated

A pattern 1865 quarter in copper, bearing "In God We Trust." (Judd-426)

A pattern half dollar of 1865, with "In God We Trust," struck in copper. (Judd-430)

A pattern 1865 dollar, with the motto, in copper. (Judd-435)

dollar. This over-dated coin was "discovered" when it was sold in the October 1977 Fairfield Collection auction by Bowers and Ruddy. The coin was bought out of the auction by noted collector and researcher Harry W. Bass Jr. It was on display along with other coins from Bass's collection for many years at the American Numismatic Association Museum in Colorado Springs. The Fairfield auction catalog stated that the 1865 was struck over 1866 and a small picture insert of the enlarged date was included with the lot description. Walter Breen, in his *Complete Encyclopedia of U.S. and Colonial Coins*, published in 1988, highlighted the coin as evidence that that coin and the other 1865 transitionals were restrikes made in later years. Breen commented:

> At least seven short silver proof sets (quarter, half, and dollar) and two short gold proof sets (half eagle, eagle, and double eagle) were issued dated 1865, in the exact designs adopted in 1866, together with a larger number of copper and aluminum proof from the same dies (for collectors, not VIP's). For generations the silver and gold coins were accepted as true transitional issues (and traded at very high prices); but in recent years their status has been thrown into doubt because of discovery of a single silver dollar dated 1865 with motto, overstruck on another dollar dated 1866, with both dates plain enough to show in an auction catalog's halftone illustration ("Fairfield"). This event forced reexamination of other denominations from these sets. Though the half dollar's reverse die has not been identified, the dollar's reverse is that of the two later regular proof varieties of 1866 and the two earlier of 1867, suggesting that the whole group was made up at that time—for Mint Director Linderman and Robert Coulton Davis.[10]

A $5 pattern of 1865, in copper, with the motto. (Judd-446)

A $10 eagle pattern of 1865, with motto, in copper. (Judd-450)

An 1865 double eagle pattern, with motto, in copper. (Judd-453)

However, the picture in the catalog that Breen relied upon was not detailed enough to be conclusive and could have been misleading.

Then in 2001 a museum sylloge of the Bass Collection at the American Numismatic Association was written by Q. David Bowers and pub-

The Judd-434 overdate.

lished. At that time the coin was again examined, and it was concluded that the 1865 date was not struck over 1866 but rather over 1853. "Die Notes and Comments" in the sylloge referencing the coin stated:

> This specimen exhibits an interesting feature at the date. Apparently, this coin was struck over another Liberty Seated dollar. In the catalogue of the Fairfield Collection, where this rare die anomaly was first discussed, it was noted that the under-type was a dollar of 1866, suggesting that the present specimen is a back-dated piece, and was struck in 1866 and made especially for a collector of that era (as was the extremely rare 1866 dollar without the motto on the reverse, of which just two specimens are known). Careful examination of the present piece suggest that the under-type may be a dollar of 1853 (!), as the numerals at the date suggest a 5 3, rather than a 6 6.[11]

This then threw Breen's thesis into doubt, as the coin could have been made in 1865 using an 1853 dollar as a makeshift planchet.

Then in 2004 yet another over-dated 1865 With Motto coin was discovered. It was a quarter dollar (Judd-425) that was struck over an 1840-O quarter. It was in a Heritage auction, and the cataloger did not notice or note the overdate in the auction-lot description. Nor did the PCGS graders who slabbed the coin before the sale catch it. This coin, along with the supposed 1853-overstruck 1865 dollar raised the thought that someone (a Mint employee, perhaps?) desiring examples in silver had secretly brought into the mint older silver coins to use as planchets. Did he (or they?) take the opportunity when the copper examples were struck to make some silver examples, in late 1865? It could have been done by simply placing the older silver coins in the press. That thought is somewhat reinforced by the fact that the overstruck silver coins were not placed in perfect alignment. The dollar strike was fairly closely aligned with the underlying coin's design, but the quarter was off by several degrees of rotation, suggesting that the job may have been done in haste. What might have been the motivation for making these overstrikes? Did the perpetrator simply want a personal souvenir? Was it to produce a coin that could be sold for a personal profit?

Finally, in another twist to further complicate the story, the dollar was de-accessioned from the Harry W. Bass Jr. Collection at the ANA Money Museum and sold along with a number of other patterns by Heritage Auctions at the ANA

An 1865 pattern dollar similar to this one, minted in silver, bearing the motto "In God We Trust," but struck over an 1866 dollar, called into question the entire 1865 pattern "transitional" series having been made in 1865. (Judd-434)

Details of a Judd-425 quarter dollar, with motto, struck in silver over an 1840-O quarter. Note in the close-up that the overstruck date is off by a few degrees from the original coin. Also note the very clear O mintmark on the reverse. (Judd-425)

World's Fair of Money convention in August 2014. This provided the opportunity again for the coin to be closely examined. The evidence was conclusive that the coin was indeed struck over an 1866-dated dollar! So the 1865 transitional patterns, or at least that one dollar pattern, may well have been made after 1865.

This evidence, however, does not preclude the possibility that the quarter was made in 1865, as it is over an 1840-O quarter, making it at least possible that it was made in 1865 as dated.

Furthermore, other 1865 quarters, halves, and dollars exist in silver that are not overstrikes.

Contrary to Breen's comment about the die evidence indicating the coins to be later restrikes, subsequent research does not support that conclusion for the 1865 coins.

Documentary evidence besides Pollock's December 15 letter to McCulloch supports the idea that only copper examples were produced in 1865. It seems many requests for the new With Motto coins were received around the end of 1865, and Pollock's responses provide us some further information. One example is a letter written from Pollock to Assistant Secretary of the Treasury William Chandler and dated December 30, 1865:

> Your letter of the 22nd enclosing letter of Mr. R. Amond requesting copies of the
> motto coins in copper has been received. It would give me pleasure to comply with
> your request for Mr. Amond and Senator Doolittle, but as only five copies were
> struck in copper, for the Sec. of the Treasury and the Mint, it is not in my power
> to do so. The numbers of applications is large, but as we are preparing proof sets
> in silver and gold including the motto coins, which will be ready sometime in Jan-
> uary for sale, we will then be able to gratify those who desire the specimens.[12]

This informs us not only that the coins were struck in copper but also that only five
sets had been made. Does the letter prove that only copper specimens were struck?
Pollock's letter indicates that Mr. Amond was "requesting motto coins in copper."
Could Pollock have been responding narrowly, only addressing copper coins and saying five sets had been produced and that none were available for Amond? And could
it be that coins in silver might have been made but not mentioned in this letter?
Another letter from Pollock to Hugh McCulloch, also dated December 30, addresses
a request from the Netherlands for an exchange of coins with the U.S. Mint.

> Your letter of the 29th instant, in reference to an exchange of coins of the U.S.
> for a like collection made from the coinage of the Netherlands has been
> received. It would give me much pleasure to forward coins of the U.S. in
> exchange, but respectfully suggest that this be postponed until the proof sets of
> 1866 with the motto included can be prepared, they will be ready for delivery
> sometime in January next, about the 20th. If however the Netherlands Minis-
> ter desires the exchange to be made at once, I will forward the proof coins of
> 1865, gold & silver, now on hand.[13]

This too could be read to imply that no 1865 Proof coins in silver with the
motto yet existed and that the Netherlands ambassador should wait until the 1866-
dated Proof sets were available. It could also be interpreted that Pollock didn't
want to provide pattern coins for the exchange, but rather regular-issue Proof
coins that would be made in early 1866.

Yet another item that sheds some light on the 1865 With Motto patterns is from
a letter written by Pollock near the end of his life. A paper about Pollock published
by the Northumberland County Pennsylvania Historical Society in 1936, written by
Frederick Godcharles, relates the story that Albert Williams, who had been an official of the Mint under Director Pollock, was asked if Salmon P. Chase had caused
"In God We Trust" to be placed on U.S. coins. Williams believed that Pollock,
rather than Chase, deserved the credit, and promised to write to Pollock to clarify
the situation. He did so, and Pollock responded in a letter as follows:

> In answer to your inquiries about the motto "In God We Trust", permit me to
> say that I was appointed Director of the United States Mint in 1861, by President

Lincoln; the Hon. S.P. Chase was Secty. of the Treasury. Early in the year 1864, believing that the recognition of our Nation's God on our national coins was a national as well as personal religious duty—particularly as we were then in the midst of a fearful war and struggle for our nation's unity and life, I corresponded with the Secretary, Mr. Chase, and urged the propriety of placing upon the coins of the United States the motto "In God We Trust" or "God Our Trust." After some correspondence, Mr. Chase approved my suggestions, and in 1864 or early in 1865, I prepared a bill to be submitted to Congress authorizing the motto "In God We Trust" (approved by Secretary Chase) to be placed upon all coins of the United States (gold and silver) large enough to contain the motto. The bill passed both House and Senate unanimously. In 1865, before the final passage of the bill, specimen coins with the motto were struck and placed in the cabinet of the United States Mint, and some were sent to the Secretary. In 1866 the regular coinage of gold and silver coin with the motto was commenced, and has continued ever since on all the coins large enough to contain the motto except the nickel five cent piece, from which it was omitted by my successor, after my retirement from that office, why, I cannot answer.

James Pollock[14]

This letter is interesting in that it makes no mention of Reverend Watkinson's letter or of Chase's memo to Pollock or the "God Our Trust" specimens of 1861 to 1863, or of the two-cent piece of 1864. In it Pollock seems to credit himself with coming up with the whole idea. The letter is undated but is likely from 1886 or later (Pollock died in 1890). Perhaps the passage of nearly a generation since those events had dimmed Pollock's memory and inclined him to take the full credit for the project. He does mention specimen coins with the motto being struck in 1865 and placed in the Mint cabinet. He does not specify whether they were only in copper.

So, what are we led to conclude? We are certain that 1865 With Motto coins were struck in copper in late 1865, as both the December 15 letter to McCulloch and the December 30 letter to Chandler clearly so state. But what of silver and gold examples? The documentary evidence tends to lean against them being officially produced in 1865, but might not be conclusive. The die evidence does not preclude at least some, if not most, of them being produced in 1865. An excellent article by Dick Osborne in the Spring 2018 issue of the *Gobrecht Journal* sheds more light on this matter, concluding that earlier die-state examples of Judd-434 may have indeed been struck in 1865. The fact is that the 1865-dated coins do exist in copper, silver, gold, and, in some cases, aluminum. And so the question remains, awaiting further discoveries and research. Walter Breen may have summed up the situation best about the 1865 as well as the 1863 and 1864 With Motto coins when he wrote, "Whatever their time and occasion of manufacture, these coins will remain prized as great rarities."[15]

1863 and 1864
IN GOD WE TRUST Patterns

Pattern quarters, halves, and dollars with "In God We Trust" dated 1863 and 1864 also exist. There is less debate and controversy surrounding them, as it can be pretty firmly established that they were struck in later years, perhaps 1867 or even later. There is significant die evidence of their times of origin being later than the dates they bear. Beyond the die evidence, however, the documentary evidence is decisive. James Pollock's December 15 letter by itself clearly states that the dies for these With Motto coins were made. "In pursuance of this authority [i.e., the March 3, 1865, legislation) I directed the Engraver of the mint to prepare dies, with the motto, for such gold and silver coins as would admit of the addition." Hence the dies did not exist before 1865.

Pollock's annual Mint director's report for June 30, 1865 (cited in chapter 10), also confirms that the dies for the With Motto coinage did not exist before 1865. In discussing his actions following passage of the Mint Act of March 3, 1865, he stated: "The direction was at once given to prepare the necessary dies, and it is confidently expected that before the close of the calendar year, the gold and silver coins will have impressed upon them . . . the distinct and unequivocal recognition of the Sovereignty of God. . . ."

A Gallery of 1863 Pattern "In God We Trust" Coinage

An 1863-dated quarter pattern with the motto, almost certainly struck later in the 1860s. (Judd-335)

An 1863-dated half dollar pattern with the motto. (Judd-342)

A dollar pattern dated 1863, bearing the motto. (Judd-345)

This leads to the firm conclusion that no dies with "In God We Trust" existed for any coin except the two-cent piece before 1865.

All three years of the "transitional" With Motto coins were struck in silver and in copper, and some were struck in aluminum also. The fact that the 1865 patterns included the gold denominations lends more credence to their legitimacy, while the 1863 and 1864 examples did not include the gold denominations but only coins of one dollar and smaller denominations.

All of them—the 1863, 1864, and 1865 With Motto patterns, whether copper, silver, aluminum, or gold—are rare coins. As for the 1865 quarter dollar in copper (Judd-426), the major grading services document fewer than a dozen certification events. Of course, some of these could be resubmissions of the same coins, so this doesn't necessarily mean there are nine or ten or a dozen individual pieces in existence. The Pollock pattern book enumerates only three examples. In silver (Judd-425) the coin has about a dozen certification events. Pollock lists five specimens. There is reportedly a unique example in aluminum that sold in 1960.

For the 1865 half dollar With Motto coins in copper (Judd-430) some eleven certifications are reported in the Judd book. The Pollock book lists twelve examples. In silver (Judd-429) Judd lists ten certifications.

A Gallery of 1864 Pattern "In God We Trust" Coinage

A quarter pattern with the motto, dated 1864. (Judd-386)

An 1864 half dollar with the motto. (Judd-391)

A dollar with the motto, dated 1864. (Judd-396)

Treasury Secretary Hugh McCulloch and a silver half dollar and nickel three- and five-cent coins of the era.

1866 Motto Coinage and the Introduction of Nickel Three-Cent and Five-Cent Coins

A s in past years, Mint Director James Pollock, in his annual report of 1866, highlighted the issue of the religious motto on the coinage, this time in celebration:

> The motto "In God We Trust" authorized by the Act of Congress of March 3, 1865, has been placed upon all the gold and silver coins of the United States, susceptible of such addition, since the commencement of the current year. "Happy is that Nation, whose God is the Lord."

Mintage of the new motto coinage began in January of 1866. The design was of course the same as that displayed on the 1865 With Motto patterns, with IN GOD WE TRUST on a ribbon above the eagle.

1866 San Francisco No Motto Coins

Though most regular-issue coins of 1866 bore the motto, there are some exceptions without it that have interesting stories behind them. Obverse dies dated 1866 were sent from Philadelphia, where the dies were all made, to the San Francisco Mint in the fall and arrived there just before the end of 1865. However, the new reverse dies with the motto, as we know, were not completed until near year-end. Given the slow transport to the West Coast, the dies did not reach the San Francisco Mint until mid-April of 1866. A letter from the superintendent of the San Francisco Mint to Pollock acknowledged the receipt of the dies and appreciation for the new motto:

> I have to acknowledge the receipt of your letter of the 17th and the box of dies to which it refers, having the desired and excellent motto authorized by act of Con-

gress, expressive of our dependence upon Providence. The adoption of this sentiment upon our national coins in this crisis is appropriate and will hence have a salutary effect upon the religious feeling of the people. I think you are entitled to the special thanks of the country for your agency in causing its introduction.[1]

Before April, out of necessity then, before receiving the new reverse dies, the San Francisco Mint staff paired the new 1866-dated obverse dies with the older No Motto reverse dies that it had on hand. As a result a number of 1866-S

A Gallery of 1866 With Motto Coinage

1866 quarter dollar, with
the motto IN GOD WE TRUST.

1866 dollar, With Motto.

1866 half dollar,
With Motto.

1866 half eagle, With Motto.

1866 double eagle, With Motto.

1866 eagle, With Motto.

coins were struck without "In God We Trust." In particular half dollars and $5, $10, and $20 gold pieces were produced. Sixty thousand halves were coined before the new reverse dies arrived. Among the gold denominations, 9,000 $5 coins, 8,500 $10 coins, and 120,000 $20 coins with no motto were struck. At that time in San Francisco there were few coin collectors to save and preserve high-grade examples. As a result the No Motto San Francisco coins are very rare in Uncirculated grades.

A Gallery of 1866-S No Motto Coinage

1866-S No Motto half eagle. About 9,000 of these were struck. The coin is rare in high grade.

1866-S half dollar with no IN GOD WE TRUST motto on the reverse. About 60,000 No Motto halves were struck before May of 1866, when the new "In God We Trust" reverse dies arrived in San Francisco and were put in use.

1866-S No Motto eagle. A similar number as the half eagle, about 9,000 coins, were struck.

1866-S No Motto double eagle. Although 120,000 were struck, this is a rare coin in high grade.

1866 Philadelphia No Motto Fantasy Pieces

Besides the 1866-S No Motto coins there also exist 1866 quarter dollar, half dollar, and dollar coins struck in Philadelphia without the motto. The quarter and half dollar are unique—only one of each known—while two of the dollars are known. The circumstances of their production are mysterious. Researchers have laid out several theories, but the general belief is that they were made by Mint employees as a favor for Robert Coulton Davis. Davis was a Philadelphia druggist who collected coins and evidently did favors for people at the Mint. Numismatic historian Walter Breen contended that Davis provided laudanum (a tincture of opium) to some of the staff, and therefore Davis was provided with "almost any old patterns and restrikes or other fantasy coins he wished even to making up many to order."[2] This may be true or it may be one of the stories from Breen's notorious imagination. (Q. David Bowers calls it a "Breenism," noting: "At the time laudanum or any other opiate could be bought by anyone, including children, at any drugstore; no prescription needed."[3]) Some efforts at determining the year the coins were struck have been made by studying the die characteristics, but they appear to have been inconclusive. Nevertheless the belief that the 1866 No Motto pieces were made for Davis is supported by the fact that the quarter and the half were in Davis's collection that was sold in January, 1890, by New York Coin & Stamp Company. The general belief is that Davis had both the dollars as well as the quarter and half dollar, but that the dollars were sold somehow in a separate transaction outside the 1890 auction. The quarter is traced to a May 1915 U.S. Stamp and Coin Company sale without the half or a dollar. The pedigrees of the coins are traced by various people but are contradictory and confusing. It is clear that one or another of them passed through several major collections over the years, including those of H.O. Granberg, William Woodin, Waldo Newcomer, Wayte Raymond, and others. Evidently at one stage Colonel E.H.R. Green, the prolific collector, partially reassembled the set with the quarter, the half, and one of the dollars. Abe Kosoff obtained them from Green's collection. Kosoff sold the coins to King Farouk of Egypt and then later bought them out of Farouk's sale in 1954 following the Egyptian king's overthrow. The quarter and half sold as one lot and the dollar in a separate lot. This was the first time all three had sold in a single public sale. In the 1961 Hydeman Sale handled by Kosoff, the quarter and the half were sold. The dollar was sold at some point by Kosoff to Willis DuPont, an heir to the DuPont chemical company fortune. DuPont also obtained the quarter and the half dollar, reuniting the three coins.

Then on October 5, 1967, the DuPont home in Coconut Grove, Florida, was entered by five armed men. The home had an elaborate alarm system that had not been activated that evening, and a door had been left unlocked, allowing the entry.

The DuPont family was held at gunpoint with Miren, Willis's wife, being forced to open a safe. Besides cash and jewelry DuPont's coin collection, consisting of some 7,000 items, was hauled off in Mrs. DuPont's red Cadillac convertible. The collection included many great rarities including two 1804 dollars and a Brasher doubloon, along with the 1866 No Motto coins. Those coins were missing for more than thirty years. In late 1999 the half dollar turned up at a Los Angeles–area coin shop together with a group of low-grade common pieces. Shortly thereafter the quarter also was found in a group of coins that had been purchased by Superior Coins, also in Los Angeles. Both coins were returned to the DuPonts.

In 2003 the other No Motto dollar that had not belonged to DuPont was sold at public auction. This coin had its own interesting history, having been acquired by Stephen Nagy, a Philadelphia dealer; it had resided in several noted collections. It was displayed with major publicity at the 1979 American Numismatic Association convention in Detroit and subsequently was loaned to the Money Museum at the National Bank of Detroit, where it was on public view for a time. Then in 2003 it appeared at public auction through American Numismatic Rarities, a major coin-auction firm. This drew news coverage and the September 2003 issue of *Coin World* contained an article about the motto-less dollar as well as the story of the DuPont coins. The article was seen by a librarian in Maine who had taken a group of coins some years before as collateral for a personal loan to an acquaintance. When he

A Gallery of the Fantastical
1866 No Motto Coinage

1866 No Motto
quarter dollar. (Judd-536)

1866 No Motto
half dollar.
(Judd-538)

1866 No Motto
dollar. (Judd-540)

read the article, he realized that he had a coin just like the one sold by ANR, and that it likely was the DuPont specimen. He contacted ANR, located in nearby New Hampshire. Two of ANR's numismatists, John Pack and John Kraljevich, visited him and confirmed that it was indeed the DuPont coin. Arrangements were made to send it to the American Numismatic Association, which returned it to the DuPont family. The family put the entire set—the quarter, half, and dollar—on loan to the ANA Money Museum in Colorado Springs, where it remained for several years. Then in November of 2014 the DuPonts donated the coins to the Smithsonian's National Numismatic Collection to be put on permanent display.

The journey of the 1866 No Motto coins has become one of the legendary stories of American numismatics.

Nickel Three-Cent and Five-Cent Pieces

As noted in chapter 9, Joseph Wharton's work with nickel and his 1864 paper promoting its use in coinage had their effect. Beyond the practical advantages that he argued for, his political influence was substantial. Wharton's friends in Congress won support from Representative John Kasson, the House Coinage, Weights, and Measures committee chairman, who earlier had thrown his weight in favor of eliminating nickel from the cent.[4] Kasson had changed his opinion about nickel probably because the idea that a nickel three-cent coin could replace the unpopular three-cent fractional note was appealing. This was the background to the Act of March 3, 1865, that authorized the three-cent piece, made of 25 percent nickel and 75 percent copper. It also contained a provision that prohibited further issuance of fractional currency denominated under 5¢. This provision would tend to lead to the use of the coin and fairly rapid disappearance of the disliked low-value fractional currency.

Of course this was the legislation to which James Pollock was able to attach his provision for including "In God We Trust" on coins beyond the two-cent piece.

One wonders if Pollock didn't moderate his own earlier opposition to nickel in some kind of agreement with Kasson to get the motto provision in the bill. This thought is supported by the letter cited in chapter 9, dated February 6, 1865, from Pollock to Kasson. It covered not only the motto, as earlier quoted, but also the nickel three-cent piece, implicitly linking the two issues:

> I enclosed as suggested a draft of a bill authorizing the introduction of the Motto "In God We Trust" upon the gold and silver coins of the United States. I also enclosed a specimen of a three cent piece nickel and copper (25% & 75%) struck this day as an experiment. I cannot at the present furnish the draft of the law necessary to authorize the coinage. The metal is harsh, hard to work,

The influential Representative John Kasson changed his approach to nickel-alloy coins over time.

Joseph Wharton pursued —and won—his goal of nickel-alloy coinage.

damaging the machinery and therefore I would not recommend under any circumstances the coinage of any other denominations, of this metal, than the
three cent pieces. I will write to the Secretary of the Treasury and forward to
him a copy of the bill for the new coinage when we have ascertained the date.

This letter might be read to imply that Pollock and Kasson had discussed these
issues earlier, perhaps in person, and had agreed that Pollock would go along with
a nickel coin and that Kasson would go along with an expansion of the motto's
placement on coins beyond the two-cent piece. The last sentence of Pollock's letter seems to indicate that they had come to this arrangement without the involvement of Secretary of the Treasury William Fessenden. They would seek his
approval, and Pollock would draft the proposed bill that Kasson would sponsor
and which would become the Act of March 3, 1865. Per the letter, Pollock made
it clear that he did not agree to any denomination in nickel beyond the three-cent
piece. Soon after, however, Pollock had a change of heart on this point. On February 15, just nine days after his earlier letter, he wrote again to Kasson:

> Enclosed is a copy of the bill relating to the coinage of the three, five, or ten
> cent pieces from the alloy of copper and nickel, which I this day sent to the
> Secretary of the Treasury and which I presume he will communicate to you, if
> he approves the suggestions. I recommend the three cent piece, the five is not
> objectionable, but beyond 5 it is not advisable to do. The alloy is hard to work,
> but can be controlled and made profitable. If the new alloy is adaptable, the
> coins will be a popular substitute of the 3 or 5 cent notes. This matter will be
> before you officially by the Secretary of the Treasury. I have no doubt it will
> receive the favorable action of the House and Senate.[5]

Even though Pollock had dropped his objection to a nickel five-cent coin, the bill only authorized the three-cent piece. The three-cent nickel coin was put into production soon after the bill was passed. The coins eventually were used to retire more than 17 million of the three-cent fractional notes.[6]

Chief Engraver James B. Longacre designed the new coin. It was a fairly simple design with an allegorical head of Liberty wearing a cap on the obverse and a Roman numeral III surrounded by a wreath on the reverse.

Though technically Pollock had the authority under the legislation to add "In God We Trust" to this coin (so long as he had concurrence of the Treasury secretary), he must have deemed it too small to properly accommodate the motto.

A large portion of the 1865 three-cent nickel coins were struck with clashed dies.

Over the summer and autumn of 1865 discussions went on about the issue of using nickel for larger denominations than the three-cent piece. Joseph Wharton continued to raise the matter. He wrote to Hugh McCulloch, the new secretary of the Treasury, and, in a lengthy letter dated August 23, argued that more of the Fractional Currency notes should be retired:

The three-cent piece struck in 25 percent nickel, 75 percent copper beginning in 1865. It was successful in replacing the three-cent Fractional Currency bills, which were deemed a nuisance. The coin was struck until 1889, though in low numbers in the last few years of its production.

> It is, I think expected by the country and desired by yourself that our present small currency system should shortly be reorganized by the substitution of coins for paper and, as I have given the subject some attention, I venture to offer the following suggestions. Of course, whatever steps may be taken must be such as will be compatible with and suitable to a return to specie paying times.

Among Wharton's several suggestions were:

1. Fractional 25¢ and 50¢ Fractional Currency should be continued until specie payment could be resumed, at which time coinage of silver quarters and half dollars would be resumed.

2. The 5¢ and 10¢ Fractional Currency notes should be replaced by coins with the same copper-nickel content as the three-cent piece (though, not surprisingly, he was open to increasing the nickel proportion to 33 percent from 25 percent).

3. The two-cent piece should be discontinued, leaving the minor coinage to consist of the cent in bronze, and the three-cent, five-cent, and ten-cent coins in copper-nickel, all of them to be easily distinguishable from one another.

4. To facilitate the fast replacement of the paper notes with the coins, Jay Cooke and Co. could be hired to distribute the new coins. Cooke's reimbursement could be a half year's interest on the government's profits from the coins.[7]

McCulloch replied to Wharton on August 25. We do not have a copy of his letter, but we can deduce generally what he said from Wharton's subsequent letter of August 28 back to McCulloch. McCulloch may have concurred with Wharton about producing copper-nickel five-cent and ten-cent pieces as an interim measure to eliminate the Fractional Currency notes, but it seems he may also have expressed a preference for returning to silver half dimes and dimes when things had settled down and specie payments resumed. Wharton's responding letter to McCulloch strongly argued for the nickel coins as permanent replacements:

I have received your letter of the 25th instant replying to mine of the 23rd and now I write to endeavor to impress upon your mind that the nickel alloy coins are not proposed as a mere makeshift for the present moment, but as the best possible system for the specie paying times as well. A return to silver for the 5 cent and 10 cent coins is not in my opinion desirable, for aside from the great and useless waste of a precious metal by the wear and loss of so small coins, the public should not be exposed to the insufferable inconvenience of a withdrawal of the entire small money of the country whenever specie may command a premium.[8]

Jay Cooke in a wartime portrait. To speed the replacement of Fractional Currency notes with coins, Joseph Wharton recommended the logistical aid of Cooke, who had already proven his resourcefulness as the "Financier of the Civil War."

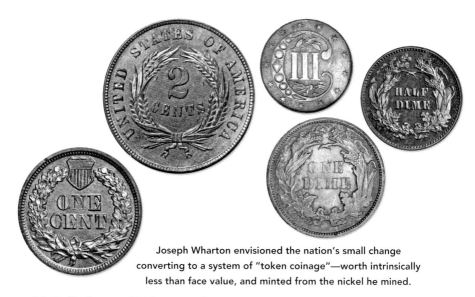

Joseph Wharton envisioned the nation's small change converting to a system of "token coinage"—worth intrinsically less than face value, and minted from the nickel he mined.

McCulloch passed Wharton's letter on to Director Pollock, evidently asking for his comments. On September 7 Pollock responded to McCulloch in a fairly lengthy letter:

I have the honor to acknowledge the receipt of your letter of the 29th with the enclosing letter from J.P. Wharton Esqr. of Philadelphia on the subject of substituting tokens or coins of nickel alloy for paper notes and silver coins under the denomination of ten cents. I have given the proposal of Mr. Wharton full consideration and have often discussed the questions with him in private conversations.

I cannot and do not agree with Mr. Wharton in his advocated policy of substituting tokens for paper or silver as a permanent measure of government to meet an emergency such as that we have recently experienced with silver in full supply for coins of all denominations and with our intrinsic value equal to its legal value in our coinage. Why an inferior alloy should be substituted for the small coins is more than I can comprehend. . . .

We have already introduced three cent pieces from nickel alloy and find it a convenient coin and a good substitute for the three cent note. This coin should be retained as it is more convenient in size and weight than the silver coin of the same denomination. The silver three cent piece has never been a popular coin as it is too small and light and easily lost. Any other substitution of the nickel alloy for silver as a permanent measure should not be adopted. In my annual report, just prepared and which will be submitted to you in a few weeks, *on this subject I remark that from this same nickel alloy a coin of the denomination of five cents would be a popular substitute for the five cent note and could easily be made. This suggestion however is respectfully submitted in view of the probable withdrawal of the small denominations of the fractional paper currency and as preparation to aid in its accomplishment.* This to continue only until the resumption of the specie payment or for a fixed and limited period in a country abounding in the precious metals and with silver in time of peace generally in excess of all demands for coinage or other purposes. *"Tokens" or coins of inferior alloy should not be permitted permanently to take the place of silver in coinage of pieces above the denomination of three cents. . . .*

Mr. Wharton suggests that the two cent bronze coin should be discontinued to make room for the nickel three cent, five cent and ten cents. The fact is that the two cent coin is more in demand now than the three cent nickel, and for all the purposes of small change more convenient and the profits fully equal if not greater than the nickel coin. Therefore I do not agree with his suggestion in this matter.

Mr. Wharton is an intelligent and truly loyal gentleman. Yet as a manufacturer of nickel his view on this subject seems somewhat affected by that circumstance. I do not see the force of his arguments nor appreciate the correctness of his conclusions. The adoption of his suggestion would not be any use.[9]

To sum up Pollock's letter: He agreed with Wharton that the nickel three-cent piece should be retained permanently and silver dropped for that coin. He favored a five-cent coin made of nickel but only temporarily, not as a permanent substitute for the silver half dime. When specie payments were resumed the five-cent coin should again be of silver. He argued that the bronze two-cent piece should be retained.

As Pollock had promised in his letter, his annual report was soon issued, coming out on September 28 of 1865. In it he reported the passage of the Act of March 3, authorizing the nickel three-cent piece and its issuance and placement in circulation. "It is neat in appearance—convenient in size, and will become a popular coin." He then reiterated what he said in his letter to McCulloch, almost word for word, regarding the potential for a five-cent coin in nickel to be issued to help in retiring the five-cent fractional paper note, but not to be permanent. Rather the nickel coin would be replaced by silver coinage once specie payments resumed.

By late 1865 / early 1866, with Pollock buying in to the concept of a nickel five-cent coin, with Kasson and Congress on board, and with continuing pressure from Wharton, the coin became inevitable. Pollock began preparing a bill to authorize it. Longacre began work on pattern pieces, even well before the passage of authorizing legislation, so as to have some proposed designs for Pollock and McCulloch to consider.[10] That authorizing bill was the Mint Act of May 16, 1866. It was passed by both houses of Congress without debate. It included a provision that five-cent fractional notes would no longer be issued, therefore ensuring the circulation of the new coins.

Twelve days later, on May 28, Pollock wrote a letter to McCulloch enclosing four patterns:

Sir, I have the honor to forward for your selection and approval specimens of the five cent piece, the coinage of which has been recently authorized.

No. 1: Obverse,-the "Union Shield resting on tied arrows," peace, &c. Motto "In God We Trust," and date. Reverse, – 13 stars set in rays, U.S. of America, and figure &c. "5 cents." A neat and unique design, and differs from the devices on all of our other coinage. This specimen is in my opinion before all the others in artistic beauty, significance, and diversity. I would respectfully recommend its adoption.

No. 2: Obverse – "Head of Washington," Motto, "In God We Trust," and date &c. Reverse – same as No. 1; a neat and elegant design.

No. 3: Obverse – "Head of Washington," U.S. of America and date. Reverse – Wreath and figure &c. "5 cents."

No. 4: Obverse – "Head of Washington," Motto, "In God We Trust," and date. Reverse. Wreath and figure "5."

The above are respectfully submitted for your consideration. Be pleased to notify me of your decision as early as is convenient, so that the dies may be prepared for the specimen selected.[11]

From Pollock's descriptions we can try to match up the relevant Judd reference numbers.

No. 1 is almost certainly Judd-497. This design is the same as that adopted for regular coinage except that the date is split between the 18 and the 66 by the ball at the base of the shield. It could be Judd-510 from the viewpoint of the design

An 1866 Shield nickel pattern nearly identical to the design adopted for the regular coinage, except that the date is split by the ball at the base of the shield. (Judd-497)

Another 1866-dated Shield nickel pattern, identical to the adopted design but struck in copper. (Judd-510)

but, according to Judd, the pattern is known only in copper or bronze. J-510 is virtually the same as the design adopted for regular issue as the date is not split. There was an example sold by Bowers and Merena in 1996 that was made in an unknown metal, possibly steel or pure nickel. Judd-497 seems therefore most likely to have been the specimen enclosed by Pollock.

No. 2 is almost certainly Judd-473. According to Judd, it is relatively plentiful, with perhaps 20 to 25 known specimens.

No. 3 is a mystery as no design shown in Judd exactly matches Pollock's description. It could refer to Judd-527 or -528, but those pieces lack CENTS on their reverses. Pollock's letter points out the text "5 cents." Furthermore, Judd notes "No specimen verified in recent generations" for either Judd-527 or -528.

No. 4 is Judd-467 or -470. Pollock's description is compatible with both. Judd-467 is quite rare, with probably fewer than five known. Judd-470, on the other hand, is relatively common, with some two dozen likely extant.

Judd-497 (left) has a centering dot on the reverse. Judd-510 (right) lacks this feature. This could indicate that it was a later restrike and not likely one of the patterns enclosed by Pollock for McCulloch's examination.

An 1866 Washington Head nickel five-cent pattern. It was likely included in the group of patterns sent by Pollock to McCulloch for his consideration. (Judd-473)

An 1866 Washington Head
nickel five-cent pattern. (Judd-470)

Besides the four pattern coins referenced and enclosed in Director Pollock's letter, Longacre produced several others that were not presented to Secretary McCulloch. Most were combinations of three obverses (Shield, and two styles of Washington Head) and three reverses (Stars and Rays, and two styles of Wreath). The combinations then were varied with "In God We Trust" or "United States of America" on the obverses or reverses. Besides "In God We Trust" some of the patterns displayed "God And Our Country," the motto that had been on the 1863 Washington Head two-cent patterns. It is possible that some of the nickel patterns may have been later restrikes. But the evidence for this or for the dies being combined in ways not originally intended is sketchy. It is possible that some were indeed struck in later years but definite conclusions for this having been done, and/or by whom, await further research.

Judd-486.

Also interesting was an 1866 nickel pattern (Judd-486) produced by Longacre with a portrait of Abraham Lincoln, the president martyred less than a year earlier. This was rejected by Pollock and not included in the specimens sent to McCulloch. It was reported that Pollock was concerned about a negative reaction in the South to having a portrait of Lincoln on the new coin.[12] Pollock clearly favored the Shield obverse with the Stars and Rays reverse in preference to the Head of Washington. He may simply have been averse to portrayal of an actual person, favoring instead some allegorical symbol, in this case the shield. In 1864 as well he had preferred the Shield design for the two-cent piece over the Head of Washington.

Some believe the case of Spencer Clark maneuvering to get his picture on the five-cent Third Issue Fractional Currency note (discussed in chapter 6) had made government officials and Congress especially wary of placement of the image of a real person, living or dead, on coins or paper currency.

In any case, it is clear that McCulloch concurred with Pollock's choice of the Shield obverse and Stars and Rays reverse. The motto "In God We Trust" was placed on the coin. The size of the nickel five-cent piece was much larger than the tiny silver half dime which, along with the dime, was deemed too small to accommodate the motto.

The silver half dime and dime—pictured here at actual size—were too small to feature the addition of the motto "In God We Trust."

Prototypes and Transitionals

Just as with so many of the other pattern coins during these times of changeover in designs and metals, there is confusion if not controversy about which are genuine "prototypes" or "transitionals" and which are restrikes, some done years later. Such is the case with the 1865-dated Shield nickels.

Some of these are patterns that have virtually the same design as the regular-issue 1866 coins with stars and rays on the reverse. These are known both in nickel (Judd-416) and in copper (Judd-417).

There were also 1865-dated patterns with the same Shield obverse but with no rays between the stars on the reverse, as would be adopted in 1867. These are struck in nickel (Judd-418). None are known in copper, though a Judd number is assigned (Judd-419) leaving the possibility that one or more might exist.

The general consensus is that at least some of the 1865-dated coins with stars and rays (Judd-416 and -417) were indeed struck in 1865 and are genuine prototypes, and that others were restrikes made in 1869 or 1870. The means of distinguishing them from one another lies in a centering dot in the loop of the numeral 5 on the reverse of the coin.

Note that both of these 1865 patterns (Judd-416 at left, and Judd-417 at right) have a centering dot within the 5. This lends credence among some experts that they were actually struck in 1865.

These 1865-dated patterns without the rays on the reverse were almost certainly struck in later years. At least part of the evidence for this is the lack of a centering dot in the 5. (Judd-418)

This dot also exists on the early 1866 Shield nickels, leading to the conclusion that they were from the same dies. Those that do not have the dot were almost certainly produced much later. Walter Breen[13] and Saul Teichman (at uspatterns.com) agree on this point. Both the Judd-416 pattern in nickel and the Judd-417 in copper are quite rare, with estimates of about two dozen for the former and one dozen for the latter known.

Detail of a Proof 1866 Shield nickel. Note the centering dot in the upper portion of the loop in the 5.

On the other hand, Q. David Bowers, in his *Guide Book of Shield and Liberty Head Nickels*, argues that the 1865-dated patterns were struck later than 1865. As evidence he says that the die punch for the large 5 on the reverse of the new coins was produced by an outside supplier to the Mint during 1866, making it impossible for the dies to have been made during 1865.[14]

As for Judd-418, the 1865-dated Shield nickel without rays among the stars, the common belief is that it was produced in a later time, probably about 1869. This belief is justified by the knowledge that the rays were not removed from the regular issues until 1867. They were removed likely to improve the striking characteristics of the coins, though there was also the story that there was public outcry against the design as it reminded people of the "stars and bars" of the Confederacy. Secretary McCulloch himself apparently urged removal of the rays in late 1866. In any case there is no evidence that dies for the Without Rays design existed in 1865. In addition, the Judd-418 coins lack a centering dot on the reverse. There are about a dozen of these patterns extant.

The Enduring Nickel

And so the nickel five-cent piece came into being, composed of 25 percent nickel and 75 percent copper. This coin and this composition would endure (with a temporary detour to a silver-manganese alloy during World War II) to our present day, a highly successful device. It has gone through three basic design changes in the 150-plus years since the Shield and Rays (the Liberty Head nickel, the Indian Head or Buffalo nickel, and the Jefferson nickel). This is despite James Pollock's intention that it only be an interim solution until specie payments resumed and silver half dimes would resume their place as the choice for the five-cent denomination. The five-cent coin has become known as the "nickel." Silver has long since disappeared from U.S. coinage, but nickel continues on. The prime mover who brought this coin into being was Joseph Wharton. However, we must also perhaps credit James Pollock's strong desire to have "In God We Trust" placed upon more denominations than the two-cent piece. His apparent willingness to overlook his own aversion to nickel as a coining metal to achieve that goal may have facilitated its authorization and initial production.

Neither the bronze two-cent piece nor the nickel three-cent coin survived long, the former discontinued in 1873 and the latter in 1889. Their demise was not related to their bronze or nickel content but rather to their lack of demand in commerce.

The silver three-cent piece and the silver half dime were both continued until 1873 in parallel with their nickel brethren of the same denominations. Their production persisted, though in low mintage numbers, with the thought still being that nickel was only an interim substitute and that those denominations would eventually be struck again in silver. This, however, was not to be, as nickel proved to be a satisfactory metal for these coins and long outlasted the silver pieces.

Nickel five-cent coins of the Liberty Head (1883–1912),
Buffalo (1913–1938), and Jefferson (1938 to date) designs.

CHAPTER 15

Pollock Departs

As noted at the beginning of the last chapter, in his 1866 annual report, Mint Director James Pollock celebrated the placement of "In God We Trust" on not only the two-cent piece but on all of the larger silver and gold coins. "Happy is that Nation, whose God is the Lord." He also discussed the new five-cent nickel coin:

> The coinage of the five cent piece nickel and copper alloy has been commenced, as authorized by the Act of Congress. The withdrawal of the five cent note has created a great demand for the new coin, and every effort has been made to meet it. The substitution of this coin for the paper currency of the same denomination is generally approved, and well received by the people.

The annual report was as of the fiscal year ending June 30, 1866, and it was issued on September 18, 1866. At the same time, other events were moving that brought dramatic changes, one of which was the resignation of James Pollock, the Mint's director.

With the end of the war in April 1865, the Southern states began reorganizing their state and local governments. It soon became evident that many in the Southern leadership were unrepentant. They began passing local laws that were reinstating de-facto forms of slavery. These laws often took the form of repressive labor rules and "black codes" that were punitive toward newly freed slaves. Black Americans were prohibited from serving on juries, from testifying against whites, from bearing arms. Unemployed black Americans were arrested for vagrancy, often forcing them into taking jobs with only nominal pay. Furthermore, they were prohibited from holding large public gatherings.

Opposite page: James Pollock as Mint director. He would resign in the autumn of 1866 over deep philosophical differences with President Andrew Johnson.

President Andrew Johnson and Republicans in Congress divided deeply over Reconstruction policy in the South and on other issues, leading to his impeachment trial in the Senate in 1868.

In December 1865 the Southern states sent representatives to Congress for the first time after the war. The Republicans there were dismayed to see that those sent were unreconstructed former Confederates. Among them was the Confederate vice president, Alexander Stephens, some four ex-Confederate generals, eight colonels, six former cabinet members, and other prominent officials known for their roles and hardline attitudes during the war.

The Republicans, through procedural means, prevented their being seated. Then in April of 1866 the Congress passed a civil-rights act to negate the black codes. President Andrew Johnson vetoed the measure and Congress over-rode his veto by one vote.

Johnson was not a Republican. He had been chosen by Abraham Lincoln as his vice president because of his status as a "War Democrat" who supported the Union and might provide credence and votes for a unity ticket in the 1864 election. It soon became apparent that his ideas for reconstruction of the South were far more generous than many in the Republican leadership favored. The term "Radical Republicans" was applied to much of the party leadership. These included men such as Thaddeus Stevens and Charles Sumner, who had favored abolition before the war and who wanted to secure rights for freed slaves afterward.

In June of 1866 Congress passed the 14th Amendment to the Constitution, which guaranteed civil liberties, including voting rights, for freed slaves. President Johnson opposed it on the grounds that it should not apply to the Southern states since they had no representatives in Congress. He encouraged Southern states not to ratify the amendment. The Southern states, heartened by this, nearly all declined to ratify. Johnson began working to form a new party, the National Union Party, that would oppose the Republican efforts.

This then was the status of national politics in summer and autumn of 1866. James Pollock, a loyal Republican and longtime opponent of slavery, became disillusioned with Johnson and on September 14, 1866, wrote his letter of resignation to the president:

Sept. 14, 1866

Andrew Johnson, President of the United States.

Sir:

I hereby tender to you my resignation of the office of Director of the U.S. Mint, which I hold under the appointment and commission of our late and ever to be lamented President Abraham Lincoln.

I cannot approve your policy as defined by yourself in your late public speeches and practically illustrated in deeds of violence and blood by its advocates and defenders in Memphis, New Orleans, and elsewhere.

I cordially and unhesitatingly approve of the constitutional Amendment proposed by Congress. They embody the true policy of reconstruction, and just and more magnanimous than treason had any right to expect, or in justice to demand. This adoption, in my opinion, would at once restore harmony and peace to every section of our country.

I desire the earliest possible reconstruction of the Union upon the basis of truth, honor, justice, liberty, and equality. This will be done, and I will labor earnestly for its accomplishment; but in the name of the patriot dead of the late war, and the living and loyal millions who then stood and still stand by the nation's flag, I protest against giving to the late rebellious states the right to make laws for their antagonists; to govern the true friends of the Union, whilst in their hate of freedom, they disregard the rights of emancipated millions, and deny to the loyal citizens of the United States the ordinary privileges of American Citizenship.

I cannot sacrifice my manhood for office. Nor will I approve, under any circumstances, that which every sentiment and feeling of my heart condemns. I regret the necessity that compels me to address you thus. I could say more, I can say no less. Longer silence would be dishonor.

Yours Very Truly,

Jas. Pollock[1]

Rather than sending his resignation letter directly to President Johnson, he sent it via Secretary of the Treasury Hugh McCulloch. This was due to a rule instituted by John Quincy Adams in August 1825 which forbade direct communication by the Mint director to the president. Therefore, Pollock enclosed the resignation letter to Johnson with what was in effect a cover letter to McCulloch, as follows:

Sept 18th, 1866

Hon. Hugh McCulloch

Secretary of the Treasury.

Sir:

I herewith enclose to you, for the President, my resignation as Director of the Mint of the United States, to take effect at his pleasure. Prepared on the 14th inst. I delayed sending it until his return to Washington.

In view of the developments of the past few months, I cannot, with every desire to do so, sustain his administration. I cannot sacrifice my conscientious convictions for office or its emoluments, and therefore resign.

In regard to yourself permit me to say that our personal and official relations have been pleasant and agreeable, and I regret the necessity that compels a separation.

Yours Very Truly,
Jas. Pollock[2]

Pollock returned to private legal practice following his resignation. In the meantime relations between President Johnson and Congress deteriorated further, ultimately leading to an impeachment trial in 1868 presided over by Supreme Court Chief Justice Salmon Chase. Johnson survived the trial by a single vote in the Senate. However, his political career was effectively over. In 1868 the Democrats nominated Horatio Seymour of New York, who was defeated in the November 1868 election by the Republican candidate, General Ulysses S. Grant.

The official Mint Director medal issued for James Pollock (portrait sculpted by Chief Engraver William Barber).

Following Pollock's departure in September of 1866, William Millward of Pennsylvania (a U.S. House representative before the war, then U.S. marshal for the eastern district of Pennsylvania during the war) became director of the Mint in October. He held the office only for six months and was not confirmed by the Senate. Following his tenure, Henry Linderman was named director by Johnson. Linderman was a Democrat, so it made sense politically that Johnson would name him to the post. Then with Grant's election Pollock was reappointed to the director's post in Philadelphia, replacing Linderman in May of 1869. Linderman went on to handle special projects, tour the branch mints, and study Mint procedures. Pollock continued as director until March of 1873. At that time the Mint's management structure was reorganized under the Coinage Act of 1873. This change was largely engineered by Linderman, without Pollock's knowledge. The Mint was made a bureau of the Department of the Treasury, and the Mint directorship was relocated to Washington, overseeing all of the mints, not just Philadelphia. The head of the Philadelphia Mint was then titled *superintendent*, as were the heads of the other mints, all reporting to the director in Washington. Pollock doubted the wisdom of this restructuring and, in a letter to the secretary of the Treasury dated January 28, 1870, gave his opinion of the proposed change:

> . . . . Now apart from all personal considerations, whoever may be Director of the mints, &c., his office should not be in Washington, but in one of the principal mints of the United States. The Director, to be efficient and fitted for his duties, should know the daily operations of a mint from actual personal inspection, should see and know the details of its working, be personally familiar with all the requirements of its respective departments. This he could not do if his office is to be at Washington, however roving his commission may be. He must depend for all his information in relation to mints and assay offices upon the superintendents of these establishments, and any opinion he may form must come from those officers who are in daily contact with the actual operations of the mint. . . . There is no use and no advantage, then, in the proposed directorship. It would be the creation of a new office not required by any consideration of public interest, and consequently the useless expenditure of government funds.[3]

Former Mint director James Ross Snowden also was consulted about the changes and he concurred with Pollock, stating in a March 10, 1870, letter that a director could not manage the mints efficiently from a distant city (i.e., Washington).[4]

Nevertheless the changes were passed by Congress in the Mint Act of 1873, and Henry Linderman was given the directorship in Washington. This may have been promoted by the nickel interests in Congress, as Linderman was seen as more favorable to expansion of nickel coinage.[5] He was from the same area of Pennsylvania as

Henry Linderman was a medical doctor before the Civil War, then chief clerk of the Mint in Philadelphia, then a stockbroker, before serving twice (1867–1869 and 1873–1878) as director of the Mint.

Joseph Wharton and had espoused nickel usage. His appointment was made despite his being a Democrat. He was deemed knowledgeable about the Mint operations and had many supporters.

James Pollock remained with the Mint in Philadelphia, as superintendent reporting to Linderman in Washington until the latter retired in December 1878. (Pollock himself would retire in 1879.) In 1878 he oversaw the introduction of the Morgan silver dollar and worked to see that it bore "In God We Trust." When certain dollar patterns by both George T. Morgan and William Barber were being considered for the design, at least one did not have the motto. In a letter from Pollock to Linderman dated August 11, 1876, Pollock expressed his opinion:

> . . . . I herewith return the letter from Senator Sherman. I confess my surprise that No. 1 without the motto "In God We Trust" was approved. I hope the day will never come when that motto will be omitted from our coins. In the hour of our nation's trial the Congress of the U.S., unanimously, authorized it—the true patriotic and Christian sentiment of the country approved, and will approve, and may you never consent to its removal. Mr. Barber agrees with me in these opinions.[6]

Of course the famous design by Morgan was chosen, and it did indeed have "In God We Trust" on the reverse, above the eagle.

By the late 1870s one might have expected that pretty much everyone was on board for the motto, as it had been an established fact on U.S. coinage for more than a decade. However, in 1876 an interesting letter from Archibald Loudon

Snowden (chief coiner at the Philadelphia Mint and nephew of former Mint director J.R. Snowden) to Director Henry Linderman implied not everyone was enthusiastic about it but the general public approved of it, and "Hell itself" might be let loose if it were removed:

> [In new designs] I would omit "In God We Trust" because it is very cumbersome and doesn't please God much, I don't think—as I think he trusts more for the conversion of the world upon the faith of the people as exemplified in their lives, rather than the devices upon the coinage of the world. Indeed, it is a sign . . . of the degeneracy of times, when external manipulation of piety and faith take the place of the simple unostentatious faith and modest piety of our fathers. . . . However, it might not be well to run contrary to the people of the country. . . . If this message were taken from our coinage, many would conclude that Hell itself was let loose.[7]

Pollock remained active after his 1879 departure from the Mint, serving for four years as naval officer of the Port of Philadelphia. In 1886 he was appointed federal chief supervisor of elections. In the meantime he continued his various volunteer activities related to education. Among them was serving as president of the Lafayette College board of directors and president of the board of trustees of the Pennsylvania Military Academy. He continued as vice president of the American Sunday School Union, where he served for fifty years. He was also president of the council of the Pennsylvania Industrial Home for the Blind.

James Pollock passed away April 19, 1890, at age 79. His wife Sarah (Sally) had preceded him in death in 1886. They are buried in the cemetery at Milton, Pennsylvania. His tombstone reads:

JAMES POLLOCK
Born September 11, 1810.
Died April 19, 1890.
Governor of Pennsylvania
1834–1857
In God we trust

Clearly James Pollock regarded the coinage motto as one of his major life achievements.

The silver dollar designed by Mint engraver George T. Morgan, 1878.

CHAPTER 16

Sacred and Profane

In earlier chapters references were made to various pattern coins struck or re-struck at later times than the dates on the coins suggest. Insights into who did the restrikes, and their motivations, are part of the story, much of which was first disclosed through the research of Don Taxay in his books *Counterfeit, Mis-Struck, and Unofficial U.S. Coins* (1963) and *The U.S. Mint and Coinage* (1966). In the first book the chapter entitled "A Workshop for their Gain" is especially enlightening as to illicit activities within the Mint that brought about production of some of these coins.

Sorting out which coins were "original" (i.e., struck in the year shown on the coin and for official purposes) and which were not is in some cases easy, but in others difficult or impossible. Certainly some of the "God Our Trust" half dollars and eagles of 1861, 1862, and 1863, as well as the "God Our Trust" two-cent pieces of 1863, were struck under official auspices. Treasury Secretary Salmon Chase had directed Mint Director James Pollock to "cause a device to be prepared . . . with a motto expressing . . . this national recognition" (referring to "the trust of our people in God"). Pollock in his official role had supervised that project, the result being the "God Our Trust" coins. In this regard they were official and produced for, from Chase's and Pollock's viewpoints, moral, even "sacred," purposes. The same can be said for the 1865 "In God We Trust" pattern quarter, half dollar, dollar, $5, $10, and $20 pieces. They were officially sanctioned by the Mint Act of March 3, 1865. However, as we saw earlier, it is suspect as to whether the 1865-dated coins were all struck in 1865. An example of the 1865 With Motto dollar is struck on an over-dated 1866 dollar. Some documentary evidence indicates that only copper specimens were officially struck in 1865. Definitive answers about these coins might never be found, or perhaps they await future research and discoveries.

Various other coins of the era, however, clearly had no official sanction and were definitely made in a later time. In particular the 1863 and 1864 "In God We Trust" quarter, half, and dollar patterns were clearly done after the fact and almost certainly for "profane" reasons. Those reasons were likely mercenary, as there was

Opposite page: A transitional pattern coin—struck in copper in 1865, from the regular $20 dies for 1866. (Judd-453)

no reason for them to have been made beyond their private sale outside the Mint to take advantage of collector demand, for the financial gain of whichever Mint employees were involved.

Such shenanigans were not new to the Mint. Among the most notable were the activities of Franklin Peale. Peale joined the Mint in 1833 and worked his way into the position of chief coiner by 1839. He succeeded Adam Eckfeldt, the highly respected employee whose tenure dated back to the very foundations of the Philadelphia Mint in the early 1790s. The chief coiner was responsible for striking regular coinage and also official medals given to individuals recognized by Congress for commendable actions or accomplishments. Peale went beyond those official duties and began producing medals for sale to private interests, using Mint equipment, employees, and materials. So far as is known, he kept the profits for himself. This went on for some years, under multiple directors, with Director Robert M. Patterson keeping a blind eye to his activities despite complaints from some employees. A later director, James R. Snowden, informed the secretary of the Treasury of these irregularities, and he issued directives in an effort to prevent them. Eventually Peale was dismissed for running his personal business within the Mint.[1]

The most notable scandal, however, involved the 1804 dollar. Its complex story is best related in a book written by Eric P. Newman and Kenneth Bressett, *The Fantastic 1804 Dollar*. Their pioneering research published the essence of the real history of this famous rarity. The coin was struck in a small quantity in late 1834 along with an 1804-dated eagle ($10 gold piece), for inclusion in complete sets of United States coins for diplomatic gifts and presentation by the State Department. The director of the Mint in 1834 was Samuel Moore. As he was directed to produce complete sets of U.S. coins for a diplomatic mission, he realized that two denominations, the dollar and the $10 gold piece, had not been produced for many years and were unavailable to be included in denomination sets. He felt his instructions required all denominations should be included. Investigating the Mint's records, Moore learned the last time the dollar

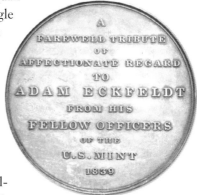

Adam Eckfeldt, chief coiner of the early Philadelphia Mint, was the first of several generations of his family to work for the Mint.

and $10 coins had been made was 1804. He therefore had dies made and coins produced bearing the date of 1804 in those denominations, to fill out the sets. Perhaps eight examples of the dollar were made at that time. What Moore did not realize was that, while the Mint records showed some dollar coins struck in 1804, they did not bear the date 1804. Instead they were dated 1803 or earlier, as the old dies were carried over into 1804 usage. The 1804-dated dollar coins struck in 1834 were therefore the first ones ever made.

Unlike the dollars, there actually had been $10 coins struck in 1804 and dated 1804. The restrikes ordered done by Moore have differences that make it easy to distinguish them from the original 1804 $10 pieces. In particular the digit 4 in the restrikes' date have no crosslet, as do the originals. Also, the rim dentilation on the coins differs.

Director Moore was acting with good intentions in having the Mint prepare dies and strike ante-dated coins, as he was endeavoring to meet the needs of the State Department. But strictly speaking he was breaking regulations that prohibited coins being dated prior to their actual year of production. Several examples of the 1804 dollar were retained by the Mint and later even displayed in the Mint Cabinet and used as an illustration in a Mint publication in 1842. A few collectors thus became aware of the 1804 dollars in the 1840s, and some acquired specimens through various means, including swapping with the Mint in exchange for rare items it needed for its collection. There was demand for the 1804-dated dollars by collectors as they worked to complete date sets of that denomination. Likely few collectors at that time realized these coins had actually been struck some 30 years after 1804. By 1858 there was a significant rise

The Dexter/Pogue specimen of the 1804 dollar, the "King of American Coins," sold for $3,290,000 in 2017.

An original 1804 gold eagle has a crosslet 4 in the date.

The date of a restrike 1804 gold eagle has a plain 4.

in interest in collecting U.S. coins. This increased popularity was related to the changeover from large-sized copper cents to small cents in 1856 and 1857. Americans strove to assemble collections of the fast-disappearing large cents. The Mint reacted to the demand for rare dates and for pattern coins. The director, James Snowden, wrote a letter to Treasury Secretary Howell Cobb in January of 1859:

Sir,

We are daily pressed upon, by Collectors of Coins from all parts of the country either by letter or in person, for specimens of pattern pieces of coins, and rare types. A few of these having been in every case issued, some of them got into the hands of dealers and are sold at excessive prices. I propose, with your approbation, to check this traffic, and at the same time to gratify a taste which has lately greatly increased in this country, and seems to be increasing every day, namely, by striking some of each kind and affixing a price to them, so that the profits may enure to the benefit of the Mint Cabinet of Coins and ores which is the property of the U. States; and exact account of which will be kept and rendered to the Department.

    I have the honor to be

    With great respect,

    Your faithful servant

James Ross Snowden
Director of the mint[2]

While Snowden's letter sought the Treasury secretary's buy-in to produce and sell numismatic rarities, it also clearly implied that this activity had already been going on, and that Snowden was aware of it. There is no known response from Cobb to Snowden's letter.

In the meantime the illicit activity went on. One employee's name that is often associated with the activity is that of Theodore Eckfeldt. He was the grandson of Adam Eckfeldt and son of George Eckfeldt, foreman of the engraving department. Several members of the Eckfeldt family were employed by the Mint over many years, even into the twentieth century. Theodore worked in the coining department under Peale.

Adam Eckfeldt, the grandfather, actually worked gratis at the Mint after his retirement, doing a lot of the work that Peale should have handled—probably freeing Peale's time for his private medal business.

Then Peale discovered that Theodore was guilty of theft, and he therefore dismissed him. Probably at the grandfather's behest they together wrote up an affidavit attesting to Theodore's honesty and worthiness as an employee. This was done, almost certainly, as an accommodation to the grandfather and to allow Theodore to find other employment outside the Mint.

Then, some years later, Theodore applied to work again at the Mint. He was hired perhaps on the strength of the affidavit he had been

James Ross Snowden, director of the Mint, 1853 to 1861.

provided years earlier. His new job was as night watchman, a position of considerable trust![3] Walter Breen, in conjecture that was picked up by Taxay but has since been debunked, held that it was in this position that Theodore was able to locate old dies and carry on so-called midnight minting. In this theoretical scenario, Eckfeldt struck more 1804 dollars and sold them to collectors. (In a September 1997 *Numismatist* article, "Untangling the Tale of the Midnight Minter," numismatic researcher Pete Smith dug deeper into the story and concluded "enough rare pieces got out of the Mint over a sufficient period to suspect the involvement of several insiders . . . with the approval of higher Mint officials." Smith stated "There was no Midnight Minter" and that it is time to retire the story, which has led a generation of researchers in the wrong direction. There is ongoing research on the topic that may eventually help clear up this tangled tale.)

Snowden, the director, was aware of and involved in extraofficial minting activities. Other rarities were also produced, including 1827 quarters and certain hard-to-find half cents. Snowden used some of the rarities to trade for other coins, and issued a circular to this effect prior to spring 1859. In particular he collected George Washington pieces dating from the late eighteenth century. He did this both for the Mint's collection and for his own personal collection.

Eventually collectors, especially those already possessing 1804 dollars, began to notice an increasing number of these supposed great rarities coming on the market. Furthermore, collectors and dealers began to note die characteristics that made them realize something was amiss. W. Elliot Woodward, a prominent Boston dealer, noted there was no edge lettering on some of the coins, while earlier ones had it. Another dealer, Ebenezer Mason, later recalled being offered three 1804 dollars by young Eckfeldt for $70 each, as well as numerous rare half cents. Questions were raised and the Mint, in some embarrassment, endeavored to recall and buy back the unofficial products and to put in place some measures to secure older dies.[4] Theodore Eckfeldt, whatever the extent of his involvement beyond selling the restrikes and fantasy coins, was apparently not seriously reprimanded.

This then was the situation of extraneous minting activities when James Pollock became Mint director. Collectors were becoming upset at what was happening, and some took the opportunity of having a new man in charge to express their concerns. Members of the Boston Numismatic Society wrote a letter to Pollock calling his attention to the situation. The letter was dated November 12, 1861.

> The undersigned, a committee of the Boston Numismatic Society, were instructed to call your attention to the abuses which have of late years been practiced at the Mint of the United States whereby a number of pattern pieces and coins from dies of former years have been freely struck and disposed of by Employees of the Mint to dealers who have in turn disposed of them at great prices. Two years since Members of this society were offered specimens of the

Dollar of 1804 of which, previously, only three or four examples were known; on applying to the Director of the Mint, he peremptorily replied that none had been struck; further investigation resulted in the fact being proven that three specimens had been struck, two of which had been sold for $75.00 each; various pattern pieces, in large number, have also been issued without the sanction of the proper officers. Under these circumstances, we respectfully urge the expediency of destroying the dies of the current coin, and also of pattern pieces at the close of each year.

Pollock, new to the job, and probably not fully aware of what had gone on, responded with a somewhat ambiguous letter on November 21:

Gentlemen,

Yours of the 12th inst. has been rec'd. The abuses to which you refer, if they have ever had an existence, can no longer be practiced in this Institution. The practice of striking pattern pieces and coins from dies of former years cannot be too strongly condemned, and great care is now taken to prevent the recurrence of any such abuse. All the dies of former years are secured in such a manner that it is impossible for anyone to obtain possession of them without the knowledge of the Director. The dies of the past few years have also been destroyed.

He did not admit to knowledge of abuses prior to his administration, but he was saying that, if they had occurred, he would prevent it from happening again.[5]

It is hard to know for sure, but it appears that the abuses were fewer during Pollock's time as director. He may have collected coins himself but, unlike Snowden before him and Henry Linderman after him, Pollock may not have had the hunger for numismatic rarities that Linderman in particular was noted for.[6] There are no blatant examples of restrikes that can be connected to him. He was known for his ethics and almost certainly would not have sought any personal financial gain through his position. Any abuses there may have been during his time were likely carried out by subordinates, unbeknownst to him.

Henry Linderman was the nephew of Senator Richard Brodhead, Democrat of Pennsylvania. Through Brodhead's influence Linderman obtained his first job at the Mint in 1853 as chief clerk. He held that position until 1864 (he was succeeded by James Pollock's son), when he left to become a banker and broker. He returned to the Mint in May 1867 as director, upon appointment by President Andrew Johnson following Pollock's resignation.[7] When he took office, Linderman found two boxes of dies sealed in 1859 or 1860, when Snowden had been director. This storage had been done right after the scandal of the sales of 1804 dollars to various collectors. Claiming the inventory list had been lost, Linderman decided to open the boxes. He listed the dies contained in them, the first being the obverse die of the 1804 dollar. Various other older regular-coinage dies and pattern dies were also in the boxes. Though the 1804 dollar die was probably not used for more restrikes, Linderman may have been involved in, or at least aware of, applying edge lettering on some of the coins struck in 1858. These were the 1804 dollars sold by Theodore Eckfeldt and then rebought by the Mint to quiet the scandal. Instead of being destroyed they were "improved" with the edge lettering. The lack of edge lettering had been one of the reasons collectors and dealers realized those struck in 1858 were not genuine. With the application of edge lettering it seems at least one of these coins was again offered to collectors in 1869. It is believed more were sold in the early 1870s through dealers such as John Haseltine and the Chapman Brothers. These things occurred under Director Linderman's watch, and the abuses of restrikes and sales of pattern coins resumed. A few months prior to his death he was under investigation by a congressional subcommittee for official misconduct, but he died in January of 1879 before the case was concluded. Most interesting is that in 1887, some years following his death, his wife had his coin collection auctioned. It contained, among other things, one of the 1804 dollars! It also contained various 1861, 1862, and 1863 God Our Trust halves and eagles struck in copper. The Treasury Department recognized that these were "of unusual character" and seized many of them.[8]

The relevance of the 1804 dollars to our story is evidence that among other items struck up and peddled to dealers and collectors (by Mint employees such as Theodore Eckfeldt) were "God Our Trust" pieces. The Boston dealer, Woodward, noted in the preface of his auction catalog for the Ferguson Haines Collection (October 1880):

> The note on page 39 will be observed, and I take the liberty here of calling the attention of Numismatic Societies and collectors of the subject there touched upon, in the hope that it may be agitated until mint officials will consent to do their duty, as laid down by authority for the regulation of their conduct in regard to their distribution of pattern pieces.

Henry Linderman, like other Mint directors of the 1860s and earlier, was aware of rarities being produced unofficially.

Woodward then referred to the sale of goloid pattern sets of 1879 in large quantities and at varying prices. On page 39 of the catalog, however, he commented more specifically on the sale of rarities and patterns. He began in reference to lot 921, an 1802 dime.

> The piece is undoubtedly the rarest of the American silver series—not only that, but it must remain so, as the dies are no longer in existence. Judging from my own experience, I believe that the purchaser of an 1804 dollar, or any one of many of the rarest of American coins, has no guarantee that the son of some future director or chief coiner of the Mint will not, at an unexpected moment, place a quantity on the market. "What man has done, man may do"; and the ways of the Mint of the United States are past finding out, though transactions, such as restriking 1804 dollars, 1827 quarter dollars, and rare half cents, and speculations in rare experimental coins, designed, engraved, and struck at the expense of the government, have become too frequent not to be well understood. What the lords of the treasury will do next is "what no feller can find out." We will wait and see.
>
> As Government is fond of illustrating its reports, as a frontispiece, is suggested a view of a son of a late official of the Mint, as he appeared at the store of the writer, when on a peddling expedition from Philadelphia to Boston, he drew from his pocket rolls of "God Our Trust" patterns and urged their purchase at wholesale, after sundry sets had been disposed of at one hundred dollars each to collectors of rare coins, with the assurance that only a very few had been struck, and that the dies had been destroyed.

It is interesting that later in the same sale catalog three "God Our Trust" halves were listed, one dated 1862 and two dated 1863. An early sale (May 1864) that included "God Our Trust" pieces was the Woodward sale of the John F. McCoy collection that included examples of the 1862 With Motto halves in silver and eagles in bronze; and 1863 halves in silver and eagles in bronze. An even earlier appearance was in the Woodward sale of May 1863, which included the two types (Scroll and Plain Letters) of "God Our Trust" halves in silver and both types of "God Our Trust" eagles in copper, all dated 1862. It is hard to know how the coins ended up in these auctions. Perhaps they were the products of surreptitious minting, or, more likely, they were examples that had been provided by Pollock to congressmen or other officials as part of his efforts to promote the motto.

But it is Woodward's 1880 commentary of "rolls" of "God Our Trust" patterns being peddled illicitly that put a taint on the series over the years with the general impression that they had been produced (and continued to exist) in very high numbers. Walter Breen, in his monograph on United States eagles, stated that for the 1862-dated eagles "Several hundred pieces were struck—possibly nearer a thousand or more—in copper with the two GOD OUR TRUST reverses of 1861." For the 1863 examples he stated that "many" were made.

There are two points to be made here. First, the 1862 and 1863 "God Our Trust" patterns exist in much higher numbers than do the 1861 pieces. The 1861s are true rarities, particularly when taking into account that there are High Date and Low Date varieties of the eagles, and date-position varieties of the Scroll Type halves. There may be only three or four known of each individual variety of the halves. The lack of 1861s in the early auction records also lends credence to their rarity. Second, even for the 1862 and 1863 "God Our Trust" halves and eagles, auction records and certifications indicate that the numbers of surviving coins are far lower than Woodward's or Breen's comments imply.

"God Our Trust" Patterns

Date	Judd #	Denom.	Variety	Metal	Auctions *	Since	Certification Events †	Total §
1861	J-277	Half dollar	Scroll	Silver	5	1999	3 NGC + 7 PCGS	10
1861	J-278	Half dollar	Scroll	Copper	9	2000	13 NGC + 10 PCGS	23
1861	J-279	Half dollar	Plain Letters	Silver	8	1999	5 NGC + 7 PCGS	12
1861	J-280	Half dollar	Plain Letters	Copper	6	1997	8 NGC + 9 PCGS	17
1861	J-285	Eagle	Scroll	Copper	14	1996	11 NGC + 12 PCGS	23
1861	J-287	Eagle	Plain Letters	Copper	8	1992	9 NGC + 7 PCGS	16
1862	J-293	Half dollar	Scroll	Silver	24	1996	15 NGC + 20 PCGS	35
1862	J-294	Half dollar	Scroll	Copper	20	1996	9 NGC + 10 PCGS	19
1862	J-295	Half dollar	Plain Letters	Silver	32	1990	13 NGC + 25 PCGS	38
1862	J-296	Half dollar	Plain Letters	Copper	22	1994	10 NGC + 15 PCGS	25
1862	J-297	Eagle	Scroll	Copper	34	1990	15 NGC + 27 PCGS	42
1862	J-298	Eagle	Plain Letters	Copper	21	1992	14 NGC + 19 PCGS	33
1863	J-338	Half dollar	Scroll	Silver	46	1992	15 NGC + 25 PCGS	40
1863	J-339	Half dollar	Scroll	Copper	26	1990	10 NGC + 19 PCGS	29
1863	J-340	Half dollar	Plain Letters	Silver	32	1999	15 NGC + 27 PCGS	42
1863	J-341	Half dollar	Plain Letters	Copper	22	1999	12 NGC + 23 PCGS	35
1863	J-350	Eagle	Scroll	Copper	16	1992	9 NGC + 17 PCGS	26
1863	J-352	Eagle	Plain Letters	Copper	17	1992	12 NGC + 18 PCGS	30

* The auction appearance numbers are drawn from the Newman Numismatic Portal listings for patterns sold in recent decades. † NGC data + PCGS data, compiled August 2019. Note that one individual coin, submitted for grading multiple times, could account for multiple certification events. § Combined NGC and PCGS certification events.

It is a given that the number of surviving coins over time has to be smaller than the number struck. In most cases of ordinary circulating coins the ratio of survivors to the number struck is extremely small. For most coins produced a hundred years ago or more (Morgan silver dollars being one exception), the surviving population is likely significantly less than 1 percent. The coins were made to be used and circulated. Ordinary wear as well as such things as changing precious-metals prices can lead to scrapping of coinage and take their toll on the supply of any given coin over time. If we think about the regular-issue circulation-strike 1861 half dollars, some 2.9 million were produced. Q. David Bowers, in his *Guide Book of Liberty Seated Silver Coins*, estimates that there are perhaps 600 examples in Mint State condition (MS-60 through MS-65). There are many more in circulated grades, but a collector would likely be hard put to find more than a couple of thousand in all conditions, a miniscule survival rate.

In the case of pattern coins, however, that ratio of survivors to number struck is much higher. These coins were not intended to circulate and were prized by collectors who endeavored to preserve them and pass them down to future generations of collectors. To measure surviving quantities for them is guesswork, as we don't have a definite number that were originally struck. But it seems highly unlikely that there were "rolls and rolls" of the "God Our Trust" pieces made and even less likely, given the surviving numbers, that there were a thousand of the 1862 pattern eagles struck, as Breen speculates.

Another way of thinking about possible numbers of restrikes is to compare what scanty information we have of definite official strikes with the estimated number of survivors. We have the excerpt from George Eckfeldt's journal regarding the 1863 half dollars. His November 16, 1863, entry stated, "Struck 30 sets of silver 'In God is Our Trust' half dollars and 20 sets in copper for Gov. Pollock. Date 1863." If we look at the auction figures for these 1863 halves, the Scroll Type in silver (Judd-338) shows 46 appearances since 1992. The 1863 Plain Letters type in silver (Judd-340) shows 32 appearances since 1999. So we see 16 more appearances for the Scroll Type compared with what we know were struck on November 16, and 2 more appearances than Eckfeldt's journal shows for the Plain Letters type. The copper examples show 26 auction appearances for the Scroll Type (Judd-339) since 1990 versus 20 per Eckfeldt, and 22 appearances for the Plain Letters type (Judd-341) since 1993, just 2 over Eckfeldt's number. Of course, we know some of the auction appearances are almost certainly of the same individual coins auctioned repeatedly, but we have no way, without comparing pictures of all the auctioned coins, of determining those numbers. We also do not know if more of these coins were officially struck on other dates besides November 16 but not entered in Eckfeldt's journal. Similar numbers can be seen for the "God Our Trust" eagles in copper. These numbers lead us to the belief that there could indeed have been restrikes, but that their numbers were not large.[9]

To summarize and to try to arrive at some overall conclusions: During the 1840s Franklin Peale ran his own medals business out of the Mint with the knowledge of Mint officialdom, perhaps setting some precedent for shady dealings. The occasion to produce 1804 dollars in 1834 for the State Department purposes provided William Dubois, curator of the Mint's collection, material for trading for rarities that the Mint did not have, especially Washington medals. It also benefited the Mint director, James Ross Snowden, who had his own personal collection of these medals. By 1858, when demand for rarities increased, Mint employees evidently did extensive restriking and selling of earlier rarities, including 1804 dollars. This became a scandal as collectors and dealers realized what was going on. There was some effort on the part of Snowden to rectify the situation, but it may have been more for window dressing than of substance. When James Pollock became director the business was evidently mostly shut down. With the ascension of Henry Linderman to the director's position in 1867, it seems the gates opened for extensive extracurricular minting and sales. This was likely the period, 1867 to 1869, when most of the restrikes of the patterns we are concerned with were made. These included not only the "God Our Trust" coins but also the 1863 and 1864 (and perhaps some 1865) "In God We Trust" transitionals. Die characteristics of these coins tend to confirm this for the 1863 and 1864 patterns. More 1804 dollars were sold, and such oddities as complete denomination sets were struck in aluminum and copper, apparently for Linderman. Some of the aluminum sets were ordered by Treasury Secretary Hugh McCulloch. The 1863-dated "In God We Trust" two-cent "transitional" piece is believed to have been made around this time as well, based on various die characteristics.

Theodore Roosevelt, interested in improving art in the United States, focused part of his presidency on introducing new and more attractive coin designs.

CHAPTER 17

Teddy Roosevelt and "In God We Trust"

Teddy Roosevelt was a patron and promoter of the arts. He took an interest in the beautification of Washington D.C., and worked for a restoration of the White House (in his day known as the Executive Mansion). He also was involved in establishment of a national art gallery. He was regarded in the art community as "the greatest friend of art to reside in the White House since Thomas Jefferson."[1] Henry James, the writer, related the story of his attending the Annual Diplomatic Reception and the "supper" following it. James was flattered to be placed at the table among so many representatives of empire. He noted that Augustus Saint-Gaudens was seated in a prominent position next to Mrs. Roosevelt. He later wrote, "Democracy still reigned at the heart of the Republic; art mattered here as much as politics."[2]

Roosevelt espoused American themes in art, decorating the White House dining room with bison heads rather than those of non-native animals. Among his artistic interests were the coins of ancient Greece, which he regarded as very beautiful.[3] It is not clear when he got the idea to have U.S. coinage redesigned to bring

Augustus Saint-Gaudens, renowned as a great American artist, at work in his studio.

beauty on everyday objects to the people. It is clear, though, that he became serious about it following his election in November of 1904. He had first become president following William McKinley's assassination in September of 1901, so the 1904 election was the first that he won in his own right. His election brought about the need for an inaugural medal, and he sought the involvement of the famous sculptor Augustus Saint-Gaudens in its creation. He had known the New Hampshire–based artist since 1901 and admired his work.

Saint-Gaudens did the drawings for the medal, though much of the actual execution work on it was done by Adolph Weinman, another noted sculptor of the time. Weinman went on to later design the Winged Liberty Head ("Mercury") dime and the Liberty Walking half dollar, both of which debuted in 1916.[4]

President Roosevelt was pleased with the design of the inaugural medal and immediately began soliciting Saint-Gaudens to think about U.S. coinage redesign. Even before the medal was completed he wrote to the secretary of the Treasury, Leslie Shaw, on December 27, 1904.[5]

> My dear Secretary Shaw:
>
> I think our coinage is artistically of atrocious hideousness. Would it be possible, without asking the permission of Congress, to employ a man like Saint-Gaudens to give us a coinage that would have some beauty?

Saint-Gaudens had been reluctant to become involved with the Mint and coinage as he had a bad experience working with them in the early 1890s when he designed an award medal for the World's Columbian Exposition in Chicago. In particular, his medal had a nude male figure on the reverse that Mint officials deemed offensive, and he had been required to make changes. But his work with Roosevelt on the inaugural medal made him confident in presidential support, and he was willing to give the coinage a try. Under the laws of the time the silver coinage designs were not eligible for a change for another several years. The five-cent nickel could not be changed until 1908 or after. This left the gold coins and the one-cent piece as the logical candidates for change. Saint-Gaudens ultimately was commissioned to do the $10 gold eagle and the $20 gold double eagle. Roosevelt's vision was to produce U.S. coins in very high relief, as had the ancient Greeks. Mint officials threw up objections to this, doubting the technical feasibility of striking such coins in the quantities required, as well as the commercial considerations such as whether they would stack properly. Mint officials clearly resented the encroachment of outsiders in the design process.[6] A great deal of back and forth went on over this, and ultimately the regular circulating $20 piece in particular had a much lower relief than that originally envisioned by Roosevelt and Saint-Gaudens.[7]

On November 22, 1905, in the course of correspondence with Treasury Secretary Shaw, Saint-Gaudens brought up the coins' mottoes and asked if he might add either

Augustus Saint-Gaudens's unofficial presidential inaugural medal for Theodore Roosevelt.

Justice or *Law* to the word *Liberty*. The latter had been required since 1792, the very beginnings of U.S. coinage. Saint-Gaudens also asked if "In God We Trust" was required, as he wanted as few inscriptions as possible, believing they would detract from the design. Roosevelt was in accord with this, believing that simplicity was an element of the ancient coins he admired.[8]

The legalities surrounding the motto were somewhat murky. As we know, the original legislation that brought about "In God We Trust" was the Act of April 22, 1864. It enabled the two-cent piece and did not specify any particular words for a motto. It simply said that "devices of said coins shall be fixed by the director of the mint, with the approval of the Secretary of the Treasury." Salmon Chase and James Pollock had come up with "In God We Trust" without any congressional input or even knowledge on the part of Congress. The Act of March 3, 1865, which enabled the motto to be placed on coins beyond the two-cent piece, was explicit in the words "In God We Trust," authorizing that "it shall be lawful for the director of the mint with the approval of the Secretary of the Treasury to cause the motto, 'In God We Trust', to be placed upon such coins hereafter issued as shall admit of such legend thereon." The next relevant legislation, the Act of February 13, 1873, section 18, repeated much the same language, stating that "the director of the mint, with the approval of the Secretary of the Treasury, may cause the motto 'In God We Trust' to be inscribed upon such coins as shall admit of such motto." Significantly this act also included a provision requiring that "E Pluribus Unum" be placed on coins. This brought that motto, dropped from U.S. coinage in 1837, back into the picture for coins besides the Liberty Head double eagles (it had been on a ribbon on the reverse since the beginning of the circulating $20 denomination in 1850).

Then further legislation, the Revised Statutes Section 3617, was enacted on June 22, 1874. It provided that:

Upon the coins there shall be the following devices and legends: Upon one side there shall be an impression emblematic of Liberty, with an inscription of the word "Liberty" and the year of the coinage, and on the reverse shall be the figure or representation of an eagle, with the inscriptions, "United States of America" and "E Pluribus Unum" and designations of the value of the coin; but on the gold one dollar and three dollar piece, the dime, five, three, and one cent piece the figure of the eagle shall be omitted. . . ."[9]

This information was provided at Roosevelt's request by Mint Director George Evan Roberts. Perhaps surprisingly, "In God We Trust" was not mentioned in the June 1874 legislation. Roberts stated that then–Treasury "Secretary [George] Boutwell, referred the preparation of those [things] relating to coinage and paper money to John Jay Knox, Comptroller of the Currency, and Dr. [Henry] R. Linderman, Director of the Mint, who eliminated the clause relative to 'In God We Trust' from the statute. Their action was approved by Secretary Boutwell and adopted by Congress."[10] Boutwell retired from the Treasury post near the end of 1873 to fill a vacancy in the Senate. He was replaced by William Richardson. Since the Revised Statutes were enacted on June 22, 1874, we cannot be sure whether Boutwell or Richardson actually referred the drafting to Linderman, but definitely it was passed under Richardson's watch. In any case it seems clear that Linderman is the one who dropped the motto clause back in 1873–1874.

There were no new coins issued in the years immediately following this legislation. The next change was the introduction of the Morgan silver dollar in 1878. At that time Secretary of the Treasury John Sherman recognized that the law was ambiguous regarding the motto, as earlier legislation gave discretion to the Mint director and secretary of the Treasury to include it, while the 1874 legislation made no mention of it. He was concerned to the point that he consulted with President Rutherford B. Hayes about how to proceed. The conclusion was to include "In God We Trust" on the new dollar as well as "E Pluribus Unum."[11] We recall from chapter 14 that in August 1876 James Pollock, who was still superintendent of the Philadelphia Mint, had urged Director Linderman to choose a design for the new dollar that would retain the motto: "In the hour of nation's trial the Congress of the

Augustus Saint-Gaudens, the noted sculptor who designed the new $10 and $20 gold pieces. He preferred dropping "In God We Trust" from the new coins to avoid distraction from his motifs.

U.S., unanimously, approved it—the true patriotic and Christian sentiment of the country approved, and will approve, and may you never consent to its removal."

In 1883 the five-cent nickel came up for redesign. The Shield design initiated in 1866, while Pollock was still Mint director, bore "In God We Trust." As planning proceeded to replace the design in the 1880s, pattern coins were produced based on ideas by Charles Barber, the Mint's chief engraver. In 1881 two patterns, cataloged as Judd-1671 and Judd-1674a, were identical to one another except that one had "In God We Trust" and the other did not.

In 1882 several more pattern designs were struck, some with the motto, some without. Then in 1883 yet more patterns were produced before a final design was agreed upon. None of these bore "In God We Trust." The adopted design, known as the Liberty Head, did not therefore have the religious motto but did bear "E Pluribus Unum." It seems there was no notable public reaction to this. Perhaps public attention was distracted by the coin's not carrying the word "Cents," leading to fraudsters gold-plating and edge-reeding the new coins and passing them as $5 gold pieces—the so-called Racketeer nickels.

An 1881 five-cent pattern
struck in nickel. (Judd-1671)

A similar design, but with "In
God We Trust."(Judd-1674a)

The Liberty Head nickel design introduced in 1883. Note that initially it did not
have CENTS beneath the Roman numeral V, but the word was added later in 1883.
The coin did not bear "In God We Trust" as its predecessor, the Shield nickel, had.

Pollock, by that time long gone from the Mint, was troubled by the dropping of the motto and alluded to Barber's Liberty Head nickel in his 1886 letter cited in chapter 12, saying that "In 1866 the regular coinage of gold and silver coin with the motto was commenced, and has continued ever since on all the coins large enough to contain the motto except the nickel five cent piece, from which it was omitted by my successor, after my retirement from that office, why, I cannot answer."

In any case, while the law and precedents were unclear and perhaps conflicting, it could clearly be concluded that "In God We Trust" was not a mandatory requirement. Treasury Secretary Shaw likely communicated this thought to Saint-Gaudens, who left the motto off his sketches for the new coins.

Teddy Roosevelt had believed the inclusion of "Justice" was acceptable if Saint-Gaudens desired it, but it ultimately was not used. It also seems Roosevelt remained concerned about the legalities of dropping "In God We Trust" and, in April of 1907, had his secretary write Mint Director George Evans Roberts for assurance and confirmation on this point. Roberts sent to the White House a copy of the 1896 *Mint Director's Report*, which elaborated on the history of the religious motto and implied there was no legal requirement for it.[12]

Out of various 1905–1907 correspondence among President Roosevelt, Saint-Gaudens, Secretary Shaw, and Director Roberts, it seems all parties were in accord that the motto could and should be left off. And so, as the coins were designed and began production in 1907, there was no "In God We Trust" on either the $10 eagle or the $20 double eagle. The $10 piece did include "E Pluribus Unum" on the reverse and "Liberty" in the Indian's headdress on the obverse, while the $20 piece carried nothing beyond the mandatory "Liberty" on the surfaces of the coin. However, since "E Pluribus Unum" was legally required, it was lettered unobtrusively on the coin's edge, so as not to interfere with Saint-Gaudens's design.

Sketches and a plaster by Augustus Saint-Gaudens for the new gold coins of 1907.

Roosevelt was proud of the new coins. He had feared congressional interference with what he termed his "pet crime," and had intentionally arranged the timing of their introduction to be while Congress was recessed. In his mind the "crime" was introducing innovative designs to the coins and effectively overriding the Old Guard at the Mint—those who resented outside influences in their domain. He likely did not expect any negative reaction to come from elimination of the motto.

The coins were issued in December of 1907. Even before they were in the public's hands the word had got out that they did not have "In God We Trust" on them. The *New York Times* reported this on November 7, and public reaction was immediate. Letters and postcards were addressed to the White House, the Treasury secretary, and Congress, as well as to the Mint itself.[13] Much of the reaction that was carried in the papers came from church groups and other organizations, such as the Women's Christian Temperance Union, that were offended by the motto's omission.

The criticism was largely targeted at Roosevelt. Though Saint-Gaudens had really been the one to bring up removal of the motto for the artistic purpose of avoiding distractions in the fields of the coins, the president is the one who caught the heat. There were various reasons for this. Saint-Gaudens had passed away in August from cancer and escaped the public criticism that arose in November and after. Beyond this there was some unhappiness with Roosevelt by this time. He had been in office for nearly two terms, and his opponents were weary of controversies often resulting from his authoritarian approach to issues.

Earlier in 1907 a collapse in financial markets had led to a recession, the Panic of 1907. American financier J.P. Morgan, recognizing the seriousness of the situation, had organized a group of bankers to provide liquidity to the markets and narrowly avoid total collapse. This too was taking its toll on the president's popularity, and the downturn was frequently called the "Roosevelt Panic." Mark Twain made a connection between the recession and the removal of the motto with a joke noted by various newspapers, including this one in the *Alamance Gleaner*, a North Carolina paper.

Mr. Clemens said that he was grateful that Congress was about to restore to the coinage the words "In God We Trust." He continued: "I knew that we would get into difficulty if we left those words off and straightaway the trouble came. The prosperity of the whole nation went down in a pile when we ceased to trust God in that conspicuous and well-advertised way. If Pierpont Morgan hadn't stepped in just then—! Now that we have resumed our trust in God we will discharge Mr. Morgan from his high office of honor."

After his election in 1904, the president had said that he regarded the three years he had held the office after William McKinley's death (autumn of 1901 through 1904) as a first term and that he would respect the precedent established by Washington to not serve more than two terms. By so saying he had made himself a lame duck, likely giving up much of a president's capacity to enforce his will with Congress.

Augustus Saint-Gaudens's $20 gold design, originally crafted in detailed ultra high relief (pictured here), was modified by his assistant, Henry Hering, after the artist died in August 1907. Then the Mint's chief engraver, Charles Barber, flattened the design and made other artistic changes, resulting in a much less visually dramatic coin being struck for general circulation. Still, it was an improvement over the old Liberty Head design.

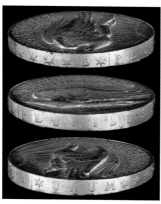

The legend E PLURIBUS UNUM was placed on the edge of the $20 gold coin.

The artist's $10 gold coin designs, in their final minted form.

Roosevelt reacted to the criticism, as in so many of his controversies, with a hard line. He told a friend that the controversy had become a matter of considerable worry to him, but that he could not "help but feeling that (the removal) was the right action from the standpoint of good taste, and indeed a little more than good taste."[14] On November 11, 1907, he wrote a letter to a minister spelling out his thoughts on the issue:

Dear Sir:

When the question of the new coinage came up we looked into the law and found there was no warrant therein for putting "In God We Trust" on the coins. As the custom, although without legal warrant, had grown up, however, I might have felt at liberty to keep the inscription had I approved of its being on the coinage. But as I did not approve of it, I did not direct that it should again be put on. Of course the matter of the law is absolutely in the hands of Congress, and any direction of Congress in the matter will be immediately obeyed. At present, as I have said, there is no warrant in law for the inscription.

My own feeling in the matter is due to my very firm conviction that to put such a motto on coins, or to use it in any kindred manner, not only does no good but does positive harm, and is in effect irreverence which comes dangerously close to sacrilege. A beautiful and solemn sentence such as the one in question should be treated and uttered only with that fine reverence which necessarily implies a certain exaltation of spirit. Any use which tends to cheapen it, and above all, any use which tends to secure its being treated in a spirit of levity, is from every standpoint profoundly regretted. It is a motto which it is indeed well to have inscribed on our great national monuments, in our temples of justice, in our legislative halls, and in buildings such as those at West Point and Annapolis—in short, wherever it will tend to arouse and inspire a lofty emotion in those who look thereon. But it seems to me eminently unwise to cheapen such a motto by use on coins, just as it would be to cheapen it by use on postage stamps, or in advertisements. As regards its usage on the coinage we have actual experience by which to go. In all my life I have never heard any human being speak reverently of this motto on the coins or show any sign of its having appealed to any high emotion in him. But I have literally hundreds of times heard it used as an occasion of, and incitement to, the sneering ridicule which it is above all things undesirable that so beautiful and exalted a phrase should excite. For example, throughout the long contest extending over several decades, on the free coinage question, the existence of this motto on the coins was a constant source of jest and ridicule; and this was unavoidable. Everyone must remember the innumerable cartoons and articles based on phrases like "In God we trust for the other eight cents"; "In God we trust for the short weight", "In God we trust for the thirty-seven cents we do not pay"; and so on and so forth. Surely I am well within bounds when I say that a use of the phrase which invites constant levity of this type is most undesirable. If Congress alters the law and directs me to replace on the coins the sentence in question, the direction will immediately put into effect; but I very earnestly trust that the religious sentiment of the country, the spirit of reverence in the country, will prevent any such action being taken.

Sincerely yours,

Roosevelt sent the same letter to eight other people and the letter appeared in the *New York Times* on November 13, 1907. It was widely distributed in other papers around the country. The letter did not calm the critics. If anything it brought more attention, and the outcry increased. Beyond church leaders many in the general public regarded the removal as an act of blasphemy and "a backward step." There were suggestions that the eagle on the coins should be replaced by a teddy bear over an inscription "In Theodore We Trust."[15] The November 17 *New York Sun* carried a poem sent by a reader:

In God We Trust	In God We Trust
Oh, no we don't	Upon Our Coins!
That is, we mustn't say so;	Oh, sacrilegious people!
Such sentiment is out of date	God is not needed in this nation;
At least so says the potentate	We have the great Administration;
And He's the country and the State	And he's enough for all creation
Our Teddy	Our Teddy

At an Episcopal diocesan convention on November 13 in New York the issue was raised in a resolution to denounce the removal of the motto. In an article (largely repeating reportage by the *New York Times*) the *Detroit Free Press* reported the proceedings.

MINISTERS HIT AT PRESIDENT

Denounce Removal of Motto From Coins, Notwithstanding Roosevelt's Letter.

EXECUTIVE DEEMS USE OF WORDS SACRILEGE

"In God We Trust" Should Be Uttered Only With Exalted Reverence.

New York, November 13. – At the Episcopal diocesan convention at the Cathedral of St. John the Divine a resolution was introduced this afternoon denouncing the action of the government in taking the motto "In God We Trust" from the coins and demanding its restoration.

The resolution which was introduced by Rev. Dr. Grosvenor of the Church of the Incarnation after the president's letter had been made public was received with an outburst of applause. An effort to have it laid on the table was defeated by an almost unanimous vote.

Later the resolution was again brought forward and finally passed by a vote of 131 to 81, after a debate of nearly two hours, during which several attempts were made to "dodge it" as one clergyman, Rev. Dr. Townsend, put it. Friends of President Roosevelt fought bitterly against its passage.

A coterie of laymen was prominent in the supporting of the antagonism to the resolution. Two motions to lay it on the table were defeated with a vote so close that a count was needed. Then an attempt was made to have the consideration indefinitely postponed, and then as a last resource, it was tried to have the vote on the resolution itself put off until tomorrow. All attempts failed, however, and the resolution was carried.

On November 14 the *Philadelphia Inquirer* reported that the Board of Publications and Sabbath School Works of the Presbyterian Church was also sending a protest to Washington. It indicated some divided opinions, just as the Episcopalians had experienced, but the majority ruled and the protest was sent.

PRESBYTERIAN PROTEST WILL BE FORWARDED

Notwithstanding the public letter from President Roosevelt setting forth his reasons for ordering the words, "In God We Trust," omitted from the new gold coins, it was said yesterday afternoon in the office of Rev. Dr. Alexander Henry, secretary of the Board of Publication and Sabbath School Work of the Presbyterian Church, that the petition to President Roosevelt, authorized by the Presbytery of Philadelphia North, at their meeting at Bristol, Wednesday, would be forwarded to Washington as soon as prepared.

All ministers of the Presbyterian Church do not seem to agree with the Presbytery North in the matter, however. The Rev. Charles D. Wood, pastor of the Second Presbyterian Church, said yesterday that he considered the words, "In God We Trust," on the new gold coins unnecessary.

"President Roosevelt has taken just about the right stand on this matter," said Dr. Wood. "While I have never heard of any one ridicule the words, it seems to me the use of the solemn words in such worldly connections was not called for."

Several other pastors, directly connected with the Presbyterian Board of Publication work, yesterday concurred with Dr. Wood in his opinion.

The committee appointed by the Presbytery North consists of Revs. Dr. Alexander Henry, Robert H. Mackie and William H. Roberts. The two latter are prominent laymen of the Presbyterian Church.

The *Detroit Free Press*, November 14, 1907, carried an article reporting that a group of Chicago lawyers was contradicting the president's claim that there was no legal "warrant" for the motto. They cited the Act of March 2, 1865.

The congressional recess ended December 2, 1907. As the congressmen returned they were met with demands from constituents to do something about the motto issue.[16] One prominent Philadelphia attorney and Episcopal layman, Frederick Carroll Brewster, was motivated to issue and distribute a pamphlet that called the motto's removal "unconstitutional" and under the authority of Congress, not the president. He urged Congress to reassert its authority and restore "In God We Trust."[17]

The Democrats, eager to embarrass Roosevelt in any way possible, introduced six different bills to respond to popular demands to put back the motto. One Democrat from Texas, Morris Shepard, on

The cartoonists got to work, as seen here on the front page of the *Detroit Free Press*, November 14, 1907.

January 7, 1908, spoke about it on the floor for more than half an hour. His words, preserved in the *Congressional Record*, said the motto was "a sentence summarizing the history and reflecting the character of the American people." Furthermore the president had replaced the sacred symbol on the coins with a design "which shows on the one side a woman in savage headdress and on the other a Roman eagle in predatory flight—the one side a degradation of woman and the other an eulogy of war."

President Theodore Roosevelt was publicly criticized for the omission of "In God We Trust."

The Republicans, realizing the Democrats were taking control of the issue, quickly made sure that a bill of their own was given preference by the House Committee on Coinage, Weights, and Measures. They chose to push a bill introduced by Congressman Hampton Moore of Pennsylvania. The bill itself had been drafted by F. Carroll Brewster, the attorney who had produced the pamphlet critical of Roosevelt. He was Moore's constituent. The Republicans, however, were fearful that even if they passed legislation restoring the motto, Roosevelt would veto it. If they over-rode a veto it would create even more embarrassment to the party. Moore was known to be a friend of the president's and he was persuaded to call on Roosevelt to see what his intentions were. Moore did so, hoping (as he said) that Roosevelt "would take a suggestion from me as a friend."[17] They had a difficult discussion, and Roosevelt initially seemed intransigent, but Moore argued that the religious community was shaken by his action and that the president himself was being put in a false light as personally lacking a religious faith. Roosevelt then relented and called Thomas Carter, a Republican senator from Montana, into the meeting and stated to both of them:

> The Congressman (Moore) says the House Committee wants to pass a bill restoring the motto to the coin. I tell him it is not necessary; it is rot; but the Congressman says there is a misapprehension as to the religious purport of it— it is so easy to stir up a sensation and misconstrue the President's motives—and the Committee is agitated as to the effect of a veto. I repeat, it is rot, pure rot; but I am telling the Congressman if Congress wants to pass a bill re-establishing the motto, I shall not veto it. You may as well know it in the Senate too.[18]

On the strength of the president's saying he didn't intend to veto the bill, Congress moved ahead. On February 19 the House committee voted to favorably report a bill to the full House. The *New York Times* reported that in committee an amendment was proposed, tongue in cheek, to add a different motto to the paper currency.

TO RESTORE IN GOD WE TRUST

House Committee Votes to Report Bill Putting Motto on Gold Coins.

Washington, Feb. 19—The motto "In God We Trust" will likely go back on the gold coins, as the House Committee on Coinage, Weights, and Measures to-day voted to report favorably a bill to restore the words.

Mr. Wallace's amendment, "to require that on all the paper money there be inscribed the words 'I know that my Redeemer liveth,'" was lost.

The motion was lost in the laughter.

Another article, in the *Warren Times Mirror*, from Warren, Pennsylvania, gave a more in-depth report on the committee session and vote.

Congress Passing Few Bills.

The number of bills on the house calendar so far this session is very small in comparison with preceding congresses and in the face of the fact, too, that already 18,000 measures have been introduced in that body. In the senate 5,000 bills have been offered. This breaks the record in both branches. Members have been particularly anxious to let people in their districts know that they have accomplished something because their reelections are at stake. So few bills have passed that there has been a contention as to who is to be credited with the distinction of having moved the Coinage, Weights, and Measures committee to take favorable action on the measure to restore the coins of the United States the motto "In God We Trust." At times there has been so little to write about that one fellow who was employed to act as a sort of press agent for a Democratic member serving his first term was very hard pinched for booming material, so he announced to the voters of the district that the congressman could justly claim to be the leader in the movement to restore the motto to the coin of the land.

A search of the records showed that the representative referred to had not even introduced a bill on the subject, although a member of the coinage committee. It turned out that Representative Ollie James of Kentucky happened to be the first on to put in an "In God We Trust" bill, and, as the religious folks were complaining of the omission of the motto, other congressmen later rushed in bills also.

From it we see that congressmen were eager to be seen supporting restoration of the motto. The *North Carolinian* in Raleigh, North Carolina, on March 26, 1908, reported the overwhelming passage (with only five votes opposed) in the full House for the restoration of the motto. The reporter also observed the discomfort of Roosevelt's congressman son-in-law, Nicholas Longworth (married to his daughter Alice), in casting his vote on the issue, wanting to offend neither his father-in-law nor the popular opinion of his constituents.

The Senate then passed the bill on May 13, and it was signed by the president on May 18. The law stated:

> Be it enacted by the Senate and House of Representatives of the United States
> of American in Congress assembled, That the motto "In God We Trust" here-
> tofore inscribed on certain denominations of the gold and silver coins of the
> United States of America, shall hereafter be inscribed upon all such gold and
> silver coins of said denominations as heretofore.

And so the episode ended with the motto restored. What are the lessons from
it? Certainly the public reaction made the politicians realize there was such support for the motto that it should not be lightly dropped or trifled with. In a sense
any controversy requires two viewpoints, and there certainly were in this case.
Editorials in the *Chicago Tribune* and the *Cleveland Plain Dealer* agreed with the
president that associating God with "filthy lucre" was sacrilegious rather than
pious. The *New York Times* and other papers agreed with Roosevelt that the motto,
by being on coins, was exposed to jest and ridicule. A Presbyterian paper, the
Westminster, said the president was right for omitting the motto "until the ethical
level of business in the U.S. warranted the use of God's name as the symbol of
commerce."

Clearly, however, a majority of opinion objected to its removal. Some observers
felt it was evidence of the secular trend of the age. Just as there had been, decades
earlier, discussions of the omission of the Deity from the Constitution, there were
references to the French Revolution where "in 1790 they decreed that God did
not exist." The fact that the various atheist societies supported the motto's removal
led many to believe that it was all part of an atheist plot.

In later years, President Roosevelt commented in his autobiography regarding
the incident and the new coins:

> In addition certain things were done of which the economic bearing was more
> remote, but which bore directly on our welfare, because they add to the beauty
> and therefore the joy of life. Securing the great artist, Saint-Gaudens, to give
> us the most beautiful coinage since the decay of Hellenistic Greece was one
> such act. In this case I had power myself to employ Saint-Gaudens. The first,
> and most beautiful, of his coins were coined in thousands before Congress
> assembled or could intervene, and a great and permanent improvement was
> made in the beauty of the coinage.[19]

An interesting sidebar of the dispute was publication of various newspaper articles describing how the motto had come to be. Some of the coverage was fairly
accurate. An article in the *Brooklyn Daily Eagle* on November 17 was titled "O
Tempora! O Mores!" (roughly, "Oh, what times! Oh, what customs!"). It was in the
form of a letter to the editor written by James Kohler, who was an acquaintance of
James Pollock's and understood something of the role of Pollock in the story.

"O TEMPORA! O MORES!"
Mr. Kohler Regrets the Decadence of Morals
in Public Life—Preachment on Coin Motto.

To the Editor of the Brooklyn Eagle:

Considerable fuss is being made in certain quarters over President Roosevelt's order to omit from our future coinage the words "In God We Trust." It is very evident that we do not, in these days, trust in God so much as we did when our coins first bore the inscription. Napoleon said that God was on the side of the army that had the best artillery, and Blucher, in praying before the battle of Waterloo, said, "God, we do not ask that you help us, but we do ask that you do not help the other side."

Certain it is that the God of to-day is not the God of fifty years ago. But it is not wise for man to annihilate his God. The better his God is, the better man himself becomes, for no stream rises higher than its source, and the great thing that humanity should be proud of is that while God is unchanging, our idea of God is becoming more human as we ourselves improve. Eventually we will evolve a God whose justice is synonymous with a square deal, and we may try to establish a square deal on earth.

It was not Abraham Lincoln who ordered "In God We Trust" placed on our coins, but James Pollock, a close friend of Lincoln's, and, at the time the inscription originated, director of the mint at Philadelphia. Mr. Pollock certainly did not think that the inscription meant nothing. (The "crime of '73" had not yet been committed.) He put it there because he thoroughly believed in and trusted God. He was religious in the deepest and best sense of the word—a thoroughly honorable, upright man and scholar of the old school.

When I was born James Pollock was Governor of Pennsylvania; his home residence was the town where I was born, and my middle name, because of my parents' great regard for the man, was registered Pollock in the little Lutheran church where I was baptized.

James Pollock, who was the first anti-slavery Republican governor of Pennsylvania, afterward served in Congress, and put through Congress the bill for building the Union Pacific Railroad, and, with Abraham Lincoln, selected Council Bluffs, Ia., as the starting point of that railroad.

I well remember, many years ago, that much regret was experienced in pulpit, press, and forum, over the fact that we had left God out of the Constitution. The idea of putting God on our coins was for the distinct purpose of having this nation recognize in some way the existence of a Supreme Ruler.

I well remember the great presidential campaigns between Lincoln and McClellan, between Grant and Seymour and Grant and Greeley, where Republican Pennsylvania was stirred to its depths. Governor Pollock was one of the great orators of those days, and when he was booked to speak in his home town the farmers for miles came in to hear him. I think I must have heard Governor Pollock speak at least twenty times. I know that when I first heard Henry Ward Beecher in Plymouth Church in 1873, I was at once reminded of Governor Pollock of Pennsylvania.

The thing that I regret is not that we have taken the inscription "In God We Trust" off our coins, but that we have ceased to raise the kind of men that lived when the inscription was first ordered. In those days honesty in politics inspired and commanded universal respect; in these days politics furnishes no market at all for honest. Indeed, honesty, nowadays, is a rare article, either in business or politics.

Along about 1878, on my way home to Pennsylvania, I stopped over in Philadelphia and called at the mint to see Governor Pollock. I remember his advice, that what-

ever I undertook, I should stay out of politics. I have never yet been in politics, although I have been pretty close to strong political currents here and elsewhere, and I every day find plenty of evidence of what must have been in his mind when he gave me that advice, vis., that honest and success in politics are far from being the handmaidens they once were. And now "In God We Trust" is to be taken off our coins.

James P. Kohler
Brooklyn, November 15, 1907

Another article, in the *Philadelphia Inquirer*, November 14, gave credit to Pollock for the motto but completely botched the history by saying that Pollock had received the "permission of President Buchanan" for it!

EX-GOVERNOR POLLOCK RESPONSIBLE FOR MOTTO

It does not seem likely that "In God We Trust" will appear again on the coins. It was pointed out at the Mint yesterday that Congress had never authorized the inscription, it having been placed on United States coins by order of James Pollock, once Governor of Pennsylvania, when he had charge of the Mint. He was Governor from January 16, 1855, to January 19, 1858, and he died on

April 19, 1890, having figured largely in the history of this State during this period.

It is said that he secured the permission of President Buchanan to have the inscription placed on American coin which President Roosevelt has now forbidden on the grounds that he thinks it is irreverent and therefore out of place.

Perhaps the most amazing piece was carried in the *Evening Star* of Independence, Kansas (November 27, 1907), referencing the account of J.B. Work, a Chicagoan who had been an acquaintance of Dr. Linderman's. In his account, Linderman was the man responsible for the motto, with Work himself playing a role!

MOTTO

"In God We Trust" Only Recently Discarded.

From Coins of the United States, and How the Tabooed Sentiment Originally Came to Be Used by the American Government, After Civil War.

Since President Roosevelt decreed that the familiar "In God We Trust" must come off the United States coins, where it has come to be as familiar as the figure of liberty, there has been considerable inquiry as to how it

got on the coins in the first place. It is well known that the motto first appeared shortly after the war, but a well-known Chicagoan, J.B. Work, a veteran of the war, a member of the G.A.R., and at present in the office of the superintendent of public service of Cook county, happened to be intimately associated with Dr. Lindeman [*sic*], the director of the United States Mint, when the latter ordered the motto placed upon the coins, says the Chicago Inter-Ocean.

"It happened that shortly after the war," said Mr. Work recently discussing how the motto was first adopted, "that I was something of a coin collector, and being down in Virginia, where I often ran across old coins more or less valuable, I used to take a trip up to Washington every now and then to consult with Dr. Lindeman [*sic*], whom I knew well. Whenever I found a coin that I was anxious to know the origin of I used to go to Washington and submit it to the director in the hope that he would be able to throw some light upon it. He was usually able to and in that way I often got some important information which was of great use to numismatists.

"It happened that one day I was in the office of Dr. [Linderman], near the time when the government was about to resume specie payments. He pulled a handful of coins from the drawer and showed them to me. It was at that time that the silver coins mostly bore the motto 'E Pluribus Unum,' which was adopted just previous to Calhoun's attempt at nullification. The object of it was to emphasize the unity of the states. Dr. [Linderman] said that he had been thinking of placing the motto 'In God We Trust' on the coins, because there was no mention of God in the constitution, and he thought there should be some recognition of the Deity, in that we were a Christian nation. He asked me what I thought of it, and I told him that I considered it a very good idea.

"So Dr. [Linderman] sent out a sort of feeler, which is what they often do in Washington when they want to ascertain public sentiment on any contemplated act. He let it be known that this action was contemplated, and in a remarkably short time he began to get letters from all over the country approving the course he had taken. The newspapers contained editorials showing that the sentiment was overwhelmingly in favor of it, and thereafter the motto was placed on the coins and has remained there ever since. Distinguished theologians and ministers strongly advocated it, and that is the reason why the motto which President Roosevelt has caused to be removed became a part of the United States coinage.

The first coins struck off in 1794 contained the figure of the liberty pole and cap, which was the emblem of liberty in this country before we had a flag of any kind. This was finally done away with; then the motto 'E Pluribus Unum' came to be used, and finally 'In God We Trust.'"

After very public criticism, "In God We Trust" was incorporated into Saint-Gaudens's designs in 1908.

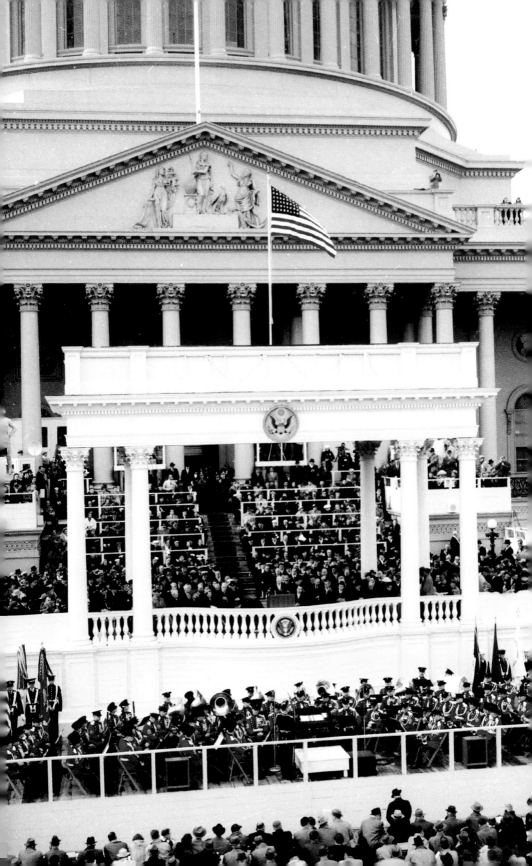

CHAPTER 18

The Revival of the 1950s and the "Unwritten Constitution"

T he United States in the early 1950s experienced an upsurge in religious sensibility. This was manifested in various ways. Church membership grew dramatically. As discussed in chapter 1, the percentage of the population who claimed church or synagogue membership had grown gradually in the nineteenth century but, at least as measured by those claiming official membership, remained at fairly low levels. In 1900 it was at about 36 percent, growing to 43 percent in 1920 and rising further to 49 percent in 1940. After World War II the increase accelerated, reaching 57 percent in 1950 and a peak by 1960 of 69 percent.

This growth was coincident with increased expressions of religious sentiment in public affairs. Of most interest to our present subject, the motto "In God We Trust" gained in visibility and usage during this period, becoming the official motto of the nation. The rise in religiosity and use of religious symbols during this time is often attributed to the Cold War and efforts to distinguish the Western world, the United States in particular, from the overt atheism of Communism in the Soviet Union and China. This was undoubtedly a factor, but there was more to the story.[1] Details of that story are told in a book by history professor Kevin Kruse, *One Nation Under God*. Much of this chapter is drawn from that book.

Opposite page: President Dwight D. Eisenhower delivering his inaugural address on the east portico of the U.S. Capitol, January 21, 1957.

In the late 1930s and early 1940s American business leadership realized that the image of commerce and the business community had been badly damaged by President Franklin Roosevelt and the New Deal, for overt political purposes. The Roosevelt administration's success in painting business as an evil force was leading, in the view of businessmen, to greater concentration and control of commerce by government. Part of the New Deal method in denigrating business was the use of religious and biblical imagery. It seems FDR delighted in using religious language to cast aspersions and shame on his opponents. There are many examples of this. When criticizing Republican promotion of privatization of public utilities (a favorite cause of Wendell Willkie, FDR's 1940 presidential-campaign opponent), Roosevelt said, "There is a history and a sermon on the subject of water power, and I preach from the Old Testament. The text is 'Though Shalt Not Steal.'" Roosevelt blamed the Great Depression on "many amongst us who have made obeisance to Mammon." For the financial industry he said that because of New Deal policies "the money changers have fled from their high seats in the temple of our civilization. We may now restore the temple to ancient truths."[2] In his second inaugural address in 1937 he implicitly portrayed himself as Moses leading his people out of the wilderness. "Shall we pause now and turn our back on the road that lies ahead? Shall we call this the promised land? . . . . Or shall we continue on our way . . . to reach our happy valley?"[3]

The basic message was that the New Deal's plans for instituting its social programs was "the Christian thing to do."[4]

President Franklin D. Roosevelt used religious language to promote his policies.

Various business organizations and individuals began to cooperate to counter the New Dealers' line. The National Association of Manufacturers and J. Howard Pew of Sun Oil, among others, were prominent in the efforts. Through the 1930s they met with only limited success, particularly in failing to sway many clergy to their cause. Then an organization was begun in the early 1940s by James Fifield, the minister of the First Congregational Church of Los Angeles. Fifield had been successful in quadrupling the church's membership in the late 1930s, making it the largest Congregational church in the world. He had raised enough money to eliminate the church's large debt while building an outreach program through radio and other media that reached large numbers of people with a fairly simplified gospel message that had broad appeal. About 1940 Fifield began to focus more directly on the religious community. His organization, Spiritual Mobilization, worked to involve its member clergy in stressing the danger of overcentralized government, its undermining of individual initiative, the dignity of the individual, and personal morality.[5] The organization began a publication called *Faith and Freedom*. It was written mainly by and for ministers. It was effective in promoting the counterarguments to the New Deal in a relatively low-key and non-partisan way.

Under Fifield and his followers' guidance, business- and church-related organizations began to coordinate their activities. They ran essay contests, radio programs, and various events surrounding Independence Day, stressing the need for spiritual foundations to the nation's freedom. These activities were coordinated and labeled as "Freedom Under God" celebrations. A notable example were the activities sponsored on the Sunday before Independence Day and including Independence Day in 1951. Thousands of clergymen offered sermons around the theme on that Sunday morning. These were encouraged by the *Faith and Freedom* publication, which offered prizes for the best sermons submitted to it. Then on that same Sunday evening CBS Radio carried a nationwide broadcast put together by Fifield and his friend the movie mogul Cecil B. DeMille. It included such Hollywood stars as Jimmy Stewart, Bing Crosby, Gloria Swanson, Lionel Barrymore (who read the preamble to the Declaration of Independence), and others who all stressed the general theme that "Freedom under God will save our country." Linking the celebration of independence, the program expressed the thought that the Founding Fathers had been motivated in large part by their religious faith.[6]

It is most interesting that these efforts were reminiscent of those of the Civil War, when North and South contested who was more "on God's side." Indeed that contest led to the Confederate constitution's inclusion of "Almighty God" and ultimately to "In God We Trust" appearing on federal coinage, as well as the efforts of the National Reform Association to change the federal Constitution. In the case of the business community vs. the New Deal during the twentieth century, it was deemed just as important to command the high ground in use of religious symbols as it had been in mid-nineteenth-century Civil War America. Both ends of the political spectrum in the 1950s were eager to promote their religious bona fides. This led to, among other things, greater prominence for "In God We Trust."

In about 1949, the young evangelist Billy Graham began to emerge on the national stage. His well-delivered sermons at large revivals in major cities urged personal salvation but also the salvation of the nation from the "religion of Communism."

In some ways Graham brought the various themes of religious salvation, national freedom, personal freedom, and free enterprise together to become intermingled and mutually supportive by the early 1950s.

Then the movement and the man met as Dwight Eisenhower announced his candidacy for president in 1952. As a retired military man who had never belonged to a church or espoused any denominational affiliation, Eisenhower did not appear on the surface to be an advocate for religion. He rarely even attended church services during his adult career. On the face of it he may not have looked like a person who would work for a national religious revival or be a partner with the business community as it sought to link business in the public mind with religious morality. Eisenhower and his brothers, however, had been raised in a Christian home where prayer and Bible reading were routine. His paternal grandfather had been a minister in the River Brethren Church, an offshoot of the Mennonites. His mother had been Lutheran but converted to the River Brethren when she married his father. Among the teachings of their church was abstinence from alcohol and tobacco. It also renounced violence and supported conscientious objection to military service for its members. His mother expressed disappointment when her son went off to West Point to be a soldier. Furthermore he became a chain smoker. Nevertheless, the religious upbringing had had its effects. Eisenhower wrote in 1952 that "while my brothers and I have always been a little bit 'non-conformist' in the business of actual membership of a particular sect or denomination, we are all very earnestly and very seriously religious. We could not help being so considering our upbringing." An aide of the general during World War II recalled that Eisenhower could "quote scripture by the yard" to make points at staff meetings.[7]

In the late 1940s and early 1950s it seems Eisenhower came to feel that the United States was losing its spiritual anchor. He became acquainted with the evangelist Billy Graham through an introduction by Sid Richardson, the Texas oilman who was a major political supporter of Eisenhower's. Graham, through encouragement from Richardson, urged the general to run for president. At Eisenhower's request Graham began advising him on spiritual matters. Graham, while not

Evangelist Billy Graham.

officially endorsing him, helped add appropriate religious content to his speeches.

Eisenhower by 1952 still had not joined any specific church and commented to a friend that "While I have no objection whatsoever to joining a particular group, the fact is that the only reason for doing so from my viewpoint is the ease it provides in answering questions. It is easier to say 'I am a Presbyterian' than to say 'I am a Christian but I do not belong to any denomination.'"[8] This is reminiscent of Abraham Lincoln's thoughts on the matter: "When any church will inscribe over its altar as its sole qualification for membership the Savior's condensed statement of the substance of the law and Gospel, Thou shalt love the Lord thy God with all thy heart, and with all thy soul, and with all thy mind, and thy neighbor as thyself, that church I will join with all my heart and soul."[9]

Nevertheless Billy Graham urged Eisenhower to choose a denomination, if only for appearance's sake. He decided to do so but waited until after the election in November of 1952, so as not to appear "to use the church politically." After he was elected by a landslide of 442 to 89 electoral votes he followed through in early 1953, being baptized and joining the Presbyterian Church, probably choosing it because his wife, Mamie, was a Presbyterian. The minister at the National Presbyterian Church in Washington promised to be discreet and keep all of this quiet. Later Eisenhower complained, "We were scarcely home before the fact was being publicized by the pastor, to the hilt." Eisenhower sent his press secretary to "go tell that goddam minister that if he gives out one more story about my religious faith I won't join his goddam church."[10]

Eisenhower wanted to put his mandate to work in reviving the spiritual life of the country. He met with Billy Graham and Sid Richardson shortly after the election and told them, "I think one of the reasons I was elected was to help lead this country spiritually. . . . We need a spiritual renewal."[11] Shortly after that meeting Eisenhower delivered a speech at the Waldorf Astoria in New York. It was filled with references to that spiritual renewal. "[If] we are to be strong, we must be strong first in our spiritual convictions." He said, "Americans have to go back to the very fundamentals of all things. And one of them is that we are a religious people. Even those among us who are, in my opinion, so silly as to doubt the existence of any Almighty, are still members of a religious civilization, because the Founding Fathers said it was a religious concept that they were trying to translate into the political world." He called attention to the use of the term "Creator" in the Declaration

of Independence. But his most notable line was that "our form of government has no sense unless it is founded in a deeply-felt religious faith, and I don't care what it is." This line drew much comment, both negative and positive. Many believed his intent was to express that the mainstream faiths of America (Protestantism, Catholicism, and Judaism) were similar to one another in affirming general spiritual ideals and moral values of the nation.[12] There was a vagueness in this that his supporters believed was intentional, as he was seeking a kind of lowest common denominator of religious faith to support national unity and give him a rapport with all religious groups.

Even before Eisenhower's inauguration, on February 5, 1953, a National Prayer Breakfast was organized as an offshoot of a previous existing Senate Prayer Breakfast. A capacity crowd of more than 500 attended and included Supreme Court justices, senators, representatives, Cabinet members, and ambassadors, as well as prominent businesspeople. Chief Justice Fred Vinson commented that he had "never felt or seen anything like this in all my years here in Washington." The breakfast led to similar prayer meetings and discussion groups being formed in various government departments.[13]

In his Inaugural Address Eisenhower offered a prayer: "Almighty God, as we stand here at this moment my future associates in the Executive branch of Government join me in beseeching that Thou will make full complete our dedication to the service of the people in this throng, and their fellow citizens everywhere."

Among his early actions, Eisenhower began opening Cabinet meetings with prayer. He deemed this appropriate as Congress opened its sessions this way. However, in the early days of the administration this wasn't yet routine, and he was known to sometimes forget it. According to a secretary he once came out of a Cabinet meeting and said, "Jesus Christ, we forgot the prayer!"[14]

One of the first concrete changes made to national ceremonialism during the Eisenhower administration involved the Pledge of Allegiance. The background and evolution of this familiar recitation in schools and at public events is relatively little known. It was written by Francis Bellamy, a Baptist minister from Rome, New York. Besides being a minister he was an active socialist, being one of the founders of the Society of Christian Socialists, a group dedicated to the idea that socialism and Christianity had the same aims and that Christ's teachings would lead to some form of socialism. In 1891 he took a job with *Youth's Companion Magazine* and became involved with commemoration events in 1892 of the 400th anniversary of Columbus's discovery of America. Among the plans for commemoration was to have every schoolhouse in the country display the American flag and to have students go through a brief ceremony celebrating the flag and the nation. The idea caught on, and Bellamy met with President Benjamin Harrison, who endorsed the plans. Bellamy spent about two hours drafting a pledge to be said at these commemoration ceremonies:

Opposite page: President Dwight D. Eisenhower.

"I pledge allegiance to my Flag and to the Republic for which it stands—one Nation indivisible—with Liberty and Justice for all."[15] It seems it was widely used during the Columbus Day celebrations in 1892. In subsequent years, however, there were several such flag pledges that were written and used around the country. Different schools used different pledges and usage was inconsistent even within individual schools. After World War I there was an effort to select a single pledge. In 1923 and 1924 there were National Flag Conferences that worked on this and other protocols surrounding the flag. Bellamy offered his pledge as an option but modified it from saying "my Flag" to "the Flag of the United States of America." This was in response to the large number of immigrants coming into the country and the schools during this period; it would make clear which flag they were addressing, i.e., not the flag of the country they had recently left. This pledge within a short time became a standard part of U.S. school life as students recited it before classes began every day. In December of 1945 Congress made it the official pledge to the American flag.[16]

In April of 1951 the Knights of Columbus, the Catholic fraternal group, proposed adding "under God" after the words "one nation" in the pledge. This was likely thought of in the environment of the "Freedom Under God" activities of the early 1950s. The organization sent copies of its proposal to President Harry Truman, other officials, and members of Congress. One congressman in particular picked up the idea and promoted it. He was Louis Rabaut, a Democrat from Detroit and a

Schoolchildren reciting the Pledge of Allegiance in New York City, 1943.

Opposite page:
A World War I–era Knights of Columbus poster illustrating the military's trust in God.

KNIGHTS·OF·COLVMBVS

ALFOUR-KER

devout Catholic. In a way these events marked a change, as most of the earlier efforts for such religious symbolism had come from Protestants. The Catholics were now joining in. Rabaut pushed for support in Congress, but no action was taken. Then another event tipped Rabaut's proposal over the top. George Docherty, the minister of the New York Avenue Presbyterian Church in Washington, D.C., preached a sermon in May of 1952 noting that the Pledge of Allegiance lacked any reference to God. Though his sermon was praised by his congregation, nothing came of it. Nevertheless he kept the idea in mind and in February of 1954 he learned that President Eisenhower would be attending his church service for the annual "Lincoln Sunday" event. Docherty got his old sermon out and brushed it up for the service to be heard by the president and Mrs. Eisenhower.

Docherty in his message stated that the Pledge of Allegiance was missing something. He said rhetorically that he could "hear young Muscovites repeat a similar pledge to their hammer-and-sickle flag in Moscow with equal solemnity." Placing "Under God" in the pledge would distinguish it and show "the definitive character of the American way of life." Not surprisingly, the sermon created something of a sensation, convincing Eisenhower that action should be taken. Rabaut's bill was resurrected in Congress and was quickly joined by 16 other bills to the same end. Representatives and senators scrambled to co-sponsor or in some way have their names associated with its passage. Seven of the related bills were from Democrats, eight from Republicans, and one from an Independent. It was one of the few things in that session to receive bipartisan support! All sides wanted to present themselves as being in tune with God's will. The bill was signed into law by President Eisenhower on Flag Day, June 14, 1954.[17] Schoolchildren have ever since recited:

> I pledge allegiance to the Flag of the United States of America, and to the Republic for which it stands, One Nation under God, indivisible, with liberty and justice for all.

George Docherty (left) with President Eisenhower, February 1954.

Representative Louis Rabaut of Michigan pushed for "under God" being added to the Pledge of Allegiance.

"In God We Trust" came in for more attention during this period. In 1952 a popular newspaper column for stamp collectors written by Ernest Kehr proposed creating a postage stamp imprinted with the motto. If on the coins, why not on the stamps? Kehr succeeded in having other newspapers and magazines, as well as television and radio stations, promote his idea. Eventually he convinced the American Legion to pass a resolution of support. Through these means the matter was introduced in Congress with liberal Democrat Mike Mansfield sponsoring it in the Senate and conservative Republican Charles Potter in the House. Mansfield was a Catholic and Potter a Protestant. So this issue, like

The "In God We Trust" postage-stamp design introduced by President Eisenhower in 1954.

the Pledge of Allegiance, united people both politically and religiously. Congressman Rabaut, who had got the ball rolling for the Pledge, joined in this effort but, in addition to a stamp bearing "In God We Trust," he wanted all postal cancellation marks to also carry the motto, saying that "Use of the motto as a cancellation mark would give it a wider distribution and bring it more constantly to the attention of our people." The stamp was approved, and the Post Office issued an 8¢ stamp with the motto in April of 1954. It was the first stamp to be introduced by a president, as Eisenhower personally attended the official ceremony. It was deemed to be the largest ceremony of its kind in Post Office history. The stamp proved very popular and sold in large numbers.

In the meantime Rabaut pressed his case for the motto on all postal cancellations. When his proposal languished he suggested instead that cancellations carry "Pray for Peace." This received more support from both Congress and the Post Office, and was adopted.

The successes and popularity of "Under God" in the pledge in June 1954 and "In God We Trust" on the postage stamp in April 1954 led to a push for "In God We Trust" on U.S. paper currency. In some ways it is surprising that this hadn't been done when the motto was put on coins in the 1860s. There is one report that, when presented with the idea, President Lincoln had turned it down. Quoting Scripture he had joked, "Silver and gold have I none, but such as I have give I thee." He may have been referencing his own doubts about paper money unbacked by silver or gold.[18]

One individual is credited with getting the ball rolling again on this issue. He was Matthew Rothert, a prominent coin collector from Arkansas. Rothert had founded a furniture-manufacturing company in the late 1920s and was a well-known businessman in the state. At a Sunday morning church service in 1953, the collection plate was passed by him. He was suddenly struck with the realization that while the coins in the plate bore "In God We Trust," the paper currency did not. He became an advocate for adding the motto to the currency, believing its placement would give the message wider circulation. He said, "I realized that the circulation of American coins was limited to the boundaries of the country, while U.S. paper money circulated worldwide."[19] He began giving talks on the subject and promoting the idea through letters to newspapers and congressmen. Through his business influence he drew the attention of his own senator, William J. Fulbright, to the subject. Also through his membership and influence in the American Numismatic Association he succeeded in having the organization pass a resolution at its annual convention held in Cleveland on August 21, 1954. (Rothert later became president of the ANA from 1965 to 1967.)

At about the same time Rothert was promoting the motto on currency, the American Legion followed up with a nearly identical resolution at its convention held in Washington. Donald Carroll, the state commander of the Legion in Florida, became especially enthusiastic about the idea and convinced his congressman, Charles Bennett, to sponsor it in Congress. Bennett, a Democrat, represented his Florida district for 44 years and was known for his efforts to improve ethics in

Matthew Rothert at the 1967 opening of the new American Numismatic Association headquarters. One Sunday in church he noticed as the collection plate passed him that the paper currency lacked "In God We Trust," and he began a campaign to have it added.

Congress and government in general. He was an active member of the Disciples of Christ and had been leader of a prayer breakfast group. A colleague was known to have commented that he was "a little too pious."

Bennett was successful in building congressional support for the motto and began soliciting support from the administration. It seems the Treasury secretary, George Humphrey, may have initially resisted the idea on the grounds of high costs involved in changing the designs on the currency. However, President Eisenhower expressed support, and that led to Humphrey and the Treasury Department lending whatever help was needed with Congress. Bennett's bill was well received in the House Committee on Banking and Currency

Representative Charles E. Bennett was known as "Mr. Clean" for his work on congressional ethics.

with one exception, Abraham Multer, a Jewish representative from Brooklyn. While he supported religion in public life he said he felt "very strongly that it was a mistake to put it on coins in the first place and this is perpetuating a grievous error. . . . I don't believe it has inspired one single person to be more religious because we have these words on our currency. . . . If we are going to have religious concepts—and I am in favor of them—I don't think the place to put them is on our currency or on our coins." Nevertheless he did not officially oppose the bill, and it passed out of committee unanimously. The full House passed the bill with almost no debate on June 7, 1955.[20]

In the Senate the groundwork had already been laid by William Fulbright, who had been sold on the project by his constituent, Matthew Rothert. Fulbright, a liberal Democrat, was chairman of the Banking and Commerce Committee. Fulbright's bill, identical to the House bill, passed the committee unanimously and was reported to the full Senate. The bill then passed the full Senate, also unanimously, on June 29. President Eisenhower signed the bill July 11.

Due to ongoing installation of new printing presses at the Bureau of Engraving and Printing, the new notes bearing "In God We Trust" did not come into circulation until 1957.

Well before the new currency even appeared in public, soon after Eisenhower signed the bill in 1955, Congressman Bennett began working for a congressional resolution declaring "In God We Trust" to be the official national motto! He introduced the bill July 21, 1955. Initially it didn't have support, but by February of 1956 he was able to have it moved through the relevant House Judiciary subcommittee.

Matthew Rothert was famous, especially among coin and paper-money collectors, for his role in the placement of "In God We Trust" on U.S. paper currency. He was frequently asked to autograph notes as he did just under the motto on this $50 bill.

He acted as a witness (the only witness) before the subcommittee and said: "In sponsoring this legislation, it is my position that it would be valuable to our country to have a clearly designated national motto of inspirational quality and in plain popularly accepted English." It is interesting that Bennett cited the final stanza of "The Star Spangled Banner", i.e., "And this be our motto, 'In God is our trust.'" It is unlikely that Bennett was aware that James B. Longacre and James Pollock had also used that stanza to derive "In God We Trust." It seems rather that Bennett cited the national anthem as a bit of flattery to gain support from Emanuel Celler, the powerful House member and chairman of the subcommittee. Celler had been instrumental in establishing "The Star Spangled Banner" as the official national anthem way back in 1931.[21] The effort to win Celler over was successful, and he moved the bill through his committee quickly. By April 17, 1956, the full House passed Bennett's bill.

There had been little or no opposition expressed in the House proceedings, but some organizations, the American Civil Liberties Union in particular, raised objections in the Senate. The ACLU sent a letter to the Senate Judiciary subcommittee: "In our opinion, this change would be at the very least an approach toward the infringement upon the Constitutional guarantee that there shall be no establishment of religion in this country," and it "would also, through the implicit authority of the national motto, constitute a religious test for government employees." There was support in the Senate for the bill, and it was evidently pushed through fairly quickly before any further opposition could be mounted. The full Senate passed it on July 23, 1956. President Eisenhower signed it into law on July 30.[22]

So, as Kevin Kruse points out in his book, "In little more than two years time, 'In God We Trust' had surged to public notice, first taking a place of prominence on stamps and currency, and then edging its way past 'E Pluribus Unum' to become the nation's first official motto."

Beyond the increased public use of these religious allusions, another effort appeared to take advantage of this favorable atmosphere toward Christian/religious sentiment. It came almost as a ghost from the past as the National Reform Association reemerged to again promote its 90-year-old effort to amend the Constitution. In 1954 the organization's head official, a Presbyterian minister, J. Renwick Patterson, provided the Senate with a long list of practices that showed that "the spiritual has been woven into the fabric of American life" as a kind of unwritten law. His list included public prayers delivered at presidential inaugurations, prayers before congressional sessions, military chaplains, and tax-exempt status for religious organizations. Patterson said:

> All of these things testify to the place Christianity had had in the past and continues to have in our national life. . . . But when it comes to our Constitution, our fundamental law, there is complete silence regarding God. He isn't even mentioned. There is no recognition, no acknowledgement. In our Constitution there is absolutely nothing to undergird and give legal sanction to the religious practices mentioned above.

The Constitution, Patterson argued, should be amended to support these and other religious practices. His words echoed those of 90 years earlier.

In May of 1954, Republican senator Ralph Flanders, from Vermont, presented a bill to a Judiciary subcommittee for the following amendment to the Constitution:

> This Nation devoutly recognizes the authority and law of Jesus Christ, Savior and Ruler of nations through whom are bestowed the blessings of Almighty God.

Flanders did not obtain approval for his Christian amendment. The effort failed, as those before it had. Nevertheless the adoption of the motto "In God We Trust," of "One Nation Under God," and the other changes toward religion in this era had created a kind of "Unwritten Constitution" favorable to religious expression in the public sphere.[23]

Congressman Emanuel Celler, who represented New York from 1923 to 1973, helped smooth the way for "In God We Trust" becoming the national motto.

CHAPTER 19

Challenges to "In God We Trust"

W ith the passing of the 1950s and the arrival of the 1960s some challenges and testing of earlier religious measures began. Some challenges sought a rollback of the mixing of politics and religion, but in
other cases the challenges were not to existing practices but rather to their further
extensions. An example of this was the court case of *Engel vs. Vitale*. This case
involved the New York Board of Regents, which oversaw public education in the
State of New York. In 1951 the board became interested in the "moral and spiritual training in the schools" and recommended schools introduce prayer before
classes began each day. To assist the schools in this effort the board composed a
suggested prayer to be used. It read: "Almighty God, we acknowledge our dependence upon Thee, and we beg Thy blessings upon us, our parents, our teachers,
and our Country." This was adopted by many of the schools in the state and
became known as "The Regents' Prayer." Some schools did not follow the recommendation at all while others adopted the recommendation for prayer but chose
alternative prayers or variations of the Regents' version. This practice continued
through the 1950s, and in 1955 the board also recommended that schools should
foster spiritual and moral values through students' studying various documents
such as the Declaration of Independence and presidential speeches.[1]

Eventually these policies, particularly the prayer, led to splits along sectarian lines
in particular school districts. In suburban Long Island one district, the Herrick
Union District, experienced such a split, mainly between a Catholic majority and a
Jewish minority. In 1956 and 1957 unsuccessful efforts were made on the local school
board to adopt the Regents' Prayer, but in 1958 a turnover in the board membership
led to approval. This created a reaction in the growing Jewish community, which
opposed use of the prayer, and led to *Engel vs. Vitale*. The case worked its way up
through the New York courts in the late 1950s and early 1960s, with the school
board's pro-prayer position winning at every level. Eventually in 1962 it reached the

Opposite page: Madalyn Murray O'Hair, likely the most noted atheist of recent times.

U.S. Supreme Court. Here the school board's case was overruled in a 6 to 1 decision declaring the prayer a violation of the First Amendment's Establishment Clause. (Two justices did not vote, due to illness.) Justice Hugo Black drafted the opinion for the majority. In a lengthy and detailed opinion he spelled out that part of the reason the Pilgrims and others had fled to America was to escape such governmentally mandated prayers in Europe.[2]

Black caught the public's outrage over the ruling, receiving thousands of letters, telegrams, and phone calls. Among the letters was one from California worrying about a slippery slope from the ruling: "Next God will be taken out of the oath of the President; out

Supreme Court Justice Hugo L. Black wrote the majority opinion for *Engel vs. Vitale*, which ruled against mandated school prayer.

of the courts; out of the National Anthem, the salute to the flag, off the coin of the U.S.; out of the Battle Hymn of the Republic; prayer will be taken out of the House and Senate; the national observance of a Day of Thanksgiving to God abandoned; Christmas and the Christian Sabbath will be objected and vetoed by our Supreme Court as embarrassing to somebody."[3]

Indeed the letter writer from California had a point: though the court had ruled that prayers could not be said to open a school day, how was it that sessions of Congress and even of the Supreme Court itself could be opened with prayer, as indeed

Justice William Douglas (seen here on the day of his swearing-in, with his son) pondered the constitutionality of *any* undertaking of "governmental aids to religion"—including "In God We Trust" on currency.

they were? Black had included a footnote in his decision in which he said, "There is of course nothing in this decision reached here that is inconsistent with the fact that school children and others are officially encouraged to express love for our country by reciting historical documents such as the Declaration of Independence which contain references to the Deity . . . or with the fact that there are many manifestations in our public life of belief in God." Furthermore "such patriotic or ceremonial occasions bear no true resemblance to the unquestioned religious exercise that the State of New York has sponsored in this instance."[4] Likely Black felt this commentary mitigated any contradictions of the court's ruling with public officials' prayer.

Congressional Counterprotest

It was no surprise that there was an outcry regarding the *Engel* decision with most of the public opposing it. In the House the reaction resulted in a symbolic action being taken. Fred Marshall, a representative from Minnesota, proposed placing "In God We Trust" behind and above the Speaker's chair in the House chamber. This was passed swiftly and unanimously. Another representative, William Randolph from Missouri, made sure the connection with the court decision was clear, saying it was "in a not so subtle way our answer to the recent decision of the U.S. Supreme Court order banning the Regents' Prayer from the New York State schools." The motto was added in September of 1962. The Senate chamber already had the motto inscribed over its south entrance, with "E Pluribus Unum" on the other side over the presiding officer's chair.

And so the Supreme Court ruling banning officially sponsored prayer in schools led to more prominent display and official recognition for "In God We Trust" as a kind of protest on the part of Congress against the ruling.

The display of the motto in the House chamber came into play during President Donald Trump's January 30, 2018, State of the Union Address. In it he stated, "We all share the same home, the same heart, the same destiny, and the same American flag. Together we are rediscovering the American way. In America, we know that faith and family, not government and bureaucracy, are the center of American life. Our motto is 'In God We Trust.'"

Speaker of the House Paul Ryan, seated in the speaker's chair behind the president, pointed his finger up to where the motto is inscribed on the wall. There was general applause for the president's line, with even Democratic leader Nancy Pelosi applauding, one of the few times she did so during his address.

In his book *Dark Agenda: The War to Destroy Christian America*, David Horowitz points out that, while the motto remains on the wall of the actual chamber of the House, the U.S. Capitol Visitor Center replica version of the speaker's rostrum omits it. The Visitor Center was completed in 2008 at a cost of $621 million for the purpose of reducing or eliminating tourist traffic from the actual House and Senate chambers. Also photos on display of the chamber cropped out the motto, until protests from some conservative lawmakers forced uncropped pictures showing the motto to be used. Other displays in the Visitor Center state that the official motto of the United States is "E Pluribus Unum," just as President Obama had claimed.

Justice William Douglas disagreed with Black's thinking on this issue and wrote a separate opinion. In it he said he agreed with the unconstitutionality of the New York prayer but also said, "If however we would strike down a New York requirement that public school teachers open each day with prayer, I think we could not consistently open each of our own sessions with prayer. That's the kernel of my problem." He pointed out that many "governmental aids to religion" including religious proclamations by presidents, the use of "In God We Trust" on currency, and the addition of "Under God" to the Pledge of Allegiance were problematic. He said, "I think it is an unconstitutional undertaking whatever form it takes."

The lone dissenting justice, Potter Stewart, said something similar, pointing out the contradictions of the majority ruling. "Is the Court suggesting that the Constitution permits judges and Congressmen and the President to join in prayer, but prohibits school children from doing so?" He doubted that the religious observances that were common in government and schools established anything like an "official religion." These thoughts, though similar to Douglas's, led him to vote in an opposite direction and to uphold school prayer as the means of preventing the contradiction with official public prayer.[5]

Douglas's solution to eliminating the contradiction would have been to eliminate all public religious observances while Stewart likely would have made everything, including school prayer, constitutional. Further cases brought to the court would attempt to deal with this contradiction, but the contradiction remains to this day.

The *Engel vs. Vitale* decision led logically to another case the following year, 1963. This was *Abington School District vs. Schempp*. The case involved Bible-reading in schools. A Pennsylvania state statute required that teachers read 10 Bible verses every morning to their students without comment. A quarter of the states in the U.S. had mandatory Bible-reading as Pennsylvania did. Another quarter had legal provisions permitting voluntary readings but not requiring them. Yet another quarter had no laws relating to the practice but de facto permitted it. Approximately another quarter had laws specifically prohibiting such Bible readings in their schools. Most of the states either mandating or permitting the practices were in the Northeast and South, and many had had such Bible readings since the nineteenth century.

The *Abington* case involved a student, Ellory Schempp, whose family was Unitarian and who objected to his being required to listen to the readings. The American Civil Liberties Union supported Schempp, and a U.S. District Court in Philadelphia ruled against the school requirements. The school appealed, leading eventually to the Supreme Court. At the same time another case, very similar to *Abington*, reached the Court. This was a case from Maryland brought by Madalyn

Murray (later O'Hair), involving her son, William, who also had been exposed to mandatory Bible readings at his public school in Baltimore. The ACLU had earlier supported that case but dropped it finding Madalyn Murray, a strict atheist, too abrasive to work with and likely not presenting a sympathetic image to the courts. Murray therefore pushed the case to the Court on her own, and stated, "The ACLU can go to hell and take their opinions with them."

Because the two cases (*Schempp* and *Murray*) were so similar, the Court decided to combine them and hear them in 1963. The Court ruled against the schools and the practice of Bible readings. The reaction was more muted than in the *Engel* prayer case as it was largely expected. However, there was something of a denominational split as the Jewish establishment and mainline Protestant denominational leadership actually expressed support for the ruling, while the Catholic hierarchy and Fundamentalist Protestants objected to it. It was also noted that while the mainline Protestant leadership showed support, a large portion of their lay congregations disagreed and feared that all religion in public life would ultimately be lost.[6]

Justice Tom Clark wrote the majority opinion (decided 8 to 1), but other justices also wrote four different but concurring opinions. Justice William Brennan in particular seemed sensitive to the fears that religion would be driven from the public domain, and tried to spell out in his concurrence what was permissible. He said, for example, "'In God We Trust' was simply interwoven so deeply into the fabric of our civil polity that its present use may well not present that type of involvement which the First Amendment prohibits." In similar fashion the phrase "Under God" in the Pledge "may merely recognize the historical fact that our Nation was believed to have been founded under God."[7]

Madalyn Murray O'Hair

Madalyn Murray O'Hair is almost certainly the most famous (or infamous) atheist of recent times. She was born Madalyn Elizabeth Mays in 1919 in suburban Pittsburgh. She attended the University of Toledo and later the University of Pittsburgh. She met and married John Henry Roths in October of 1941. With the Japanese attack on Pearl Harbor occurring in December, just weeks after they married, the nation was mobilized and John went into the U.S. Marines. Madalyn also joined the war effort, in the Women's Army Corps, attending Officer Candidate School and learning top-secret cryptographic code skills. She was sent to North Africa and later to Europe. While in the military she met and fell in love with an Eighth Air Force pilot,

William Murray. She became pregnant by him, but he too was already married, making for an impossible situation. When she returned from the military her husband was willing to remain with her and adopt the child as his own. However, she proceeded to divorce him, giving the newborn baby the name of the father, William Murray, and adopting Murray as her own name as well. She returned to college (Ashland College in Ohio) under the GI Bill and graduated in 1948. She moved to Texas and worked as a probation officer while attending law school at South Texas College of Law, where she earned a degree but failed to pass the bar exam. She had a second baby with a neighbor and named the child John Garth Murray.

Even before her fame as an atheist, Madalyn Murray was known for her foul-mouthed expressions and slovenly appearance, which often made it difficult for her to maintain employment.

She followed her parents in a move to Baltimore, Maryland, and there soon found her destiny as an atheist activist. As she accompanied her son Bill to the local Baltimore junior high school in the fall of 1960 to register him, she was struck by how quiet the school was. She saw that the students were all standing quietly reciting "The Lord's Prayer." She immediately went to the administrative office and demanded that her son not be subjected to any mandatory prayer. She told the principal that her son would be starting school and "I'm an atheist and I don't want him taught any gawd damned prayers." She learned the school also held mandatory Bible readings. She was able to gather a great deal of publicity for her demands against the readings and eventually brought a lawsuit that ultimately led to her Supreme Court case *Schempp and Murray* in 1963. This was a landmark victory for separation of state and religion as Bible readings in school were deemed unconstitutional. Though she was only somewhat secondarily involved with the case, her name was attached to the decision. The Schempp family was not interested in the publicity surrounding the victory, while Madalyn played her role up to the hilt. She began receiving donations for her efforts from atheist supporters and went on to found the American Atheist Society as well as numerous other related groups. She began publishing *The American Atheist*. She gathered more notoriety as she filed numerous lawsuits against a whole range of what she deemed religiously tainted activities.

In 1965 she married Richard O'Hair and added his name to hers, arriving at how she is best known, Madalyn Murray O'Hair.

In 1995 she, her son John Garth Murray, and her granddaughter disappeared. By that time O'Hair's son Bill had become estranged from her and had become a Christian

Notwithstanding Justice Brennan's reference in the 1963 Schempp and Murray case to "In God We Trust" as being constitutional because it had "ceased to have

evangelist. Local law enforcement in Austin, Texas, where she then lived and operated her various organizations, were not aggressive in searching for her as she had repeatedly irritated them with complaints and charges of anti-atheist bias. Furthermore, large sums of money were missing from the organizations' coffers, and there were rumors that she had fled the country with the money to escape various lawsuits against her as well as tax-fraud charges by the IRS. The police believed she would eventually turn up in New Zealand or some other distant place. The disappearance remained a mystery for nearly two years. But in the end some enterprising reporters were able to break the case and learned that O'Hair, her son, and her granddaughter had been kidnapped by a former employee and his cohorts, were forced to withdraw funds for the kidnappers, and then were murdered by those

The 50th-anniversary issue of *American Atheist*, founded by Madalyn Murray O'Hair. The cover highlights her opposition to "In God We Trust," with "In God We Do Not Trust" next to her image on a $50 bill.

kidnappers. Their bodies were mutilated and buried in a remote area of the Texas Hill Country. The kidnappers/murderers were eventually brought to trial and convicted, ending an amazing saga for Mrs. O'Hair, often deemed "the most hated woman in America."[8]

O'Hair wrote numerous atheist tracts. Among these was "A Brief History of Religious Mottoes on United States Currency and Coins." It was a well-researched piece covering accurately the story of Mark Watkinson's letter, along with Salmon Chase's and James Pollock's roles. O'Hair highlighted the two-cent piece as being the first coin with "In God We Trust," and the motto's later addition to other coins in 1866. She related Theodore Roosevelt's story connected with the $10 and $20 gold pieces and the legalities surrounding these. She also covered placement of the motto on paper currency, including Matthew Rothert's part in the story.

O'Hair's main reason for writing the piece was to demonstrate the religious origins of "In God We Trust" in history, demonstrating that it was, in her view, an establishment of religion. (The tract was published by O'Hair's American Atheist Press and is still available in print through that organization.)

religious meaning," the motto was challenged in 1970 in a case brought by Stefan Ray Aronow in a federal district court in California. The court ruled that Aronow lacked standing as he could not demonstrate that he had suffered harm from the motto. However, he appealed to the Ninth Circuit, which agreed he lacked standing but nevertheless ruled on the merits of the case. Aronow's case challenged "the use of expressions of trust in God by the United States Government on its coinage, currency, official documents, and publications." Aronow claimed that the motto and its usage violated the Establishment Clause of the Constitution. The court determined that the motto isn't actually religious and that its presence on a bill or coin did not carry any religious significance. The ruling stated:

> It is quite obvious that the national motto and the slogan on coinage and currency "In God We Trust" has nothing whatsoever to do with the establishment of religion. Its use is of a patriotic or ceremonial character and bears no true resemblance to a governmental sponsorship of a religious exercise. . . . It is not easy to discern any religious significance attendant the payment of a bill with coin or currency on which has been imprinted "In God We Trust" or the study of a government publication or document bearing that slogan. In fact, such secular uses of the motto was viewed as sacrilegious and irreverent by President Theodore Roosevelt. Yet Congress has directed such uses. While "ceremonial" and "patriotic" may not be particularly apt words to describe the category of the national motto, it is excluded from First Amendment significance because the motto has no theological or ritualistic impact. As stated by the Congressional report, it has "spiritual and psychological value" and "inspirational quality."[9]

In an interesting and perhaps confusing turn, the court cited Teddy Roosevelt's objection to having the motto on coins as the commercial context sullied and diminished its religious sentiment. Aronow appealed to the Supreme Court, but the Court declined to hear the case, in effect agreeing with the Ninth Circuit's decision.[10]

There have been various other challenges to the motto since *Aronow*, most notably *O'Hair vs. Blumenthal* in 1978. Madalyn Murray O'Hair, the famous atheist activist, sued Treasury Secretary Michael Blumenthal, arguing use of "In God We Trust" on national coins and paper currency and its designation as the national motto were a violation of the First Amendment. The case was heard in U.S. District Court in Austin and was rejected; the court cited *Aronow* as deeming the motto not in violation of the First Amendment.

Another related case in 1977 reached the Supreme Court: *Wooley vs. Maynard*. In this case the court ruled in a 6-to-3 decision that stated New Hampshire (in this case) could not require display of a state motto on vehicle license plates. The court explicitly commented in its opinion that the ruling did not affect the motto on coinage or currency:

It has been suggested that today's holding will be read as sanctioning obliteration of the National Motto, "In God We Trust," from United States coins and currency. That question is not before us today but we note that currency, which is passed from hand to hand, differs in significant respects from an automobile, which is readily associated with its operator. Currency is generally carried in a purse or pocket and need not be displayed by the public. The bearer of currency is thus not required to publicly advertise the National Motto.

In this case, Chief Justice William Rehnquist, in a dissent from the license-plate ruling, commented on the motto:

> I cannot imagine that the statutes proscribing defacement of U.S. currency impinge upon the First Amendment rights of an atheist. The fact that an atheist carries and uses U.S. currency does not, in any meaningful sense, convey any affirmation of belief on his part in the motto "In God We Trust."[11]

A concept which underlies these cases from the 1970s had been voiced in a 1961 lecture at Brown University, delivered by Eugene Rostow, the dean of Yale University Law School. In his lecture he coined the term "Ceremonial Deism." By this he meant that phrases such as "In God We Trust" and "One Nation Under God" were so general as to be supported by a wide religious spectrum including Protestants, Catholics, and Jews. These phrases were ceremonial and "ornamental" without meaningful substance. Rostow deemed them to be "so conventional and uncontroversial as to be constitutional." There was wide concurrence with Rostow's thoughts. The American Civil Liberties Union and other related organizations generally did not contest the concept.

Nevertheless, various suits contesting the constitutionality of the motto have continued to be brought. An example was in 2013 as the Freedom From Religion Foundation (the FFRF, a national non-profit educational organization of atheists and agnostics) filed such a suit in a New York federal district court. A noted contemporary atheist, Michael Newdow, seems in some respect to have picked up the mantle of Madalyn Murray O'Hair and has filed various suits dating back some years, contesting

Michael Newdow is an emergency-room physician who also has a law degree. He has brought various suits against "In God We Trust" and clearly intends to continue the fight against the motto.

the constitutionality of the motto. Newdow works as an emergency-room physician in California but leverages his University of Michigan law degree for atheist causes. He represented the FFRF and several other plaintiffs in court. He argued that the plaintiffs in the case were "forced to proselytize—by an act of Congress—for a deity they don't believe in whenever they handle money."[12]

Robert Zimmerman, the pastor of the Prospect Hill Baptist Church (from whence Reverend Mark Watkinson wrote his letter to Treasury Secretary Salmon Chase proposing a religious motto on U.S. coinage), was quoted in the March 2006 issue of *Coinage Magazine* saying that atheist Michael Newdow's 2006 anti–"In God We Trust" lawsuit was "just more lunacy as far as I am concerned."

In an interesting twist several of the other plaintiffs were coin collectors, termed *numismatists* in the case. They were included to help establish damages. Among them was Newdow's mother, Rosalyn. She was deemed a numismatist who bought coin sets from the U.S. Mint for more than 40 years, but because of the "In God We Trust" verbiage "she has felt obligated to stop purchasing these sets, thus being deprived of the pleasure and the investment opportunity" she would otherwise partake of. Another numismatist, Kenneth Bronstein, had purchased coins from the U.S. Mint for nearly 60 years. But because of the coins bearing the offensive motto, he opted to stop purchasing these coins, thus being deprived of an investment opportunity as well as the enjoyment of the hobby. Another plaintiff complained that he found "In God We Trust" on the coins and currency so alienating that "he has altered his behavior to use as little cash as possible."

Judge Harold Baer of the district court rejected the claims. In his ruling he said:

> The Supreme Court has repeatedly assumed the motto's secular purpose and effect, and all circuit courts that have considered this issue—namely the Ninth, Fifth, Tenth, and D.C. Circuits—have found no constitutional violation in the motto's inclusion on currency. Each circuit court that has considered the issue found no Establishment Clause violation in the motto's placement on currency, finding ceremonial or secular purposes and no religious effect or endorsement.
>
> While Plaintiffs may be inconvenienced or offended by the appearance of the motto on currency, these burdens are a far cry from the coercion, penalty, or denial of benefits required under the "substantial burden" standard. As such the inclusion of the motto on currency does not present a violation to the Free Exercise Clause or the Religious Freedom Restoration Act.[13]

Despite the failure of this and other cases that have challenged the motto, Newdow has been persistent; he filed another similar case in an Ohio court in 2016.

It would seem "In God We Trust" has thus far been sheltered from serious constitutional challenge based on the concept of "Ceremonial Deism." However, an article from 1996 in the *Columbia Law Review*, titled "Rethinking the Constitutionality of Ceremonial Deism," contests this assumption. Its author, Stephen Epstein, listed 10 manifestations of Ceremonial Deism:

Legislative prayers

Prayers at presidential inaugurations

Presidential addresses invoking the name of God

Invocations in the courts; "God save the United States and this honorable court"

Oaths of public office including the use of the Bible

Use of A.D. (Anno Domini) in the dating of public documents

Thanksgiving and Christmas as national holidays

National days of prayer

Addition of "Under God" in the Pledge of Allegiance

"In God We Trust" as the national motto

Epstein then wrote that:

To date, every court that has analyzed these types of governmental appeals to the Deity, albeit in Christian or Judeo-Christian form rather than Muslim form, has assumed as axiomatic that they do not encroach upon the Establishment Clause of the First Amendment. While striking down a mildly theistic New York school prayer in 1962 (Engel), the passive display of the Ten Commandments in Kentucky in 1980, and a moment of silence law in Alabama in the 1985, the Supreme Court has held explicitly, or implied in dicta, that the forms of "ceremonial deism" described above are immune from constitutional scrutiny. . . . How then can Christians and Jews reconcile this feeling of exclusion with approval of a state of affairs in 1996 in which non-Christians, non-Jews, and non-religionists have no constitutional basis for attacking "ceremonial" Christian or Judeo-Christian forms of government expression? More to the point, how can the Supreme Court continue to countenance these practices?

The America of 1996 is one in which the endorsement test, not originalism, asks the right questions. If there is to be freedom of religion in this country today of the type the Framers contemplated 220 years ago, some practices that seemed perfectly permissible then cannot be perfectly permissible now.

Oliver W. Holmes stated: It is revolting to have no better reason for a rule of law than that it was laid down in the time of Henry IV. It is still more revolting if the grounds upon which it was laid down have vanished long since, and the rule simply persists from blind imitation of the past.

Then Epstein addressed individually each form of the ceremonial deism that he had laid out. For the motto, he said the following:

> Although, like the Pledge of Allegiance, the effect of "In God We Trust" is not as pronounced as the other endorsements, its pervasiveness on currency serves as a daily reminder to those who do not believe in a monotheistic god "that they are outsiders, not full members of the political community" and instills in them a perception of "disapproval of their individual religious choices. That this message is non-coercive and non-sectarian does not lessen the endorsement."

Epstein argued that these various forms, including the motto, need to be eliminated soon lest within the not too distant future, Christians and Jews may be subject to saying "In Allah We Trust" or substituting "Under Buddha" for "Under God" in the Pledge of Allegiance as the demographics of the nation continue to change. He cites statistics showing that as of 1996, when he wrote the article, about 80 percent of the U.S. population was Christian or Jewish, with increasing proportions of Muslims and Buddhists as well as non-believers.[14]

While Epstein's thesis may be valid in the long run, his statistics may be somewhat misleading. It does not seem that 20 percent of the population in 1996 were non-Christian in the sense of being Islamic or Buddhist. A study in 2014 by Pew Research Center showed the breakdown generationally of religious affiliation. The chart below illustrates the results of the survey:[15]

	Silent Generation (Born 1928–1945)	Baby Boomers (1946–1964)	Gen X (1965–1980)	Older Millennials (1980–1989)	Young Millennials (1990–1996)
Total Christian%	85	78	70	57	56
Protestant	57	52	45	38	36
Evangelical	30	28	25	22	19
Mainline	22	17	13	10	11
Black	5	7	7	6	6
Catholic	24	23	21	16	16
Other Christian	3	3	4	3	3
Other Faiths	4	5	6	8	8
Unaffiliated	11	17	23	34	36

Clearly all religious affiliations are declining generationally as young Americans are less likely to identify with these various categories except for "Other Faiths" and "Unaffiliated." Other faiths (Muslims, Buddhists, Hindus, et al.), which Epstein highlighted in his writing, doubled between older and younger responders, but remained at a low 8 percent. The most marked difference among generations was among "Unaffiliated," rising from 11 to 36 percent—a significant

The design of the silver Franklin half dollar, minted from
1948 to 1963, made bold use of the national motto.

increase and a significant number in absolute terms. The question is what "Unaf-filiated" means. Are these people who remain "religious" but don't identify with any of the standard categories, or are they "unreligious," perhaps atheists? It may be that the culture is reverting to something akin to the colonial era, in which a large portion of the population did not identify with any denominational affiliation but probably had some religious sense.

This thought is supported by a 2019 Gallup survey indicating that the percentage of Americans belonging to a church or other formal religious institution has fallen to 50 percent, down from 70 percent in 1999. The poll, however, indicates that 77 percent of Americans identify with some religious group even if they are not formal members or do not attend services regularly. This 77 percent represents a decline from 90 percent in 1998, but still is a significant majority.[16]

If those who hold some religious sense remain a large majority, perhaps there will be continued support for "In God We Trust" as the national motto for some time to come. If not, then Stephen Epstein may be right and, over some period of time, its support may fade and legal challenges might chip away at the Ceremonial Deism concept that so far has given the motto legal shelter.

Two coins (a Roosevelt dime and Washington quarter) of 1963, the year *Schempp and Murray* was adjudicated by the U.S. Supreme Court.

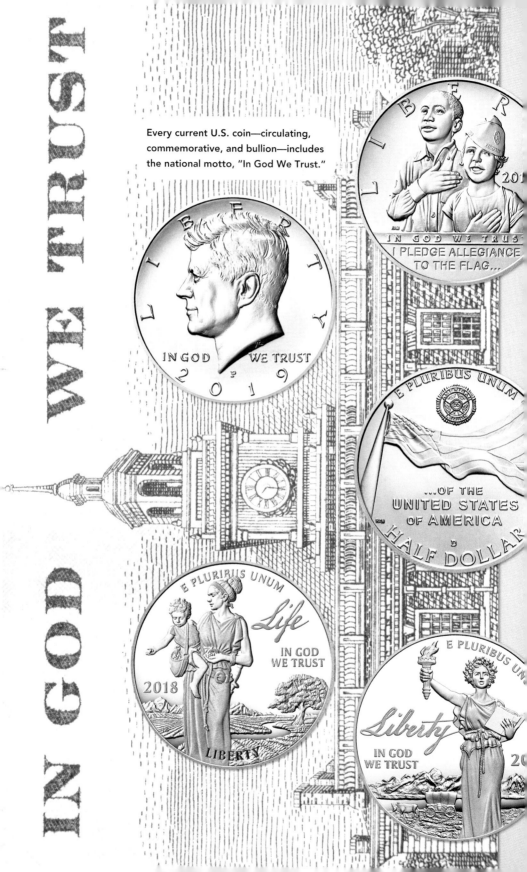

IN GOD WE TRUST

Every current U.S. coin—circulating, commemorative, and bullion—includes the national motto, "In God We Trust."

CHAPTER 20

Incidents in Recent Years Regarding the Motto and Its Future

W hile litigation has plagued the national motto, "In God We Trust," and will likely continue to challenge it in the future, removing it from U.S. coinage anytime soon would likely bring an outcry from large segments of the public. A suggestion of this can be found in the case of the Presidential dollar series that ran from 2007 to 2016. The legislation authorizing these coins was the Presidential $1 Coin Act of 2005. It called for four presidents per year to be honored with coins bearing their individual likenesses, beginning with George Washington. The act was passed unanimously in the Senate and by an overwhelming majority in the House. It was signed into law by President George W. Bush on December 22, 2005.

The bill contained a provision stating: "The inscription of the year of minting or issuance of the coin and the inscriptions 'E Pluribus Unum' and 'In God We Trust' shall be edge incused into the coin." The Mint highlighted this feature in a press release dated January 25, 2007: "For the first time since the 1930s, coin inscriptions such as 'E Pluribus Unum' and 'In God We Trust' will be prominently inscribed on the edge of the coins."

The first two years of Presidential dollars (2007 and 2008) had the motto "In God We Trust" incused on the edge of the coins.

This point was missed by many Americans, however, and as the George Washington dollar coins appeared in early 2007 without the mottoes or even the date or mintmark on the face of the coin (where people were accustomed to seeing them), emails began circulating complaining of the absence of "In God We Trust." An example was, "Here is another way of phasing God out of America" and calling for a boycott of the coins.[1] They were termed "Godless dollars" and created a public furor. Another email posting stated:

> This simple action (i.e. boycotting the coins) will make a strong statement. Please help do this. Refuse to accept these when they are handed to you. I received one from the Post Office as change and I asked for a dollar bill instead. The lady just smiled and said "way to go." So she had read the emails. Please help out . . . our world is in enough trouble without this too!!!!!
>
> U.S. Government to release new Dollar Coins. You guessed it, "IN GOD WE TRUST" IS GONE!!!

Compounding the confusion and public frustration was the fact that production problems at the Mint left the edge lettering completely off of quantities of the new coins, likely tens of thousands of them. These coins truly were "Godless." Even

A "Godless" dollar, with the national motto left off by mistake.

though the quantities of coins lacking the edge lettering were not insignificant, later estimated to be 50,000, this was a miniscule percentage of the more than 340 million Washington dollars struck. The misstruck coins were initially a sensation among collectors and some sold for more than $500 each. However, as the realization dawned that they had been made in numbers sufficient to meet collector demand for them, the price fell to $50 and less. Even worse, some sharpers began grinding off the edge lettering of correctly struck coins and fraudulently selling them as Godless errors. The Mint, in some embarrassment, announced on March 7, 2007, that an "unspecified quantity" of coins without the motto had got out, but that it was working to correct the error for future production. However, when the second Presidential coin, the John Adams dollar, came out, again some were found to be lacking the edge lettering. This led to another round of public complaints and doubts about government motivations regarding the national motto. By the end of 2007, Congress acted to address the public complaints and enacted legislation stating that "In God We Trust" must appear on the obverse or reverse of future coins, not on the edge. By 2009, when the William Henry Harrison dollar was issued, "In God We Trust" was prominently displayed on the obverse of the coin. The date, mintmark, and "E Pluribus Unum" continued to be placed on the edge.[2]

Another incident that illustrates the potential for negative reaction to any threat or demeaning of "In God We Trust" is that caused by a speech in 2011 by President Barack Obama in front of a group of Indonesian students. In it he referred to an Indonesian saying that he deemed analogous to the "United States national motto, 'E Pluribus Unum.'" Of course, the official U.S. motto is not "E Pluribus Unum" but "In God We Trust." There was an immediate outcry against the president's words. According-ing to critics, he was either ignorant of the real motto or trying to denigrate it in favor of a different, secular one. The House of Representatives acted by passing a non-binding reso-lution reaffirming the status of "In God We Trust" as the U.S.

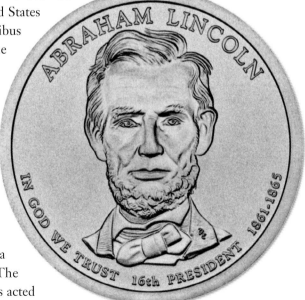

Starting in 2009, the Presidential dollar coins featured "In God We Trust" on the obverse.

national motto, as it had been established by Congress in 1956. Many Democrats, including the president, complained about the Republican House wasting time on such a measure when there was more important work to be done. Nevertheless, the House vote was 396 to 9 for reaffirming the motto. This certainly indicates that even the Democrats were leery of voting against "In God We Trust."[3]

President Obama said the Congress had too much time on its hands and should be acting on his American Jobs Act. He rhetorically asked Republican Speaker of the House John Boehner, "In the House of Representatives, what have you guys been doing, John? You've been debating a commemorative coin for baseball. You've had legislation reaffirming that 'In God We Trust' is our motto. That's not putting people back to work. I trust in God, but God wants to see us help ourselves by putting people back to work."

President Obama's stating "E Pluribus Unum" to be the national motto was in contrast to his immediate predecessor President George W. Bush's honoring the 50th anniversary of "In God We Trust" as the national motto in 2006. He held a ceremony, stating:[4]

> On the 50th anniversary of our national motto "In God We Trust" we reflect on these words that guide millions of Americans, recognize the blessing of the Creator, and offer our thanks for His great gift of liberty.
>
> From its earliest days, the United States has been a nation of faith. During the War of 1812, as the morning light revealed that the battle-torn American flag still flew above Fort McHenry, Francis Scott Key penned, "And this be our motto: 'In God is Our Trust.'" His poem became our national anthem, reminding generations of Americans to "Praise the Power that hath made and preserved us as a nation." On July 30, 1956, President Dwight Eisenhower signed the law officially establishing 'In God We Trust' as our national motto.
>
> Today our country stands strong as a beacon of religious freedom. Our citizens, whatever their faith or background, worship freely and millions answer the universal call to love their neighbors and serve a cause greater than self.
>
> As we commemorate the 50th anniversary of our national motto and remember with thanksgiving God's mercies throughout our history, we recognize a divine plan that stands above all human plans and continue to seek His will.
>
> Now therefore I, George W. Bush, president of the United States of America, do hereby proclaim July 30, 2006, as the 50th anniversary of our national motto, "In God We Trust." I call upon the people of the United States to observe this day with appropriate programs, ceremonies, and activities.
>
> In witness whereof, I have hereunto set my hand this twenty-seventh day of July, in the year of our Lord two thousand six, and of the independence of the United States of America the two hundred and thirty-first.
>
> *George W. Bush*

President Bush's words were classic examples of "Ceremonial Deism." The contrast between Bush and Obama in this regard likely shows a growing political gap between the two major political parties regarding expression of religious sensibility. This marks a change from the 1950s, when both parties were eager to participate in such demonstrations.

Certainly the expression of Ceremonial Deism continues to the present day as in a graduation address on May 13, 2017, at Liberty University, where President Donald Trump stated the following:

> America had always been the land of dreams because America is a nation of true believers. When the Pilgrims landed at Plymouth they prayed. When the founders wrote the Declaration of Independence, they invoked our Creator four times, because in America we don't worship government, we worship God. That is why our elected officials put their hand on the Bible and say "So help me God," as they take the oath of office. *It is why our currency proudly declares "In God We Trust" and it is why we proudly proclaim that we are "One Nation Under God" every time we say the Pledge of Allegiance.*

A recent phenomenon involving the motto may shed light on the way some Americans think about it and its possible future role. In November 2015 the Texas attorney general issued a legal opinion that police cars showing the motto don't violate the First Amendment's Establishment Clause. His opinion was issued in response to the Freedom From Religion Foundation's challenging various local police departments in Texas, and in other states, with warnings against placing the motto on their police vehicles. A Texas town, Childress, had placed the motto on its police cruisers and then received letters from the FFRF stating that "Piety should not be synonymous with patriotism. But godliness has been equated with good citizenship since this unconstitutional and misguided law passed in 1956."[5] Apparently the letters contained some implied threat of litigation. In response the Childress police chief was quoted as saying: "They can go fly a kite!"

The *Washington Post* carried an article in August of 2015 stating that various police officers and sheriff's deputies as well as firefighters in Illinois, Kentucky, North Carolina, and other states had begun to display the motto on their vehicles. In Bonifay, Florida, the police department placed stickers with the motto on their patrol cars. The action brought out a local atheist group to protest. However, the protesters were met by 300 supporters of the motto bumper stickers.[6]

The FFRF is active in sending letters to every department it knows that displays the motto. The Foundation's president has said, "It is inappropriate for the sheriff's office to display 'In God We Trust' on county property. The fact that these stickers were privately funded indicates that you know it is inappropriate for the government to fund religious statements."

The Original Motto Project, mentioned earlier as providing stamps to over-print "In God We Trust" with "E Pluribus Unum" on the backs of the paper cur-rency, has offered to provide bumper stickers with "E Pluribus Unum" for local police departments to place on their cars instead of "In God We Trust."

It seems in some cases, where municipalities have in the past had crosses or other religious symbols as part of their city logos, but have been forced by activist groups to remove them, the "In God We Trust" stickers have been used in the belief that that motto will stand up under legal challenge.

A sheriff in Stone County, Missouri, said, "There has been no better time than now to display our national motto. I am very humbled by the amount of support behind it."

The *Livingston Daily*, a suburban Detroit newspaper, carried an article on the topic in September 2016. It cited Livingston County's use of the motto on many of its police cars, placed there voluntarily by individual sheriff's deputies. An under-sheriff was quoted as saying, "We've had people follow our deputies and say it is awesome. Some specifically came in and said 'That's awesome.'" However, as with other depart-ments, the FFRF has raised objections, with one of its legal staff writing a letter to the county sheriff objecting to the motto display and saying she had received a complaint from a person questioning the Sheriff's Department decision. She wrote, "I think putting statements about believing in a god alienates everyone who is agnostic or atheist." The under-sheriff is quoted in response as saying, "One cool thing about the Sheriff's Department is the sheriff responds to and is elected by the people; that's the only law enforcement that is that way. They are truly beholden to the people, not the government or a set of councilmen. We need to know what the citizens are thinking and how they feel, and the decal is very representative of our citizenry and I cannot tell you how many hundreds, if not thousands, have made positive comments." The FFRF, however, said that the Sheriff's Department had stated in an email that the stickers were placed on the cars for "religious heritage," which, according to the FFRF, "demonstrates there is a religious purpose which definitely makes it unconsti-tutional." The Sheriff's Department responded that "The courts recognize our reli-gious heritage, and as a result adopted 'In God We Trust' as our national motto. This is all part of our heritage and history. There are way too many people out there trying to rewrite or ignore history/heritage, and this is terribly unfortunate because to understand how we are where we are, we have to understand how we got here."

It seems previously the Livingston County Sheriff's Department had a decal ref-erencing the Bible verse John 15:13, which says, "There is no greater love than to give up one's life for one's friends." Many of the deputies felt this was appropriate for their law-enforcement work. However, the county attorney believed it to be legally dubious so it was dropped and its place taken by "In God We Trust," which the county attorney said was "OK." The FFRF said they would like to bring a legal challenge to these stickers but need a police officer to act as a plaintiff for a lawsuit. So far they have been unable to find one, but they say, "People are being bullied out of a lawsuit," fearful of community backlash.[7]

A billboard in Botetourt County, Virginia, erected after the September 11, 2001, terrorist attacks.

The comments by Livingston County deputies and others might lead us to think that one function of the motto is almost a protest against the secular trends that many people believe are being imposed by the elites of government (and of Hollywood?) to remove any religious expression from the public domain and to deny the significance of religion in the nation's history.

In March of 2017, the Tennessee state legislature was considering legislation requiring all Tennessee license plates to bear "In God We Trust." The state attorney general commented that such a law would be "constitutionally suspect" but would be defensible if citizens were given the option of having one, instead of being forced to get one.[8]

A more recent trend is that of several states passing legislation requiring display of "In God We Trust" in public schools. This is an ongoing phenomenon that is closely followed by the "Original Motto" group referred to in chapter 5. The Original Motto supporters protest, and in some cases file legal objections to, the legislation in the various states passing them. It would seem, however, that such state legislation is likely protected under the Ceremonial Deism concept.

The motto tends to appear more in times of crisis or national stress. It frequently appeared on billboards following the September 11, 2001, terrorist attacks. In this use it may have implied for many people less of a religious connotation and more of an expression of national unity, something to rally around.

And so, as we conclude our story, we can only speculate about the future of "In God We Trust" in our national life. It is certain it will continue to attract legal challenges in an increasingly secular nation. It may, as Stephen Epstein's 1996 *Columbia Law Review* article urged, eventually lose its legal protection under the "Ceremonial Deism" argument as other religions, or the non-religious, increase demographically. We can also expect, however, that it will have its supporters and any serious effort to eliminate it will create great controversy.

One wonders what Reverend Mark Watkinson would make of the situation. He likely would not understand why there should be controversy around such a motto. But, as has been said many times, "The past is another country."

NOTES
Chapter One

1. *Montgomery Weekly Mail.* The paper was widely read in Montgomery, Alabama, and surrounding areas. It was published between 1854 and 1871.
2. Lee, Charles Robert, *The Confederate Constitution*, University of North Carolina Press, 1963, pp. 63–64. Also in Jefferson Davis's enormous work, *Rise and Fall of the Confederacy.* Davis quotes the new constitution in its first and in its final forms, comparing it with the old federal document.
3. Green, Steven K., *The Bible, the School, and the Constitution*, Oxford University Press, 2012, p. 145.
4. Holmes, David L., *The Faiths of the Founding Fathers*, Oxford University Press, 2006, pp. 34–35.
5. Kramnick, Isaac, and Laurence Moore, *The Godless Constitution*, W.W. Norton & Company, 2005, p. 118.
6. Beeman, Richard, *Plain Honest Men*, Random House, 2009, pp. 180–181.
7. Holmes, pp. 62–63.
8. Ibid., p. 248.
9. There are various references dealing with the Great Awakenings. Among them are *The Great Awakening: The Roots of Evangelical Christianity in Colonial America*, by Thomas S. Kidd, Yale University Press, 2007; *A Religious History of the American People*, by Sidney Ahlstrom, Yale University Press, 1973, pp. 280–330. Also xroads.virginia.edu., "The Second Great Awakening and the Rise of Evangelism," chapter from *Liquid Fire Within Me*, Master's thesis, University of Virginia, by Ian Frederick Finseth, 1995.
10. Waldman, Steven, *Founding Faith*, Random House, 2008, p. 133; and Meacham, Jon, *American Gospel*, Random House, 2006, p. 96.
11. Ellsworth, Oliver, "On a Religious Test for Holding Public Office," *Annals of America*, pp. 169–172.
12. Meacham, Jon, *American Gospel*, Random House, 2006, p. 97.
13. Waldman, p. 135.
14. Kramnick and Moore, p. 144.
15. Goen, Clarence C., *Broken Churches, Broken Nation: Denominational Schisms and the Coming of the Civil War*, Mercer University Press, 1985, p. 57.
16. Ibid., pp. 43–63.
17. Simpson, Robert D., "From Blacksmith to Bishop," *The Interpreter*, United Methodist Communication, July–August 1995; and Custer, Chester E., *The United Methodist*

Primer, Revised Edition, Discipleship Resources, 1993. Also Goen, pp. 55–57.
18. Wolf, William J., *The Almost Chosen People: A Study of the Religion of Abraham Lincoln*, Doubleday and Co., 1959. Wolf describes Lincoln's religious faith and deep knowledge of the Bible and also his reluctance to formally join any church.
19. Goen, pp. 49–50. The Presbyterians were considered the elite of the evangelical denominations, and they tended to dominate the leadership of several interdenominational organizations including the American Bible Society and the American Sunday School Union.
20. Morris, Robert, *William Morgan: On Political Anti-Masonry, Its Rise, Growth, and Decadence*, 1883.
21. Goen, pp. 47–48. Also xroads.virginia.edu., "Social Reform."
22. Chesebrough, David, *Clergy Dissent in the Old South, 1830–1865*, Southern Illinois University Press, 1996, p. 8.
23. Stewart, James Brewer, *Holy Warriors: The Abolitionists and American Slavery*, Hill and Wang, 1996, p. 70. Also an in-depth biography of Lewis Tappan and his activities is *Lewis Tappan and the Evangelical War Against Slavery*, by Bertram Wyatt-Brown, 1969, Case Western University Press.
24. Miller, Randall, Harry Stout, and Charles Wilson, *Religion and the American Civil War*, Oxford University Press, 1998, pp. 234–235.
25. Goen, pp. 68–107. Also Chesebrough, pp. 3–5.
26. Both the Clay and the Calhoun quotes are drawn from Chesebrough, chapter entitled "The Stance of the Majority," and from Goen, pp. 104–106.
27. Chesebrough, p. 16.
28. Adger, John B., and John Girardeau, *Collected Writings of James Henley Thornwell, 1871–1873.* Also Palmer, Benjamin, *The Life and Letters of James Henley Thornwell*, 1875. Thornwell's quote regarding the constitution is from his paper, "Our Danger and Our Duty."
29. Wikipedia, sermon by Palmer, December 29, 1860, at First Presbyterian Church, New Orleans.
30. Duncan, Christopher, *Benjamin Morgan Palmer, Southern Presbyterian Divine*, 2008, PhD dissertation, Auburn University. Also Goldfield, David, *America Aflame*, Bloomsbury Press, 2011, pp. 191–193. Also *The Life and Letters of Benjamin M. Palmer*, by Thomas Johnson, 1906, Cumberland Press.

31. Rable, George C., *God's Almost Chosen People*, University of North Carolina Press, 2010, pp. 62–63.

32. Stout, Harry, *Upon the Altar of the Nation*, Penguin Books, 2007, pp. 49–51.

33. Bushnell's sermon is cited in many sources indicating the impact it had on Northerners. See Stout, pp. 70–71, and Rable, p. 79. Also Woodworth, Steven, *While God is Marching On*, University Press of Kansas, 2001, p. 96.

Chapter Two

1. Much of this information was provided by the Prospect Hill Baptist Church, which produced a small history on the 150th anniversary of the church. It outlines Reverend Mark Watkinson's role in the creation of a religious motto. The church also provided the author with a copy of a December 26, 1964, article from the Delaware County *Daily Times* that gave good biographical information on Watkinson. Much of the information contained in it was based on research by Samuel H. Newsome, president of the Delaware County Historical Society at that time and by Harmed B. Cole of the Delaware County Coin Club. Also Mrs. Harry Bond, the last living descendant of Reverend Watkinson, provided information on her grandfather. Furthermore, a book entitled *The History of Ridley Township*, written by Keith Lockhart, a local police officer, was available. It was published by the local board of commissioners in 1987 in observance of the tricentennial of the township. Pp. 11–15 and p. 21 specifically cover Reverend Watkinson and his letter to Secretary Chase.

2. Adamson, N.E., *History of Court Street Baptist Church of Portsmouth, Virginia*, Printcraft Press, Portsmouth, Virginia, 1939, pp. 42–45.

3. *Court Street Baptist Church Minute Book*, November 29, 1860. The *Minute Book* is held at the Virginia Baptist Historical Society on the campus of the University of Richmond.

4. Porter, David D. Admiral, *Naval History of the Civil War*, H.J. Richards & Co., 1887, pp. 31–32.

5. Ibid., p. 32.

6. *Minute Book*, May 10, 1861.

7. Burdette, Roger W., *Renaissance of American Coinage*, Seneca Mill Press, 2006, pp. 185–186.

8. *Delaware County Daily Times*, December 26, 1964.

9. *Report of the Director of the Mint*, Fiscal Year End, June 30, 1896, Government Printing Office, 1897, pp. 106–108. In 1896, the Department of the Treasury found materials in its files relating to "In God We Trust" and printed them in the Mint director's annual report. These included copies of Reverend Mark Watkinson's letter to Salmon Chase, Chase's memo to Mint Director James Pollock, and various other correspondence relating to the subject. It appears this was the first time these materials had been published and become known to the general public.

10. I am grateful to my fellow Chicago Coin Club member Bill Burd for providing me this Chase Manhattan Bank Museum brochure that he acquired many years ago.

11. Adamson, pp. 47–48.

12. *Minute Book*, July 12, 1863.

13. Burdette, pp. 187–188.

14. *Minute Book*, September 13, 1863.

15. Ibid., September 20, 1863.

16. Adamson, pp. 50–51. The *Minute Book* entry of July 8, 1871, confirms this.

17. *Religious Herald*, October 11, 1877.

Chapter Three

1. Schuckers, J.W., *The Life and Public Services of Salmon Portland Chase*, D. Appleton & Co., 1874, p. 5. J.W. Schuckers had been a Treasury Department clerk under Chase and worked as his secretary for a time. Chase's daughter, Kate, provided her father's private letters and other material to Schuckers following her father's death. Schuckers wrote and published the first biography of Chase. It was sympathetic to Chase (as Kate had expected) and remains a key source of primary documentation about him.

2. Blue, Frederick J., *Salmon P. Chase: A Life in Politics*, Kent State University Press, 1987, pp. 3–6; Schuckers, pp. 5–18. Details about Philander Chase can be found on the Kenyon University web site.

3. Blue, p. 7.

4. Stowe, Harriet Beecher, *Men of Our Times*, 1868, pp. 246–247. Stowe, author of *Uncle Tom's Cabin*, wrote this book after the war. She interviewed some 18 leaders of the prewar and war periods. She then wrote short biographies of each of them, and assembled them in this book.

5. Hart, Albert B., *Salmon Portland Chase*, Houghton Mifflin & Co, 1899, pp. 11–12. Also Blue, pp. 10–11.

6. Niven, John, *Salmon P. Chase: A Biography*, Oxford University Press, 1995, pp. 36–38.

7. Ibid., pp. 41–43.

8. Blue, pp. 23–25.

9. Hart, pp. 52–53.

10. Quoted from Chase's diary, in Warden, Robert B., *An Account of the Private Life and Public Services of Salmon Portland Chase*, p. 290.

11. Niven, pp. 71–76.

12. Blue, p. 16.
13. Ibid., p. 84.
14. Niven, p. 96.
15. Ibid., pp. 143–144.
16. Blue, pp. 93–95.
17. *Annals of America*, vol. 8, p. 254.
18. Niven, pp. 156–161.
19. Ibid., 172–175.
20. Ibid., pp. 177–179.
21. *Mint Director's Report*, 1896, p. 108.

Chapter Four

1. U.S. Mint archives, Record Group 104. I am grateful to Robert W. Julian for locating and providing a copy of this letter that was previously unknown to me.
2. U.S. Mint archives, Record Group 104, courtesy of Robert W. Julian.
3. The closest thing to a biography of James Pollock was written as an unpublished Master's thesis by Dorothy J. Roughton in 1956 at Penn State University, Department of History. Her thesis is entitled "James Pollock, Governor of the Keystone State, 1855–1858." As its title implies, its main focus is on his governorship, but it does provide substantial information on his earlier life and his career following the governorship.
4. Drawn from the Sarah Hepburn Pollock autobiography. It is a 100-page handwritten document held in the Pollock family archives in the Special Collections section of the library at Penn State.
5. Roughton thesis and the Pennsylvania Archives, Papers of the Governors, vol. vii, pp. 785–797.
6. McClure, A.K., *Old Time Notes of Pennsylvania*, John C. Winston Company, 1905, pp. 230–232.
7. Kieffer, Rev. W.T. Linn DD, *A History of the First Presbyterian Church of Milton, Pa.*, 1935, p. 146. The quote from McClure is contained in the church history.
8. Pollock Family Archives, Special Collections, Penn State University Library, letter dated January 1, 1857.
9. Tooley, Mark, *The Peace that Almost Was: The Forgotten Story of the Washington Peace Conference and the Final Attempt to Avert the Civil War*, Google Books, 2015.

Chapter Five

1. U.S. Mint Archives, Record Group 104, letter dated December 13, 1861, from Longacre to Pollock.
2. U.S. Mint Archives, Record Group 104, letter dated December 26, 1861, from Pollock to Chase.

Chapter Six

1. Schuckers, J.W., *The Life and Public Services of Salmon Portland Chase*, D. Appleton & Co., 1874, pp. 212–215.
2. *Historical Statistics of the United States from Colonial Times to 1970*, part 2, p. 888.
3. Two excellent sources of information about the tax and tariff measures as well as the bond and currency issues undertaken by Chase and the Congress are: Schuckers (*The Life and Public Services of Salmon Portland Chase*), chapter XXV, pp. 216–225, chapter XXVI, pp. 229–234, chapter XXVII, pp. 238–257; and *The Greenbacks*, by Otto Gresham, chapter X, "Financing the Union," pp. 140–149. The latter book, published in 1927 by The Book Press Inc., gives insights into the politics and economics of the Civil War from a firsthand perspective. Otto Gresham's father, Walter Q. Gresham, had been financial agent for the State of Indiana and had been privy to many of the discussions regarding financing and currency for the war.
4. Friedberg, Robert, *Paper Money of the United States*, Coin and Currency Institute Inc., p. 11.
5. Friedberg, Arthur and Ira, *A Guide Book of United States Paper Money*, Whitman Publishing, 2005, pp. 12–17.
6. Schuckers, pp. 217–228.
7. The fullest telling of Jay Cooke's story is *Jay Cooke: Financier of the Civil War*, by Ellis P. Oberholtzer, George W. Jacobs & Co., 1907.
8. Schuckers, p. 237.
9. Gresham, Otto, *The Greenbacks*, The Book Press, 1927, p. 150.
10. Schuckers, pp. 243–244.
11. Ibid., p. 244.
12. "The Gold Standard Now" web site, "Civil War and Greenbacks."
13. Friedberg (*Guide Book*), pp. 13–14.
14. Friedman, Milton, and Anna Schwartz, *A Monetary History of the United States*, Princeton University Press, 1963, pp. 46–47.
15. Goodwin, Jason, *Greenback*, Henry Holt & Co., 2003, p. 222.
16. Wikipedia, Clark.
17. Goodwin, p. 219.
18. Ibid., pp. 236–241.
19. Ibid., pp. 242–244.
20. Blue, Frederick J., *Salmon P. Chase: A Life in Politics*, p. 230.
21. Schwartz, Ted, *A History of United States Coinage*, A.S. Barnes & Co., Inc., 1980, p. 187.
22. Gresham, pp. 145–146.
23. Mihm, Stephen, *A Nation of Counterfeiters*, Harvard University Press, 2007. This book

relates the story of obsolete currency and the massive counterfeiting of the era.

24. Office of the Comptroller of the Currency, *Lincoln and the Founding of the National Banking System*. This is available in print from the OCC and also available on their web site (OCC.treas.gov).
25. Sharkey, Robert P., *Money, Class, and Party: An Economic Study of Civil War and Reconstruction*, The Johns Hopkins Press, 1959, p. 224.
26. Ibid., pp. 225–226.
27. Sherman, John, *Recollections*, p. 298.
28. Blue, p. 160.
29. Sharkey, pp. 225–228.
30. Blue, p. 161.
31. Friedman, p. 19.
32. Flaherty, Edward, *A Brief History of Central Banking in the United States*, contained in the web site "American History from Revolution to Reconstruction and Beyond."
33. Gordon, John Steele, "The High Cost of War," in *Barron's*, April 4, 2011.
34. Mihm, pp. 319–330. Counterfeit Confederate paper money is also explored in depth in Tremmel, George B., *A Guide Book of Counterfeit Confederate Currency*, Whitman Publishing, 2007.

Chapter Seven

1. Mint Archives, Record Group 104, letter by Pollock to Chase, June 16, 1862.
2. *Mint Director's Annual Report*, October 27, 1862.
3. Julian, Robert W., *The Numismatist*, December 2005, p. 35.
4. Carothers, Neil, *Fractional Money: A History of Small Coins and Fractional Paper Currency of the United States*, John Wiley & Sons, Inc., 1930, p. 338.
5. Taxay, Don, *The U.S. Mint and Coinage*, Arco Publishing, 1966, pp. 176–177.
6. Schwartz, Ted, *A History of United States Coinage*, A.S Barnes & Co., Inc., 1980, pp. 176–177. Schwartz gives a good description of the Canadian part of the movement of coins out of the United States.
7. Bowers, Q. David, *A Guide Book of Civil War Tokens*, Whitman Publishing, 2013, p. 25.
8. Carothers, p. 218.
9. Ibid., p. 219.
10. Breen, *Complete Encyclopedia of U.S. and Colonial Proof Coins*, p. 401.
11. Kravitz, Robert, J., *A Collector's Guide to Postage and Fractional Currency*, Arkives Press, p. 12.
12. Reed, Fred III, *Civil War Encased Stamps*, BNR Press, 1988, pp. 45–46.

13. Ibid., 48–49.
14. Ibid., p. 48.
15. Ibid., pp. 54–55.
16. Goodwin, Jason, *Greenback*, Henry Holt & Co., 2003, pp. 222–224.
17. Ibid., p. 224.
18. Reed, *Civil War Encased Stamps*, pp. 48–49. Fred Reed also has written a book dealing specifically with postage stamp envelopes, entitled *Civil War Stamp Envelopes, the Issuers and Their Times*.
19. Reed, *Civil War Encased Stamps*, p. 80.
20. Ibid., quoted on p. 75.
21. Ibid., p. 78.
22. Ibid., pp. 76–77.
23. Ibid., p. 78.
24. Carothers, p. 177.
25. Kravitz, pp. 13–15.
26. Cassel, David, *United States Pattern Postage Currency Coins*, 2000, pp. 7–23. Cassel's book, self-published in limited quantity, provides an in-depth analysis of the Postage Currency coins and contains three articles written by professional numismatist Douglas Winter providing the background for Eckfeldt and Dubois's experiments and promotion of the pieces with Chase. The articles by Winter originally appeared in 1985 beginning with the May 15 issue of *Coin World*. Winter also provides possible reasons for why Chase rejected the idea of these coins. Among those reasons was the general acceptance by the public of the paper Fractional Currency, which reduced the pressure to make changes to the coinage.
26. Judd, J. Hewitt, *United States Pattern, Experimental, and Trial Pieces*, Western Publishing Company, 1977, pp. 71–72.
27. Cassel, pp. 14–21.
28. Taxay, p. 231.
29. Carothers, p. 219.
30. Ibid., pp. 175–176.

Chapter Eight

1. Carothers, Neil, *Fractional Money: A History of Small Coins and Fractional Paper Currency of the United States*, John Wiley & Sons, Inc., 1930, p. 187.
2. Ibid., p. 188.
3. Julian, Robert W., *The Numismatist*, December 200 5, pp. 34–35.
4. U.S. Mint Archives, Record Group, 408, Pollock letters.
5. Bowers, *A Guide Book of Civil War Tokens*, Whitman Publishing, 2013, pp. 7–8.
6. See Hetrich, Guttag, and Taxay.
7. Cited in Erlenkotter, Donald, Civil War Token Society *Journal*, Fall 2010, p. 18.

8. Bowers, *A Guide Book of Civil War Tokens*, p. 34. Bowers cites a *Baltimore Sun* newspaper article dated October 31, 1863, discussing the arrest of a Philadelphia innkeeper "on a charge of passing tokens for money." The article did not include the final disposition of the case.

9. Snow, Rick, "Sesquicentennial of the Bronze Cent," *Longacre's Ledger*, December 2013, pp. 10–13.

10. Ibid., p. 11.

11. Mint Archives, quoted in Flynn, Kevin, *The Authoritative Reference on Two Cents Coins*, pp. 192–193.

12. Mint Archives, Record Group 104, letter from Chase to Pollock, December 9, 1863.

13. uspatterns.com web site, Research Center, Half Dollars, Judd-338. The excerpts from George Eckfeldt's journal shown on the web site are courtesy of Alan Meghrig, who owns the unpublished journal.

14. Ibid., Research Center, Eagles, Judd-349 and -351.

15. Mint Archives, Record Group 104, letter from Pollock to Chase, December 15, 1863.

Chapter Nine

1. Rable, George C., *God's Almost Chosen People*, University of North Carolina Press, 2010, p. 79.

2. Kramnick, Isaac and R. Laurence Moore, *The Godless Constitution*, W.W. Norton & Co., 1996, p. 145.

3. Ibid.

4. Green, Steven K., *The Bible, the School, and the Constitution*, Oxford University Press, 2012, p. 140.

5. McAllister, David, *Christian Civil Government in America*, sixth edition, revised by T.H. Acheson and William Parsons, National Reform Association, 1927, pp. 20–21.

6. Kramnick, p. 146.

7. Ibid., p. 141. The quote from Lincoln was originally reported by Thomas Sproull, editor of *The Reformed Presbyterian and Covenanter*, in the November 1865 issue entitled "Reminiscence of President Lincoln." That the Lincoln quotation was published after his assassination and other factors have led some to believe the quote to be apocryphal. In particular Stewart Jacoby in a University of Michigan PhD dissertation, "The Religious Amendment Movement," p. 111, argues this case. If the quote is authentic, the assumption is that Lincoln was referring to securing emancipation during his first term and that he hoped to secure a Christian amendment during his second term. It is unclear if their interpretation and reporting of Lincoln's words was justified or wishful thinking, but at any rate the group took heart from their meeting.

8. Green, p. 142.

9. *Diary of Gideon Welles*, vol. II, p. 190.

10. Jacoby, Susan, *Freethinkers: A History of American Secularism*, Metropolitan Books, Henry Holt & Co., 2004, p. 351.

11. Originally from a Master's thesis by Steven K. Green entitled "The National Reform Association and Religious Amendments to the Constitution, 1864–1876," pp. 48–55, University of North Carolina, 1987. Later included in Green's book *The Bible, the School, and the Constitution*.

12. *Slate*, November 17, 2011.

13. Palmer, Benjamin M., *The Life and Letters of James Henley Thornwell*, Whittet and Shepperson, 1875, Richmond, Virginia, p. 508.

14. Ibid.

Chapter Ten

1. Snow, Rick, "Sesquicentennial of the Bronze Cent," *Longacre's Ledger*, December 2013, pp. 10–13.

2. National Mining Hall of Fame and Museum web site (MiningHallOfFame.org).

3. Mint Archives, Record Group 104, quoted in Flynn, *Authoritative Reference on Liberty Seated Dollars*, p. 193, letter from Pollock to Chase dated January 27, 1864.

4. Julian, *Numismatist*, December 2005, p. 36, letter from Wharton to Chase, February 15, 1864.

5. Mint Archives, quoted in Flynn, *Authoritative Reference on Liberty Seated Dollars*, p. 194. Letter from Wharton to Pollock, dated March 5, 1864.

6. Mint Archives, Record Group 104, letter from Pollock to Chase dated March 2, 1864.

7. Taxay, Don, *The U.S. Mint and Coinage*, Arco Publishing, 1966, p. 241. Also cited in Snow, *Longacre's Ledger*, December 2013, p. 12.

8. Mint Archives, Record Group 104, letter from Pollock to Chase, March 17, 1864.

9. Taxay, p. 241.

10. *Longacre's Ledger*, volume 23.3, issue 89, December 2013, pp. 15–20.

11. Taxay, pp. 241–242.

12. National Mining Hall of Fame and Museum web site (MiningHallOfFame.org). A fuller biography of Wharton is *Joseph Wharton: Quaker Industrial Pioneer*, by W. Ross Yates, Lehigh University Press, 1987.

Chapter Eleven

1. Flynn, Kevin, *The Authoritative Reference to Two Cents Coins*, p. 218. The ad is quoted by Flynn.
2. Carothers, Neil, *Fractional Money: A History of Small Coins and Fractional Paper Currency of the United States*, p. 200.
3. Bowers, *A Guide Book of Civil War Tokens*, p. 40.
4. Fuld, George and Melvin, *Patriotic Civil War Tokens*, Krause Publications, 1982, p. 6.
5. Bowers, *A Guide Book of Civil War Tokens*, p. 40.
6. Mint Archives, Record Group 104, quoted in Flynn (*The Authoritative Reference on Two Cents Coins*), p. 195.
7. Ibid. (Flynn, p. 196).
8. Ibid. (Flynn, pp. 160–161).
9. Ibid. (Flynn, p. 192).
10. Julian, Robert W., "All About the Two Cents," *The Numismatist*, December 2009, p. 37.
11. Breen, *Complete Encyclopedia of U.S. and Colonial Proof Coins*, p. 120.
12. *Coin World*, February 15, 2016, p. 38.
13. Vermeule, Cornelius, *Numismatic Art in America: Aesthetics of the United State Coinage*, originally published in 1971, updated and republished by Whitman Publishing, 2007.
14. Flynn, *Authoritative Reference on Seated Dollars*, p. 187.

Chapter Twelve

1. Breen, *Complete Encyclopedia of U.S. and Colonial Coins*, p. 353.
2. Phelps, Mary Merwin, *Kate Chase, Dominant Daughter*, Thomas Y. Crowell Company, 1935, p. 240.
3. Oller, John, *American Queen*, Da Capo Press, 2014, p. 5.
4. Lamphier, Peg, *Kate Chase and William Sprague: Politics and Gender in a Civil War Marriage*, University of Nebraska Press, 2003, p. 42.
5. Ibid., p. 39.
6. Phelps, p. 100.
7. Leech, Margaret, *Reveille in Washington, 1860–1865*, Harper Brothers, 1941, p. 281.
8. Oller, pp. 60–62.
9. Leech, p. 281–282.
10. Lamphier, pp. 48–49; Phelps, p. 99.
11. Lamphier, pp. 50–51.
12. Leech, p. 281.
13. C-Span, "Booknotes" interview by Bryan Lamb with John Niven, author of *Salmon P. Chase, A Biography*, May 28, 1995.
14. Lamphier, pp. 60-63.
15. Ross, Ishbel, *Proud Kate: Portrait of an Ambitious Woman*, Harper Brothers, 1953, p. 140.
16. Lamphier, p. 62.
17. Ross, p. 124.
18. *Encyclopedia Brunoniana* (publication of Brown University), written by Martha Metchell, 1993.
19. *History of the One Hundred and Twenty-Fifth Regiment, Pennsylvania Volunteers, 1862–1863*, written and assembled by Regimental Committee, J. B. Lippincott Company, 1906, pp. 167–169.
20. Ibid., p. 151.
21. Ibid., p. 152.
22. Sears, Stephen, *Landscape Turned Red*, Houghton Mifflin, Harcourt, 2003, pp. 224–225.
23. Gardiner, Richard E., *The Ultimate Originations of "In God We Trust,"* circa 2000, pp. 1–4.

Chapter Thirteen

1. From the Pollock family archive in the Special Collections area at Penn State University.
2. Schuckers, *The Life and Public Services of Salmon Portland Chase*, p. 509.
3. Blue, Frederick J., *Salmon P. Chase: A Life in Politics*, pp. 235–236.
4. Niven, *Salmon P. Chase: A Biography*, pp. 363–368.
5. Sokoloff, Alice Hunt, *Kate Chase for the Defense*, Dodd, Mead & Company, 1971, p. 106.
6. Schuckers, p. 649.
7. Taxay, *The U.S. Mint and Coinage*, p. 231.
8. Kate Chase's story is dramatic. She enjoyed the heights of wealth and influence but ultimately experienced deep poverty and deprivation. Her story has attracted numerous biographers, probably not just because of her fall from the heights but also for her intelligence, great ambitions, and strivings especially on behalf of her father. Among the biographies are *Kate Chase, Dominant Daughter*, published in 1935, by Mary Merwin Phelps; *So Fell the Angels*, 1956, by Thomas Belden; *Proud Kate*, by the popular biographer Ishbel Ross, published in 1953; *Kate Chase & William Sprague*, by Peg Lamphier, 2003; *Kate Chase for the Defense*, by Alice Sakoloff, 1971; and *American Queen*, by John Oller, 2015. It is likely there will be more in the future. There was a well-reviewed novel called *Mrs. Lincoln's Rival*, by Jennifer Chiaverini, published in 2014. As noted in the text

there were plans for a movie about her to be made in the 1940s, which never came to fruition. We can hope that some ambitious scriptwriter/moviemaker will take up such a project in the future.

9. Mint archives, Record Group 104.
10. Breen, *Complete Encyclopedia of U.S. and Colonial Coins*, p. 404.
11. Bowers, Q. David, *The Harry W. Bass Jr., Museum Sylloge*, Harry W. Bass Jr. Foundation, 1999–2001, p. 412.
12. Mint archives, Record Group 104. Also quoted in Flynn, *Authoritative Reference on Liberty Seated Dollars*, p. 191.
13. Flynn, *Authoritative Reference on Liberty Seated Dollars*, p. 191.
14. Godcharles, Frederick, "Governor James Pollock," presentation to the Northumberland County (Pennsylvania) Historical Society, May 19, 1936, *Proceedings and Addresses*, volume VIII.
15. Breen, *Complete Encyclopedia of U.S. and Colonial Coins*, p. 404.

Chapter Fourteen

1. Mint archives, Record Group 104. Quoted in Flynn, *Authoritative Reference on Liberty Seated Dollars*, p. 192.
2. Breen, Walter, *Complete Encyclopedia of U.S. and Colonial Coins*, pp. 351–352.
3. Bowers, Q. David, correspondence with the author, July 2019.
4. Taxay, *The U.S. Mint and Coinage*, pp. 243–244.
5. Mint archives, Record Group 104. Quoted in Flynn, *Experiments in Aluminum Coinage*, p. 40.
6. Breen, *Complete Encyclopedia of U.S. and Colonial Coins*, pp. 242–243.
7. Mint archives, Record Group 104. Quoted in Flynn, *Experiments in Aluminum Coinage*, p. 41.
8. Ibid., p. 42.
9. Ibid., pp. 42–43.
10. Breen, *Complete Encyclopedia of U.S. and Colonial Coins*, pp. 246–247.
11. Bowers, *A Guide Book of Shield and Liberty Head Nickels*, p. 216.
12. Breen, *Complete Encyclopedia of U.S. and Colonial Coins*, p. 247.
13. Breen, *Encyclopedia of United States Colonial and Proof Coins*, p. 127.
14. Bowers, *A Guide Book of Shield and Liberty Head Nickels*, p. 216.

Chapter Fifteen

1. Mint archives, Record Group 104. Quoted in Flynn, *Authoritative Reference on Liberty Seated Dollars*, p. 194.

2. Mint archives, Record Group 104. Thanks to Robert W. Julian for providing a copy of this letter and an explanation of the rule set up by John Quincy Adams.
3. Taxay, *The U.S. Mint and Coinage*, pp. 250–251.
4. Ibid., p. 251.
5. Ibid., pp. 252–253.
6. Ibid., p. 270.
7. Mint archives, "Special file of H.R. Linderman," quoted in Burdette, *Renaissance of American Coinage*, p. 192. Letter from A. Loudon Snowden to H.R. Linderman, dated May 23, 1876.

Chapter Sixteen

1. Q. David Bowers observes: "The Peale situation is very complicated; certain officials, such as Jacob Reese Eckfeldt and William DuBois, later came to Peale's defense." (Correspondence with the author, July 2019.)
2. Taxay, Don, *Counterfeit, Mis-struck, and Unofficial U.S. Coins*, p. 280.
3. Taxay, *The U.S. Mint and Coinage*, p. 191.
4. Taxay, *Counterfeit, Mis-struck, and Unofficial U.S. Coins*, pp. 82–87.
5. Ibid., pp. 89–90.
6. Numismatic historian Robert W. Julian has told the author that he heard from some sources that Pollock did have a collection of both standard issues and patterns.
7. *Pennsylvania Magazine of History and Biography*, 1927, p. 92.
8. Taxay, *Counterfeit, Mis-struck, and Unofficial U.S. Coins*, pp. 98–100.
9. We are indebted to Alan Meghrig, who owns George Eckfeldt's journal. It remains unpublished but Alan has placed certain quotes from it on the uspatterns.com web site, under the "Photo Gallery" section of the site.

Chapter Seventeen

1. Gatewood, Willard A. Jr., *Theodore Roosevelt and the Art of Controversy*, Louisiana State University Press, 1970, pp. 213–214.
2. Morris, Edmund, *Theodore Rex*, Random House, 2002, p. 370.
3. Gatewood, Willard B. Jr., *Theodore Roosevelt and the Art of Controversy*, pp. 212–214.
4. Moran, Michael F., *Striking Change: The Great Artistic Collaboration Between Theodore Roosevelt and August Saint-Gaudens*, Whitman Publishing, 2008, pp. 353–354.
5. Burdette, *Renaissance of American Coinage*, p. 30.
6. Gatewood, p. 218.
7. Moran, pp. 319–321.
8. Gatewood, p. 218.

9. Revised Statutes, Section 3617, quoted in the *Des Moines Register*, November 17, 1907.
10. Burdette, p. 192.
11. *Des Moines Register*, November 17, 1907.
12. *Mint Director's Report* of 1896.
13. Burdette, p. 193.
14. Gatewood, pp. 227–228.
15. Ibid., 228–229.
16. Ibid., 222–223.
17. Ibid., p. 231.
18. Ibid., p. 232, and *Roosevelt and the Old Guard*, p. 207.
19. Roosevelt, Theodore, *An Autobiography*, 1920, Charles Scribner & Sons, p. 420.

Chapter Eighteen

1. Kruse, Kevin, *One Nation Under God*, Basic Books, 2015, p. xv.
2. Ibid., pp. 4–5.
3. Ibid., p. 39.
4. Ibid., p. 5.
5. Ibid., p. 19.
6. Ibid., p. 27.
7. Ibid., p. 58.
8. Ibid., p. 72.
9. Wolf, William J., *The Almost Chosen People: A Study of the Religion of Abraham Lincoln*, Doubleday & Co., 1959, pp. 74–75. Also, the book *Lincoln's Youth*, by Louis Warren, published in 1959, gives insight into the origins of Lincoln's views toward churches and church doctrine. According to Louis Warren, when Lincoln was a boy, he and his father attended the Baptist Church near their home in Southern Indiana. However, the church was constantly riven with doctrinal disputes that caused both father and son to become disillusioned with such narrow sectarian differences.
10. Kruse, pp. 72–73.
11. Graham, Billy, *Just as I Am*, Harper San Francisco, 1997, p. 199.
12. Kruse, pp. 67–68.
13. Ibid., pp. 78–79.
14. Ibid., p. xii.
15. Ellis, Richard J., *To the Flag: The Unlikely History of the Pledge of Allegiance*, University of Kansas Press, 2005, pp. 24–33.
16. Ibid., pp. 54–71.
17. Kruse, pp. 100–110.
18. Ibid., p. 112.
19. Emmaus Walk web site quotes a 1985 newspaper interview with Rothert.
20. Kruse, pp. 113–119.
21. Ibid., pp. 121–122.
22. Ibid., p. 123.
23. Ibid., pp. 97–99.

Chapter Nineteen

1. Kruse, Kevin, *One Nation Under God*, Basic Books, 2015, pp. 170–171.
2. Ibid., pp. 173–181.
3. Ibid., p. 182.
4. Ibid., pp. 181–182.
5. Ibid., pp. 170–186.
6. Ibid., pp. 192–201.
7. Ibid., p. 199.
8. There have been a number of books written about Madalyn Murray O'Hair, including *Ungodly: The Passions, Torments, and Murder of Atheist Madalyn Murray O'Hair*, by Ted Dracos, Free Press; *America's Most Hated Woman: The Life and Gruesome Death of Madalyn Murray O'Hair*, Continuum International Publishing Group, Inc.; and *The Atheist: Madalyn Murray O'Hair*, by Bryan Le Beau, New York University Press, 2003.
9. *Aronow vs. United States*, 432 F2d 243 (Ninth Circuit, October 6, 1970).
10. Original Motto Project web site.
11. *Wooley vs. Maynard*, 430 U.S. 705.
12. *Huffington Post*, March 15, 2013.
13. Friendly Atheist web site, September 2013.
14. *Columbia Law Review*, volume 96, no. 8, December, 1996, pp. 2083–2174.
15. Pew Research Center, 2014.
16. *Politics*, April 18, 2019. Article by Jeffrey M. Jones summarizing the poll.

Chapter Twenty

1. Brooks Johnson, FactCheck.Org, May 27, 2009; also, Christensen, Brett, HoaxSlayer.net, March 13, 2007. Various versions of this and similar emails were circulating in 2007. Where and by whom they were generated is unknown.
2. FactCheck.org, May 29, 2009.
3. *Newsmax Finance* article by professional numismatist Mike Fuljenz, 2017.
4. White House press release, July 27, 2006.
5. *Constitution Daily*, November 9, 2015, article by Scott Bomboy.
6. *Washington Post*, August 5, 2015, article by Elahe Izadi.
7. *Livingston Daily*, September 17, 2016, article by Lisa Roose-Church.
8. Associated Press, March 27, 2017. Of course, the 1977 *Wooley vs. Maynard* case ruled that requiring the motto on automobile license plates was unconstitutional. Voluntary inclusion on individual plates is still legal in some states.

GLOSSARY

Over the years numismatists have developed special jargon to describe coins, paper currency, tokens, and medals. This glossary includes terms that are used frequently by collectors and researchers, and/or that have a special meaning other than their ordinary dictionary definitions.

alloy—a combination of two or more metals.

authentication—examination of a coin or medal to determine its genuineness.

bronze—an alloy of copper, zinc, and tin.

certification—the process by which a coin is authenticated, graded, and encapsulated in plastic by a professional third-party firm (neither the owner of the coin nor its potential buyer).

circulation strike—a coin intended for use in commerce, as opposed to a Proof or other presentation piece.

Civil War token—a privately produced token made during the Civil War as a substitute for regular legal-tender one-cent coins.

designer—the artist who creates a coin's design. Often different from its engraver.

die—a piece of metal, usually hardened steel, with an incuse reverse image of a coinage design, used for stamping coins.

double eagle—the United States twenty-dollar gold coin.

eagle—the United States ten-dollar gold coin.

edge—the periphery of a coin, often with reeding, lettering, or ornamentation.

engraver—the person who engraves or sculpts a model for use in translating a coin's design to a coinage die.

Gresham's Law—the monetary principle that "bad money drives out good"—that is, if there are two forms of legal tender in circulation, with the same face value, the one made of the more valuable commodity will be hoarded and disappear from circulation. E.g., a paper dollar bill will be spent before a silver dollar; both will be spent before a gold dollar coin.

half eagle—the United States five-dollar gold coin.

hub—a positive-image punch used to impress a coin's design into a die used for coinage production.

inscription—a legend or lettering on a coin or paper money.

legal tender—money officially issued and recognized for redemption by an authorized agency or government.

legend—a principal inscription on a coin or paper money.

mintmark—a small letter or other mark on a coin, indicating the mint at which it was struck; e.g., D for the Denver Mint.

motto—an inspirational word or phrase used on a coin or paper money.

National Bank—A commercial bank incorporated under the laws of the federal government and given a federal charter number pursuant to the National Banking Act of 1863 and its amendments. Regulated by the comptroller of the currency, an officer of the Treasury Department.

National Bank Note—A note bearing the imprint of a specific National Bank and its location, plus the signatures of bank officials, in addition to federal signatures and information.

obverse—the front or face side of a coin.

overdate—a coinage date made by superimposing one or more numerals on a previously dated die.

pattern—an experimental or trial coin, generally of a new or proposed design, denomination, or alloy.

pedigree—provenance; the record of previous owners of a rare coin or piece of paper money.

planchet—a blank piece of metal on which a coin design is stamped.

Proof—a coin struck for collectors by the Mint, using specially prepared dies and planchets, and typically struck multiple times in the coinage press, under greater than normal pressure.

quarter eagle—the United States $2.50 gold coin.

reverse—the back side of a coin.

rim—the raised circumference portion of a coin that protects its design from wear.

scrip—Privately issued paper currency intended for temporary use during an emergency (e.g., wartime) or to facilitate local trade.

seigniorage—the profit made by a government by issuing coins; the difference between their face value and their production costs.

third-party certification—authentication, grading, and encapsulation of a coin or piece of paper money by a professional independent firm (neither its buyer nor its seller).

token—a privately issued piece of money, typically with an accepted exchange value for goods or services, but not an official (legal-tender) government-issued coin.

type—a series of coins defined by a shared distinguishing design, composition, denomination, or other elements; e.g., Indian Head cents of 1859 to 1909.

variety—a minor design feature that sets a coin apart from other issues of that type; e.g., a variety of coin might have its motto in plain letters rather than spelled out on a scroll.

Selected Bibliography

Adamson, N.E., *History of the Court Street Baptist Church of Portsmouth, Virginia*, Printcraft Press, Portsmouth, Virginia, 1939.

Adger, John B. and Girardeau, John, *Collected Writings of James Henley Thornwell*, 1871–1873.

Ahlstrom, Sidney, *A Religious History of the American People*, Yale University Press, 1973.

Beeman, Richard, *Plain Honest Men*, Random House, 2009.

Blue, Frederick J., *Salmon P. Chase: A Life in Politics*, Kent State University Press, 1987.

Bowers, Q. David, *Engravers, Minters, and Distributors of Civil War Tokens*, Civil War Token Society, 2018.

———. *A Guide Book of Civil War Tokens*, Whitman Publishing, 2013 and later editions.

———. *A Guide Book of Double Eagle Gold Coins*, Whitman Publishing, 2004 and later editions.

———. *A Guide Book of Shield and Liberty Head Nickels*, Whitman Publishing, 2006.

Breen, Walter, *Walter Breen's Complete Encyclopedia of U.S. and Colonial Coins*, Doubleday, 1988.

———. *Encyclopedia of United States and Colonial Proof Coins 1722–1989*, FCI Press, Inc., 1977.

Burdette, Roger W., *Renaissance of American Coinage*, Seneca Mill Press, 2006.

Bureau of the Census, "Historical Statistics of the United States from Colonial Times to 1970," Part 2.

Carothers, Neil, *Fractional Money: A History of Small Coins and Fractional Paper Currency of the United States*, John Wiley & Sons, Inc., 1930.

Cassel, David, *United States Pattern Postage Currency Coins*, self-published, 2000.

Chesebrough, David, *Clergy Dissent in the Old South, 1830–1865*, Southern Illinois University Press, 1996.

Davis, Jefferson, *Rise and Fall of the Confederacy*, Appleton & Co., 1881.

Dracos, Ted, *Ungodly: The Passions, Torments, and Murder of Atheist Madalyn Murray O'Hair*, Penguin Publishing, 2004.

Duncan, Christopher, "Benjamin Morgan Palmer: Southern Presbyterian Divine," 2008 PhD dissertation, Auburn University.

Ellis, Richard J., *To the Flag: The Unlikely History of the Pledge of Allegiance*, University of Kansas Press, 2005.

Flaherty, Edward, "A Brief History of Central Banking in the United States," contained in the web site "American History from Revolution to Reconstruction and Beyond," University of Groningen (www.let.rug.nl/usa).

Flynn, Kevin, *The Authoritative Reference on Two Cents Coins*, Deuces Wild, Kyle Vick, 2011.

———. *The Authoritative Reference on Liberty Seated Dollars*, self-published, 2014.

———. *Experiments in Aluminum Coinage*, Kyle Vick, 2013.

Friedberg, Arthur and Ira, *A Guidebook of United States Paper Money*, Whitman Publishing, 2005 and later editions.

Friedberg, Robert, *Paper Money of the United States*, Coin and Currency Institute Inc., 1953 and later editions.

Friedman, Milton and Anna Schwartz, *A Monetary History of the United States*, Princeton University Press, 1963.

Fuld, George and Melvin, *Civil War Tokens*, Krause Publications, 1982.

Gatewood, Willard B. Jr., *Theodore Roosevelt and the Art of Controversy*, Louisiana State University Press, 1970.

Godcharles, Frederick, "Governor James Pollock," presentation to the Northumberland County Pennsylvania Historical Society, May 19, 1936, *Proceedings and Addresses*, volume VIII.

Goen, Clarence C., *Broken Churches, Broken Nation: Denominational Schisms and the Coming of the Civil War*, Mercer University Press, 1985.

Goodwin, Jason, *Greenback*, Henry Holt & Co., 2003.

Gordon, John Steele, "The High Cost of War," published in *Barrons*, April 4, 2011.

Green, Steven K., *The Bible, the School, and the Constitution*, Oxford University Press, 2006.

Gresham, Otto, *Financing the Union*, The Book Press Inc., 1927.

Hart, Albert B., *Salmon Portland Chase*, Houghton Mifflin & Co, 1899.

Holmes, David L., *The Faiths of the Founding Fathers*, Oxford University Press, 2006.

Horowitz, David, *Dark Agenda*, Humanix Books, 2018.

Jacoby, Susan, *Freethinkers: A History of American Secularism*, Metropolitan Books, Henry Holt & Co., 2004.

Julian, Robert W., *The Numismatist*, December 2009.

Judd, J. Hewitt, *United States Pattern, Experimental, and Trial Pieces*, Whitman Publishing, 1977 and later editions.

Kidd, Thomas S., *The Great Awakening: The Roots of Evangelical Christianity in Colonial America*, Yale University Press, 2007.

Kramnick, Isaac and Moore, Lawrence, *The Godless Constitution*, W.W. Norton & Company, 2005.

Kravitz, Robert J., *A Collector's Guide to Postage and Fractional Currency*, Arkives Press, 2003.

Kruse, Kevin, *One Nation Under God*, Basic Books, 2015.

Lamphier, Peg, *Kate Chase and William Sprague: Politics and Gender in a Civil War Marriage*, University of Nebraska Press, 2003.

LeBeau, Bryan, *The Atheist: Madalyn Murray O'Hair*, New York University Press, 2003.

Lee, Charles Robert, *The Confederate Constitution*, University of North Carolina Press, 1963.

Leech, Margaret, *Reveille in Washington, 1860–1865*, Harper Brothers, 1941.

McAllister, David, *Christian Civil Government in America*, revised by T.H. Acheson and William Parsons, 6th edition, National Reform Association, 1927.

McClure, A.K., *Old Times Notes of Pennsylvania*, John C. Winston Company, 1905.

Meacham, Jon, *American Gospel*, Random House, 2006.

Metchall, Martha, article in "Encyclopedia Brunoniana" a publication of Brown University, 1993.

Mihm, Stephen, *A Nation of Counterfeiters*, Harvard University Press, 2007.

Miller, Randall, Harry Stout, and Charles Wilson, *Religion and the American Civil War*, Oxford University Press, 1998.

Morris, Edmund, *Theodore Rex*, Random House, 2002.

Morris, Robert, *William Morgan, or, Political anti-Masonry: Its Rise, Growth, and Decadence*, Robert Macoy, New York, 1883.

Niven, John, *Salmon P. Chase: A Biography*, Oxford University Press, 1995.

Oberholtzer, Ellis P., *Jay Cooke, Financier of the Civil War*, George W. Jacobs & Co., 1907.

Office of the Comptroller of the Currency, *Lincoln and the Founding of the National Banking System*. Available from the OCC both in hardcopy and on their web site.

Oller, John, *American Queen*, DaCapo Press, 2014.

Palmer, Benjamin, *The Life and Letters of James Henley Thornwell*, Kessinger Legacy Reprints, 1875.

Phelps, Mary Merwin, *Kate Chase, Dominant Daughter*, Thomas Y. Crowell Company, 1935.

Pollock, Andrew W. III, *United States Patterns and Related Issues*, Bowers and Merena Galleries, 1994.

Porter, David D. Admiral, *Naval History of the Civil War*, H.J. Richards & Co., 1887.

Rable, George C., *God's Almost Chosen People*, University of North Carolina Press, 2010.

Reed, Fred III, *Civil War Encased Stamps*, BNR Press, 1988.

Roosevelt, Theodore, *An Autobiography*, Charles Scribner & Sons, 1920.

Ross, Ishbel, *Proud Kate: Portrait of an Ambitious Woman*, Harper Brothers, 1953.

Roughton, Dorothy, "James Pollock, Governor of the Keystone State, 1855–1858," unpublished Master's thesis, Penn State University Department of History, Special Collections library, 1956.

Schuckers, J.W., *The Life and Public Services of Salmon Portland Chase*, D. Appleton & Co., 1874.

Schwartz, Ted, *A History of United States Coinage*, A.S. Barnes & Co., Inc., 1980.

Sears, Stephen, *Landscape Turned Red*, Houghton Mifflin, Harcourt, 2003.

Sharkey, Robert, *Money, Class, and Power: An Economic Study of Civil War and Reconstruction*, John Hopkins Press, 1959.

Sherman, John, *Recollections of Forty Years in the House, Senate and Cabinet*, The Werner Company, Chicago, 1895.

Simpson, Robert D., "From Blacksmith to Bishop," *The Interpreter*, United Methodist Communication, July–August 1995.

Snow, Rick, "Sesquicentennial of the Bronze Cent," *Longacre's Ledger*, December 2013.

Sokoloff, Alice Hunt, *Kate Chase for the Defense*, Dodd, Mead & Company, 1971.

Stewart, James Brewer, *Holy Warriors: The Abolitionists and American Slavery*, Hill and Wang, 1996.

Stout, Harry, *Upon the Altar of the Nation*, Penguin Books, 2007.

Stowe, Harriet Beecher, *Men of Our Times*, Hartford Publishing Co., 1868.

Taxay, Don, *Counterfeit, Mis-struck, and Unofficial U.S. Coins*, Arco Publishing, 1963.

———. *U.S. Mint and Coinage*, Arco Publishing, 1966.

Waldman, Steven, *Founding Faith*, Random House, 2008.

Warren, Louis A., *Lincoln's Youth, Indiana Years, 1816–1830*, Indiana Historical Society Press, 1959.

Wolf, William J., *The Almost Chosen People: A Study of the Religion of Abraham Lincoln*, Doubleday & Co., 1959.

Woodworth, Steven, *While God is Marching On*, University Press of Kansas, 2001.

Wyatt-Brown, Bertram, *Lewis Tappan and the Evangelical War Against Slavery*, Case Western University Press, 1969.

Yeoman, R.S, edited by Q. David Bowers, Kenneth Bressett, and Jeff Garrett, *A Guide Book of United States Coins*, Whitman Publishing, annual editions 1946 to date.

ABOUT THE AUTHOR

William (Bill) Bierly was raised on a farm near Walkerton, Indiana. As a child he heard stories from his grandparents about two of his great-grandfathers who had served in the Civil War. This led to a lifelong interest in that war and that period of history. At about age eight he began collecting coins from circulating change. Following high school Bierly attended Northwestern University for two years and then completed a degree in sociology and economic development with a minor in Chinese studies at Indiana University. He then worked in India for two years as a Peace Corps volunteer in a dairy development project. Back in the United States his interest in coins was rekindled. He soon went abroad again, working for three years in Osaka, Japan. Then in the United States he operated a small business for five years, sold it, and entered graduate school, earning an MBA in finance from Indiana University and embarking on a 25-year career in commercial banking. With

his overseas experience Bierly focused on international banking, particularly Japanese corporate business and Asian correspondent banking. He began his career at National Bank of Detroit and he worked with J.P. Morgan Chase for much of his career; at various times at the bank's Detroit, Chicago, and Columbus, Ohio, offices, as well as traveling often to Asia.

While thus engaged, Bierly continued to pursue his coin hobby, eventually specializing in Civil War–era coinage, in particular pattern coins. Today he is active in several coin groups and clubs, most notably the Central States Numismatic Society, the American Numismatic Association, the American Numismatic Society, the Chicago Coin Club, the Michigan State Numismatic Society, and the Pennsylvania Association of Numismatists, as well as the Civil War Token Society and the Liberty Seated Collectors Club. He sometimes exhibits his collection at major coin shows and frequently volunteers as an exhibit judge.

Bierly resides in La Porte, Indiana. He has two children, Emma and Ken, as well as a granddaughter, Kiki.

CREDITS AND ACKNOWLEDGMENTS

There are so many organizations and people to whom I am indebted for assistance in the writing of this book that I am sure I will unintentionally and inadvertently neglect some. Please forgive me for such omissions.

First I must acknowledge the indispensable assistance provided me by the **Central States Numismatic Society**. The organization's leaders and members have had my respect for many years as I participated in their excellent program of exhibits and presentations. As I was giving thought to writing a book on the topic of how "In God We Trust" came about on our coinage I became aware of their program of grants for authors. **Ray Lockwood**, their education director, encouraged me to apply and I was fortunate enough to receive their assistance. That grant enabled me to travel for research and get far more deeply into the details of the story than I otherwise would have been able to do. CSNS's educational programs and outreach are, in my opinion, unmatched in the numismatic community.

I had collected pattern coins beginning in the 1970s and focused on those of the Civil war era, particularly those of 1861, 1862, and 1863 bearing the motto "God Our Trust" and those termed "transitionals" of 1863, 1864, and 1865. I collected them without understanding their origins or historical backgrounds. By the mid- to late 1990s I began to realize there was a story behind these coins. Around this time I became acquainted with **John Kraljevich** through our mutual friend, **John Pack**. Kraljevich, learning of my interest in this story, provided me with a copy of an undergraduate paper he had written while at the University of Virginia. The paper was entitled "Relieve Us from the Ignominy of Heathenism: The Significance of the National Motto on United States Coins and Currency." He had used the archives extensively in his writing. The paper was a revelation to me as I realized there was archival material available through which the story could be explored and told. John's paper, as much as anything, got me on the path to this book.

I took the opportunity of a trip to Philadelphia in about 2000 to travel out to Prospect Park, Pennsylvania, and the **Prospect Hill Baptist Church** from whence Reverend Mark Watkinson in 1861 wrote a letter to Treasury Secretary Salmon Chase proposing a religious reference on the coinage. There I acquired a book written by **Keith Lockhart**, a local historian. The book, *A History of Ridley Township*, provided information about Reverend Watkinson. Later I contacted the church to seek further material. **Ron Lindenmuth**, the church treasurer at that time, provided me with a very helpful local newspaper article from 1964 which contained detailed information about Watkinson as well as useful summaries of the church's history.

As I worked to learn more of the historical religious context of the Civil War I visited the **Indiana University** library in Bloomington several times. The staff was most helpful in assisting me in locating sources about the Great Awakenings. They also provided copies of certain Mint director reports. As I became more serious about writing this book and received encouragement and the grant funding from CSNS I traveled to Milton, Pennsylvania, Mint Director James Pollock's hometown. I met with **George Venios** and **Jessica Hess**. George and Jessica have been active in the local history of Milton; they wrote a small book about Pollock and his role in "In God We Trust." The information they provided me was invaluable. Also George told me of the Pollock family archive located at **Penn State University**. I visited this archive twice and gathered insights into Pollock's life; this contributed significantly to this book. The staff there, at the Special Collections section of the Penn State library, went above and beyond duty in helping me.

As for Reverend Watkinson: Besides material provided by the Prospect Hill Baptist Church, I was able to visit the **Virginia Baptist Historical Society**, located on the campus of the University of Richmond. The Society's research assistant, **Darlene Slate Herod**, generously provided me access to the Minute Book of the Court Street Baptist Church, where Watkinson had been during a crucial period early in the Civil War. I also traveled to Portsmouth, Virginia, where the **Court Street Church** is located. The pastor there, **Dr. Wilbur Kersey**, was most helpful and kind to me. He has been at the church since 1959. He and his wife Katharine have established a highly regarded elementary and middle school in conjunction with the church. I was able to join the congregation for a Sunday morning worship service and was very much impressed with Dr. Kersey's sermon. I am certain Reverend Watkinson would be proud that his former church is in such capable hands.

Early in my writing process I met **Kevin Flynn**, the writer of numerous numismatic books. He gave me much guidance and advice. I found his books useful in my own research as they contain many archival letters relating to the story.

As the writing of the book took shape, **Gerry Tebbin**, a longtime friend from Columbus, Ohio, reviewed what I had written and gave me encouragement to keep going. Later **Dennis Forgue**, a friend knowledgeable in U.S. currency, read my chapters dealing with Civil War–era money and gave constructive and encouraging comments.

Most important, as I neared completion of the book, **Bob Julian** most generously spent time with me discussing it and reading it in its entirety. He greatly encouraged me to drive toward its final chapters. His knowledge of the archival records of the Mint and Treasury is probably without peer. He provided me with letters written among Chase, Watkinson, and Pollock previously unknown to me and unseen in any earlier literature of which I am aware. I am very grateful to him for his help and encouragement.

I belong to several numismatic organizations. My fellow members of the **Chicago Coin Club** have been supportive and helpful during this entire process. In particular fellow member **Bob Leonard** gave me great advice based on his writing experience and most helpfully introduced me to **Dennis Tucker** of **Whitman Publishing**. Also fellow members of the **Pennsylvania Association of Numismatists** have been extremely generous in the research for this book. In particular **Tom Uram** of PAN introduced me to George Venios in Milton, leading me deeper into the story of James Pollock and the origins of "In God We Trust." Tom also introduced me to **Mike Fuljenz**, who has done good work on the story of the motto.

I also want to thank **Len Augsburger** for keeping an eye out for material relevant to the motto as he did research at the Smithsonian and other places for his own writing. He went out of his way to provide me with items he ran across.

I also want to thank family member (cousin) David Cramer for his willing assistance on various technical computer issues that I encountered during the writing of this book. I would have thrown in the towel in frustration several times without his knowledgeable and patient assistance.

Tom Mulvaney, from whom I took a coin photography class several years ago at an ANA Summer Seminar, has become a friend and willingly photographed a number of my pattern coins for inclusion in the book.

To the above people and many others unnamed I express my deep appreciation. Without them the book would have been impossible.

The publisher would like to thank the following: **Mark Borckardt** advised on Mint director portraiture. **Q. David Bowers** reviewed the entire manuscript and provided valuable feedback, in addition to writing the foreword, sharing several historical images from his personal archives, and granting permission to access the archives of Stack's Bowers Galleries. Artist **Barry Brown Jr.** created portraits of Reverend Mark Watkinson and of Madalyn Murray O'Hair, two diametrically opposed personalities in the story of "In God We Trust." The **Bureau of Engraving and Printing** provided several images. Some philatelic images are from the **Estate of Bernard Heller**. **Emily Hemming**, associate director of media relations for the **Wharton School**, provided image-research assistance. **Heritage Auctions** shared images from its numismatic archives. **Robert W. Julian** shared portraits of Treasury officers from his collection. **McKenzie Lemhouse**, library specialist at the **South Caroliniana Library**, assisted with image-hunting advice. **Liberty Presbyterian Church**, Delaware, Ohio (**DeAnne Miller**, communications coordinator), provided an image. The **Library of Congress** was invaluable as a source of diverse historical imagery. The **National Archives and Records Administration** provided several images. The **New York Public Library** provided several images. The Smithsonian's **National Numismatic Collection**, **National Portrait Gallery**, and **National Postal Museum** each provided images. The **Pennsylvania Association of Numismatists** (**Thomas Uram**, president, and **Patrick McBride**, journal editor) provided images. The **Pennsylvania Capitol Preservation Committee** (**Hayley Moyer**, retail/office administrator) provided a portrait. **Stack's Bowers Galleries** generously opened its image archives of coins, tokens, and paper money. **Swarthmore College (Friends Historical Library; Celia Caust-Ellenbogen**, archivist) provided portraits of Joseph Wharton. **Jon Sullivan** of Sullivan Numismatics shared an image. **Saul Teichman** (uspatterns.com) shared information and images. The **United States Mint** provided several images. The **University Archives and Records Center of the University of Pennsylvania** (**J.M. Duffin**, senior archivist and office manager; and **Timothy J. Horning**, public services archivist) assisted with image research on Joseph Wharton. The **Wadsworth Atheneum Museum of Art** (**Stacey Stachow**, manager of the museum shop and rights and reproductions coordinator) provided an image. **Sydnei Wheat** was important in the book's image research and gathering.

Image Credits. Images are credited by page number. Where multiple images are found on a given page, they are credited by location on the page, starting with number 1 at upper left and reading left to right, top to bottom. BEP = Bureau of Engraving and Printing. LOC = Library of Congress. NARA = National Archives and Records Administration. NNC = National Numismatic Collection, Smithsonian Institution. NYPL = New York Public Library.

Front Matter: Pgs x–xi, Whitman Publishing Archives. Pg xiv, (letter), National Archives and Record Administration; (coins), Stack's Bowers Galleries.

Chapter One: Pg 3, Library of Congress. Pg 6, LOC. Pg 8, LOC. Pg 9, LOC. Pg 11, Liberty Presbyterian Church. Pg 13, LOC. Pg 14, New York Public Library. Pg 15, LOC. Pg 16.1, LOC. Pg 16.2–3, Stack's Bowers Galleries. Pg 17.1, LOC. Pg 17.2, LOC. Pg 19, The South Caroliniana Library, University of South Carolina Archives, Digital Collections; from Palmer, Benjamin, *The Life and Letters of James Henley Thornwell*, Whittet and Shepperson, 1875. Pg 20, Carte de visite photograph of Rev. Benjamin Morgan Palmer, as located in the Thomas Dwight Witherspoon Manuscript Collection [MS083], PCA Historical Center, St. Louis, MO. Used by permission. Pg 22, LOC. Pg 23, Jared B. Flagg, American, 1820–1899; Reverend Horace Bushnell, 1847; Oil on canvas, 34-1/8 x 29-1/4 in. (86.7 x 74.3 cm); Wadsworth Atheneum Museum of Art, Hartford, CT; source unknown; endowed by Charles N. Flagg, 1850.10. Photography credit: Allen Phillips / Wadsworth Atheneum.

Chapter Two: Pg 24, Barry Brown Jr. / Whitman Publishing. Pg 26, author. Pg 27, LOC. Pg 30, LOC. Pg 34, NARA. Pg 35.1–2, NARA. Pg 36.1–2, Stack's Bowers Galleries. Pg 38, Bureau of Engraving and Printing. Pg 41.1–2, author.

Chapter Three: Pg 42, LOC. Pg 44, author. Pg 45, LOC. Pg 46.1–2, Stack's Bowers Galleries. Pg 46.3 and 47.2, LOC. Pg 47.1, LOC. Pg 48.1, author. Pg 48.2, Oregon Historical Society. Pg 50.1–2, Stack's Bowers Galleries. Pg 51, LOC. Pg 52, LOC. Pg 54, LOC. Pg 55.1–3, NARA.

Chapter Four: Pg 56, Brian Hunt and Pennsylvania Capitol Preservation Committee. Pg 57, Q. David Bowers. Pg 60, Jessica Hess and George Venios, from *Honoring Milton*. Pg 61, Yale Collection of Western Americana, Beinecke Rare Book and Manuscript Library, Yale University, New Haven, Connecticut. Pg 62, LOC. Pg 63, LOC. Pg 64, Penn State University. Pg 65, Robert W. Julian.

Chapter Five: Pg 68, LOC. Pg 70.1–6, Stack's Bowers Galleries. Pg 72.1, LOC. Pg 72.2, NARA. Pg 72.3, Ilyashenko Olksiy / Shutterstock. Pg 72.4, author. Pg 73 (portrait), Whitman Publishing Archives; (coins), Stack's Bowers Galleries. Pg 75.1–9, Stack's Bowers Galleries. Pg 76.1–9, Stack's Bowers Galleries. Pg 77.1, Stack's Bowers Galleries. Pg 77.2, uspatterns.com. Pg 77.3–4, Stack's Bowers Galleries.

Chapter Six: Pg 78, LOC. Pg 79, LOC. Pg 80.1–2, Stack's Bowers Galleries. Pg 83, Whitman Publishing Archives. Pg 90, LOC. Pg 92.1–2, National Numismatic Collection, Smithsonian Institution. Pg 93.1–4, NNC. Pg 95, LOC. Pg 96, Stack's Bowers Galleries. Pg 97, LOC. Pg 98.1–3, Stack's Bowers Galleries. Pg 99.1–3, Stack's Bowers Galleries. Pg 100, Stack's Bowers Galleries. Pg 101, Beyond My Ken / Wikimedia. Pg 103.1, LOC. Pg 103.2, author. Pg 104.1–2, Stack's Bowers Galleries. Pg 105, RTRO / Alamy Stock Photo. Pg 107.1–2, Stack's Bowers Galleries.

Chapter Seven: Pg 108, LOC. Pg 110.1–2, Stack's Bowers Galleries. Pg 112.1–3 and 7–12, Stack's Bowers Galleries. Pg 112.4–6, Heritage Auctions. Pg 115.1–4, National Postal Museum, Smithsonian Institution. Pg 117, LOC. Pg 119.1–2, Stack's Bowers Galleries. Pg 119.3–4, NNC. Pg 121, Stack's Bowers Galleries. Pg 124.1–2, Whitman Publishing Archives. Pg 127, LOC.

Chapter Eight: Pg 128 (lithograph), LOC; (tokens), Stack's Bowers Galleries. Pg 130.1–6, Stack's Bowers Galleries. Pg 134.1–11, Q. David Bowers. Pg 135.1–2, Stack's Bowers Galleries. Pg 136, Stack's Bowers Galleries. Pg 141.1–6, Stack's Bowers Galleries. Pg 142.1–12, Stack's Bowers Galleries.

Chapter Nine: Pg 144, National Portrait Gallery, Smithsonian Institution. Pg 147, LOC. Pg 148, LOC. Pg 150, LOC. Pg 153, LOC.

Chapter Ten: Pg 154 (background), Whitman Publishing Archives. Pg 154.1 and 154.4, Swarthmore College (Friends Historical Library). Pg 154.2, LOC. Pg 154.3, University Archives and Records Center, University of Pennsylvania. Pg 156, LOC. Pg 161.1–2, Stack's Bowers Galleries. Pg 163, Whitman Publishing Archives.

Chapter Eleven: Pg 164.1, Estate of Bernard Heller. Pg 164.2–3, Stack's Bowers Galleries. Pg 167.1–4, Stack's Bowers Galleries. Pg 169.1–6, Stack's Bowers Galleries. Pg 170.1–2, Stack's Bowers Galleries. Pg 171.1–3, Whitman Publishing Archives. Pg 177.1, LOC. Pg 177.2–3, United States Mint.

Chapter Twelve: Pg 180, Courtesy of George Venios, Milton, Pennsylvania. Pg 181.1–2, Stack's Bowers Galleries. Pg 183.1, NYPL. Pg 183.2, LOC. Pg 185, LOC. Pg 186, LOC. Pg 187, LOC. Pg 189, NARA. Pg 193, LOC. Pg 194, LOC. Pg 195, Courtesy of George Venios, Milton, Pennsylvania. Pg 197.1, NYPL. Pg 197.2, author.

Chapter Thirteen: Pg 198, LOC. Pg 199, U.S. Treasury Department. Pg 201, LOC. Pg 203.1–2, LOC. Pg 204, LOC. Pg 206, Litererarian1912 / Wikimedia. Pg 207, LOC. Pg 210.1–6, Author's collection, photographed by Tom Mulvaney. Pg 211.1–6, Author's collection, photographed by Tom Mulvaney. Pg 212, author. Pg 213.1–4, Author's collection, photographed by Tom Mulvaney. Pg 216.1–6, Author's collection, photographed by Tom Mulvaney. Pg 217.1–6, Author's collection, photographed by Tom Mulvaney.

Chapter Fourteen: Pg 219.1 (portrait), LOC. Pg 219.2–4, Stack's Bowers Galleries. Pg 220.1–12, Heritage Auctions. Pg 221.1–8, Stack's Bowers Galleries. Pg 223.1–6, Stack's Bowers Galleries. Pg 225.1, LOC. Pg 225.2, Whitman Publishing Archives. Pg 226.1–2, Stack's Bowers Galleries. Pg 227, *Century Illustrated*. Pg 228.1–5, Stack's Bowers Galleries. Pg 230.1–3, Stack's Bowers Galleries. Pg 230.4–5, Heritage Auctions. Pg 231.1, Stack's Bowers Galleries. Pg 231.2, Heritage Auctions. Pg

231.3–6, Heritage Auctions. Pg 232.1–2, Heritage Auctions. Pg 232.3–6, Stack's Bowers Galleries. Pg 233.1–9, Heritage Auctions. Pg 234, Stack's Bowers Galleries. Pg 235.1–6, Stack's Bowers Galleries.

Chapter Fifteen: Pg 236, Robert W. Julian. Pg 238.1, Stack's Bowers Galleries. Pg 238.2, Bureau of Engraving and Printing. Pg 240, Stack's Bowers Galleries. Pg 242.1, Stack's Bowers Galleries. Pg 242.2, LOC. Pg 243.1–3, Stack's Bowers Galleries.

Chapter Sixteen: Pg 244.1 (Andersonville flag), Joseph Sohm / Shutterstock. Pg 244.2 (coin), Stack's Bowers Galleries. Pg 246.1–2, Stack's Bowers Galleries. Pg 247.1–2, Stack's Bowers Galleries. Pg 247.3, Stack's Bowers Galleries. Pg 247.4, Q. David Bowers. Pg 248.1–2, Stack's Bowers Galleries. Pg 251, LOC.

Chapter Seventeen: Pg 256, LOC. Pg 257, LOC. Pg 259.1–2, Stack's Bowers Galleries. Pg 260, National Park Service, Saint-Gaudens National Historic Site. Pg 261.1–2, Stack's Bowers Galleries. Pg 261.3, uspatterns.com. Pg 261.4–7, Stack's Bowers Galleries. Pg 262.1, Rauner Special Collections Library. Pg 262.2, National Park Service, Saint-Gaudens National Historic Site. Pg 264.1–2, Stack's Bowers Galleries. Pg 264.3, NNC. Pg 264.4–5, Stack's Bowers Galleries. Pg 267, *Detroit Free Press*. Pg 268, LOC. Pg 273.1–2, Stack's Bowers Galleries.

Chapter Eighteen: Pg 274, LOC. Pg 276, LOC. Pg 279, LOC. Pg 280, White House. Pg 282, LOC. Pg 283, LOC. Pg 284.1, public domain, courtesy of personal collection of Hilltoppers. Pg 284.2, LOC. Pg 285, Alexander Zam / Shutterstock. Pg 286, Q. David Bowers. Pg 287, Florida State Archives. Pg 288, author's collection. Pg 289, LOC.

Chapter Nineteen: Pg 290, Barry Brown Jr. / Whitman Publishing. Pg 292.1–2, LOC. Pg 297, *American Atheist* magazine. Pg 299, Kallahar at English Wikipedia. Pg 300, Prospect Hill Baptist Church. Pg 303.1–4, Stack's Bowers Galleries.

Chapter Twenty: Pg 304 (background), BW Folsom / Shutterstock; (coins), United States Mint. Pg 305.1–3, United States Mint. Pg 306, Jon Sullivan, Sullivan Numismatics. Pg 307, United States Mint. Pg 311, Taber Andrew Bain.

INDEX